Lecture Notes in Computer Science 10319

Commenced Publication in 1973
Founding and Former Series Editors:
Gerhard Goos, Juris Hartmanis, and Jan van Leeuwen

More information about this series at http://www.springer.com/series/7408

Jean-Marie Jacquet · Mieke Massink (Eds.)

Coordination Models and Languages

19th IFIP WG 6.1 International Conference, COORDINATION 2017
Held as Part of the 12th International Federated Conference
on Distributed Computing Techniques, DisCoTec 2017
Neuchâtel, Switzerland, June 19–22, 2017
Proceedings

 Springer

Editors
Jean-Marie Jacquet ⓘ
University of Namur
Namur
Belgium

Mieke Massink ⓘ
CNR-ISTI
Pisa
Italy

ISSN 0302-9743   ISSN 1611-3349 (electronic)
Lecture Notes in Computer Science
ISBN 978-3-319-59745-4   ISBN 978-3-319-59746-1 (eBook)
DOI 10.1007/978-3-319-59746-1

Library of Congress Control Number: 2017942989

LNCS Sublibrary: SL2 – Programming and Software Engineering

Printed on acid-free paper

This Springer imprint is published by Springer Nature
The registered company is Springer International Publishing AG
The registered company address is: Gewerbestrasse 11, 6330 Cham, Switzerland

Foreword

The 12th International Federated Conference on Distributed Computing Techniques (DisCoTec) took place in Neuchâtel, Switzerland, during June 19–22, 2017. It was organized by the Institute of Computer Science of the University of Neuchâtel.

The DisCoTec series is one of the major events sponsored by the International Federation for Information Processing (IFIP). It comprises three conferences:

- COORDINATION, the IFIP WG6.1 International Conference on Coordination Models and Languages
- DAIS, the IFIP WG6.1 International Conference on Distributed Applications and Interoperable Systems
- FORTE, the IFIP WG6.1 International Conference on Formal Techniques for Distributed Objects, Components and Systems

Together, these conferences cover a broad spectrum of distributed computing subjects, ranging from theoretical foundations and formal description techniques to systems research issues.

Each day of the federated event began with a plenary speaker nominated by one of the conferences. The three invited speakers were Prof. Giovanna Di Marzo Serugendo (UniGE, Switzerland), Dr. Marko Vukolić (IBM Research, Switzerland), and Dr. Rupak Majumdar (MPI, Germany).

Associated with the federated event were also three satellite events that took place during June 21–22, 2017:

- The 10th Workshop on Interaction and Concurrency Experience (ICE)
- The 4th Workshop on Security in Highly Connected IT Systems (SHCIS)
- The EBSIS-sponsored session on Dependability and Interoperability with Event-Based Systems (DIEBS)

Sincere thanks go to the chairs and members of the Program and Steering Committees of the aforementioned conferences and workshops for their highly appreciated efforts. The organization of DisCoTec 2017 was only possible thanks to the dedicated work of the Organizing Committee, including Ivan Lanese (publicity chair), Romain Rouvoy (workshop chair), Peter Kropf (finance chair), and Aurélien Havet (webmaster), as well as all the students and colleagues who volunteered their time to help. Finally, many thanks go to IFIP WG6.1 for sponsoring this event, Springer's *Lecture Notes in Computer Science* for their support and sponsorship, and EasyChair for providing the reviewing infrastructure.

April 2017

Pascal Felber
Valerio Schiavoni

Preface

Modern information systems rely increasingly on combining concurrent, distributed, mobile, adaptive, reconfigurable, and heterogeneous components. New models, architectures, languages, and verification techniques are necessary to cope with the complexity induced by these systems. Coordination models and languages have emerged as a successful approach to that end, in that they provide abstractions that cleanly separate behavior from communication, therefore increasing modularity, simplifying reasoning, and ultimately enhancing software development. Building on the success of the previous editions, this volume contains the papers presented at Coordination 2017, the 19th IFIP WG 6.1 International Conference on Coordination Models and Languages held in Neuchâtel, Switzerland, during June 19–22, 2017, as part of the federated DisCoTeC conference. Coordination itself is part of a series whose proceedings have been published since 1996 in Springer's *Lecture Notes in Computer Science* (LNCS).

The Program Committee (PC) of Coordination 2017 consisted of 33 prominent researchers from 18 different countries. In all, 31 submissions were received out of 37 submitted abstracts. Each submission was reviewed by three independent referees. The review process included an in-depth discussion phase during which the merits of all the papers were discussed. Based on quality, originality, clarity, and relevance criteria, the PC finally selected 13 contributions for presentation and publication in the proceedings. The program was further enhanced by an invited talk by Giovanna Di Marzo Serugendo from the University of Geneva, entitled "Spatial Edge Services," an extended abstract of which is included in the these proceedings.

Many people contributed to the success of Coordination 2017. We first of all would like to thank the authors for submitting high-quality papers. We also thank the Program Committee members for their effort and time to read and discuss the papers and we equally acknowledge the help of the additional reviewers who evaluated submissions in their area of expertise. Furthermore, we wish to thank the Steering Committee of Coordination and the Steering Board of DisCoTeC for their support and in particular Giovanna Di Marzo Serugendo for her keynote address.

It is also our pleasure to thank Pascal Felber, the general chair of DisCoTec, Valerio Schiavoni, the organizing chair of DisCoTec, Ivan Lanese, the publicity chair of DisCoTec, and Francesco Tiezzi, the publicity chair of Coordination 2017. We would also like to thank the providers of the EasyChair conference management system, whose facilities greatly helped us run the review process and facilitate the preparation of the proceedings. With respect to the latter, we also warmly thank Anna Kramer, from Springer, for her help in producing the proceedings. Finally, we are indebted to the conference attendees for keeping the Coordination research community lively and interactive, and ultimately ensuring the success of this conference series.

June 2017

Jean-Marie Jacquet
Mieke Massink

Organization

Conference Chairs

Jean-Marie Jacquet   University of Namur, Belgium
Mieke Massink   CNR-ISTI, Italy

Publicity Chair

Francesco Tiezzi   University of Camerino, Italy

Program Committee

Gul Agha   University of Illinois at Urbana-Champaign, USA
Farhad Arbab   CWI and Leiden University, The Netherlands
Jacob Beal   Raytheon BBN Technologies, USA
Simon Bliudze   EPFL, Switzerland
Frank de Boer   CWI and Leiden University, The Netherlands
Antonio Brogi   University of Pisa, Italy
Roberto Bruni   University of Pisa, Italy
Vincenzo Ciancia   CNR-ISTI, Pisa, Italy
Dave Clarke   Uppsala University, Sweden
Ferruccio Damiani   Università di Torino, Italy
Wolfgang De Meuter   Vrije Universiteit Brussel, Belgium
Rocco De Nicola   IMT, School for Advanced Studies Lucca, Italy
Schahram Dustdar   TU Wien, Austria
José Luiz Fiadeiro   Royal Holloway, University of London, UK
Stephen Gilmore   University of Edinburgh, UK
Paola Inverardi   Università dell'Aquila, Italy
Jean-Marie Jacquet   University of Namur, Belgium
Ramtin Khosravi   University of Tehran, Iran
Eva Kühn   Vienna University of Technology, Austria
Alberto Lluch Lafuente   Technical University of Denmark, Denmark
Michele Loreti   Università degli Studi di Firenze, Italy
Mieke Massink   CNR-ISTI, Italy
Hernan Melgratti   Universidad de Buenos Aires, Argentina
Andrea Omicini   University of Bologna, Italy
Ernesto Pimentel   University of Malaga, Spain
Gwen Salaün   University of Grenoble Alpes, France
Marjan Sirjani   Malardalen University, Reykjavik University, Iceland
Carolyn Talcott   SRI International, California, USA
Emilio Tuosto   University of Leicester, UK
Vasco T. Vasconcelos   LaSiGE and University of Lisbon, Portugal

Erik de Vink	Eindhoven University of Technology, The Netherlands
Mirko Viroli	University of Bologna, Italy
Takuo Watanabe	Tokyo Institute of Technology, Japan
Danny Weyns	Katholieke Universiteit Leuven, Belgium
Martin Wirsing	Ludwig-Maximilians-Universität München, Germany

Steering Committee

Gul Agha	University of Illinois at Urbana-Champaign, USA
Farhad Arbab	CWI and Leiden University, The Netherlands
Dave Clarke	Uppsala University, Sweden
Wolfgang De Meuter	Vrije Universiteit Brussel, Belgium
Rocco De Nicola	IMT, School for Advanced Studies Lucca, Italy
Tom Holvoet	KU Leuven, Belgium
Jean-Marie Jacquet	University of Namur, Belgium
Christine Julien	The University of Texas at Austin, USA
Eva Kühn	Vienna University of Technology, Austria
Alberto Lluch Lafuente	Technical University of Denmark, Denmark
Jose Proenca	University of Minho, Portugal
Rosario Pugliese	University of Florence, Italy
Marjan Sirjani	Reykjavik University, Iceland
Carolyn Talcott	SRI International, California, USA
Vasco T. Vasconcelos	LaSiGE and University of Lisbon, Portugal
Mirko Viroli	University of Bologna, Italy
Gianluigi Zavattaro	University of Bologna, Italy

Additional Reviewers

Yehia Abd Alrahman	Ehsan Khamespanah	Sophie Therese Radschek
Maryam Bagheri	Dimitrios Kouzapas	Guido Salvaneschi
Roberto Casadei	Diego Latella	Atul Sandur
Stefan Craß	Anastasia Mavridou	Chris Shaver
Joeri De Koster	Florian Myter	Jacopo Soldani
Kasper Dokter	Luca Padovani	Quentin Stievenart
Philipp Haller	Karl Palmskog	Hugo Torres Vieira
Ahmad Ibrahim	Danilo Pianini	
Ali Jafari	Martin Planer	

Contents

Verification

Invited Talk

Invited Talk

Spatial Edge Services - From Coordination Model to Actual Applications

Giovanna Di Marzo Serugendo[(✉)]

Centre Universitaire d'Informatique, Institute of Services Science,
University of Geneva, Geneva, Switzerland
giovanna.dimarzo@unige.ch

Abstract. Ubiquitous and context-aware sensors are increasing in number and aim at providing comfort and better life quality. They are spatially distributed and their computation capacity is still under-exploited. *Spatial Edge Service* are a new generation of services exploiting IoT and spatially distributed data. They result from collective and decentralised interactions of multiple computing entities. They rely on a logic and chemical-based coordination model. Spatial edge services provide innovation capabilities for the software industry, connected objects manufacturers and edge computing industry. This paper provides and overview of Spatial Edge Services, their underlying coordination model, a set of development tools, a series of case studies scenarios and future visions.

1 Introduction

Mobile phones, laptops, tablets locally connected to each other form huge computing and storage infrastructures, currently under-exploited, but available on motorways, city-centers, inside buildings, etc. Those infrastructures pave the way for a new category of services based on data propagation among devices, e.g. car traffic control service through propagation of data from one car to another, information dissemination in a crowd to better steer the crowd towards points of interest or emergency exits, and alternative communication infrastructures in case of environmental disasters. Such services are time-related: they may last just for a very short time for a specific purpose exploiting current contextual data, as well as space-related: these services have a meaning because the data they rely on or the data they spread is spatially distributed over a geographic area.

Traditional service-oriented approaches allow programmers to combine together into a new service diverse functionalities provided themselves under the form of services. Typical approaches involve Web services or rely on APIs mashups. Composition of services is generally foreseen at design-time, adaptation happens by choosing the actual services at run-time. Current service-oriented approaches are not suited for the new generation of services, working on smart environments or exploiting Internet of Things scenarios. They do not cope with the dynamicity involved by the underlying mobile and changing computing infrastructures, the spatiality of the considered data, or time-related

© IFIP International Federation for Information Processing 2017
Published by Springer International Publishing AG 2017. All Rights Reserved
J.-M. Jacquet and M. Massink (Eds.): COORDINATION 2017, LNCS 10319, pp. 3–17, 2017.
DOI: 10.1007/978-3-319-59746-1_1

issues. There is a need for a paradigm shift in the notion of services along two dimensions: (1) services make sense because they are spatially distributed, their functionality is provided as the result of the interactions among several entities, possibly distributed across several computational nodes; (2) services are built on demand, e.g. users can query diffused clouds of data in a smart city, to retrieve the closest vacant parking place, sensors, "things" and services spontaneously collaborate to provide the answer to the query. We call such services *spatial edge services*. This paper summarises our research works related to the notion of spatial services.

2 Spatial Edge Services

Spatial edge services are a new generation of services that exploit spatially distributed data, enable smart environments, or exploit Internet of Things (IoT) scenarios. This is a new category of decentralised services based on data propagation among mobile devices and where the functionality of the service is provided as the result of the collective interactions among multiple entities, involving processes and calculations taking place across several spatially (geographically) distributed computational entities (i.e. sensors, mobile or stationary computational nodes, actuators). Spatial edge services are built and composed on-demand. Spatial edge services are based on Spatial Computing [29]. Spatial computing thrives on decentralised computation, in a way similar to edge computing, fog computing or jungle computing, where computation is pushed at the edge of the network, away from centralised clouds, closer to end-users [23]. Spatial services bring an engineering dimension to spatial computing as they provide ready to use services that can be deployed on-demand over physical environments by higher-level services or applications. A spatial service is built dynamically through collaboration with other services [17]. Spatial edge services have time- and space-enabled capabilities: deposit data at geographic locations, retrieve data, aggregate data, provide information to users, evaporate information, or act on the environment. Geographically distributed data collectively provides a specific meaning (e.g. artificial gradient).

Bio-inspired mechanisms. Self-organisation, as exhibited by natural systems, provides an appealing approach to engineer spatial services where the functionality and coordination arises from the interactions among several autonomous entities; no central control is required; and some robustness properties and adaptation in dynamic large-scale environments are naturally provided. Self-organisation is achieved by the use of self-organising mechanisms [21] (Fig. 1), i.e., rules that autonomous entities employ to coordinate their behaviour, usually following information gathered from their local environment. One of the main ideas behind spatial service is to provide the above mechanisms under the form of services, ready to use by other services. Therefore, among spatial services, we distinguish on the one hand, Spatial User Services (like finding a vacant parking place), and Spatial System Services, those services that implement spatial self-organisation mechanisms like spreading or gradient for example.

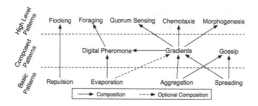

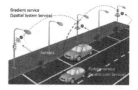

Fig. 1. Self-organising mechanisms   **Fig. 2.** Spatial services

Spatial system services. [17] bring an engineering dimension to spatial computing as they provide ready to use services that can be deployed on-demand over physical environments by higher-level services or applications. Spatial system services are based on self-organising mechanisms [21], they are time- and space-related, work on a decentralised and autonomous manner, and are naturally robust to some environmental perturbations, even though not to any perturbation or environmental change [15]. Figure 1 depicts these self-organising mechanisms as well as their inter-relations (e.g. gossip uses spreading and aggregation).

Spatial user services are the services offered at the application level (for example the services offered by a smart city like help for parking, visually impaired visitor guided across a campus). They are provided through dynamic selection of underlying spatial system services. Figure 2 shows an example of such service, parking place sensors communicate with the nearest street lamp. Information about empty places spread, thanks to the Gradient system service among street lamps, until it reaches the user requesting that information.

Chemical-based coordination platform. Spatial services rely on the SAPERE coordination model that is built on chemical reactions and active shared tuple spaces [30] and its corresponding middleware [4]. Depending on their nature and location, objects are attached to diverse computational nodes (e.g. cars, smartphones, raspberry pi, etc.). Each computational node runs an instance of the coordination platform. Software agents run in the node and interact on behalf of objects (e.g. lamps, cameras, etc.), services, or applications with the coordination platform. They inject or retrieve information to/from the platform, and are sensitive to data present in the platform. Software agents also act on the objects (e.g. switch on/off a lamp, turn surveillance camera), update data spread by a spatial service, or provide a parking place location. Figure 3 depicts the case of a computational node, running an instance of the coordination platform. Computational nodes are connected through low-level connection mechanisms.

3 Design Patterns

Bio-inspired mechanisms. In biological systems, complex emergent behaviour can be achieved by letting agents follow a set of basic rules while having

Fig. 3. Coordination model

only partial knowledge of the environment. Typical bio-inspired self-organising mechanisms are those using stigmergy, like ant foraging for coordinating behaviour, schooling and flocking for coordinating movements, or gradients based systems [5,18].

Bio-inspired design patterns. To ease the use of bio-inspired mechanisms and to apply them more systematically, a series of authors proposed descriptions of these mechanisms under the form of design patterns [1,14,22,25,27]. Results show that the bio-inspired decentralised approaches achieve better results (in terms of robustness, optimisation and adaptability) than more traditional approaches based on formal modelling. To ease engineering of artificial bio-inspired systems, we described a catalogue of bio-inspired mechanisms in terms of modular and reusable design patterns organised into different layers [21], shown on Fig. 1. The mechanisms presented are uniformly described and framed using a software design pattern structure identifying when and how to use each pattern, and describing the relationship between the different mechanisms and their respective boundaries. This catalogue of mechanisms is a step forward to engineering self-organising systems in a systematic way.

4   Suite of Spatial Services

Despite the interest in building self-organising systems, there is currently no established way of designing and programming self-organising systems or applications in a systematic way. Applications are developed in an ad-hoc manner and the functionality of the application is closely entangled with the underlying self-organising mechanism. To implement a crowd steering application using digital pheromones, in addition to programming the crowd steering application functionality it is also necessary to implement the behaviour of the digital pheromone itself. We then consider that for engineering self-organising systems it is important to separate the concerns at different levels: (1) Separate functionality of an application from the underlying mechanisms it uses; (2) Delegate underlying mechanisms and their non-functional, self-managing aspects to the underlying environment.

Self-organising mechanisms as services. In consequence, we propose that self-organising mechanisms (e.g. gradients, digital pheromone or gossip) be provided to higher-level services or applications as ready-to-use services. This involves the design and implementation of a computational environment that provides reliable low-level self-organising mechanisms in the form of services, reusable by applications. This allows the implementation of self-organising applications in a modular way, favours reuse of mechanisms by decoupling them from the application functionality and delegating responsibilities for them to the computational environment.

Core service. Following the relationship among self-organising mechanisms, Core services provided at the level of the infrastructure or computational environment are: Spreading, Aggregation, Evaporation, Static Gradients. Higher-level services, developed by re-using and extending low-level self-organising services provided by the infrastructure, are: Dynamic Gradients, Chemotaxis, Remote Query and Retrieval (a composed service that spreads a query using the Gradient or Dynamic Gradient service and uses the Chemotaxis service to bring back information from remote nodes [19]). We propose to program self-organising systems using services that implement self-organising mechanisms, abstracting away the implementation of those low-level mechanisms for the developer and favouring the re-use of code.

Higher-level services. At the lower level, the computational environment provides reliable "Core" services, i.e. low-level self-organising mechanisms and proposes them to higher-level services or to applications in the form of ready-to-use "services" (e.g. spreading or evaporation). The implementation of higher-level self-organising services (e.g. digital pheromone or dynamic gradient) uses and exploits those low-level services. Higher-level services are themselves ready to be used by actual applications. Finally, applications exploit both high-level and low-level self-organising services. Their implementation happens then in a modular way, reusing self-organising mechanisms, decoupling them from the application functionality, as shown in Fig. 4.

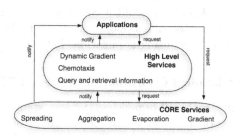

Fig. 4. Spatial services

5   Coordination Models

Coordination models have proven useful for designing and implementing distributed systems. They are appealing for developing collective adaptive systems working in a decentralised manner, interacting with their local environment, since the shared tuple space on which they are based is a powerful paradigm to implement bio-inspired mechanisms (e.g. stigmergy). Coordination infrastructures provide the basic mechanisms and the necessary middleware to implement and deploy coordinated systems. Different categories of coordination models have been developed: chemically-inspired models work as rewrite systems, where states are interpreted as chemical substances, and where molecules represent the coordinated entities that interact according to some reaction rules [30]. Physics-based models, are instead inspired by the way physical masses and particles move and self-organise according to gravitational and electromagnetic fields [2, 26].

5.1 SAPERE

Our work derives from the SAPERE model [3], a coordination model for multi-agent pervasive systems inspired by chemical reactions. It is based on four main concepts: *Live Semantic Annotations* (LSAs), *LSA Tuple Space, agents* and *eco-laws*. LSA are tuples of types $(name, value)$ used to store applications data. For example, a tuple of type $(date, 04/04/1988)$ can be used to define a hypothetical date. LSAs belonging to a computing node are stored in a shared container named LSA Tuple Space. Each LSA is associated with an agent, an external entity that implements some domain-specific logic. For example, agents can represent sensors, services or general applications that want to interact with the LSA space - injecting or retrieving LSAs from the LSA space. Inside the shared container, tuples react in a virtual chemical way by using a predefined set of coordination rules named *eco-laws*, which can (i) instantiate relationships among LSAs (*Bonding* eco-law), (ii) aggregate them (*Aggregate* eco-law), (iii) delete them and (*Decay* eco-law) and (iv) spread them across remote LSA Tuples Spaces (*Spreading* eco-law). When a tuple is modified by an *eco-law*, its relative agent is notified. The implementation of the SAPERE model (Fig. 5(a)), named SAPERE middleware permitted the development of several kinds of real distributed self-adaptive and self-organising applications [30].

5.2 Logic-Based Chemical Coordination Model (LFCM)

A well-known difficulty with self-organising systems stems from the analysis, validation and verification (at design-time or run-time) of so-called emergent properties - i.e. properties that can be observed at a global level but that none of the interacting entities exhibit on its own. Few coordination models integrate features supporting the validation of emergent properties, none of them relying on the chemical metaphor. Recently we extended SAPERE and defined a coordination model based on logic inference named Logic Fragments Coordination Model (LFCM) [10] as well as its semantics [12] (Fig. 5(b)). Logic Fragments are combinations of logic programs defining interactions among agents distributed over the nodes of the system. They are able to accommodate various types of logics, ranging from classical up to many-valued paraconsistent ones. The logical formalisation makes it possible to express coordination in a rigorous and predictable way, both at design-time and run-time. Our logic-based coordination model allows agents to inject logic fragments into the shared space. An additional eco-law, the logic fragement eco-law interprets those fragments based on the current tuples in the tuple space (including neighbouring ones). Those fragments actually define on-the-fly ad hoc chemical reactions that apply on matching data tuples present in the system, removing tuples and producing new tuples, possibly producing also new logic fragments. Our model is defined independently of any specific logic, an actual instantiation and implementation of the model can use its own logic(s). We also defined a spatial language to verify graph-based spatial properties of self-organising systems [6], a multi-valued logic [7] and an approximate reasoning [13]. The language encapsulates Logic Fragments in statements that are evaluated in a distributed manner at run-time, involving several system entities at the same time. The corresponding middleware for two-valued logic is available. LFCM is composed of the following elements (Fig. 6):

- *Agents:* autonomous entities representing applications, services and sensors.
- *Tuple space:* shared space for all the agents running on the same node of the system. The Tuple Space stores information under the form of tuples, which can be *passive* (e.g. contextual-information, data input for service invocation, etc.) and *active* (logic fragments).
- *Logic fragments:* combinations of logic programs manipulating passive data stored in the Tuple Space and introduced either by Agents or generated by other logic fragments. They can be injected, removed and copied among nodes of the system at run-time. We consider many-valued logics with *true, false, unknown* and *inconsistent* logical values.

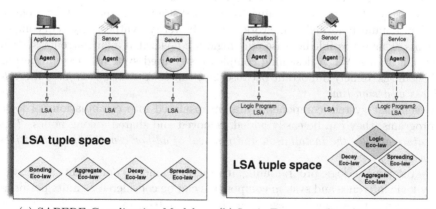

(a) SAPERE Coordination Model   (b) Logic Fragment Coordination Model

Fig. 5. Coordination models

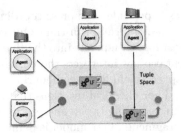

Fig. 6. Components of the Logic Fragment Coordination Model. Green tuples represent passive data injected by Agents, red ones depict information generated by logic fragments. (Color figure online)

LFCM combines the benefits of chemical-based coordination models and formal methods, offering a framework to rigorously design and implement self-organising systems. In the LFCM logical formulae are represented by combinations of logic programs, whereas the execution flow is controlled through predicates and operators defining how logic programs are interpreted and how data is manipulated through predicates (e.g. to create, aggregate, delete and spread information).

- When designing complex coordination mechanisms, great emphasis is put on the definition of the logic part, enforcing a rigorous formalisation of the algorithm while hiding most of implementation details. In such a way, code of system units becomes an essential set of logical rules defining the behaviour of components with respect to the distributed state of the system. This aspect ensures that *the set of spontaneous interactions taking place in the system is the one that is logically entailed from the rules.*
- The usage of logic programming to design system units makes it possible to adopt a uniform formal framework to specify, verify, synthesise system components. This is possible because pure logic can be used as a language for system specifications. When designing complex distributed systems these properties become extremely important because *they can be exploited to enforce correctness at design-time.*
- Given that system components are encapsulated into combinations of logic programs, they can be easily added, removed and shared among nodes. *This feature enables the installation and removal of ad-hoc coordination primitives on-the-fly.*
- By resorting to logic programming, interactions among components are driven by logic inference and system components can be considered as units performing formal reasoning processes on the distributed state of the system. By resorting to this feature, *components can be exploited to evaluate distributed system properties at run-time* [11].

6 Prototyping Platforms

TheOne-SAPERE. TheOne-SAPERE is a prototyping tool [20] that integrates the SAPERE middleware within The Opportunistic Network Environment (The One) simulator [24], allowing us to prototype and validate applications with realistic scenarios before deploying them. Indeed, it allows on the one hand to simulate a large number of computational nodes movements and their communications, placing them in various configurations allowing stochastic evaluation of parameters. On the other hand, each node is equipped with the actual SAPERE middleware (actual code), allowing to execute from within the simulation actual spatial system services (gradient, spreading, evaporation, etc.), thus providing actual results relating to spatial system services behaviour (Fig. 7). The corresponding video is available on-line[1].

TheOne-LFCM. Following the above idea, we similarly developed a corresponding simulator, called TheOne-LFCM, involving the actual LFCM middleware in each simulated node.

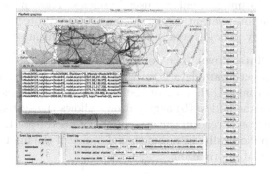

Fig. 7. TheOne-SAPERE

7 Developed Applications

We discuss here a series of applications actually deployed on tablets and smartphones. For more IoT applications, see [16].

Confidential channel. The Confidential Channel service [8] provides an encrypted channel for routing confidential communication between devices in a mobile ad-hoc network. The computational power and memory available in mobile devices, is increasing dramatically, and allows now the use of traditional encrypting techniques that some years ago were available only in wired computers, such as laptops or PCs. Therefore, the Secure Channel service uses RSA encryption on top of Dynamic Gradient and Chemotaxis services in order to ensure and maintain confidential communication and routing even in complex

---

[1] http://youtu.be/EGbPq2rejmM.

mobile networks. Using a Gradient service, node A sends a public key and a request for information. They are both propagated to all nodes in the network along with additional gradient information about the sender's distance (e.g. number of hops). When the Gradient reaches node B, the latter retrieves the query and the public key. B encrypts the information using the received public key and sends back the encrypted information using the Chemotaxis service using the shortest available path. The gradient structure is updated periodically in order to deal with network's topology changes. We subsequently developed a chat over the confidential channel.

SmartContent. This is a novel approach for content protection and privacy. Documents are active and context-aware documents that sense and analyse their current context, e.g. location, noise, neighbouring devices, social network, expiration time, etc. Based on user provided policies, they grant, deny or limit access and manipulation actions, or destroy themselves if necessary. The implementation leverages the SAPERE middleware. Context information (GPS location, camera picture, etc.) is provided as tuples in the SAPERE middleware. Specific agents, wrapping documents, enforce users' policies. They are sensitive (bond) to context information relevant to the document they protect and enact when necessary the privacy policy (revealing or not the document) [9].

Context-aware data flows. The goal of this demonstration is to show-case self-organising context-aware data flows with a particular emphasis on the self-organising mechanisms [21] that are at the heart of it: (a) diffusion - propagates information among the nodes; (b) aggregation - allows the system to reduce the amount of information spread in the system or obtained from the environment; (c) evaporation - periodically decreases the relevance of the information in order to get rid of outdated information.

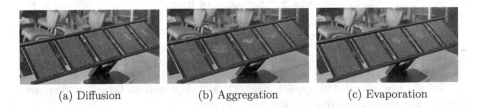

(a) Diffusion   (b) Aggregation   (c) Evaporation

Fig. 8. Self-organising mechanisms - concepts

In the first part of the demonstration, data flows of pictures spread, in a P2P fashion, from one tablet to the other. Data flows are sensitive to their context as follows: tapping tablets causes a new data flow to spread from one tablet to the neighbouring one (Fig. 8(a)); similarly swiping creates a new flow in the direction of the swipe; several flows meeting at the same time in the same tablet aggregate with each other. Here a simple aggregation is chosen, where one of the two flows is stopped (shown as an explosion in the demonstration) (Fig. 8(b)).

Figure 8(c) shows an example of evaporation, with time data relevance fades away and ultimately information disappears. In the second part of the demonstration, data flows become services used to retrieve a friend in a crowd. A query first spreads from tablet to tablet following the gradient principle - a type of diffusion with a notion of distance [21]; once the message has reached the friend, the answer follows back the path created by the gradient. This demonstration has been featured at the ICT'13 Conference in Vilnius, the video is available here[2].

Tracking mobile objects/runners - querying IoT. Runners are sensed along the racetrack and their positions spread continuously in order to provide a real-time tracking. A variety of devices (beacons), and nodes (raspberry pi and smartphones) are exchanging data using Bluetooth Low Energy (BLE) to track mobile objects in a peer-to-peer network. Let us consider that each runner is equipped with a small device that emits continuously a signal. We also deploy several nodes along the path sensing and relaying these signals. People in the crowd with a smartphone and an appropriate mobile application request informations about their favourite runners and receive a response in real-time. In other words, people track their favourite runners while they are running and follow their performance during the race.

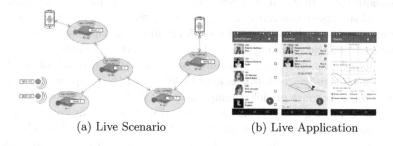

(a) Live Scenario   (b) Live Application

Fig. 9. Tracking runners

Each competitor runs with a beacon that emits a BLE signal. A beacon identifies a runner by communicating its runner identifier to its surrounding environment. Several nodes, running a SAPERE application built over the SAPERE middleware, are deployed along the path to sense BLE signals and compute their position in the race, their location on the map, and the time they have been running. Every node spreads received signals and people in the crowd interact across a peer-to-peer network to request information about their favourite runners (Fig. 9(a)). People track their favourite players while they are running and know about their performance live during the race (Fig. 9(b)). The information remains spatially available in the area only during the time when the event takes place. A complete description and full details can be found here [28].

---

[2] http://youtu.be/4S4J5wYvdNk.

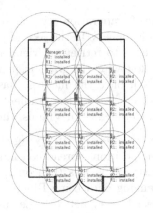

Fig. 10. Warehouse and communicating shelf units.

Assessing IoT properties on-the-fly. We show here how to resort to the Logic Fragment Coordination Model to design and implement a distributed monitoring spatial edge service for an industrial warehouse in order to avoid safety hazards arising from potential interactions among chemical compounds. The model of the warehouse system includes: Containers (e.g. tanks); Shelf units supporting the physical storage of containers in a particular point of the warehouse; Policies constraints on physical positions of containers implementing safety regulations (e.g. proximity relations among chemical compounds, etc.). Policies can be established, replaced or removed at run-time. By resorting to a many-valued logic, policies can be *strongly violated, weakly violated, weakly accepted* and *strongly accepted*. Our warehouse model is composed of 12 shelf units connected in a grid network; shelf units must be considered as autonomous agent entities, able to perform computations and communicate with each other (Fig. 10). The monitoring service triggers an alarm signal when one or several policies are violated on a particular shelf unit.

Whenever a policy is violated on a shelf unit, its associated logic fragment generates a tuple of type *Alam(Rule)*, where *Rule* is the identifier of the policy. An additional logic fragment (controller of the system) aggregates all tuples of type *Alarm(Rule)*, generating a tuple *Alarm* with a logical level that represents the level of criticality of the violated policies.

8   Future Works

Future works involve multiple paths: integrating learning aspects within agents, analysing QoS for each of the different spatial services involved in an application and their impact on each other, pursuing current efforts on privacy and security, actually building spatial services on demand, arising from existing services, sensors and actuators.

Acknowledgements. This work has been supported by the EU-FP7-FET Proactive project SAPERE Self-aware Pervasive Service Ecosystems, under contract no. 256873. It is the result of the joint work of the SAPERE team. I would like to particularly thank the Geneva team, namely: Akla Esso Tchao, Jose Luis Fernandez-Marquez, Francesco Luca De Angelis, Houssem Ben Mahfoudh, Roberto Tomaylla.

References

1. Babaoglu, O., Canright, G., Deutsch, A., Caro, G.A.D., Ducatelle, F., Gambardella, L.M., Ganguly, N., Jelasity, M., Montemanni, R., Montresor, A., Urnes, T.: Design patterns from biology for distributed computing. ACM Trans. Auton. Adapt. Sys. **1**, 26–66 (2006)
2. Beal, J., Bachrach, J.: Infrastructure for engineered emergence on sensor/actuator networks. IEEE Intell. Syst. **21**(2), 10–19 (2006)
3. Castelli, G., Mamei, M., Rosi, A., Zambonelli, F.: Pervasive middleware goes social: the sapere approach. In: Proceedings of the 2011 Fifth IEEE Conference on Self-Adaptive and Self-Organizing Systems Workshops, SASOW 2011, pp. 9–14 (2011)
4. Castelli, G., Mamei, M., Rosi, A., Zambonelli, F.: Engineering pervasive service ecosystems: the sapere approach. ACM Trans. Auton. Adapt. Syst. **10**(1), 1:1–1:27 (2015). http://doi.acm.org/10.1145/2700321
5. de Castro, L.N.: Fundamentals of Natural Computing: Basic Concepts, Algorithms, and Applications (Chapman & Hall/Crc Computer and Information Sciences). Chapman & Hall/CRC (2006)
6. De Angelis, F., Di Marzo Serugendo, G.: A logic language for run time assessment of spatial properties in self-organizing systems. In: IEEE International Conference on Self-Adaptive and Self-Organizing Systems Workshops, pp. 86–91 (2015)
7. De Angelis, F., Di Marzo Serugendo, G., Szałas, A.: Graded rule-based reasoning. Accepted to International Journal of Approximate Reasoning (2017, to appear)
8. De Angelis, F., Fernandez-Marquez, J.L., Di Marzo Serugendo, G.: Secure channel for manets - demonstration. In: IEEE International Conference on Self-Adaptive and Self-Organizing Systems (SASO2013). IEEE Computer Society (2013)
9. De Angelis, F.L., Di Marzo Serugendo, G.: Smartcontent - self-protected context-aware active documents for mobile environments. Electronics **6**(1), 1–22 (2017). http://www.mdpi.com/2079-9292/6/1/17
10. Angelis, F.L., Marzo Serugendo, G.: Logic fragments: a coordination model based on logic inference. In: Holvoet, T., Viroli, M. (eds.) COORDINATION 2015. LNCS, vol. 9037, pp. 35–48. Springer, Cham (2015). doi:10.1007/978-3-319-19282-6_3
11. De Angelis, F.L., Di Marzo Serugendo, G.: A logic language for run time assessment of spatial properties in self-organizing systems. On: 9th IEEE Conference on Self-Adaptive and Self-Organizing Systems Workshops (SASOW). IEEE (2015)
12. De Angelis, F.L., Di Marzo Serugendo, G.: Logic fragments: coordinating entities with logic programs. In: 7th International Symposium On Leveraging Applications of Formal Methods Verification and Validation (ISOLA) (2016)
13. De Angelis, F.L., Di Marzo Serugendo, G., Dunin-Keplicz, B., Szałas, A.: Heterogeneous approximate reasoning with graded truth values. In: International Joint Conference on Rough Sets (2017)

14. De Wolf, T., Holvoet, T.: Design patterns for decentralised coordination in self-organising emergent systems. Eng. Self-Organising Syst. **4335**, 28–49 (2007)
15. Marzo Serugendo, G.: Robustness and dependability of self-organizing systems - a safety engineering perspective. In: Guerraoui, R., Petit, F. (eds.) SSS 2009. LNCS, vol. 5873, pp. 254–268. Springer, Heidelberg (2009). doi:10.1007/978-3-642-05118-0_18
16. Di Marzo Serugendo, G., Abdennadher, N., Ben Mahfoudh, H., De Angelis, F.L., Tomaylla, R.: Spatial edge services. Global IoT Summit (2017)
17. Di Marzo Serugendo, G., Fernandez-Marquez, J.L., De Angelis, F.L.: Engineering spatial services: concepts, architecture, and execution models. In: Ramanathan, R., Raja, K. (eds.) Handbook of Research on Architectural Trends in Service-Driven Computing, pp. 136–159. IGI Global (2014)
18. Di Marzo Serugendo, G., Gleizes, M.P., Karageorgos, A. (eds.): Self-Organising Software - From Natural to Artificial Adaptation. Natural Computing Series, 1st edn. Springer, Heidelberg (2011)
19. Fernandez-Marquez, J.L., Tchao, A.E., Di Marzo Serugendo, G., Stevenson, G., Ye, J., Dobson, S.: Analysis of new gradient based aggregation algorithms for data-propagation in distributed networks. In: 1st International Workshop on Adaptive Service Ecosystems: Nature and Socially Inspired Solutions (ASENSIS) at 5th IEEE International Conference on Self-Adaptive and Self-Organizing Systems (SASO2012) (2012)
20. Fernandez-Marquez, J.L., Angelis, F.D., Serugendo, G.D.M., Stevenson, G., Castelli, G.: The one-sapere simulator: a prototyping tool for engineering self-organisation in pervasive environments. In: SASO, pp. 201–202. IEEE Computer Society (2014). http://dblp.uni-trier.de/db/conf/saso/saso2014.html#Fernandez-MarquezASSC14
21. Fernandez-Marquez, J.L., Serugendo, G.D.M., Montagna, S., Viroli, M., Arcos, J.L.: Description and composition of bio-inspired design patterns: a complete overview. Nat. Comput. **12**(1), 43–67 (2012)
22. Gardelli, L., Viroli, M., Omicini, A.: Design patterns for self-organizing multiagent systems. In: Proceedings of EEDAS (2007)
23. Hajibaba, M., Gorgin, S.: A review on modern distributed computing paradigms: cloud computing, jungle computing and fog computing. CIT - J. Comput. Inf. Technol. **22**(2), 69–84 (2014)
24. Keränen, A., Ott, J., Kärkkäinen, T.: The ONE Simulator for DTN protocol evaluation. In: SIMUTools 2009: Proceedings of the 2nd International Conference on Simulation Tools and Techniques. ICST, New York (2009)
25. Mamei, M., Menezes, R., Tolksdorf, R., Zambonelli, F.: Case studies for self-organization in computer science. J. Syst. Archit. **52**, 433–460 (2006)
26. Mamei, M., Zambonelli, F.: Programming pervasive and mobile computing applications: The tota approach. ACM Trans. Softw. Eng. Methodol. **18**(4), 15:1–15:56 (2009). http://doi.acm.org/10.1145/1538942.1538945
27. Nagpal, R.: A catalog of biologically-inspired primitives for engineering self-organization. In: Marzo Serugendo, G., Karageorgos, A., Rana, O.F., Zambonelli, F. (eds.) ESOA 2003. LNCS, vol. 2977, pp. 53–62. Springer, Heidelberg (2004). doi:10.1007/978-3-540-24701-2_4
28. Tomaylla, R.: Bio-Inspired approach for tracking mobile entities in a Peer to Peer MANET. An application of The SAPERE Project in Road Running events. Master's thesis, Centre Universitaire d'Informatique, University of Geneva, Geneva, Switzerland (2016)

29. Zambonelli, F., Mamei, M.: Spatial computing: an emerging paradigm for autonomic computing and communication. In: Smirnov, M. (ed.) WAC 2004. LNCS, vol. 3457, pp. 44–57. Springer, Heidelberg (2005). doi:10.1007/11520184_4

30. Zambonelli, F., Omicini, A., Anzengruber, B., Castelli, G., Angelis, F.L.D., Serugendo, G.D.M., Dobson, S., Fernandez-Marquez, J.L., Ferscha, A., Mamei, M., Mariani, S., Molesini, A., Montagna, S., Nieminen, J., Pianini, D., Risoldi, M., Rosi, A., Stevenson, G., Viroli, M., Ye, J.: Developing pervasive multi-agent systems with nature-inspired coordination. Pervasive Mobile Comput. Part B **17**, 236–252 (2015). http://www.sciencedirect.com/science/article/pii/S1574119214001904, 10 years of Pervasive Computing' In Honor of Chatschik Bisdikian

Languages and Tools

AErlang: Empowering Erlang
with Attribute-Based Communication

Rocco De Nicola[1]([⊠]), Tan Duong[2]([⊠]), Omar Inverso[2]([⊠]),
and Catia Trubiani[2]([⊠])

[1] IMT Institute for Advanced Studies Lucca, Lucca, Italy
rocco.denicola@imtlucca.it
[2] Gran Sasso Science Institute, L'Aquila, Italy
{tan.duong,omar.inverso,catia.trubiani}@gssi.it

Abstract. Attribute-based communication provides a novel mechanism to dynamically select groups of communicating entities by relying on predicates over their exposed attributes. In this paper, we embed the basic primitives for attribute-based communication into the functional concurrent language Erlang to obtain what we call AErlang, for attribute Erlang. To evaluate our prototype in terms of performance overhead and scalability we consider solutions of the *Stable Marriage Problem* based on predicates over attributes and on the classical preference lists, and use them to compare the runtime performance of AErlang with those of Erlang and X10. The outcome of the comparison shows that the overhead introduced by the new communication primitives is acceptable, and our prototype can compete performance-wise with an ad-hoc parallel solution in X10.

Keywords: Attribute-based communication · Erlang · Concurrency · Distributed programming · Collective adaptive systems · Stable marriage

1 Introduction

Collective adaptive systems (CAS) are typically large conglomerates of components which are not entirely aware of themselves as members of a collectivity and interact according to limited mutual knowledge and local rules, indirectly triggering global system evolution [14]. Eventually, despite the simplicity of the components in isolation, the global behaviour of the system may end up being quite sophisticated, hardly predictable to seemingly chaotic.

These classes of systems pose challenges at many levels. Reasoning about them is difficult. In fact, assessing specific properties, such as stability and convergence, or forecasting emerging behaviour is usually really hard due to non-linearity and non-determinism. Further sources of complexity are in the following distinguishing features:

© IFIP International Federation for Information Processing 2017
Published by Springer International Publishing AG 2017. All Rights Reserved
J.-M. Jacquet and M. Massink (Eds.): COORDINATION 2017, LNCS 10319, pp. 21–39, 2017.
DOI: 10.1007/978-3-319-59746-1_2

- Anonymity: the identity of components is not known;
- Open-endedness: new components may enter or leave at any time;
- Adaptivity: rôles and interests of components may change;
- Scalability: the number of components might grow very fast and large.

All these features are fairly visible, for example, in ant colonies, as well as stock markets, robot swarms, and social networks. In the presence of these features, programming may be difficult. For instance, in an anonymous and open-ended environment traditional mechanisms such as point-to-point communication are hardly acceptable. Similarly, the limited expressiveness of mainstream programming paradigms often makes it inconvenient to describe adaptive behaviour. In addition, the size of the system exacerbates this situation and on a practical standpoint is cause of concern about performance.

Some of the above issues can be addressed with adequate descriptive formalisms. Among these, *Attribute-based Communication* [2,12] is a particularly appropriate one. With this approach, components are modelled as processes exposing attributes, i.e., relevant features according to the problem domain and to the local or global behaviours of interest, and process interaction is driven by predicates over these. Communication takes place in an implicit selective multicast fashion, and interactions among components are dynamically established by taking into account "connections" as determined by predicates over their attributes. A command $send(v)@\pi$ expresses the intention of sending v to all entities satisfying predicate π while $receive(x)@\pi'$ indicates willingness to receive messages by entities satisfying predicate π' while binding the received values to x. Components can update their attributes via assignments, $[a := v]$. In this way, collectives are dynamically formed at the time of interaction by considering the sets of receiving components that satisfy the sending predicates.

Let us now consider a social network scenario where users aim at forming groups for language exchange. Such groups may be formed by only considering the language users wish to learn and the one potential partners are interested in. However in case of multiple alternatives it might be desirable to prefer people with similar age and interests, or even knowledgeable of a second language in common. Relevant attributes would then be spoken languages, age, language of interest, and so on. Predicates are built by specifying conditions on the attributes, e.g., $age \leq 25 \land language = English$. Note that here the identity of users is irrelevant for forming the groups, and no change in the predicates is required when users join or leave the system, thus anonymity and open-endedness are no longer a concern. In general, attribute-based programming allows to naturally capture the essence of a system to a very good level of abstraction without having to worry about a number of details that normally have to be taken under due consideration when using more traditional alternatives.

In this paper, we seek to leverage the benefits of attribute-based communication at a programming level while addressing the performance concerns at the same time. Our contribution is twofold.

As a first contribution, we combine attribute-based communication with functional-style programming by instantiating attribute-based programming abstractions on top of the *Erlang* programming language. We targeted *Erlang* as the host platform for our prototype language extension due to its native support for concurrency and distribution, its scalability, and the inherent modularity of functional-style programming. Its concurrency model is very lightweight and has solid foundations based on Actors [1], thus, in principle, avoids thread-and-lock problems. Moreover, it fits very well with the *AbC* process calculus [2], since both consider processes as basic units of computation that communicate via asynchronous message passing. Our prototype language extension, *AErlang*, is a middleware enabling attribute-based communication among *Erlang* processes, with the aim of preserving *Erlang*'s excellent scalability. *AErlang* plays the role of global process registry which allows processes to register and update their attributes. It also takes charge of forwarding messages from senders to receivers by evaluating the predicates they supply. In this way, programmers are relieved from the burden of working out details such as the explicit handling of attributes, the evaluation of predicates, and so on. Our attribute-based programming technique can naturally model the main distinguishing features of collective adaptive systems at no extra effort, whereas under a traditional programming setting such a task would require major and time-consuming operations.

As a second contribution, we provide a performance evaluation of our prototype in terms of efficiency and scalability. We assess the effectiveness of our prototype by using it to program a solution to *Stable Marriage* [17] that aims at matching members according to their preferences. For this problem, we consider implementations of different variants in different languages. Namely, we first consider a variant explicitly based on (predicates over) attributes and provide an implementation in *AErlang*. Then, we derive preference lists from the predicates and implement the classical algorithm in *AErlang*, *Erlang*, and *X*10, a language specifically designed to scale with the number of cores [10]. The different implementations are instrumental to compare performances of our solutions. The experimental results show that the overhead resulting from using the new communication primitives is acceptable, and our prototype successfully preserves *Erlang*'s scalability. Moreover, on very large instances the *AErlang* program for the attribute-based solution turns out to scale considerably better than a state-of-the-art parallel version based on adaptive search and implemented in *X*10 [30].

The rest of the paper is organized as follows. We describe how to extend *Erlang* with attribute-based communication constructs in Sect. 2. Example programs of *AErlang* are presented in Sect. 3. In Sect. 4 we evaluate our prototype in terms of efficiency and scalability. Related works are discussed in Sect. 5, conclusions and future research directions are provided in Sect. 6.

2   AErlang

AErlang instantiates attribute-based communication on top of the *Erlang* programming language.

Erlang [4, 35] is a concurrent functional programming language originally designed for building telecommunication systems [7] and recently successfully adapted to broader contexts, such as large-scale distributed messaging platforms [29, 31]. It supports concurrency [5] and inter-process communication natively through a compact set of powerful primitives. The *Erlang* concurrency model is based on the Actor Model [1, 20]. Actors are processes that can asynchronously exchange messages while preserving the order of outbound messages. Each process has its own unlimited mailbox for storing incoming messages that are retrieved via pattern matching. The lightweight and scalable concurrency model and the modularity of functional-style programming [22, 23] make *Erlang* particularly appropriate for building massively scalable distributed systems.

AErlang lifts *Erlang*'s send and receive communication primitives to attribute-based reasoning. In *Erlang*, the send primitive ! requires an explicit destination address (e.g., registered name, process identifier) for message passing. In contrast, *AErlang* processes are not aware of the presence and identity of each other, and communicate using predicates over attributes.

AErlang aims at relieving programmers from the burden of working out details such as the explicit handling of attributes, the evaluation of predicates, and so on, while at the same time preserving *Erlang*'s excellent scalability. Our prototype extension is implemented as a middleware that plays the role of global process registry and takes charge of forwarding messages from senders to receivers by evaluating the predicates they supply.

2.1 Programming Interface

The programming interface of our prototype is presented in Fig. 1. Processes joining the system need to register their details (e.g., process identifier, attributes) using function `register`, which takes as input a process attribute environment `Env` in form of a either a proper list or a map, i.e., pairs of attribute names and their associated values. After the registration, processes can manage their local environment by using the `setAtt` and `getAtt` functions. Processes leaving the system may actively `unregister`, and when a process unregisters, then it is no longer able to use attribute-based communication.

```
% initialization          % attribute-based           % attribute-based
aerl:start()              % send and receive           % send and receive with counting
                          to(Pred) ! Msg               Count = to(Pred) ! Msg

% join and leave
aerl:register(Env)        from(Pred),                  from(Pred,Count),
aerl:unregister()         receive                      receive
                              Pattern_1 -> Expression_1;    Pattern_1 -> Expression_1;
% environment handling        ...                          ...
aerl:setAtt(List)             Pattern_n -> Expression_n     Pattern_n -> Expression_n
aerl:getAtt(List)         end                          end
```

Fig. 1. *AErlang* programming interface.

Registered *AErlang* processes interact via attribute-based send and receive actions. Differently from standard *Erlang*, this pair of communication primitives replace source and destination identifiers with arbitrary predicates over the declared attributes. In particular, attribute-based send is used to send a message Msg to all processes whose attributes satisfy predicate Pred. On the other hand, attribute-based receive is used to receive messages sent by using attribute-based send. The receipt of a message is conditioned by the attribute values satisfying predicate Pred. A receive operation has the effect of retrieving from the receivers' mailbox any message that matches the receiving predicate.

Predicates are strings containing Boolean expressions. They can be over attribute names (*Erlang* atoms), constants (written with a prefix underscore, e.g., _constant), process-local references to attributes (written as this.a), and process-local variables representing values (written as $X) Apart from comparison operators and logical connectives, it is possible to use arithmetic operators, such as $+, *, /, -$ between predicate terms. Furthermore, predicates can contain the operator in, which denotes the membership relation between an element and a list, and allow the use of user-defined functions.

AErlang provides the possibility for processes to count with how many partners they are currently interacting and to parallelize the communication, so to increase both flexibility and performance without affecting expressiveness. Although these primitives are not originally described in the *AbC* calculus, we provide variants of attribute-based send and receive actions as shown in the rightmost column of Fig. 1. In particular, to(Pred) can return the number of selected receivers (whom the middleware forwards the message to) at communication time. On the other hand, the attribute-based multi-receive from(Pred,Count) takes this as an extra argument and blocks until the given amount of incoming messages is received. Internally the receive operation processes multiple incoming messages satisfying the receiving predicates, up to the given count. This is helpful when the sender is interested to hear back from its communication partners. Count is the number of selected receivers at communication time, which is always greater than the number of actual receivers, which in turn bounds the number of receivers willing to answer. Therefore the sender knows the maximum number of expected incoming messages before moving to the next action.

2.2   Prototype Architecture

There are two main components in *AErlang*: (i) a process registry that keeps track of process details such as the process identifier and the current status, and (ii) a message broker that undertakes the delivery of outgoing messages.

Process Registry. It is a generic server that accepts requests regarding process (un)registration and internal updates. It stores process identifiers and all the information used by the message broker to deliver messages.

Our prototype uses as the main storage back-end Mnesia, *Erlang*'s built-in distributed database. When a process joins the system, the `register` function does several things. First, the process environment is stored into an ETS table and the reference to this table is stored into the process dictionary. This information is local to the process. Second, a service request to the process registry is performed, to insert process details, including the attribute environment, into an Mnesia table. We currently store attributes in separate columns for increased performance and at the expense of some extra memory. All the above information is removed when the `unregistration` procedure is invoked.

Message Broker. It is responsible for delivering messages between processes. It is implemented as an Erlang server process listening for interactions from attribute-based send. To address potential bottlenecks arising in the presence of a very large number of processes, the message broker can be set up to run in multiple parallel threads. Similarly to the process registry, *Erlang*'s runtime system provides distribution for the message broker.

A sending action is characterized by a sending predicate, a message and sender's environment. All these elements are wrapped up into a single message and passed to the message broker. When such a message arrives, the message broker performs the following steps:

1. parse the predicates and converts them into a database query;
2. select the receivers by applying the query to the process database;
3. forward the message to all the selected receivers.

The exact behaviour depends, however, on the specific operating mode chosen at the moment of initializing *AErlang*. More specifically, there are two kinds of checks that need to be evaluated for a receiver to receive a message:

– the sending predicate is checked against the receiver's environment,
– the receiving predicate is checked against the sender's environment.

The current prototype implemented the following message forwarding strategies for the message broker: (i) *broadcast*, i.e., the broker forwards any outbound message to every components in the system, then these filter the received messages according to both the sending and receiving predicates; (ii) *pushing*, i.e., the broker only checks the sending predicates and forwards messages to selected receivers that will use the receiving predicates to decide whether to accept any incoming message; (iii) *pulling*, i.e., the broker only checks the receiving predicates and only forwards messages from selected senders; the forwarded messages are then filtered by the receiver according to the sending predicates; (iv) *push-pull*, i.e., the message broker checks for both the sending and receiving predicates before forwarding any message. The choice of one message forwarding policy over the others depends on the specific class of problems under consideration. For example, broadcast can guarantee consistency in highly dynamic systems, but it is quite expensive due to the large number of forwarded messages. On the other hand, if consistency is not the major concern, then pushing is more suitable when attributes do not change frequently, while pushpull works well when even the predicates are quite static.

3 Programming with AErlang

In this section we present attribute-based programming in AErlang. By adopting as a case study the well-known problem of Stable Marriage (SM), we begin with describing a program that implements the classical solution for this problem, and then consider progressively more elaborate variants, with the purpose of showing the convenience of using attributes and a suitable programming technique. At the end of the section we discuss how the proposed approach can be generalised to model realistic examples of collective adaptive systems such as social networks.

3.1 Stable Marriage

SM consists in finding a matching between sets of men and women, where each person has a preference list of members of the opposite gender [17]. A *matching* is a set of one-to-one assignments between men and women. Each assignment is denoted by a *pair* (m, w), where m and w indicate the two matched *partners*. A pair is *blocking* if, according to their respective preference lists, both the matched man and woman prefer someone else to their partners. A matching is *stable* if there is no blocking pair. A matching is *complete* when everybody is matched, *incomplete* otherwise.

SM has many practical applications [19], and has been intensively studied in the literature, together with its variants [24]. In the classical form, the preference lists are strictly-ordered and complete. For this, Gale and Shapley gave an efficient algorithm to find a stable matching [17]. It can be informally summarized as follows. Each man actively proposes himself to his most favourite woman according to his preference list. Whenever a man is rejected, he tries again with the next woman in the list. On the other hand, each woman continuously waits for incoming proposals. A woman without a partner immediately accepts any proposal, otherwise she compares the proposer with her current partner. She then rejects the man whom she likes less, according to her preference list. The algorithm terminates when every man has a partner.

Variations of this algorithm consider other kinds of preference list: incomplete (SMI), with ties (SMT), or both (SMTI). While the first two variants can be solved similarly to the classical case, SMTI is hard [25]. In this paper we investigate a new variant of the algorithm where the matching happens by taking into account the mutual interests of partners characteristics, rather than preference lists of identifiers. We call this variant stable marriage with attributes (SMA). Note that SMA can always be cast into SM by converting preferences over attributes to preferences over identifiers. This can be done by assigning a weight to each attribute and summing up all the attributes exposed by the identifiers to obtain the preference list.

Table 1. Correspondence between preference lists and predicate lists

men's lists	women's lists
m_1: w_1 w_2	w_1: (m_1 m_2)
m_2: w_1 w_2	w_2: m_1

men's id	men's predicates	women's id	women's predicates
m_1	$id = w_1, id = w_2$	w_1	$id = m_1$ or $id = m_2$
m_2	$id = w_1, id = w_2$	w_2	$id = m_1$

3.2 Stable Marriage with Preference List

We now consider a variant of SM known as SMTI [25], in which the preference list is incomplete and partially ordered, i.e., a man or a woman may like several people at the same level. The preference list is thus a list of sets rather than single elements and we refer to such sets as *ties*.

We model this problem in AErlang by introducing an attribute id to represent people identifiers and predicates over these to specify the preferences. As an example, Table 1 shows the predicate lists induced from a SMTI instance (on the left) where ties are enclosed by parentheses. To implement preference list we use predicates over the attribute id, where ties are modelled by predicates with logical disjunction on equality comparison. We refer to the newly derived lists on the right table as predicate lists.

We then solve the problem under this new representation of preferences by using a simple solution which is similar to the classical Gale-Shapley algorithm described in Sect. 3.1, but uses a slightly different protocol and is converted to message-passing style.

The *AErlang* program for STMI is shown in Fig. 2. Function man() takes as arguments the preference list Prefs of a man and his identifier Id. The first element in Prefs is bound to variable H by pattern matching on list (line 2). A man goes through a proposing phase from lines 3 to 14. First, he sends a propose message using "id in $H" as the sending predicate (line 3) which has the effect of contacting all women whose id belongs to the list H. He then waits for enough answers from the women he contacted using the attribute-based receive construct with counting (line 4), with the same predicate used when sending. Inside the body of this receive operation, the man is only interested in yes messages. He becomes aware of his status by checking attribute partner (line 7) to take a decision. If he has no partner, he sends a confirm message to the first woman who said yes by using her identifier W attached in the reply message. He then considers this woman as his current partner (line 10), and informs any other interested women that he is no longer available by sending them a busy message (line 12).

After the proposing phase, a man can either be alone or engaged (checked by line 15). In the first case, he does not consider any woman in the current predicate H and tries to propose himself again to the women in the remaining part of his preferences (line 16). In the second case, he takes no action unless he receives a goodbye message from his partner (lines 17–19), in which case he tries proposing himself again using his current predicate unchanged (line 21). The man keeps the predicate unchanged as it may include other women.

```
 1   man(Prefs,Id) ->                          24   woman(Prefs,Id,P) ->
 2   [H|T]=Prefs,                               25   from("bof($Prefs,$P,id)"),
 3   Count=to("id in $H") ! {propose,Id},       26   receive
 4   from("id in $H",Count),                    27     {propose,M} ->
 5   receive                                    28       to("id=$M") ! {yes,Id},
 6     {yes,W} ->                               29       from("id=$M"),
 7       case aerl:getA(partner) of             30       receive
 8         none ->                              31         confirm ->
 9             to("id=$W") ! confirm,           32           to("id=$P") ! goodbye,
10             aerl:setA(partner,W);            33           woman(Prefs,Id,M)
11         _ ->                                 34         busy ->
12             to("id=$W") ! busy               35           woman(Prefs,Id,P)
13       end                                    36       end
14   end,                                       37   end.
15   case aerl:getA(partner) of
16     none -> man(T,Id);
17     _ -> from("id=this.partner"),
18       receive
19         goodbye ->
20             aerl:setA(partner,none),
21             man(Prefs,Id)
22       end
23   end.
```

Fig. 2. Stable marriage with preference lists in AErlang (SM-aerl).

Function woman() takes as arguments a preference list Prefs, an identifier Id, and the partner's identifier P. A woman always waits for proposals from men who are better than her current partner. This comparison is performed with the bof function (line 25) that checks if a proposer preceeds the current partner P in the woman's preference list. If this is the case, then the woman sends back a yes message and waits for an confirm message from the new man M. After M confirms to her, the woman gets engaged to him by keeping M in the recursive call (line 33), after rejecting her current partner P. Otherwise, she keeps listening for other proposals (line 35).

3.3 Stable Marriage with Attributes

In this variant each person has a set of attributes describing their own characteristics and some preferences over the attributes of their potential partners. Each attribute has a finite domain, while preferences are represented by logical expressions over the attributes of the partners. For simplicity, in this section we only consider simple predicates where preferences are conjunctions of equality comparisons.

Table 2 shows an example of SMA instance of size four where each person has two attributes, which in turn have two possible values. This example points out the expressive power of attribute-based communication. In fact, our program for SMA (Fig. 3) is very similar to the program proposed in previous section (Fig. 2), and the differences are mostly accommodated by altering the predicates. In addition, men can progressively adapt their preferences to increase the chances to find a partner. For example, there is no woman in Table 2 satisfying the requirements of man m1, hence he looks for partners partially matching his

Table 2. Attributes and preferences for men and women.

Id	Wealth	Body	Preferences
m1	rich	strong	eyes=amber ∧ hair=red
m2	rich	weak	eyes=green ∧ hair=dark
m3	poor	strong	eyes=green ∧ hair=red
m4	poor	weak	eyes=amber ∧ hair=red

Id	Eyes	Hair	Preferences
w1	amber	dark	wealth=poor ∧ body=weak
w2	amber	dark	wealth=rich ∧ body=strong
w3	green	red	wealth=rich ∧ body=strong
w4	green	dark	wealth=rich ∧ body=weak

Table 3. Predicate lists for men.

Id	Relaxation of preferences		
m1	eyes=amber ∧ hair=red	eyes=amber	hair=red
m2	eyes=green ∧ hair=dark	eyes=green	hair=dark
m3	eyes=green ∧ hair=red	eyes=green	hair=red
m4	eyes=amber ∧ hair=red	eyes=amber	hair=red

initial preferences. This adaptive behaviour is achieved by transforming plain preferences into predicate lists, as shown in Table 3. For example, when man m1 relaxes his preferences and look for women with amber eyes only, then there are women w1 and w2 satisfying such predicate. We assume that the ordering of attributes within a predicate indicates their priority.

Figure 3 shows a possible AErlang implementation for SMA. Function man() takes as arguments the predicates list Prefs of a man, his Id and characteristics Atts. The first element in Prefs (i.e., the most demanding predicate) is bound to variable H by pattern matching on list (line 2). The proposing phase of a man is implemented via lines 3–14 and follows the same behaviour described in previous section.

```
1    man(Prefs,Id,Atts) ->                   24    woman(Prefs,Id,P,PA) ->
2      [H|T]=Prefs,                           25      from("bof($Prefs,$PA,wealth,body)"),
3      Count=to(H) ! {propose,Id,Atts},       26      receive
4      from(H,Count),                         27        {propose,M,MA} ->
5      receive                                28          to("id=$M") ! {yes,Id},
6        {yes,W} ->                           29          from("id=$M"),
7          case aerl:getA(partner) of         30          receive
8            none ->                          31            confirm ->
9              to("id=$W") ! confirm,         32              to("id=$P") ! goodbye,
10             aerl:setA(partner,W);          33              woman(Prefs,Id,M,MA)
11           _ ->                             34            busy ->
12             to("id=$W") ! busy             35              woman(Prefs,Id,P,PA)
13         end                                36          end
14     end,                                   37    end.
15     case aerl:getA(partner) of
16       none -> man(T,Id,Atts);
17       _ -> from("id=this.partner"),
18           receive
19             goodbye ->
20               aerl:setA(partner,none),
21               man(Prefs,Id,Atts)
22           end
23     end.
```

Fig. 3. Stable Marriage with Attributes in AErlang (SMA-aerl).

Function woman() takes as arguments the preferences Prefs, an identifier Id, in addition to arguments P and PA to keep the current partner's information. A woman waits for proposals from men whose attributes are better than her current partner. This comparison is performed with the bof boolean function (line 25) that checks if a proposer is characterized by attributes wealth, body better than the partner P characterized by the variable PA. If this function provides true as output, then the woman sends a yes message back and waits for an acknowledge message confirm from this man M. If M confirms to her, the woman gets engaged to him by keeping M and his characteristics MA in the recursive call (line 33), after rejecting her current partner P. Otherwise, she keeps listening for other proposals (line 35).

3.4   Social Networking with Attributes

By abstracting SM, we are able to deal with the more realistic setting of social networking. In fact, this domain nicely fits with our new programming abstractions that can be naturally used to express attribute-based interaction. In particular, a generalization of stable marriage can be applied to open-ended systems where many-to-many matchings are allowed and the stability requirement is dropped. This appears indeed to be quite a common case in large-scale social networks, as we are going to discuss shortly.

In the social networking domain, attributes can represent characteristics of the users, such as their hobbies, musical preferences, current location, age, spoken languages, personality, mood, groups they belong to, their contact list (if they decide to make it public). Note that some of these attributes, for example location and mood, can change dynamically.

Possible interactions between users could happen when the interests of two or more users match. For example, people could mutually look for other people to jointly participate in a certain activity according to some specific criteria which could be expressed using a predicate over the given attributes. More concretely, let us consider a language exchange scenario where initially one could only look for the language she wishes to learn and the one their potential partners are interested in. In addition, however, it might be convenient to prefer somebody with similar age and interests, or even knowledgeable of a second language in common. Possible attributes for one user joining the system are: the language that a user already knows, the language of interest, age, hobby and so on. Interaction might be naturally expressed by the following code snippets, where users advertise their own interest by sending their proposal:

```
to("language = this.interest") ! {Language, Id}
```

Another user may set up a receive waiting for somebody knowing the language that she is interested in, conditioned to the matching of the hobby and only if the potential partner is at most five years older than the user:

```
from("this.age - age < 5 and this.hobby = hobby and language =
this.interest"), receive
    {Language, Buddy} ->
        to("id = $Buddy") ! {ok, Id}
end
```

The language exchange scenario above demonstrates the high flexibility and expressiveness provided by attribute-based communication over traditional actor-to-actor communication [1]. The interactions among components flexibly arise from the sending and receiving predicates whose expressiveness allows to suitably select the communicating entities. The handling of attributes inevitably introduces a performance overhead that results to be acceptable (see Sect. 4).

Besides this we also consider the case when new pairs can join or leave the group of entities aiming at finding matching partners. Such situation can easily be dealt with when the partner selection is predicate-based, but clearly requires significant work when preferences are expressed via lists of identifiers, as these have to be recalculated whenever the set of users in the system changes.

4   Performance Evaluation

In this section we present the performance evaluation of AErlang. The conducted experimentation focuses on two main aspects: (i) the efficiency in terms of runtime overhead, see Sect. 4.1; (ii) the scalability in terms of size of the instances and hardware resources, see Sect. 4.2. Experimental results are reproducible since our prototype is publicly available[1].

4.1   Efficiency

To evaluate the efficiency of AErlang, we compared the runtime performance of SMA-aerl, SM-aerl, and SM-erl, an Erlang program implementing the same matching protocol used in SM-aerl. All three programs were used to solve the SMA problem instances. We used the pushing message forwarding policy (see Sect. 2.2) for this part of the experiments.

Firstly, we generated multiple random input instances by considering problem sizes from 100 to 500. We considered two attributes for women and two for men, each attribute having a domain of two values (like in Table 2), with a probability of occurrence ranging from 0.1 to 0.9. We used the same ranges for preferences. We selected 24 different combinations in the given probability ranges, and generated 10 instances for each combination. Since SM-erl and SM-aerl take preference lists as input, we have also converted the problem instances to use preference lists. Finally, we ran each instance 10 times and took the average execution times. The hardware environment is a machine consisting of 4 CPUs AMD Opteron 6376 2.3 GHz, 2 MB Cache, 64 GB RAM. The versions of OS and Erlang were Linux 4.4.0-62-generic and 19.1, respectively.

Table 4 reports the runtime ratio of the SM-aerl and SMA-aerl programs with respect to SM-erl. Here, columns list the instance size, whereas rows enumerate the compared variants. We observe that the ratio is always within the same order of magnitude, more precisely we found a maximum ratio of 2.99 (observed for SM-aerl vs SM-erl with 100 instance size), as highlighted by the bold entry in

---

[1] https://github.com/ArBITRAL/AErlang

Table 4. Runtime ratio AErlang vs Erlang.

	size				
	100	200	300	400	500
SM-aerl vs SM-erl	**2.99**	1.73	1.92	1.98	2.20
SMA-aerl vs SM-erl	2.21	1.36	1.36	1.43	1.65
SMA-aerl vs SM-aerl	0.73	0.71	0.72	0.72	0.75

Table 4, and a minimum one of 1.36 (observed for SMA-aerl vs SM-erl with 200 and 300 instance size). This suggests that the new programming abstractions introduce an acceptable performance overhead (always within the same order of magnitude) which is minimized when attributes are considered for predicate evaluation. In fact, in Table 4 we can notice that SMA-aerl always shows lower ratios with respect to SM-aerl. This is not affected by the instance size, i.e., with larger instance sizes the ratio remains within the min-max values observed for rather small instance sizes.

It is worth to notice that the SMA-aerl variant always outperforms SM-aerl, as showed in the last row of Table 4. I due to the different cost of predicate evaluation, in fact the former uses sending predicates whose complexity is independent from the input size (e.g., `"hair=blonde and eye=amber"`) whereas the corresponding predicates of the latter need to check membership of identifiers within ties and therefore may be as large as the size of the tie itself (e.g., `"id=w1 or id=w2 or ..."`). Note that this also holds at the receiver side.

4.2 Scalability

The scalability of our prototype is demonstrated while increasing: (i) the size of the input instances from 1 k to 5 k and comparing AErlang with AS-X10; (ii) the number of cores from 2 to 48 and comparing AErlang with its Erlang counterpart.

Comparison with AS-X10. In [30], the authors proposed adaptive search as an efficient approach to solve the SMTI and SMI problems. They model SMTI as a permutation problem and try to resolve blocking pairs until an acceptable size of the matching is achieved. Their framework, implemented in the X10 programming language (AS-X10) can handle instances up to the size of 1000 pairs with good performance and scalability on a large number of cores thanks to a fine-tuned cooperation mechanism between many parallel solvers.

In this experiment we used the inputs originally described in [18], which are generated by using their tool[2] that takes three parameters as input: (p_1) size of the instance, (p_2) probability of incompleteness, (p_3) probability of ties.

---

[2] https://github.com/dannymrock/SMTI-AS-X10.

For this comparison we optimized for performance the SM-aerl program shown in Fig. 2. In particular, we did tailor the selection mechanism of the message broker to exploit the structure of the sending predicate of men (i.e., checking the membership of an identifier within a tie is eventually expanded to disjunctions of identities checks). Note that our prototype allows arbitrarily complex expressions and function calls, however their repeated parsing and evaluation affects performance. A way to avoid this is to set the receiving predicate to true and to evaluate the function locally. Our prototype currently does not implement such mechanism, but we simulated it by simply moving the comparison function (bof) from the predicate to the local code for women. Furthermore, we used the pushpull message forwarding policy (see Sect. 2.2) as it performed best in this specific case.

We have generated two classes of instances while considering instance sizes up to 5 thousands pairs of elements and the following sets of parameters: (i) 80% of incompleteness and no-ties instances (i.e., $p_2 = 0.8$, $p_3 = 0$); (ii) 95% of incompleteness and 80% of no-ties instances (i.e., $p_2 = 0.95$, $p_3 = 0.8$). These parameters were intentionally selected to be in line with those chosen in the evaluation of the adaptive search approach, for a fair comparison [30].

This part of the experiments was run on an idle local workstation equipped with 128 GB of memory, a dual Intel Xeon processor E5-2643 v3 (12 physical cores in total) clocked at 3.40 GHz, and running a 64-bit generic Linux kernel version 4.4.0, Erlang/OTP version 19.1, and X10 version 2.4.2.

Figure 4 shows that X10 performs faster than AErlang only on small instances with 1 thousands of pairs of elements. However we do notice that when increasing the size of the instances the AErlang program turns out to scale considerably better. This gap tends to increase with size, making the AErlang program very suitable to larger instances.

Comparison with Erlang. We wrote an Erlang program for the classical algorithm by Gale-Shapley, and used it to compare runtime performance with the AErlang program for SMTI. In this experiment, AErlang is configured with pushpull message dispatching policy (see Sect. 2.2). We also used the same input generator to generate problem instances for both SMTI and SMI problems.

We ran the AErlang program for SMTI and the Erlang program for SMI to safely exclude any hidden complexity due to the management of the ties. The size of the instances is fixed to the largest available option, i.e., 10 thousands of pairs of elements, and by ranging the number of cores from 2 to 48. We ran 10 instances, 10 times each, and collected the average execution times as previously. This experiment was performed on a computing cluster [34] where we had access to nodes with 64 Intel CPUs clocked at 2.3 GHz and 110 GB of memory running a scientific Linux distribution.

The results are presented in Fig. 5, where the x-axis denotes the number of cores and the y-axis reports the execution time in seconds on a logarithmic scale. Interestingly, the pronounced fluctuations in the running times are consistent for both AErlang and Erlang programs. This suggests that performance glitches within the Erlang subsystem end up affecting our AErlang prototype too.

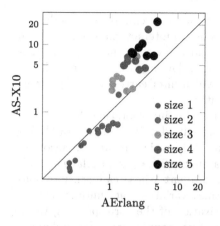

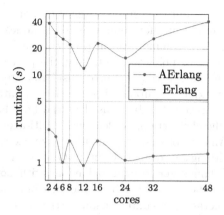

Fig. 4. AErlang vs. AS-X10

Fig. 5. AErlang vs. Erlang

Summarizing, we can conclude that introducing the attribute-based programming abstraction introduces a reasonable performance overhead. The experimental results confirm that nevertheless the scalability provided by the underlying runtime system is not significantly affected. In practice it is still possible to challenge and outperform ad-hoc state-of-art distributed algorithms conceived for large-scale systems.

5   Related Work

Attribute-based communication has been explored in the context of autonomic computing by the research centered around the SCEL paradigm [36]. It has been used to model the dynamic formation of ensembles from interacting autonomic components [12]. Notably, this novel communication paradigm can also be used to model a wide range of adaptation patterns in autonomic systems [9]. In our previous work [11] we provided a preliminary assessment of AErlang, where we used a simple program for a stable marriage variant without ties, to give a hint of what could be done with AErlang. No performance evaluation was considered. In this paper, instead, we develop an extended programming interface allowing counting and parallel message delivery, along with a comprehensive evaluation of the approach in terms of efficiency and scalability.

To the best of our knowledge, only two more efforts have been made on instantiating attribute-based communication, both on top of the Java programming language. The first work enriches the language with the primitives of the AbC calculus [3], but it only supports the broadcasting method. This simplifies the design and implementation of the message broker, it introduces communication overhead, especially in large systems. Being aware of this issue, AErlang's message broker includes three other message-dispatching strategies, allowing users to trade off depending on the application domain. The second work is jRESP [26], based instead on the SCEL paradigm, and more oriented towards autonomic and adaptive systems. jRESP designates ports with specific roles at nodes (or components) for communication. Nodes agreeing to interact via a port and can use the communication protocol (such as broadcast via a central server, multicast or point-to-point) that the port supports. The main difference with our approach is that we also consider strategies which filter early group of partners by exploiting updated predicates and attributes.

Erlang has been used as the host language for incorporating domain specific abstractions to deal with multi-agents and self-adaptive systems [13,28,33]. Among others, we mention ContextErlang [33] which is an extension of Erlang according to Context-Oriented Programming [21]. ContextErlang extends Erlang's `gen_server` behaviour with `context_agent` whose callback functions can be overridden by (functions implementing) variations at runtime. During operation, a context change triggers the activation of the corresponding variations, which leads to changing the behaviour of `context_agents`. The difference from our approach is in that we exploit exposed attributes, thus processes can adapt their behaviour implicitly using predicate-based message passing. In practice, via attributes that are updated by relying on appropriate sensors, we can model context-awareness.

The use of source-to-source transformation for extending Erlang with new primitives has been demonstrated in JErlang [32]. JErlang provides a receive-like join construct inspired from Join-Calculus [16]. Apart from transformation, their implementation intercepts the Erlang receive algorithm to incorporate the joins resolution mechanism, together with low-level optimizes inside Erlang's VM. Our AErlang prototype on the other hand focuses on mediating message passing based on predicates with appropriate handling of process attributes, and leading to user-friendly communication primitives.

6   Conclusion

In this paper, we have been experimenting with attribute-based communication and functional-style programming. We have proposed a prototype language extension, namely *AErlang*, that enables attribute-based communication among *Erlang* processes. *AErlang* conveniently combines the benefits of this novel paradigm with the efficiency and scalability of *Erlang*. Our approach copes well with the main sources of complexity of collective adaptive systems, such as anonymity, adaptivity, open-endedness, and their large size. It allows programmers to concentrate on the essence of the system being implemented, by relieving them from the burden of working out low-level details on a case-by-case basis.

We have evaluated the efficiency and scalability of our approach. Experiments compared the runtime performance of functional-style implementations for a known solution to a hard matching problem, and have shown that the overhead resulting from using the new communication primitives is acceptable, and our prototype successfully preserves *Erlang*'s efficiency and scalability.

We have also implemented a variant of the above matching problem that requires a more involved interaction pattern. We compared this variant to an ad-hoc parallel version based on adaptive search implemented in $X10$ [30] that can scale very well when increasing the number of cores. The experimental results have shown that our prototype does not currently scale well when increasing the number of cores. This is possibly partly due to known potential performance drains within the underlying *Erlang* subsystem which are being actively investigated [6,8,27]. However, *AErlang* does indeed scale considerably well on large instances, whereas these turn out to be progressively out of reach for the algorithm based on adaptive search implemented in $X10$.

Further experimentation is needed to improve *AErlang* and make it more attractive in practice. An extensive evaluation on arbitrarily large instances that use complex predicates and frequently changing attributes would be useful to assess the overall robustness. An in-depth performance evaluation to understand whether the large size of the system stresses the underlying scheduling mechanisms would be very useful. A systematic evaluation of the cost of predicate handling would be highly beneficial to improve efficiency. Indeed, since predicates can have an arbitrary complexity, their evaluation may add a significant overhead, and efficient predicate evaluation is known to be non-trivial [15]; looking for more efficient ways to handle predicate evaluation is thus very important. Lastly, handling process attributes does require complicated bookkeeping that has to take into account synchronisation, possible data inconsistencies, and so on. A comprehensive experimentation by varying the number of attributes, the size of the domains, the frequency of their updates, and their probability distribution would be very useful to devise different handling strategies according to a finer-grained classification of the attributes.

We plan to apply attribute-based communication to other concurrent languages, such as Go and Scala. Extending our experimentation across different programming environments would certainly allow a deeper investigation on the effectiveness of attribute-based communication.

References

1. Agha, G.: Actors: A Model of Concurrent Computation in Distributed Systems. MIT Press, Cambridge (1986)
2. Abd Alrahman, Y., De Nicola, R., Loreti, M.: On the power of attribute-based communication. In: Albert, E., Lanese, I. (eds.) FORTE 2016. LNCS, vol. 9688, pp. 1–18. Springer, Cham (2016). doi:10.1007/978-3-319-39570-8_1
3. Alrahman, Y.A., Loreti, M.: AbaCuS: a run-time environment of the AbC calculus (2016). https://github.com/lazkany/AbC
4. Armstrong, J.: Programming Erlang: Software for a Concurrent World. Pragmatic Bookshelf (2007)
5. Armstrong, J.: Erlang. Commun. ACM **53**(9), 68–75 (2010)
6. Aronis, S., Papaspyrou, N., Roukounaki, K., Sagonas, K., Tsiouris, Y., Venetis, I.E.: A scalability benchmark suite for Erlang/OTP. In: Proceedings of the Eleventh ACM SIGPLAN Workshop on Erlang Workshop, pp. 33–42. ACM (2012)
7. Blau, S., Rooth, J., Axell, J., Hellstrand, F., Buhrgard, M., Westin, T., Wicklund, G.: AXD 301: A new generation ATM switching system. Comput. Networks **31**(6), 559–582 (1999)

8. Boudeville, O., Cesarini, F., Chechina, N., Lundin, K., Papaspyrou, N., Sagonas, K., Thompson, S., Trinder, P., Wiger, U.: RELEASE: a high-level paradigm
   for reliable large-scale server software. In: Loidl, H.-W., Peña, R. (eds.) TFP
   2012. LNCS, vol. 7829, pp. 263–278. Springer, Heidelberg (2013). doi:10.1007/
   978-3-642-40447-4_17
9. Cesari, L., Nicola, R., Pugliese, R., Puviani, M., Tiezzi, F., Zambonelli, F.: For-
   malising adaptation patterns for autonomic ensembles. In: Fiadeiro, J.L., Liu, Z.,
   Xue, J. (eds.) FACS 2013. LNCS, vol. 8348, pp. 100–118. Springer, Cham (2014).
   doi:10.1007/978-3-319-07602-7_8
10. Charles, P., Grothoff, C., Saraswat, V., Donawa, C., Kielstra, A., Ebcioglu, K., Von
    Praun, C., Sarkar, V.: X10: an object-oriented approach to non-uniform cluster
    computing. In: ACM SIGPLAN Notices, vol. 40, pp. 519–538. ACM (2005)
11. De Nicola, R., Duong, T., Inverso, O., Trubiani, C.: AErlang at work. In: Stef-
    fen, B., Baier, C., Brand, M., Eder, J., Hinchey, M., Margaria, T. (eds.) SOF-
    SEM 2017. LNCS, vol. 10139, pp. 485–497. Springer, Cham (2017). doi:10.1007/
    978-3-319-51963-0_38
12. De Nicola, R., Loreti, M., Pugliese, R., Tiezzi, F.: A formal approach to auto-
    nomic systems programming: the SCEL language. ACM Trans. Auton. Adapt.
    Syst. (TAAS) 9(2), 7 (2014)
13. Díaz, Á.F., Earle, C.B., Fredlund, L.Å.: eJason: an implementation of Jason in
    Erlang. In: Dastani, M., Hübner, J.F., Logan, B. (eds.) ProMAS 2012. LNCS, vol.
    7837, pp. 1–16. Springer, Heidelberg (2013). doi:10.1007/978-3-642-38700-5_1
14. Ferscha, A.: Collective adaptive systems. In: ACM International Joint Conference
    on Pervasive and Ubiquitous Computing, pp. 893–895. ACM (2015)
15. Fontoura, M., Sadanandan, S., Shanmugasundaram, J., Vassilvitski, S., Vee, E.,
    Venkatesan, S., Zien, J.: Efficiently evaluating complex boolean expressions. In:
    Proceedings of the 2010 ACM SIGMOD International Conference on Management
    of data, pp. 3–14. ACM (2010)
16. Fournet, C., Gonthier, G.: The reflexive cham and the join-calculus. In: Proceedings
    of the 23rd ACM SIGPLAN-SIGACT Symposium on Principles of Programming
    Languages, pp. 372–385. ACM (1996)
17. Gale, D., Shapley, L.S.: College admissions and the stability of marriage. Am.
    Math. Monthly 69(1), 9–15 (1962)
18. Gent, I.P., Prosser, P.: An empirical study of the stable marriage problem with ties
    and incomplete lists. In: Proceedings of the 15th European Conference on Artificial
    Intelligence, pp. 141–145. IOS Press (2002)
19. Harrenstein, P., Manlove, D., Wooldridge, M.: The joy of matching. IEEE Intell.
    Syst. 28(2), 81–85 (2013)
20. Hewitt, C., Bishop, P., Steiger, R.: A universal modular actor formalism for arti-
    ficial intelligence. In: Proceedings of the 3rd International Joint Conference on
    Artificial Intelligence, pp. 235–245. Morgan Kaufmann Publishers Inc. (1973)
21. Hirschfeld, R., Costanza, P., Nierstrasz, O.: Context-oriented programming. J.
    Object Technol. 7(3), 125–151 (2008)
22. Hu, Z., Hughes, J., Wang, M.: How functional programming mattered. Ntl. Sci.
    Rev. 2(3), 349–370 (2015)
23. Hughes, J.: Why functional programming matters. Comput. J. 32(2), 98–107
    (1989)
24. Iwama, K., Miyazaki, S.: A survey of the stable marriage problem and its vari-
    ants. In: International Conference on Informatics Education and Research for
    Knowledge-Circulating Society, ICKS 2008, pp. 131–136. IEEE (2008)

25. Iwama, K., Miyazaki, S., Morita, Y., Manlove, D.: Stable marriage with incomplete lists and ties. In: Wiedermann, J., Emde Boas, P., Nielsen, M. (eds.) ICALP 1999. LNCS, vol. 1644, pp. 443–452. Springer, Heidelberg (1999). doi:10.1007/3-540-48523-6_41
26. jRESP: Java Runtime Environment for SCEL Programs. http://jresp.sourceforge.net/
27. Klaftenegger, D., Sagonas, K., Winblad, K.: On the scalability of the Erlang term storage. In: Proceedings of the Twelfth ACM SIGPLAN Workshop on Erlang, pp. 15–26. ACM (2013)
28. Krzywicki, D., Turek, W., Byrski, A., Kisiel-Dorohinicki, M.: Massively concurrent agent-based evolutionary computing. J. Comput. Sci. 11, 153–162 (2015)
29. Letuchy, E.: Facebook Chat (2008). http://web.archive.org/web/20160303044321/, https://www.facebook.com/notes/facebook-engineering/facebook-chat/14218138919/
30. Munera, D., Diaz, D., Abreu, S., Rossi, F., Saraswat, V., Codognet, P.: Solving hard stable matching problems via local search and cooperative parallelization. In: 29th AAAI Conference on Artificial Intelligence (2015)
31. O'Connell, A.: Inside Erlang, The Rare Programming Language Behind WhatsApp's Success (2014). http://web.archive.org/web/20160715132942/, http://www.fastcompany.com/3026758/inside-erlang-the-rare-programming-language-behind-whatsapps-success
32. Plociniczak, H., Eisenbach, S.: JErlang: Erlang with joins. In: Clarke, D., Agha, G. (eds.) COORDINATION 2010. LNCS, vol. 6116, pp. 61–75. Springer, Heidelberg (2010). doi:10.1007/978-3-642-13414-2_5
33. Salvaneschi, G., Ghezzi, C., Pradella, M.: ContextErlang: a language for distributed context-aware self-adaptive applications. Sci. Comput. Program. 102, 20–43 (2015)
34. Stalio, S., Di Carlo, G., Parlati, S., Spinnato, P.: Resource management on a VM based computer cluster for scientific computing. arXiv preprint arXiv:1212.4658 (2012)
35. Thompson, S., Cesarini, F.: Erlang programming: a concurrent approach to software development (2009)
36. Wirsing, M., Hölzl, M., Koch, N., Mayer, P. (eds.): Software Engineering for Collective Autonomic Systems. LNCS, vol. 8998. Springer, Cham (2015)

Simpler Coordination of JavaScript Web Workers

Marco Krauweel[1] and Sung-Shik T.Q. Jongmans[1,2](✉)

[1] Department of Computer Science, Open University of the Netherlands,
Heerlen, The Netherlands
ssj@ou.nl
[2] Department of Computing, Imperial College London, London, UK

Abstract. JavaScript is a popular sequential language for implementing Web applications. To enable concurrent execution of JavaScript code, modern JavaScript engines support the Web Workers API. Using this API, developers can spawn concurrent background workers from a distinguished main worker. These workers, which run on the same machine (e.g., to exploit multicore), interact via message-passing.

The Web Workers API is relatively low-level, which makes implementing coordination protocols among background workers laborious and error-prone. To simplify this, we propose to hide the Web Workers API behind a coordination language that provides higher-level constructs. Importantly, developers already use JavaScript together with domain-specific languages HTML (for markup/structure) and CSS (for style/design); another domain-specific language (for coordination) seamlessly fits this practice. Using the coordination language Reo, we demonstrate the advantages and feasibility of this approach by example. We also present the necessary tool support (compiler; runtime library and API; front-end).

1 Introduction

Context. *JavaScript* [7] is a sequential language originally invented to add dynamic behavior to static Web pages. Together with domain-specific languages HTML and CSS, JavaScript has become one of the most widely used languages for implementing Web application clients. In recent years, JavaScript was popularized also for writing server-side code and mobile apps. This makes JavaScript a key language in contemporary software engineering.

Single pieces of JavaScript code are executed sequentially. To concurrently execute multiple pieces of JavaScript code on the same machine (e.g., to exploit a multicore processor), modern JavaScript engines support also the *Web Workers API* [9]. This API "allows Web application authors to spawn background workers running scripts in parallel to their main page", which "allows for thread-like operation with message-passing as the coordination mechanism."

J.-M. Jacquet and M. Massink (Eds.): COORDINATION 2017, LNCS 10319, pp. 40–58, 2017.
DOI: 10.1007/978-3-319-59746-1_3

Problem. The Web Workers API is relatively low-level.

First, the Web Workers API provides no constructs for background workers to send messages directly to each other; background workers can send messages only to a distinguished main worker ("hierarchical communication" [21]). Second, the Web Workers API provides no constructs for a background worker to correlate messages sent to, and later received from, the main worker; workers cannot reply to messages. Third, the Web Workers API provides no constructs for a background worker to pause processing of the current message in anticipation of receiving the next message; background workers cannot block.

Thus, sending messages end-to-end, replying to messages, and awaiting messages, can be implemented only in terms of lower-level constructs. This is laborious and error-prone. For instance, it is already nontrivial to implement a background worker that simply needs to send a message to, and await a reply from, another background worker as part of the same task.

Contribution. To simplify implementing coordination protocols using the low-level Web Workers API, we propose to provide developers additional higher-level constructs. Such constructs have, in fact, been under development already for decades, in *coordination languages*. We therefore propose to hide the Web Workers API behind a coordination language. An observation particularly relevant to this approach is that developers already use JavaScript together with domain-specific languages HTML (for markup/structure) and CSS (for style/design); another domain-specific language (for coordination) seamlessly fits this practice.

In Sect. 2, we present preliminaries on JavaScript and the Web Workers API. In Sect. 3, we illustrate the limitations of the Web Workers API. In Sect. 4, we describe the existing coordination language *Reo* [10,11]. In Sect. 5, we demonstrate how the use of Reo to hide the Web Workers API alleviates its limitations, in theory. In Sect. 6, we present tool support (compiler; runtime library and API; front-end) for developers to implement and run coordination protocols using Reo. In Sect. 7, we demonstrate the feasibility of our approach, in practice. Section 8 concludes this paper, including related work. To our knowledge, this is the first paper that presents high-level constructs to simplify implementing coordination protocols among background workers in JavaScript and the Web Workers API.

2   JavaScript and the Web Workers API

– JavaScript provides first-class functions and the usual control constructs [7].
– The Web Workers API provides constructs for spawning *background workers* from a *main worker* and constructs for sending/receiving messages [9].

Together, JavaScript and the Web Workers API constitute an actor language in the style of *active objects*, in the taxonomy of De Koster et al. [13].

Every worker starts by performing some initial work (e.g., initializing variables). It then checks if, in the meanwhile, *events* have occurred that require processing. Examples include *message events* (i.e., receipt of a message) and *timeout events* (i.e., passage of time). If so, the worker executes *event listeners* in response, until all events have been processed; otherwise, it suspends until the next event occurs. Execution of event listeners is nonblocking and nonpreemptive: event listeners run to completion in one go, uninterleaved with other event listeners of the same worker.

A worker has an event handler for every type of event that it responds to. For instance, every background worker has a message event listener to process messages received from the main worker; as background workers cannot receive messages directly from each other, no other message event listeners are necessary. Conversely, the main worker receives messages from all background workers, and it may need to respond differently to each of them; the main worker, therefore, may have multiple message event listeners. Although many types of events exist, only message and timeout events matter in this paper, w.l.o.g.

A worker's cycle of awaiting and processing of events is called its *event loop*, and it is repeated indefinitely; pending event listeners are stored in a private FIFO queue. Furthermore, every worker has its own private heap. No memory is shared; message-passsing is the only means of communication.

```
1  var ping = new Worker("background.js");
2  var pong = new Worker("background.js");
3
4  ping.onmessage = function(e) {
5    pong.postMessage(e.data); }
6  pong.onmessage = function(e) {
7    ping.postMessage(e.data); }
8
9  ping.postMessage("pong");
```

Fig. 1. main-pp.js

```
1  onmessage = function(e) {
2    if (e.data == "ping")
3      setTimeout(function() {
4        postMessage("pong"); }, 500);
5
6    if (e.data == "pong")
7      setTimeout(function() {
8        postMessage("ping"); }, 1000);
9  };
```

Fig. 2. background.js

Example 1. Figures 1 and 2 show an example program. This program defines two background workers, called Ping and Pong, who iteratively send "ping" and "pong" to each other. Syntactically, a message event handler is a function, where parameter e represents a message event to be processed; the message is accessed through e.data. postMessage(m) sends message m. setTimeout(f,t) generates a timeout after t ms; subsequently, function f is called.

Figure 2 defines Ping (and Pong). Initially, Ping only sets his message event handler (line 1–9); subsequently, he suspends. Whenever Ping receives a "pong" message from the main worker, he resumes by sending back a "ping" message, after a 1000 ms delay (lines 6–8); subsequently, he suspends again.

Figure 1 defines the main worker. Initially, the main worker spawns Ping and Pong (lines 1–2), then it sets its message event handlers (lines 4–7), then it sends an initial "pong" message to Ping (line 9); subsequently, it suspends. Whenever the main worker receives a message from Ping or Pong, it resumes by forwarding that message to Pong or Ping; subsequently, it suspends again.

Note that the main worker must call postMessage on a particular background worker, to indicate the receiver. In contrast, background workers do not need to

```
1   var i = 0, n = 9;
2   var alice = new Worker("alice.js");
3   var bob   = new Worker("bob.js");
4   var carol = new Worker("carol.js");
5
6   alice.onmessage = function(e) {
7     bob.postMessage(e.data); };
8
9   bob.onmessage = function(e) {
10    var m = e.data;
11    if (i < n) {
12      bob.postMessage({sn: m.sn}); // ack
13      carol.postMessage(m);
14      i++;
15    } else {
16      setTimeout(function() {
17        bob.onmessage(e); }, 0);
18  } };
19
20  carol.onmessage = function(e) {
21    i--; };
```

Fig. 3. main-abc.js

```
1   var pending = [];
2
3   function fstHalf(sn, initVal) {
4     var finalVal = ...; // process initVal
5     var m = {sn: sn, val: finalVal};
6     postMessage(m);
7     pending.push(sn);
8   } // suspend until ack ...
9
10  function sndHalf(sn) { // ... resume!
11    pending.splice(pending.indexOf(sn), 1);
12    ...; // do more work
13  }
14
15  onmessage = function(e) {
16    var m = e.data;
17    if (pending.indexOf(m.sn) == -1)
18      fstHalf(m.sn, m.val);
19    else
20      sndHalf(m.sn);
21  };
```

Fig. 5. bob.js

```
1   var nextSn = 0;
2   while (true) {
3     var initVal = ...; // do init work
4     var m = {sn: nextSn++, val: initVal};
5     postMessage(m);
6   }
```

Fig. 4. alice.js

```
1   onmessage = function(e) {
2     postMessage({}); // ack
3     var m = e.data;
4     var finalVal = m.val;
5     ...; // do final work
6   };
```

Fig. 6. carol.js

call `postMessage` on the main worker; as background workers can send messages only to the main worker, no confusion can arise about who is the receiver. ☐

3 Limitations and Issues

Example 2. Figures 3, 4, 5 and 6 show an example program to illustrate the limitations of the Web Workers API, stated in Sect. 1. This program defines three background workers, called Alice, Bob, and Carol, operating in a pipeline: Alice indefinitely produces initial values and sends them to Bob, Bob processes initial values to final values and sends them to Carol, and Carol consumes final values.

Figures 4 and 6 define Alice and Carol; they are straightforward. Alice's messages record a serial number (used for bookkeeping by Bob) and an initial value.

Figure 5 defines Bob. Initially, Bob sets an empty list of pending serial numbers (line 1) and sets his message event handler (lines 15–21); subsequently he suspends. Whenever Bob receives a message, he resumes. If Bob does not recognize the serial number in the message (line 17), he starts a new processing cycle for that serial number (line 18); otherwise, he continues a previous processing cycle (line 20). In the former case, Bob processes the initial value to a final value (line 4), then he sends a message to the main worker (lines 5–6), who forwards it to Carol, then he registers the serial number (line 7); subsequently, he suspends again. In the latter case, Bob unregisters the serial number (line 11) and finalizes his processing cycle (line 12); subsequently, he suspends again.

Figure 3 defines the main worker. The main worker unconditionally forwards messages received from Alice to Bob (line 7). As such, Alice communicates to Bob via an unbounded buffer. In contrast, the main worker forwards messages received from Bob to Carol (line 13) only if the number of buffered messages i is smaller than a bound n (line 11). As such, Bob communicates with Carol via an n-capacity buffer (e.g., to avoid excessive memory usage if Carol is slower than Bob, and many large message from Bob would otherwise need to be buffered). To prevent loss of messages, the main worker acknowledges a serial number sn to Bob only once the corresponding message can be forwarded (line 12); Bob awaits this acknowledgment before beginning the second half of its processing cycle for sn. As such, the n-capacity buffer is blocking. If the main worker cannot forward a message yet, it schedules an immediate retry (lines 16–17).[1]

This example program illustrates the limitations of the Web Workers API, stated in Sect. 1. First, it illustrates that background workers cannot directly send to, and receive from, each other. In particular, background workers cannot obtain references to other background workers. Second, this example program illustrates that background workers cannot directly understand replies to messages. In particular, whenever Bob receives from the main worker a reply (acknowledgment) to an earlier message, the context in which he sent that message is gone; to Bob, the reply might just as well be a new forwarded message from Alice. This is why messages need to be explicitly tagged with a serial number and why Bob needs to do extra bookkeeping. Third, this example program illustrates that background workers cannot straightforwardly block. In particular, after Bob sends a message to the main worker, he needs to await an acknowledgment, but the only means of waiting is through suspension and resumption (event loop). As a result, Bob's processing cycle is unnaturally split into two functions.   □

The coordination protocol between Bob and Carol in the previous example is among the simplest: asynchronous communication through a blocking FIFO buffer of bounded capacity. Yet, due to limitations of the Web Workers API, the implementation of this simple coordination protocol is not that simple at all: as higher-level constructs are missing (sending message end-to-end, replying to messages, awaiting messages), key characteristics can be expressed only indirectly (through forwarding, through serial numbers, through split functions). This makes development laborious and error-prone.

Another issue is that "computation code" is entangled with "coordination code". This lack of separation and modularity between computation and coordination complicates development. For instance, *changing* the implementation of a coordination protocol typically requires global understanding of,

---

[1] This is an inefficient implementation, but we aim for simplicity here.

```
1    ...
2    var bob1 = new Worker("bob.js");
3    var bob2 = new Worker("bob.js");
4    ...
5    var pendingBobs = [bob1, bob2];
6
7    alice.onmessage = function(e) {
8      if (pendingBobs.length > 0) {
9        var bob = pendingBobs.shift();
10       bob.postMessage(e.data);
11     } else {
12       setTimeout(function(e) {
13         alice.onmessage(e); }, 0);
14   } };
15   ...
16
```

```
17   bob1.onmessage = function(e) {
18     mFromBob(e.data, bob1); };
19   bob2.onmessage = function(e) {
20     mFromBob(e.data, bob2); };
21
22   function mFromBob(m, bob) {
23     if (m == {}) {
24       pendingBobs.push(bob);
25     } else if (i < n) {
26       bob.postMessage({sn: m.sn}); // ack
27       carol.postMessage(m);
28       i++;
29     } else {
30       setTimeout(function() {
31         mFromBob(m, bob); }, 0);
32   } }
```

Fig. 7. main-abbc.js

(a) FIFO   (b) FIFOn

(c) MergerFIFOn

Fig. 8. Example connectors

and modifications to, larger parts of a program; it cannot be localized, because implementations of coordination protocols are scattered across multiple workers. Moreover, *reusing* the implementation of a coordination protocol in other programs typically requires so much effort that it is practically infeasible.

Example 3. Suppose that we want to instantiate two Bobs instead of only one (e.g., because Alice and Carol are twice as fast as Bob). Effectively, then, we need to generalize the coordination protocol between Alice and Bob to multiple readers, and the coordination protocol between Bob and Carol to multiple writers. Figure 7 shows modifications to the main worker to achieve this (see Footnote 1). Additionally, we *crucially* need to insert a **postMessage({})** call between lines 12 and 13 in Fig. 5, through which a Bob informs the main worker that he is ready for the next message. The latter illustrates that modifications cannot be localized to one specific piece of code; global understanding and modifications are necessary.   □

For more complex coordination protocols (e.g., tighter synchronization, many control states), the impact of these limitations and issues becomes only more serious. This is why we propose to provide developers additional higher-level constructs that hide the low-level Web Workers API. Next, we present an existing coordination language that achieves this aim.

4   Reo

Reo [10,11] is a graphical language for compositional construction of coordination protocols, manifested as *circuits*. Briefly, a circuit is a graph-like structure

Table 1. Common channels

Name	Syntax	Semantics
sync	$\xrightarrow[e_1 \qquad e_2]{}$	Synchronously accepts a value through e_1 and offers that value through e_2.
syncdrain	$\mathrel{\rightarrow\!\!\!-\!\!\!\leftarrow}$ $e_1 \qquad e_2$	Synchronously accepts and loses values through e_1 and e_2.
fifo1	$\xrightarrow[e_1]{}\;\Box\;\xrightarrow[e_2]{}$ $\xrightarrow[e_1]{}\;\blacksquare\;\xrightarrow[e_2]{}$	Asynchronously [accepts a value v through e_1 and stores v in a buffer], then [offers v through e_2 and clears the buffer]. A token means that a buffer is initially filled with a random v.
fifo$n$	$\xrightarrow[e_1]{}\;\boxed{n}\;\xrightarrow[e_2]{}$	Version of fifo1 with an n-capacity buffer
fifo	$\xrightarrow[e_1]{}\;\boxed{\infty}\;\xrightarrow[e_2]{}$	Version of fifo1 with an unbounded buffer

consisting of typed *channels* (decorated edges), through which values flow, and *nodes* (vertices), on which channel ends coincide. Figure 8 shows examples.

Every channel has a type, graphically indicated by (the absence of) a decoration. The type of a channel determines how values flow through it—its behavior. Every channel has two ends, each of which is either a *source end* or a *sink end*. A source end accepts values into its channel, while a *sink end* offers values out of its channel. A channel in Reo has either two source ends, or two sink ends, or a source and a sink end. Table 1 shows common channels types. Users of Reo may extend this set by defining their own channels (modeled in some formalism [18]).

The behavior of a node depends on its coincident channel ends.

– A node with only coincident source ends is a *source node*. A source node is linked to an *output port* of a worker. By performing a put(v) operation on an output port, a worker attempts to offer value v to the linked source node. As soon as each of the coincident source ends of the source node is ready to accept v, it synchronously *replicates* v into all of them, and the put returns; until then, the pending put blocks the worker.
– A node with only coincident sink ends is a *sink node*. A sink node is linked to an *input port* of a worker. By performing a get operation on an input port, a worker attempts to accept a value from the linked sink node. As soon as at least one of the coincident sink ends of the sink node is ready to offer a value, the sink node *nondeterministically selects* a value v from one of them, and the get returns v; until then, the pending get blocks the worker.
– The source and sink nodes of a circuit are its *boundary nodes* (light-gray color). A node on which both source and sink ends coincide is a *mixed node* (dark-gray color). Mixed nodes combine the behavior of source and sink nodes: synchronously, a mixed node nondeterministically selects a coincident sink end and replicates its value into all coincident source ends. Nodes cannot temporarily store, generate, or lose values.

Before a value can flow through a circuit, its channels and nodes must first reach consensus about their local behavior to ensure consistent global behavior. For instance, a node should not locally (decide to) replicate a value into the coincident source end of a fifo channel if the buffer of that channel is full.

Example 4. The circuit in Fig. 8(a) implements the coordination protocol between Alice and Bob in Example 2; the circuit in Fig. 8(b) implements the coordination protocol between Bob and Carol in Example 2. This shows that Reo is expressive enough to define both nonblocking coordination protocols (e.g., between Alice and Bob) and blocking ones (e.g., between Bob and Carol); ultimately, the programmer decides what kind of communication is needed. The circuit in Fig. 8(c) implements the coordination protocol between the two Bobs and Carol in Example 3.

The circuit in Fig. 8(c) works as follows. For a put(v) operation performed on the top-left source node to return, this node must replicate v into the coincident source end of the sync channel. This is possible only if the sync channel accepts v, which depends on whether it can synchronously offer v through its sink end to the connected mixed node. This is possible only if the mixed node accepts v, which depends both on its nondeterministic selection and on whether it can synchronously replicate v into the coincident source end of the fifo$n$ channel. The latter is possible only if the fifo$n$ channel accepts v, which depends on whether its buffer is not full. Thus, only if the mixed node makes the "right" nondeterministic selection and the buffer is not full, only then flows v *synchronously* from the top-left source node into the buffer (and put(v) returns).

Once the buffer is full, no value can flow from either of the two source nodes into the buffer. The only thing that can happen at this point is the flow of a value out of the buffer to the sink node. Subsequently, because the buffer is not full anymore, a value can flow from one of the two source nodes into the buffer. □

For Java developers to use Reo to implement and run coordination protocols, a *Reo-to-Java compiler*, a *Reo@Java runtime library*, and a *Reo@Java API* exist [16,17]. The idea is that developers implement workers as Java classes and coordination protocols as Reo circuits. Then, the Reo-to-Java compiler computes the semantics of the Reo circuits as state machines (more precisely, as *constraint automata* [12,16]), and it generates Java classes for their runtime simulation.

At runtime, every hand-written worker object, and every compiler-generated state machine object, runs in its own Java thread. Through the Reo@Java API, every worker object has access to (data structures for) ports, on which it can perform put and get operations. State machine objects monitor those ports: whenever a worker object performs a put or get on one of its ports, a designated state machine object checks whether this operation enables a transition out of its current state; every transition represents a synchronous flow of values among ports. If so, the state machine object makes the transition, distributes values accordingly among participating ports, and completes all put and get operations involved; if not, the state machine object does nothing and awaits the next put or get. In accordance with the blocking nature of put and get, the execution

```
1   function* alice(out) {              12   // (continued)
2     while (true) {                    13
3       var initVal = ...; // do init work  14   function* bob(in, out) {
4       yield out.put(initVal);         15     while (true) {
5   } }                                 16       var initVal = yield in.get();
6                                        17       var finVal = ...; // process initVal
7   function* carol(in) {               18       yield out.put(finVal);
8     while (true) {                    19       ...; // do more work
9       var finVal = yield in.get();    20   } }
10      ...; // do final work           21
11  } }                                 22
```

Fig. 9. workers-reo.js

Fig. 10. main-abc.reo

of worker objects is suspended so long as their puts and gets are pending. The Reo@Java runtime library provides an implementation of the Reo@Java API.

5   Hiding the Web Workers API Behind Reo – *In Theory*

Reo enables developers to implement coordination protocols in terms of domain-specific abstractions and higher-level constructs. As a coordination language that hides the low-level Web Workers API, use of Reo has two main implications.

The first implication is the adoption of a syntactic separation between computation and coordination: developers should implement workers in JavaScript, while they should implement coordination protocols purely in Reo. This separation leads to modularization (of workers and coordination protocols), which has well-known advantages [23], including improved changeability and reusability. The second implication is that programmers should no longer implement communications with nonblocking postMessage from the existing Web Workers API, but with blocking put and get from our new *Reo@JS API*. If necessary, as demonstrated in Example 4, put and get can effectively be made nonblocking by connecting them to a circuit with fifo buffers. Of course, nothing prevents programmers from implementing additional "covert communications" among background workers in an indirect way (e.g., using message channels or sockets), but this is against the philosophy of our approach and therefore discouraged.

Example 5. Figure 9 shows implementations of Alice, Bob, and Carol in the example program from Example 2, using the Reo@JS API instead of the Web Workers API. Alice, Bob, and Carol are now implemented as functions, with output ports and input ports as parameters. As put and get are blocking, especially function bob is significantly simpler than the code in Fig. 5 (fewer details to worry about).

Figure 10 shows implementations of the coordination protocols between Alice and Bob, and between Bob and Carol. This diagram also defines which workers the program consists of, by which functions those workers are defined, and how workers' ports are linked to boundary nodes. Using higher-level constructs to express coordination, as in Reo, developers are relieved from the burden of working with low-level constructs provided by the Web Workers API.   □

Example 6. Figure 11 shows implementations of the coordination protocols between Alice and the two Bobs, and between the two Bobs and Carol, in the example program from Example 3. The "crossed" mixed node replicates a value into only one of its coincident source ends (instead of all), selected nondeterministically.[2] Notably, Alice, the two Bobs, and Carol are defined by *exactly the same functions* as those in Fig. 9. Such reusability is one of the advantages of separating computation from coordination. Figure 12 shows an implementation of a different coordination protocol between Alice and the two Bobs, where every Bob now has its own unbounded buffer (instead of them sharing one). Making these modifications at this level of abstraction is simple; at the level of abstraction of the Web Workers API, it is not. Figure 13 shows an implementation of yet a different coordination protocol between Alice and the two Bobs, where values from Alice are divided evenly over the two buffers (not guaranteed with Fig. 12).

The circuits in Fig. 11 are built from (the two simple) circuits in Fig. 10. This shows that not only can coordination protocols be reused, but in fact, they can be further *composed* into more complex ones. In plain JavaScript and the Web Workers API, reusing and composing existing implementations of coordination protocols is practically infeasible.   □

Examples 5 and 6 show how the limitations and issues of the Web Workers API (Sect. 3) are alleviated when a coordination language, such as Reo, is used. Hiding the Web Workers API behind Reo makes both workers and coordination protocols simpler to implement, easier to change, and easier to reuse, *in theory*. To actually reap these advantages *in practice*, developers need tool support. We present such tools in the next section, to show that our approach is also feasible.

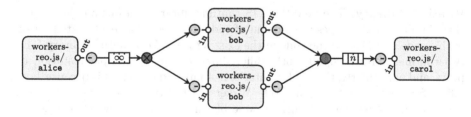

Fig. 11. main-abbc.reo

---

[2] This node is, in fact, syntactic sugar for a complexer circuit (i.e., it can be composed).

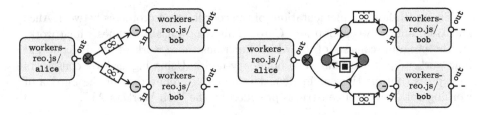

Fig. 12. main-abbc2.reo (fragment)   **Fig. 13.** main-abbc3.reo (fragment)

6 Tool Support

Overview. For developers to use Reo to implement and run coordination protocols, they need a compiler and a runtime library. The "easy part" was developing our new *Reo-to-JS compiler*, which works much in the same way as the existing Reo-to-Java compiler. The "hard part" was developing our new *Reo@JS runtime library*, which differs significantly from its Java counterpart.

Compiler. Most of the internals of the new Reo-to-JS compiler are reused from the existing Reo-to-Java compiler (see Sect. 4). In particular, computation and optimization of state machines for Reo circuits is independent of the target language and works in exactly the same way for JavaScript as for Java.

The JavaScript code generated by the Reo-to-JS compiler is also conceptually similar to the Java code generated by the Reo-to-Java compiler: in the same event-driven way as explained in Sect. 4, the generated JavaScript code simulates a computed state machine. This state machine is executed by the main worker.

The Reo-to-JS compiler also generates "wrappers" around the functions that are linked to the boundary nodes of the circuit; these wrappers are executed in separate background workers, using the Web Workers API. All necessary initialization code is also generated. Thus, the only code that developers need to write by hand are the functions that link to the boundary nodes (e.g., Fig. 9).

Runtime Library. The new Reo@JS runtime library contains auxiliary code that simplifies and reduces the amount of code that needs to be generated. Most of this code is similar to the code in the existing Reo@Java runtime library. The two runtime libraries significantly differ, however, in their implementation of ports, and particularly, the implementations of put and get. This is because Java differs from JavaScript and the Web Workers API in two significant ways: Java supports shared-memory concurrency and blocking constructs, which JavaScript and the Web Workers API do not support. Shared memory in Java enables straightforwardly linking worker objects to state machine objects by sharing the same port objects between them; this is not possible in JavaScript. Blocking operations in Java make implementing the blocking semantics of put and get straightforward; this is also not possible in JavaScript.

```
1   class InputPort { // background side
2     constructor(worker) {
3       this.w = worker;
4       this.w.onmessage = this.rcvResponse;
5     }
6
7     get() {
8       return new Promise(this.sndRequest);
9     }
10
11    sndRequest(resolve) {
12      this.r = resolve;
13      this.w.postMessage(null);
14    }
15
16    rcvResponse(e) {
17      this.r(e.data);
18  } }
```

```
1   class InputPortProxy { // main side
2     constructor(worker) {
3       this.w = worker;
4       this.w.onmessage = this.rcvRequest;
5     }
6
7     rcvRequest(e) {
8       this.get().then(this.sndResponse);
9     }
10
11    get() {
12      // ...
13      // (similar to Java version)
14    }
15
16    sndResponse(val) {
17      this.w.postMessage(val);
18  } }
```

(a)   (b)

Fig. 14. (a) input-port.js (simplified), (b) input-port-proxy.js (simpl.)

We first explain our solution to the unshared memory complication. The idea is to use *two* sets of output ports and input ports: one set for background workers, and another set for the main worker. Figures 14(a) and (b) show simplified[3] versions of the code for input ports; the code for output ports is similar. Figure 14(a) shows class InputPort, instances of which are used by background workers. At the "background side", whenever get is called, sndRequest is subsequently called (through a *promise*; see below). sndRequest essentially relays the get call to the proxy of the main worker, by sending a null message. Then, at the "main side", this null message is processed by rcvRequest, which calls the real get that is monitored by the state machine. The resulting value is eventually sent back to the background worker, where it is processed by rcvResponse.

The nonblocking operations complication is trickier to solve, because it seems impossible to implement blocking operations in JavaScript without exposing the programmer to some of the required logic. The argument is as follows. JavaScript has no blocking constructs, so we need to implement them ourselves. One option is *busy-waiting*, where an event listener that needs to block repeatedly checks the value of a variable until it is changed by another event listener of the same worker (e.g., in response to a message receipt). But, as event listeners are never preempted, they are never interleaved. This entails a causal loop that causes a busy-waiting worker to busy-wait forever: the second event listener is not executed until the busy-waiting is over, which does not happen until the variable is updated, which is what the second event listener should do. The only viable alternative to implement blocking, then, seems suspending the worker in its event loop, by ending the current event listener. Importantly, just before suspending, bookkeeping is required to register a *continuation*; otherwise, the worker does not

---

[3] Compared to Figs. 14(a) and (b), the actual implementation also supports multiple ports per workers, and it is protected against workers that perform the next get (or put) before the previous one is completed. Details appear elsewhere [20].

know how to proceed later on. It seems inevitable to place the burden of book-keeping for continuations on the developer. The main challenge is to minimize this burden, encapsulating it in the Reo@JS runtime library wherever possible.

First, we use *promises*. A `Promise` object represents the eventual result of an asynchronous computation, which may not have finished yet when the `Promise` object is created. Upon calling the constructor of a `Promise` object, an *executor (function)* is passed that defines the asynchronous computation to be performed; inside the constructor, the executor is called with a *resolve (function)* as parameter. The resolve is called once the asynchronous computation finishes. Initially, the resolve is empty. To "fill" the resolve, `then` can be called on the created `Promise` object with a *callback (function)* as parameter. If the resolve has already run at that point, the callback is immediately run; otherwise, the resolve is filled with a call to the callback (which runs as soon as the asynchronous computation finishes). Technically, `then` returns another `Promise` object, making it possible to express a sequence of seemingly blocking computations by successively calling `then`. Such a chain of `then` calls nests promises in promises, which asynchronously—interrupted in the event loop—resolve one after the other.

Example 7. As shown in Fig. 14(a), `get` returns a new `Promise` object; the same holds for `put`. Figure 15 shows what a worker looks like if developers were to express computations directly with promises. Note that the callbacks for the two `get` operations have a formal parameter `val` (which contains, conceptually, the value offered by the circuit); the actual parameter is passed on line 17, Fig. 14(a) (at which point `this.r` refers to the callback).   □

The previous example shows that using promises to implement blocking, still places a heavy burden on developers. To simplify this, we use *generators*.

```
1  function runMultiplier(
2    inputPort1, inputPort2, outputPort) {
3
4    var lhs, rhs, product;
5
6    inputPort1.get().then(
7      function(val) {
8        lhs = val;
9        return inputPort2.get();
10   }).then(
11     function(val) {
12       rhs = val;
13       product = lhs * rhs;
14       return outputPort.put(product);
15   }).then(
16     function() {
17       console.log("result: " + product);
18   });
19 }
```

Fig. 15. Promises, explicitly

```
1  function* runMultiplier(
2    inputPort1, inputPort2, outputPort) {
3
4    var lhs = yield inputPort1.get();
5    var rhs = yield inputPort2.get();
6    var product = lhs * rhs;
7    yield outputPort.put(product);
8    console.log("result: " + product);
9  }
```

Fig. 16. Promises, implicitly

```
1  function loop(generator, val) {
2    var r = generator.next(val);
3    if (!r.done) { // gener. not yet done
4      Promise.resolve(r.value).then(
5        function(nextVal) {
6          loop(generator, nextVal);
7  } );} }
8
9  loop(runMultiplier(/* ports */), null);
```

Fig. 17. Looping on promises

A generator is a function that can be exited and re-entered: whenever a `yield` is encountered during the execution of a generator, the context is saved, and the generator is exited (optionally yielding a result). When the generator is later re-entered, its saved context is restored, and it proceeds from where it left off.

We require that workers are implemented as generators instead of as normal functions (indicated with an asterix), and that `put` and `get` are always used together with `yield`. Subsequently, we can apply *promise-based asynchronous task running* [28], where every background worker calls its generator, waits until a promise from `put` or `get` is yielded, provides this promise a callback in which the generator is re-entered, and suspends; the provided callback ensures that this process repeats itself until the generator is done. Figure 17 shows this approach in code. In this way, every background worker effectively runs a loop (but with continuous interruptions through suspension and resumption) in which all code is executed in callbacks, from one `put`/`get` to the next `put`/`get`. For instance, "unrolling" the code in Fig. 16 results in the code in Fig. 15.

Using promises and generators, we largely relieve developers from the burden of bookkeeping for continuations, with concise code as a result (e.g., Fig. 9).

Front-End. We hooked our Reo-to-JS compiler into *PrDK* [16,17]. PrDK consists of plugins for Eclipse, including a graphical editor for Reo circuits that allows developers to draw Reo diagrams as the ones in Figs. 10, 11, 12 and 13, using a drag-and-drop interface. From this editor, the Reo-to-JS compiler can directly be run to generate and package all JavaScript code, for client-side execution in browsers or for server-side execution in *Node.js* (using the *tiny-worker* library [6]).

7   Hiding the Web Workers API Behind Reo – *In Practice*

Examples 5 and 6 (Sect. 5) showed that, in theory, the limitations and issues of the Web Workers API (Sect. 3) are alleviated when a coordination language, such as Reo, is used. Our example programs were still abstract, though. In this section, complementary, we report on a concrete example program that we implemented using the tools presented in Sect. 6.

Example 8. To avoid bias, we took an existing program [1] (not ours) that uses the Web Workers API. This program performs a nontrivial numerical computation, where n background workers cooperatively compute $a^b \bmod c$. This calculation is also performed, for instance, in RSA decryption, where a is the encrypted message, and where b and c constitute an agent's private key.

In the original program, first, the main worker sends a message (a, b_i, c)—a "work package"—to every background worker $1 \leq i \leq n$, such that $\sum b_i = b$. Subsequently, every background worker i computes $a^{b_i} \bmod c$ and sends back the result. Finally, the main worker aggregates these results into the final outcome. Communication between the main worker and the background workers thus follows a typical master–slaves pattern.

Using our tools, we adapted the original program to use the Reo@JS API, effectively by replacing all `postMessage` calls with `put` and `get` calls on ports. We also relieved the main worker from its original tasks of dividing the work and aggregating the results, and placed these responsibilities with two new background workers. As a result, the background workers now exactly fit Alice, the Bobs, and Carol in Example 3: Alice divides the work, the Bobs perform the work and compute the results, and Carol aggregates the results. By instantiating Alice, the Bobs, and Carol in this way, Fig. 11 is directly applicable in this case study, including all its previously explained advantages (Examples 5 and 6).

As a result of these changes, the coordination code that needed to be written manually was reduced from 145 lines to 46 lines (reduction of nearly 70%). Moreover, by implementing the coordination protocol in a separate module as a Reo circuit, it became amenable to reuse; essentially, the changes to the original program turned a specific implementation of master–slaves coordination into a reusable generic one. Thus, the effort of designing the circuit (less than an hour by a Reo expert) need not be remade in the future.   □

Example 9. Suppose that the original program "accidentally" (e.g., as the result of a programming mistake) lets the main worker send all work packages to the same background worker, so losing concurrency. As the implementation of the coordination protocol is not an explicit module in the original program, there is no obvious place to enforce that work packages should be evenly distributed among background workers.

In contrast, using Reo, we can encode such constraints in the circuit, and the compiler-generated code automatically enforces them. Figure 13 already showed such a circuit for two Bobs, which can be generalized to n. Using this circuit, if a faulty Bob performs multiple `get` operations, the circuit still ensures that the other Bobs receive a work package before the faulty Bob receives its second one, so preserving concurrency. Thus, new constraints (e.g., to improve robustness) can directly be added in our approach, due to improved changeability.   □

Example 10. As a first indication of performance, we conducted the following experiment. We took a synchronous variant of the circuit in Fig. 13 and a synchronous variant of the circuit between the two Bobs and Carol in Fig. 11, then we used the Reo-to-JS compiler to generate code, and finally we ran the resulting programs in Firefox on a machine with four hardware threads, processed by two physical cores. We experimented with synchronous circuits, because we wanted to test a worst-case scenario (asynchrony is cheaper than synchrony). The computation to be performed was always $2^{1024 \cdot 10^6} \mod 97777$. We repeated this for $1 \leq n \leq 10$ Bobs, and we averaged our timing measurements over ten runs per n; we did the same for the original program to make a comparison.

Figure 18(a) shows the begin-to-end execution times (error bars indicate standard deviation). The figure shows that scalability is quite well, so long as there is hardware parallelism to harness (up to $n = 4$). Evaluating the effectiveness of the parallelization is actually not our main concern, though; we are primarily interested in the performance of the compiler-generated protocol implementation

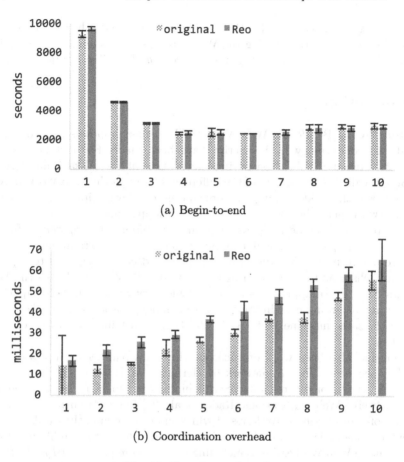

(a) Begin-to-end

(b) Coordination overhead

Fig. 18. Experimental results

relative to the hand-written one in the original program. Figure 18(b) is, thus, more interesting: it shows the execution times of *only* the coordination overhead (measured by commenting out the computations of the workers).[4] This figure shows that the compiler-generated code is on average 20% slower. Given that we have not seriously optimized our compiler and runtime library yet, we consider this a promising result: it suggests that we can have the advantages in Sect. 5 without prohibitive performance costs.   □

---

[4] Ideally, coordination overhead is completely independent of workload. In practice, however, this is not always so. The memory footprint of a workload can, for instance, affect the size of coordination overhead [16]. Generally, the larger a workload, the smaller the ratio $\frac{coordination}{computation}$, the less impact coordination overhead has on performance, and the less important minimizing such overhead becomes; at that point, other software qualities (changeability, reusability, etc.) may take precedence.

The examples in Sect. 5 and in this section, combined with the tools in Sect. 6, provide first evidence that hiding the Web Workers API behind a coordination language, such as Reo, is advantageous in theory *and* feasible in practice.

8   Conclusion

Related Work. Beside the Web Workers API, other proposals to incorporate actor-based concurrency in JavaScript have been made. For instance, Stivan et al. [26] ported the JVM-based implementation of the Akka framework to JavaScript, called *Akka.js*. One of the differences between the Web Workers API and Akka.js is that Akka.js allows actors on different JavaScript engines to communicate with each other. For Myter et al. [21], supporting both parallelism and distribution was a key design consideration in developing the *Spiders.js* framework. Spiders.js places particular emphasis on ease of programming, but not on coordination protocols. Welc et al. [27] proposed *generic workers* to support both parallelism and distribution in terms of an API very similar to the Web Workers API. These approaches are complementary to ours: in this paper, we simplify implementing coordination protocols among background workers running on the same machine, but a generalization to distributed actors would be interesting.

There has also been work on incorporating data parallelism in JavaScript, including the *River Trail* framework by Herhut et al. [14] and the *WebCL* initiative [8], which constitutes a JavaScript binding to OpenCL. In an emperical study of twelve Web applications, Radoi et al. [25] found "a surprisingly large quantity of compute-intensive loops of which many were latently parallel."

Outside academia, several libraries have been developed to simplify programming with the Web Workers API, including *q-connection* [5], *parallel.js* [4], *Hamsters.js* [2], and *operative* [3], but without emphasizing coordination protocols.

Technical differences aside, the main conceptual difference between all this related work and our proposed approach is that we emphasize the importance of coordination protocols as explicit programming artifacts, thereby enforcing syntactic separation of coordination and computation. Such a separation makes it easier to change and reuse coordination protocols.

This Work. We showed that implementing coordination protocols among background workers is difficult, because of limitations and issues with the low-level Web Workers API (Sects. 2 and 3). To make this simpler, we proposed to hide the Web Workers API behind a coordination language that provides higher-level constructs. Using Reo (Sect. 4), we demonstrated the advantages and feasibility of our approach by example (Sects. 5 and 7), and we presented the necessary tool support in terms of a compiler, a runtime library and API, and a front-end (Sect. 6). As Web application developers have a tradition of separating concerns (HTML, CSS, JavaScript), Web applications may constitute a fertile new application domain for existing coordination languages.

Future Work. We argued, by example, that use of a coordination language makes implementing coordination protocols among background workers simpler (i.e., it has particular advantages over directly using the Web Workers API). Complementary proof for this claim would consist of a set of successful real projects; we therefore aim to empirically evaluate the merits of our proposed approach, and improve our tools in the process. Optimizing the Reo-to-JS compiler and Reo@JS runtime library is also high on our list, including a study of impact on performance, which we barely touched upon in this paper.

An important aspect of the previously mentioned future work is studying the scalability of our proposed approach, both in terms of usability and performance. We expect modularity (separation of coordination and computation) to play an enabling role in dealing with complex systems, but it requires a new way of working from programmers; the consequences of this are unclear and should be better studied. Also, tools (notably, the compiler) need to ensure performance scalability as coordination protocols grow larger (i.e., involve more participants), which generally is a nontrivial technical challenge [19].

We chose to use Reo in this work, because it is strongly rooted in separation of computation and coordination. Reo, however, also has its limitations. For instance, run-time parametrization in the number of workers is not yet possible. It is therefore interesting to see if a JavaScript variant of, for instance, *Pabble* [22] (based on *multiparty session types* [15]) is more suitable.

A special case of a background worker is one that only calls an asynchronous API (e.g., the Geolocation API) and processes the result in a callback. In another experiment with our tools [20] (omitted from this paper to save space), we encountered several such distinguished background workers and already added support for them in our tool (the tool automatically generates code to make asynchronous API calls from our framework; the programmer does not need to write such boilerplate code her/himself). Further research is necessary, however, to study to what extent coordination languages can also be used to orchestrate asynchronous API calls as a solution to "callback hells", and whether there are advantages compared to existing approaches; see Philips et al. [24].

References

1. Javascript Web Workers Test. http://pmav.eu/stuff/javascript-webworkers/
2. [library]: Hamsters.js. https://github.com/austinksmith/Hamsters.js
3. [library]: operative. https://github.com/padolsey/operative
4. [library]: parallel.js. https://github.com/parallel-js/parallel.js
5. [library]: q-connection. https://github.com/kriskowal/q-connection
6. [library]: tiny-worker. https://github.com/avoidwork/tiny-worker
7. [standard] Ecma International: ECMA-262. http://www.ecma-international.org/publications/standards/Ecma-262.htm
8. [standard] Khronos Group: WebCL. https://www.khronos.org/webcl
9. [standard] W3C: Web Workers. https://www.w3.org/TR/workers
10. Arbab, F.: Reo: a channel-based coordination model for component composition. Math. Struct. Comp. Sci. **14**(3), 329–366 (2004)

11. Arbab, F.: Puff, the magic protocol. In: Agha, G., Danvy, O., Meseguer, J. (eds.) Formal Modeling: Actors, Open Systems, Biological Systems. LNCS, vol. 7000, pp. 169–206. Springer, Heidelberg (2011). doi:10.1007/978-3-642-24933-4_9

12. Baier, C., Sirjani, M., Arbab, F., Rutten, J.: Modeling component connectors in Reo by constraint automata. Sci. Comput. Program. **61**(2), 75–113 (2006)

13. De Koster, J., Van Cutsem, T., De Meuter, W.: 43 years of actors: a taxonomy of actor models and their key properties. In: Proceedings of AGERE 2016, pp. 31–40. ACM (2016)

14. Herhut, S., Hudson, R., Shpeisman, T., Sreeram, J.: River trail: a path to parallelism in JavaScript. In: Proceedings of OOPSLA 2013, pp. 729–744. ACM (2013)

15. Honda, K., Yoshida, N., Carbone, M.: Multiparty asynchronous session types. ACM SIGPLAN Notices **43**(1), 273–284 (2008). (Proceedings of POPL 2008)

16. Jongmans, S.-S.T.Q.: Automata-theoretic protocol programming. Ph.D. thesis, Leiden University (2016)

17. Jongmans, S.-S.T.Q., Arbab, F.: PrDK: protocol programming with automata. In: Chechik, M., Raskin, J.-F. (eds.) TACAS 2016. LNCS, vol. 9636, pp. 547–552. Springer, Heidelberg (2016). doi:10.1007/978-3-662-49674-9_33

18. Jongmans, S.-S.T.Q., Arbab, F.: Overview of thirty semantic formalisms for Reo. Sci. Ann. Comput. Sci. **22**(1), 201–251 (2012)

19. Jongmans, S.-S.T.Q., Arbab, F.: Can high throughput atone for high latency in compiler-generated protocol code? In: Dastani, M., Sirjani, M. (eds.) FSEN 2015. LNCS, vol. 9392, pp. 238–258. Springer, Cham (2015). doi:10.1007/978-3-319-24644-4_17

20. Krauweel, M.: Concurrent and asynchronous JavaScript programming using Reo. Master's thesis, Open University of the Netherlands (2017)

21. Myter, F., Scholliers, C., De Meuter, W.: Many spiders make a better web: a unified web-based actor framework. In: Proceedings of AGERE 2016, pp. 51–60. ACM (2016)

22. Ng, N., Yoshida, N.: Pabble: parameterised Scribble. Service Oriented Comput. Appl. **9**(3-4), 269–284 (2015)

23. Parnas, D.: On the criteria to be used in decomposing systems into modules. Commun. ACM **15**(12), 1053–1058 (1972)

24. Philips, L., De Koster, J., De Meuter, W., De Roover, C.: Dependence-driven delimited CPS transformation for JavaScript. In: Proceedings of GPCE 2016, pp. 59–69. ACM (2016)

25. Radoi, C., Herhut, S., Sreeram, J., Dig, D.: Are web applications ready for parallelism? In: Proceedings of PPoPP 2015. ACM (2015)

26. Stivan, G., Peruffo, A., Haller, P.: Akka. js: towards a portable actor runtime environment. In: Proceedings of AGERE! 2015, pp. 57–64. ACM (2015)

27. Welc, A., Hudson, R., Shpeisman, T., Adl-Tabatabai, A.R.: Generic workers: towards unified distributed and parallel Javascript programming model. In: Proceedings of PSI EtA 2010. ACM (2010)

28. Zakas, N.: Promises and Asynchronous Programming. In: Understanding ECMAScript 6, Chap. 11, 1st edn., pp. 213–241. No Starch Press (2016)

Optimally-Self-Healing Distributed Gradient Structures Through Bounded Information Speed

Giorgio Audrito[1,2]([✉]), Ferruccio Damiani[1,2], and Mirko Viroli[3]

[1] Dipartimento di Informatica, University of Torino, Torino, Italy
{giorgio.audrito,ferruccio.damiani}@unito.it
[2] Centro di Competenza per il Calcolo Scientifico, University of Torino, Torino, Italy
[3] DISI, University of Bologna, Cesena, Italy
mirko.viroli@unibo.it

Abstract. With the constant increase in the number of interconnected devices in today networks, more and more computations can be described by *spatial computing* abstractions. In this context, distances can be estimated in a fully-distributed way by the so-called *gradient* self-organisation pattern: it is a basic building block also for large-scale system coordination, frequently used to broadcast information, forecast pointwise events, as carrier for distributed sensing, and as combinator for higher-level spatial structures. However, computing gradients is very problematic in a mutable environment: existing algorithms fail in reaching adequate trade offs between accuracy and reaction speed to environment changes.

In this paper we introduce a new gradient algorithm, *BIS (Bounded Information Speed) gradient*, which uses time information to achieve a smooth and predictable reaction speed, which is proved optimal for algorithms following a single-path-communication strategy. Following a proposed methodology for empirical evaluation of performance of spatial computing algorithms, we evaluate BIS gradient and compare it with other approaches. We show that BIS achieves the best accuracy while keeping smoothness under control.

Keywords: Aggregate programming · Gradient · Information speed · Reliability · Spatial computing

1 Introduction

The increasing availability of computational devices of every sort, spread throughout our living and working environments, is creating new challenges in the engineering of complex software systems, especially in contexts like the Internet-of-Things, Cyber-Physical Systems, Pervasive Computing, and so on. *Spatial computing* abstractions have been proposed as a means to take full opportunity of

This work has been partially supported by: EU Horizon 2020 project HyVar (www.hyvar-project.eu), GA No. 644298; ICT COST Action IC1402 ARVI (www.cost-arvi.eu); Ateneo/CSP D16D15000360005 project RunVar (runvar-project.di.unito.it).

J.-M. Jacquet and M. Massink (Eds.): COORDINATION 2017, LNCS 10319, pp. 59–77, 2017.
DOI: 10.1007/978-3-319-59746-1_4

such large-scale computational infrastructures, for their ability to provide pervasive and intelligent sensing, coordination, and actuation over the physical world [5]: they provide models and mechanisms raising the abstraction layer, making it possible to more easily capture the goal of a large-scale situated system.

In this context, "collective" programs can be seen as taking as input situated data changing over time, typically perceived by (virtual or physical) sensors [9], and produce analogous data as outputs to feed (virtual or physical) actuators, having an effect on other computational components, on the physical world, or on humans in it. Such an input/output transformation is captured by a computational process iteratively executing over space and time, involving complex coordination patterns, and in need of satisfying multiple non-functional requirements: scalability, resilience to unpredictable changes, and heterogeneity and dynamism of the communication infrastructure. A key difficulty in engineering collective applications of this kind, hence, is the lack of computational frameworks and libraries of reusable algorithms with guaranteed resilience and performance to match this level of complexity in application services. Even the most basic "building block" algorithms one wants to rely upon, typically give rise to inadequate behaviour when faced with such demanding requirements.

A prototypical example of this phenomenon is given by the *shortest path* (SP) problem in a weighted network, which is fully solved in a traditional computation setting by (among many) Dijkstra's algorithm. In spatial computing, the SP problem translates into the so-called *gradient* computation [4], which amounts to computing shortest paths from all nodes to a given set of source nodes, through a fully distributed process to be iteratively executed to promptly react to any change in the environment. Gradients are known to be a basic building block for self-organising coordination [3,15,20,30], being frequently used for a variety of purposes: to broadcast information, forecast events, dynamically partition networks, ground distributed sensing [6], anticipate future events [21], and to combine into higher-level spatial structures [15]. However, the known algorithms for gradient computation are not fully satisfactory, as they involve relevant trade-offs between scalability, resiliency and precision.

In this paper we introduce a new gradient algorithm, the *BIS (Bounded Information Speed) gradient*, which highly relies on time information to achieve smooth reaction to changes with predictable speed. Given a rising speed v (i.e., increase in gradient estimate over time) as a parameter, it enforces an information propagation speed (i.e., space travelled by information over time) equal to v, so as to scale from the classic gradient (where essentially $v = 0$) to a reaction speed that we prove to be optimal (among the single-path communication algorithms) with v equal to the average information speed. If v is greater than such an average, however, a metric distortion is induced that causes the algorithm to systematically overestimate gradient values: it is thus crucial to tune correctly the parameter in order to achieve the best accuracy.

To address this problem, we compute mathematical estimates of the average single-path communication speed, and use them for validating the performance of BIS gradient with respect to the three most performant algorithms proposed

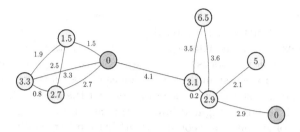

Fig. 1. Gradient computed in a sample network with two source devices.

in the spatial computing context: classic (propagating triangle inequality [30]), CRF [4] and FLEX [3]. We thus show that the BIS gradient achieves the best accuracy while keeping smoothness under control. This comparison is carried out through a general approach we propose, as an empirical evaluation methodology for the performance of all spatial computing algorithms (and gradient algorithms in particular). Finally, we present a realistic case study application of crowd steering towards multiple points of interest (POI), some of which can suddenly become unavailable—faster healing algorithms are here needed to reduce the "average travelling time" for people towards an available POI.

The remainder of this paper is organised as follows. Section 2 provides the background for this paper and discusses related works, introducing the relevant gradient algorithms. Section 3 describes the proposed BIS gradient algorithm together with the mathematical estimates of average single-path information speed. Section 4 proposes the methodology for empirical evaluation of spatial computing algorithms, compares the various gradient algorithms and tests them in the selected case study. Section 5 concludes and outlines possible directions of future research.

2   Background and Related Work

2.1   Gradient-Based Approaches

In this paper we are concerned with coordination strategies for situated networks, where the objective can be represented in terms of a global, system-level "pattern" to be achieved by local interactions between neighouring devices, showing inherent resilience with respect to unpredicted changes—in network topology, scale, inputs coming from sensors, and so on. This viewpoint is endorsed by a number of works in a recent thread of research, in the context of coordination models and languages [20,28,32], multiagent systems [10,14,29] and spatial computing [2,5,6,15,17]. In spite of various differences and peculiarities, they all promote the idea of creating complex distributed algorithms as *spatial computations*, where few basic communication and coordination mechanisms are provided to the programmer, who uses them by progressively stacking building blocks into layers of increasing complexity.

In this context, gradient data structures, or *gradients* for short, are pervasively used as key building blocks [6, 15]. They produce a map – also called a *computational field* [12, 13] – assigning to each device δ in a network N its estimated distance from the closest *source* device (an input for the problem), computed by the shortest-path through weighted links in the network (see Fig. 1).

Applications of gradients are countless. Other than to trivially estimate long-range distances (possibly according to metrics computed during execution of the algorithm), gradient computations enact an outward progressive propagation of information along optimal paths. Thus, they are used as forward "carrier" for broadcasting information, forecasting events, and dynamically partitioning networks [6]. Also, used backwards, one can make information flow back to the source, to move or steer mobile agents or data towards the source, or to summarise or average distributed information, i.e., to generally support distributed sensing [6]. Other applications include: considering future events so as to provide proactive "adaptation" [21]; managing semantic knowledge in situated environments [16], create high-level spatial structures [15], elect leaders on a spatial basis [7], and so on.

Due to their usefulness, several works also study how to establish gradients in contexts where local estimation of distances is not available [18, 19, 22], and others take them as basic example to study self-stabilisation techniques [11, 20].

2.2 Gradient-Based Implementations

According to the framework presented in [27], it is suggested to associate to fundamental building blocks (including the gradient) a library of alternative implementations, among which one has to pick the right implementation for each specific use in the application at hand. It is therefore of interest to analyse differnet trade-offs in the implementation of gradient algorithms, with the goal of identifying approaches guaranteeing reactiveness and smoothness in the way gradients (and the many applications on top) can respond to dynamic environments. In its most basic form, the gradient can be calculated through iterative application of a triangle inequality constraint in each device δ, starting with ∞ everywhere:

$$G(\delta) = \begin{cases} 0 & \text{if } source(\delta) \\ \min\{G(\delta') + w(\delta', \delta) : \ \delta' \in N \text{ linked with } \delta\} & \text{otherwise} \end{cases}$$

We call this procedure *classic* gradient. Repeated fair application[1] of this calculation in a fixed network will converge to the correct value at every point [11].[2] However, the performance of this algorithm in a mutable environment is impaired by several limitations.

---

[1] A sequence of updates is *fair* if every device updates his value infinitely often.

[2] In finite time if every device can reach a source; at the limit otherwise (in this case, distance estimates raise indefinitely towards the correct value ∞).

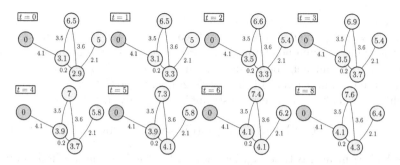

Fig. 2. Evolution after loss of the right source. In each round all devices compute in order, from the one holding the highest value to the one with the lowest. Each device rises by 0.4 every two rounds, because of the short link at the middle of the graph.

- *Speed Bias*: if devices are continuously moving, the values produced by the algorithm systematically underestimate[3] the correct value of the gradient; with an error which increases with the movement speed.
- *Rising Value*: in response to quick changes in the network (e.g., a change in the set of source devices), the algorithm can rapidly correct values that need to drop, while it is very slow in correcting values that need to rise. In other words, the algorithm can badly underestimate values for long periods of time after such changes. Precisely, the rising speed of this algorithm is bounded by the distance between the pair of closest devices: Fig. 2 shows an example of this phenomenon on a part of the network in Fig. 1. This problem is also known as *count-to-infinity* in the context of routing algorithms [25].
- *Smoothness*: in the presence of error in distance estimates, it might be preferable not to strictly follow the triangle inequality, so as to reduce the resultant flickering in the output values. Moreover, if the distance estimates are used for an higher-order coordination mechanism (e.g., for moving values towards the sources by "descending" the shortest-paths tree obtained from the gradient), then each variation in the estimates might change the resulting connection tree, effectively disrupting the outcome of the coordination for some time.

In order to overcome these limitations, several refined algorithms have been proposed. To the best of our knowledge, those that better address those problems are J. Beal's CRF gradient (Constraint and Restoring Force) [4] and FLEX gradient (Flexible) [3].

CRF Gradient. The CRF gradient [4] is designed to address the rising value problem by ignoring some *Constraints* (i.e., neighbours[4]), while assuming a *Restoring Force* inducing a uniform rise in absence of constraints. The algorithm takes as

---

[3] Sporadic overestimation is also possible, however the "minimising" nature of the algorithm propagates lower estimates and disperses higher ones.

[4] Recall that in the classic gradient, the value $G(\delta)$ is obtained by combining the "triangle-inequality" constraints $G(\delta) \leq G(\delta') + w(\delta', \delta)$ for each neighbour δ'.

parameter a fixed speed v_0, and associates a "rising speed" $v(\delta)$ to each device so that: if the value of the device is currently constrained (either by being a source or by the value of some neighbour) then $v(\delta) = 0$; otherwise if the value is *not* constrained (i.e., all neighbours have been discarded) then $v(\delta) = v_0$. Before applying the minimisation as in the classic gradient, the CRF gradient considers a neighbour δ' as "able to exert constraint" if and only if:

$$G(\delta') + w(\delta', \delta) \leq G(\delta) - \lambda(\delta', \delta) \cdot v(\delta)$$

where $\lambda(\delta', \delta)$ measures time lag, i.e., how old is the information in δ about δ'. The above condition checks whether the constraint given by δ' is able to bound the currently (i.e., not yet updated) value of the gradient *as shifted back to the time when the constraint was calculated*. If the current device is not yet rising, the condition amounts to the constraint being able to reduce the current value; otherwise it becomes more restrictive.

If some neighbour able to exert constraint exists, the value is calculated similarly to the classic gradient. Otherwise, a fixed rising speed is enforced (thus rising by $v_0 \Delta t$ where Δt is the time interval between the last two rounds).

$$G(\delta) = \begin{cases} 0 & \text{if } source(\delta) \\ \min\{G(\delta') + w(\delta', \delta) : \ \delta' \text{ exerts constraint}\} & \text{if some } \delta' \text{ exists} \\ G(\delta) + v_0 \Delta t & \text{otherwise} \end{cases}$$

Through this algorithm the rising speed is then equal to v_0, provided that v_0 is small enough, thus addressing the rising value problem.

FLEX Gradient. The FLEX gradient [3] is designed to improve smoothness through application of a "filtering function" to the outcome of the minimisation, which reduces changes while granting an overall error of at most a given parameter ϵ. Precisely, it first calculates the "maximum local slope":

$$s(\delta) = \max \left\{ \frac{G(\delta) - G(\delta')}{w(\delta', \delta)} : \ \delta' \in N \text{ linked with } \delta \right\}$$

This slope is then used to calculate the gradient estimation as:

$$G(\delta) = \begin{cases} 0 & \text{if } source(\delta) \\ G(\delta') + (1 + \epsilon)w(\delta', \delta) & \text{if } s(\delta) > 1 + \epsilon \\ G(\delta') + (1 - \epsilon)w(\delta', \delta) & \text{if } s(\delta) < 1 - \epsilon \\ G(\delta) & \text{otherwise} \end{cases}$$

where δ' is the device achieving maximum slope (according to the values available to the current device). The above formula, in other words, selects the closest value to $G(\delta)$ in the interval from $G(\delta') + (1 - \epsilon)w(\delta', \delta)$ to $G(\delta') + (1 + \epsilon)w(\delta', \delta)$, thus attempting to reduce local changes as much as possible while introducing a metric distortion below ϵ. Two further optimisations are also introduced in

FLEX gradient: first, the classical gradient formula is used instead of the above one whenever the current value is over a factor 2 from the old value, or anyway every once in a while (details can be found in [3])—this prevents a systematic error of ϵ to persist indefinitely in a static environment after a network change; second, a distorted metric $w'(\delta', \delta) = \max(w(\delta', \delta), k)$ is used, for a certain constant k—this adds some further error in the output of the algorithm, but it also ensures that the rising speed is at least k (since k becomes the shortest possible "distorted" distance between devices).

3   BIS Gradient

3.1   Information Speed

In most spatial computing abstractions, a network of devices typically perform an interaction through short-range message passing between neighbour devices. The speed achieved by information in this process constitutes an upper bound for responsiveness to environment and input changes, in a similar way to the speed of light, which is an upper bound for causal relationship between events. Depending on the pattern followed by information exchanges, we can distinguish between two main achievable speeds: *single-path* and *multi-path*.

Definition 1 (Information Speed). *The* single-path information speed *is the space travelled over time by messages through a spanning tree in the network. The* multi-path information speed *is the same quantity assuming messages are exchanged through all possible links in the network.*

Clearly, the upper bound for causal relationship in a network is given by the multi-path information speed. This communication pattern requires multiple informations to be aggregated in each node, in order to avoid a program state explosion; and is thus typical of "aggregation" algorithms (such as broadcasting and collecting). Conversely, communication in existing gradient algorithms (and in particular in the BIS gradient we shall introduce in the next subsection) is usually structured on an implicit (shortest-paths) spanning tree: messages from all neighbours are received, but only one of them is selected and passed over for subsequent computations. For this reason, in the remainder of this section we shall focus on single-path information speed and estimate its average v_{avg} in a random network. This estimate would be crucial to determine the value to be passed to BIS gradient for its parameter v.

Consider a network of computing devices, each of them running an algorithm with a certain time period P on data available from neighbour devices within a certain radius R. Let D be a random variable for the distance and T for the time interval between the event of a device sending a message and the event of another device using that message for computation. Then the average speed S achieved by information can be expressed as:[5]

---

[5] Following standard statistic notation, we use $E(X)$ for the mean and $V(X)$ for the variance of a random variable X.

$$E(S) = E\left(\frac{D}{T}\right) = \frac{E(D)}{E(T)}\left(1 + \frac{V(T)}{E(T)^2}\right)$$

truncating the bivariate Taylor expansion of the ratio function to the second order (see [26] for a complete proof of this fact).

The average distance crossed by a message can be calculated as the average radius of communication R times the average distance of a uniformly chosen random point in an n-dimensional unit ball, giving a total $E(D) = \frac{n}{n+1}R$. If devices are moving at a certain average speed v, this estimate should be adapted to take into account that messages with a certain lag T could come from a further distance up to vT. An exact calculation of the expected distance in this setting is complex and depends on many factors. However, if we assume the movement to be sufficiently uniform and restrict ourselves to algorithms with a preference for shortest-paths (as for gradients), we can just add up $\frac{v}{2}T$ to the numerator obtaining a roughly acceptable estimate $E(S) = E\left(\frac{D}{T}\right) + \frac{v}{2}$.

The average time interval between events depends heavily on the underlying specific implementation of network communication. In many spatial computing models, like field calculus [31] and Proto [2], a reasonable model of time delay would be $T = P \cdot (I + IF)$, where: P represents the period of a random device, I represents the imprecision of a single device, F represents a random phase between devices, as a uniform distribution of values in $[0, 1]$. In this model, $E(T) = \frac{3}{2}E(P)E(I) = \frac{3}{2}Q$ (where Q is the average computation period) and:

$$1 + \frac{V(T)}{E(T)^2} = \frac{E(T^2)}{E(T)^2} = \frac{E(P^2)}{E(P)^2} \cdot \frac{E\left((I + IF)^2\right)}{E(I + IF)^2} = \frac{E(P^2)}{E(P)^2} \cdot \left(1 + \frac{V(I + IF)}{E(I + IF)^2}\right)$$

$$= \frac{E(P^2)}{E(P)^2} \cdot \left(1 + \frac{V(I) + \frac{V(I)}{3} + \frac{E(I)^2}{12}}{\frac{9}{4}E(I)^2}\right) = \left(1 + \frac{V(P)}{E(P)^2}\right) \cdot \left(\frac{28}{27} + \frac{16}{27}\frac{V(I)}{E(I)^2}\right).$$

Notice that $\frac{V(X)}{E(X)^2}$ is the square of the relative standard error $\hat{\sigma}^2(X)$. Thus the average single-path information speed v_{avg} can be estimated as:

$$v_{\text{avg}} = E(S) = \frac{2}{3}\frac{n}{n+1}\frac{R}{Q}\left(1 + \hat{\sigma}^2(P)\right)\left(\frac{28}{27} + \frac{16}{27}\hat{\sigma}^2(I)\right) + \frac{v}{2} \qquad (1)$$

where v is the movement speed of devices. This equation tells us that: the speed is mainly proportional to the ratio of communication radius over computation period; the speed increases with the dimensionality of the space, i.e., is lower for devices aligned in a row and higher for devices in 3-dimensional space;[6] the speed increases with the relative error of computation periods, both among different devices and inside a single device. Equation 1 will be used later to estimate the v parameter of the BIS gradient algorithm. We remark that the average above

---

[6] Gradient algorithms have preference for shortest-path links, so that information tends to propagate linearly regardless of the dimensionality of the space. This fact does not contradict the above estimate, which assumes that transmission links are chosen randomly (assumption viable also for gradient algorithms in sparse networks).

is computed for a single hop of communication. Over multiple hops, the relative standard error decreases while the average does not change significantly. In case the network parameters (average radius of communication, computation period, etc.) cannot be assumed to be constant, a simple algorithm can still estimate v_{avg} continuously according to the formula above (by averaging the relevant quantities through low-pass filters).

3.2   Computing Gradient Through Information Speed

As exemplified in Fig. 2, in presence of a rising value problem, distance increase per round is bounded by the shortest link in the network ℓ. We accordingly obtain an average information speed proportional to $\frac{2\ell}{3Q}$ instead of $\frac{2nR}{3(n+1)Q}$, which can be arbitrarily slower as ℓ approaches zero. This fact suggests us to prevent the rising value problem by *lower bounding* the information speed to make this "slow" rise impossible.

The *Bounded Information Speed* (BIS) gradient improves over the classical gradient by enforcing a minimum information speed v requested by the user. As long as v does not surpass the average single-path communication speed, the algorithm is able to compute correct estimates of the gradient with increased responsiveness. Greater values of v induce instead a metric distortion, causing the algorithm to systematically overestimate values. In the remainder of this paper, we shall thus express v as a fraction of v_{avg} (the average single-path communication speed, which we estimate through Eq. 1).

For each device in the network, we compute both the usual gradient estimate $G(\delta)$ and a lag estimate $L(\delta)$, representing the time elapsed since the message started from a source. Lags are estimated through local time differences, so that no overall clock synchronisation is required. When considering a candidate neighbour δ' of a device δ, the time lag relative to this neighbour is:

$$L(\delta, \delta') = L(\delta') + \lambda(\delta', \delta)$$

where $\lambda(\delta', \delta)$ is the lag of the message from δ' to δ. We then take into account this value when calculating the gradient estimate relative to this neighbour:

$$G(\delta, \delta') = \max\left\{G(\delta') + w(\delta', \delta),\ vL(\delta, \delta') - r\right\}$$

where w is the distance between devices and r is the communication radius. This formula accounts to assuming that messages propagate at least at speed v, so that the gradient estimate is lower bounded by $vL(\delta, \delta')$ (with the additive constant $-r$ to ensure that some error is taken into account).

The overall estimates of $G(\delta)$ and $L(\delta)$ are then obtained by minimising $G(\delta, \delta')$ over neighbours (we assume that pairs are ordered lexicographically):

$$[G(\delta), L(\delta)] = \begin{cases} [0, 0] & \text{if } source(\delta) \\ \min\{[G(\delta, \delta'), L(\delta, \delta')] : \ \delta' \in N \text{ linked with } \delta\} & \text{otherwise} \end{cases}$$

This algorithm generalises the classic gradient algorithm, as shown in the following.

Theorem 1 (Degenerate BIS). *The BIS gradient with $v = 0$ is equivalent to the classic gradient.*

Proof. If $v = 0$, $G(\delta, \delta') = \max\{G(\delta') + w(\delta', \delta), 0 \cdot L(\delta, \delta') - r\}$ is equal to $G(\delta') + w(\delta', \delta)$ so that $L(\delta)$ is implicitly discarded.

In particular, the same result would hold for devices with no lag estimator so that $\lambda(\delta, \delta')$ is always 0. For devices with an internal timer (so that a lag estimator can be defined), tweaking the parameter v close to the average single-path information speed provides a guaranteed reactivity, which is optimal among algorithms with a single-path information flow.

Theorem 2 (Performance Bound). *Information speed in BIS gradient, calculated w.r.t. the gradient estimates, is at least v. Furthermore, values constrained by obsolete information increase at least at speed v.*

Proof. Since $G(\delta, \delta') \geq vL(\delta, \delta') - r$ for all δ', also $G(\delta) \geq vL(\delta) - r$ concluding the first part. For the second part, consider an information that started propagating from a certain source at time t_0 and is now obsolete (e.g., the source has been disconnected), and fix a device δ computing in times $t_1, \ldots, t_n$ constrained by such obsolete information. Since $L(\delta) = t_i - t_0$ in each computing round $i \leq n$, $G(\delta) \geq vL(\delta) - r = v(t_i - t_0) - r$ concluding the second part.

Theorem 3 (Optimality). *The BIS gradient with v equal to the average single-path information speed v_{avg} attains optimal reactivity among algorithms with a single-path information flow.*

Proof. As a prototypical example, consider an already stabilised network with a selected source device and its corresponding influence region, i.e., the set of devices whose distances are calculated w.r.t. the selected source (red). Suppose that the selected source device is suddenly disconnected at time $t = 0$. In any algorithm with a single-path information flow, the information about this disconnection flows through the influence region at average speed v. For example, device δ in Fig. 3 is reached by this information at time $\frac{d_0}{v}$, and it cannot change its value from d_0 before that time.

In the best case scenario, after the information about the disconnection reaches the border a new wave of information can bounce back towards the inside of the region, bringing values calculated from other sources (green). Since the shortest path from the disconnected source to the border and then back to device δ has length $d_1 + d_2$ (black arrow) and information flows at speed v, the earliest time when δ can reach the correct value is $\frac{d_1 + d_2}{v}$. Notice that this value is $d_1 + d_2$ since the distance from the border to the two sources is the same.

Then δ holds value d_0 at time $\frac{d_0}{v}$ and value $d_1 + d_2$ at time $\frac{d_1 + d_2}{v}$, effectively rising at speed $(d_1 + d_2 - d_0)/(\frac{d_1 + d_2}{v} - \frac{d_0}{v}) = v$. Since this is the best-case scenario, a faster rising speed is not possible thus proving optimality of BIS gradient.

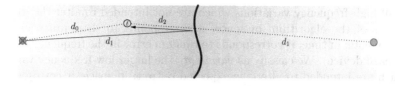

Fig. 3. Information flow upon disconnection of a source device. (Color figure online)

3.3 Reducing Volatility and Communication Cost

An improved reactivity to changes naturally translates into an increase in volatility of values, thus reducing the degree of *smoothness*. This holds true also for the BIS gradient: in a mutable environment, even calculating the exact gradient all the times would perform poorly on smoothness, since it would rapidly adapt all the values as noise and small movements take place.

In order to improve smoothness of rapidly self-healing algorithms, it is then necessary to insert a damping component. Also the FLEX gradient, designed for improved smoothness, can be seen as the embedding of the following damping function into the classical gradient computation:

$$
\mathtt{damp}(\mathtt{old}, \mathtt{new}) = \begin{cases} \mathtt{new} + \epsilon w(\delta', \delta) & \text{if } \mathtt{old} > \mathtt{new} + \epsilon w(\delta', \delta) \\ \mathtt{new} - \epsilon w(\delta', \delta) & \text{if } \mathtt{old} < \mathtt{new} - \epsilon w(\delta', \delta) \\ \mathtt{old} & \text{otherwise} \end{cases}
$$

In future works, it is therefore natural to investigate whether the insertion of this damping function (or others) into algorithms other than the classic gradient would achieve the same effect. In the next section, we shall show that this is true to some extent, allowing the BIS gradient for an improved smoothness.

4   Analysis and Verification

4.1   Performance Indicators

In order to empirically evaluate the performance of an approximated localised algorithm,[7] several aspects need to be taken into account. We divide them into *environment* characteristics, *input* properties, and *output* requirements.

Environment. A spatio-temporal computing environment is characterised by its degree of steadiness, which both in time and in space can be further specified through measures of *noise* and *variability*. We classify as *noise* the

---

[7] With *approximated localised algorithm* we denote any spatially-distributed iterative process which aim to approximate a target global *input/output* transformation (taking into account environmental data, as described in Sect. 1). For example, this is the case for *gradient* algorithms which approximate *shortest-path distances* (output) given a source set and an environmental configuration (input).

small high-frequency variations which are not intended to alter the expected output of the algorithm: in space, it corresponds to short-range brownian movements; in time, it corresponds to random error in the frequency of events (in each device). We classify as *variability* the larger low-frequency variations which are intended to alter the expected output: in space, it corresponds to long-range directional movements; in time, it corresponds to systematic error in the frequency of events (changing between devices or through time).

Input. To assess the performance of an algorithm, we need to split tests into two further possible situations: *constant* input, to isolate and measure the responses to environment variations; *discontinuous* input, where a sudden change happens at a certain point in time, to measure the healing speed of the algorithm.

Output. Given a test environment and input, we need to measure two different qualities of the output generated by the algorithm: *precision* and *smoothness*. *Precision* is the deviation from the ideal outcome: with a constant input, it measures systematic error (e.g., *speed bias* for gradient algorithms); with a discontinuous input, it measures healing speed (e.g., *rising value* for gradient algorithms). *Smoothness* is the volatility of the output values, usually measured as the integral of absolute differences between consecutive values (first derivative of the output), and aims for gradual and unidirectional changes in the output values, absorbing noise. It needs to be measured both on constant and discontinuous input.

Performance assessment of approximated localised algorithms thus requires extensive testing over several different environments, combining diverse degrees of noise and variability (both in space and in time). Among the different possibilities, we recommend to include: zero-noise zero-variability (in both space and time), in which the basic *self-stabilisation* property[8] is measured [11]; high-noise high-variability (in both space and time), in which a bottom line of guaranteed performance is measured in an extreme case; further intermediate cases, which can help differentiate how performance is affected by the different types of mutability (in space or time, as noise or variability), depending on the specific application. In each of those scenarios, performance is measured through *precision* and *smoothness*; on an input which is first constant for a long enough period of time to reach stable results, and then change discontinuously and keeps the new value constant until stable results are reached again.

4.2 Comparison Between Gradient Algorithms

In order to compare the performance of the different gradient algorithms presented in this paper, we chose an environment able to trigger the issues presented in Sect. 2:

- *speed bias*, by considering environments with increasing variability in space;

---

[8] An algorithm is *self-stabilising* if given a constant environment, it eventually reaches a correct output for any possible initial state.

- *rising value*, through arranging devices densely into a long corridor with a source at one end, so that the ratio between the longest and shortest distance between devices is high;
- *smoothness*, by measuring it in each test scenario.

Following the guidelines introduced in Sect. 4.1, we thus tested the following scenarios.

- *Environment:* we put 1000 devices with communication radius 10 m and average fire rate 1 s randomly into a 500 m × 20 m corridor, producing a network 50 hops wide. We tested this environment with increasing *variability* in space (long range movements) from 0 (none), to 1 (moderated) and 3 (high). Several conducted tests revealed that *noise* (both in space and in time) and *variability* in time did not affect significantly the behaviour of any of the considered algorithms, witnessing their intrinsic robustness. We thus only report graphs with high *noise* and time *variability* (brownian motion and 50% relative standard error in fire rate between different devices plus another 50% in each device). We modelled randomly distributed events according to a Weibull distribution [33].
- *Input:* we provided the algorithms with a single source, steadily located on the left end of the corridor until time 300, and then abruptly moved to the opposite right end. In this way, reaction to *discontinuous* input is measured (in the middle of the graphs) as well as behaviour under constant input (at the sides of the graphs).
- *Output:* for each scenario we measured *precision* as absolute error w.r.t. Euclidean distance and *smoothness* as absolute difference between values in consecutive rounds (both averaged).

Figure 4 summarises the evaluation results, which were obtained (similarly also to the experiments in next subsection) with Protelis [24] (an incarnation of the Field Calculus [13]) as programming language to code the model, Alchemist as simulator [23] and the Supercomputer OCCAM [1] to run the experiments. We tested classic, CRF, FLEX, BIS with $v = 0.5\,v_{avg}$, BIS with $v = 0.5\,v_{avg}$ and FLEX damping, BIS with $v = 0.9\,v_{avg}$, BIS with $v = 0.9\,v_{avg}$ and FLEX damping. In all cases, the tolerance of the FLEX damping was set to 10%. We run 10 instances of each scenario with different random seeds and averaged the results.

The rising value problem corresponds to the spikes in the middle of the graphs, which are considerably shorter (faster healing) for BIS gradient, even when $v = 0.5\,v_{avg}$. Speed bias is visible from the increase in error baseline under increasing space variability, and is more contained for BIS gradient (in particular when v is high). The only setting where BIS does not achieve the best precision is under constant input and zero space variability, where the error value is still small and in fact determined by the small variations reported in smoothness.

As expected, the increase in precision corresponds to a decreased smoothness, so that BIS gradient has the highest value volatility (increasing with v). Embedding the FLEX damping into BIS proves to be effective in reducing fluctuations for all values of v, so that BIS with $v = 0.5\,v_{avg}$ and FLEX damping

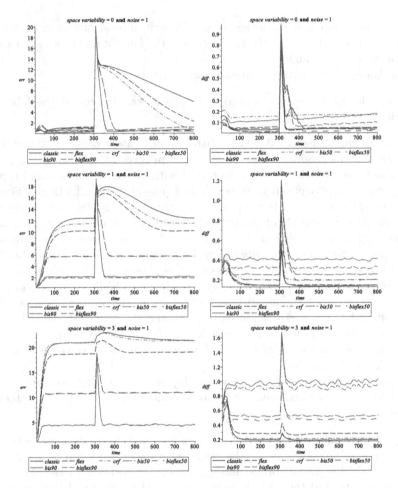

Fig. 4. Precision (left) and smoothness (right) of gradient algorithms under increasing space variability (from top to bottom) and high noise and time variability.

score better than CRF gradient and comparably similar to FLEX and classic gradients, while still achieving a much higher precision.

Overall, these results prove that BIS gradient achieves a much higher healing speed and accuracy (especially when v is high), while still keeping smoothness under control (especially when FLEX dumping is also used). This properties are readily appreciable in practical applications where inputs cannot be assumed to be constant: as we shall show in the next subsection, in these settings BIS gradient remains effective whereas other gradient algorithms fail to produce sensible results, disrupting the higher-order coordination mechanisms relying on them.

4.3 Case Study: Crowd Steering to Busy Resources

We now compare different gradient algorithms when used to implement a more complex service in a realistic scenario: classic gradient, CRF gradient, FLEX gradient and BIS gradient with $v = 0.9\,v_{\mathrm{avg}}$. We considered a *crowd steering* application run on people's smartphones and local device-to-device interaction. This service gives directions towards points-of-interest which can be invalidated: e.g., an application steering pedestrians in a large exhibition center with several food stands (restaurants), where it may happen that a restaurant suddenly becomes full. We considered a 200 m × 300 m fair ambient, containing a 7 × 2 grid of 20 m × 40 m obstacles (pavilions). On the four corners of the fair, we located restaurants of random capacity (up to 1000 people). The simulation encompassed 3000 rounds where 3000 individuals wandered randomly with a connection range of 10 m. We assumed that people get hungry (thus starting to look for a restaurant) at a random round between 50 and 1000; and that after reaching a free restaurant, they stay there for up to 1000 rounds (eating) before restarting wandering again. A 20% relative standard error in fire rate was taken into account, both between different devices and among subsequent rounds on the same device. We considered a relatively low average fire rate (5 s), in order to emphasise the differences in performance of the different gradient algorithms. We run 10 instances of each scenario with different random seeds and averaged the results. A screen shot of this scenario is presented in Fig. 5.[9]

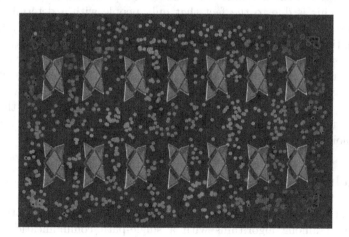

Fig. 5. A screen shot of the application scenario. The restaurant at the bottom left corner is full and the application is steering hungry (blue) people towards the other ones (as reflected by the colour hue, which is determined by the corresponding gradient). (Color figure online)

---

[9] For the sake of reproducibility, all the experiments made in this paper are available at https://bitbucket.org/gaudrito/experiment-fast-gradient.

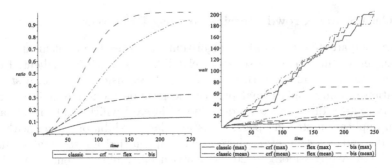

Fig. 6. Percentage of people who found a restaurant over time (left), average and maximum waiting time in minutes (right) for different gradient algorithms.

In this scenario, reactivity of the underlying gradient implementation to input changes (restaurants getting full) was proven to be crucial. Slow reactivity resulted in people reaching busy restaurants, and then waiting there until some place was let free (effectively defeating the purpose of the crowd steering application). Fast reactivity allowed people to direct themselves directly towards restaurants with free places, reducing significantly the waiting time. This behaviour is clearly pictured in Fig. 6, both by the ratio of people reaching a restaurant over time and by the maximum waiting time. The average waiting time, instead, seems to suggest a smaller difference among the performance of the different algorithms. This is due to the fact that only people with a determined waiting time are considered, i.e., which have already reached a restaurant. Thus the average waiting time is expected to keep rising until all the people have already reached a restaurant (which is far from happening for CRF and classic gradient).

Overall, these results prove that using an inefficient gradient algorithm (as e.g., classic gradient) can result in a final real-world application being unusable (as e.g., only 13% of the people were able to eat after 250 min in this case). Conversely, using BIS gradient for the underlying gradient routines represents the best choice, outperforming all the other ones by a large amount.

5   Conclusions and Future Works

We have introduced BIS gradient, a new gradient algorithm of optimal self-healing speed among algorithms with a single-path communication scheme. Mathematical estimations to guide the selection of the parameter v are provided. Thorough validation is carried out, both in a realistic case study and in isolation w.r.t. classic, CRF and FLEX gradients, showing the effectiveness of the new algorithm in a variety of contexts. We also use and suggest an empirical evaluation methodology for spatial computing algorithms, seemingly applicable to all *eventually consistent* algorithms [8] and particularly, gradients. In the future, we plan to test the present algorithm on a larger-scale case study with real data.

We believe, however, that there is still some margin for further improvements. For instance, some form of broadcast could be used to surpass the theoretical limit given by single-path communication speed. *Smoothness* could be further improved by fine-tuning other damping functions other than the one given by the FLEX gradient. The *speed bias* could be addressed directly by introducing a metric distortion dependent on the movement speed of devices (in a similar way as it is done in [19]), and several mobility models could be considered to fine-tune both the information speed estimate and the metric distortion. Additionally, it is possible that specific variants of the proposed algorithm can provide additional benefits in specific applications of the gradient pattern; in particular, we are interested in the cases where gradients are used to support distributed sensing of information in highly heterogeneous and dense environments, specifically for crowd engineering applications.

Acknowledgements. We thank the anonymous COORDINATION referees for their comments and suggestions on improving the presentation.

References

1. Aldinucci, M., Bagnasco, S., Lusso, S., Pasteris, P., Vallero, S., Rabellino, S.: The open computing cluster for advanced data manipulation (OCCAM). In: The 22nd International Conference on Computing in High Energy and Nuclear Physics (CHEP), San Francisco, USA (2016)
2. Bachrach, J., Beal, J., McLurkin, J.: Composable continuous space programs for robotic swarms. Neural Comput. Appl. **19**(6), 825–847 (2010)
3. Beal, J.: Flexible self-healing gradients. In: Proceedings of the 2009 ACM Symposium on Applied Computing, SAC 2009, pp. 1197–1201. ACM (2009)
4. Beal, J., Bachrach, J., Vickery, D., Tobenkin, M.: Fast self-healing gradients. In: Proceedings of ACM SAC 2008, pp. 1969–1975. ACM (2008)
5. Beal, J., Dulman, S., Usbeck, K., Viroli, M., Correll, N.: Organizing the aggregate: languages for spatial computing. In: Mernik, M. (ed.) Formal and Practical Aspects of Domain-Specific Languages: Recent Developments, Chap. 16, pp. 436–501. IGI Global (2013). http://arxiv.org/abs/1202.5509
6. Beal, J., Pianini, D., Viroli, M.: Aggregate programming for the Internet of Things. IEEE Computer **48**(9), 22–30 (2015)
7. Beal, J., Viroli, M.: Building blocks for aggregate programming of self-organising applications. In: 2nd FoCAS Workshop on Fundamentals of Collective Systems, pp. 8–13. IEEE CS (2014). doi:10.1109/SASOW.2014.6
8. Beal, J., Viroli, M., Pianini, D., Damiani, F.: Self-adaptation to device distribution changes. In: Cabri, G., Picard, G., Suri, N. (eds.) 10th IEEE International Conference on Self-Adaptive and Self-Organizing Systems, SASO 2016, Augsburg, Germany, 12–16 September 2016, pp. 60–69 (2016). Best paper of IEEE SASO 2016. doi:10.1109/SASO.2016.12
9. Bicocchi, N., Mamei, M., Zambonelli, F.: Self-organizing virtual macro sensors. TAAS **7**(1), 2:1–2:28 (2012)
10. Castelli, G., Mamei, M., Rosi, A., Zambonelli, F.: Engineering pervasive service ecosystems: the SAPERE approach. TAAS **10**(1), 1:1–1:27 (2015)

11. Damiani, F., Viroli, M.: Type-based self-stabilisation for computational fields. Logical Methods Comput. Sci. **11**(4) (2015). doi:10.2168/LMCS-11(4:21)
12. Damiani, F., Viroli, M., Beal, J.: A type-sound calculus of computational fields. Sci. Comput. Program. **117**, 17–44 (2016). doi:10.1016/j.scico.2015.11.005
13. Damiani, F., Viroli, M., Pianini, D., Beal, J.: Code mobility meets self-organisation: a higher-order calculus of computational fields. In: Graf, S., Viswanathan, M. (eds.) FORTE 2015. LNCS, vol. 9039, pp. 113–128. Springer, Cham (2015). doi:10.1007/978-3-319-19195-9_8
14. Elhage, N., Beal, J.: Laplacian-based consensus on spatial computers. In: van der Hoek, W., Kaminka, G.A., Lespérance, Y., Luck, M., Sen, S. (eds.) 9th International Conference on Autonomous Agents and Multiagent Systems (AAMAS 2010), Toronto, Canada, 10–14 May 2010, vol. 1–3. pp. 907–914. IFAAMAS (2010)
15. Fernandez-Marquez, J.L., Serugendo, G.D.M., Montagna, S., Viroli, M., Arcos, J.L.: Description and composition of bio-inspired design patterns: a complete overview. Natural Comput. **12**(1), 43–67 (2013)
16. Fernandez-Marquez, J.L., Tchao, A., Serugendo, G.D.M., Stevenson, G., Ye, J., Dobson, S.: Analysis of new gradient based aggregation algorithms for data-propagation in mobile networks. In: Sixth IEEE International Conference on Self-Adaptive and Self-Organizing Systems Workshops, SASOW 2012, Lyon, France, 10–14 September 2012, pp. 217–222. IEEE Computer Society (2012)
17. Giavitto, J.L., Michel, O., Cohen, J., Spicher, A.: Computation in space and space in computation. Technical report 103–2004, Univerite d'Evry, LaMI (2004)
18. Katzenelson, J.: Notes on amorphous computing. In: MIT Artificial Intelligence Laboratory. Citeseer (2000)
19. Liu, Q., Pruteanu, A., Dulman, S.: Gradient-based distance estimation for spatial computers. Comput. J. **56**(12), 1469–1499 (2013). doi:10.1093/comjnl/bxt124
20. Lluch-Lafuente, A., Loreti, M., Montanari, U.: Asynchronous distributed execution of fixpoint-based computational fields. CoRR abs/1610.00253(2016). http://arxiv.org/abs/1610.00253
21. Montagna, S., Viroli, M., Fernandez-Marquez, J.L., Di Marzo Serugendo, G.: Injecting self-organisation into pervasive service ecosystems. Mobile Netw. Appl. **18**(3), 398–412 (2013). doi:10.1007/s11036-012-0411-1
22. Nagpal, R., Shrobe, H., Bachrach, J.: Organizing a global coordinate system from local information on an ad hoc sensor network. In: Zhao, F., Guibas, L. (eds.) IPSN 2003. LNCS, vol. 2634, pp. 333–348. Springer, Heidelberg (2003). doi:10.1007/3-540-36978-3_22
23. Pianini, D., Montagna, S., Viroli, M.: Chemical-oriented simulation of computational systems with ALCHEMIST. J. Simul. **7**(3), 202–215 (2013)
24. Pianini, D., Viroli, M., Beal, J.: Protelis: practical aggregate programming. In: ACM Symposium on Applied Computing 2015, pp. 1846–1853, April 2015
25. Royer, E.M., Toh, C.: A review of current routing protocols for ad hoc mobile wireless networks. IEEE Personal Commun. **6**(2), 46–55 (1999)
26. Stuart, A., Ord, J.K.: Kendall's Advanced Theory of Statistics, vol. 1. Edward Arnold, London (1994). Copublished in the Americas by Halsted Press, Wiley, New York, 6th edn
27. Viroli, M., Beal, J., Damiani, F., Pianini, D.: Efficient engineering of complex self-organising systems by self-stabilising fields. In: IEEE 9th International Conference on Self-Adaptive and Self-Organizing Systems (SASO), pp. 81–90. IEEE (2015). doi:10.1109/SASO.2015.16

28. Viroli, M., Casadei, M.: Biochemical tuple spaces for self-organising coordination. In: Field, J., Vasconcelos, V.T. (eds.) COORDINATION 2009. LNCS, vol. 5521, pp. 143–162. Springer, Heidelberg (2009). doi:10.1007/978-3-642-02053-7_8

29. Viroli, M., Casadei, M., Montagna, S., Zambonelli, F.: Spatial coordination of pervasive services through chemical-inspired tuple spaces. ACM Trans. Auton. Adaptive Syst. **6**(2), 14:1–14:24 (2011). doi:10.1145/1968513.1968517

30. Viroli, M., Damiani, F.: A calculus of self-stabilising computational fields. In: Kühn, E., Pugliese, R. (eds.) COORDINATION 2014. LNCS, vol. 8459, pp. 163–178. Springer, Heidelberg (2014). doi:10.1007/978-3-662-43376-8_11

31. Viroli, M., Damiani, F., Beal, J.: A calculus of computational fields. In: Canal, C., Villari, M. (eds.) ESOCC 2013. CCIS, vol. 393, pp. 114–128. Springer, Heidelberg (2013). doi:10.1007/978-3-642-45364-9_11

32. Viroli, M., Pianini, D., Beal, J.: Linda in space-time: an adaptive coordination model for mobile ad-hoc environments. In: Sirjani, M. (ed.) COORDINATION 2012. LNCS, vol. 7274, pp. 212–229. Springer, Heidelberg (2012). doi:10.1007/978-3-642-30829-1_15

33. Weibull, W., et al.: A statistical distribution function of wide applicability. J. Appl. Mech. **18**(3), 293–297 (1951)

Development Tools for Rule-Based Coordination Programming in LINC

Maxime Louvel[1]([✉]), François Pacull[2], Eric Rutten[3], and Adja Ndeye Sylla[1]

[1] Univ Grenoble Alpes, CEA, Leti, 38000 Grenoble, France
{maxime.louvel,AdjaNdeye.Sylla}@cea.fr
[2] Bag-Era, Saint-Martin, France
francois.pacull@bag-era.fr
[3] Univ. Grenoble Alpes, INRIA, CNRS, Grenoble INP, LIG, 38000 Grenoble, France
Eric.Rutten@inria.fr

Abstract. During the last decades a lot of coordination models and languages have been proposed in the literature. These approaches have proven that they can greatly improve the development of distributed applications that are now common. However, to be used by many developers, there is still a gap regarding the available tools.

This paper details a set of tools that have been built to develop applications in LINC, a coordination environment rooted in Linda tuple spaces and Gamma chemical machine approaches. These tools allow developers to design better coordination rules, to monitor and update a running distributed application. The tools proposed here include design and debugging tools.

Keywords: Coordination environment · Development tools · Distributed systems

1 Introduction

Coordination models and languages [31] have been around for decades [28]. Initial works on tuple spaces with Linda [17] have paved the way to space and time decoupling between data producer and data consumer through a very simple API. The Gamma approach [3] brought the chemistry inspired programming to move away from sequential programming. Since these early works, many proposals have been made to improve them. An important trend has been to use a distributed tuple space [5,16,22,25,27,30]. Another interesting trend has been to extend the chemistry based programming to design self adaptive systems [32,37]. Coordination models have been used in many areas including mobile computing [8,27], context aware applications [19], cyber-physical systems, wireless sensor networks [10] or scientific applications [15]. Several works have tried to formalise the coordination aspects to bridge the gap with the formal methods [2,12].

One of the main challenges that is left open for the adoption of coordination paradigms by software engineers is the lack of tools [28]. There is a need

© IFIP International Federation for Information Processing 2017
Published by Springer International Publishing AG 2017. All Rights Reserved
J.-M. Jacquet and M. Massink (Eds.): COORDINATION 2017, LNCS 10319, pp. 78–96, 2017.
DOI: 10.1007/978-3-319-59746-1_5

for development tools that better capture the coordination models instead of relying only on the understanding of software engineers. There is also a need for debugging tools and tools to monitor, introspect and update applications without restarting them.

This paper presents the development tools of the coordination environment LINC [23]. LINC uses distributed tuple spaces, a rule based language and transactional reactions implementing the chemical machine. LINC is used for distributed applications, possibly large scale, that may include cyber-physical systems or the Internet of Things (IoT). This paper details the tools available to developers of LINC applications. This includes rule generation tools as well as analysis and debugging tools. The former generate correct rules based on domain specific or formal models. The latter offer run time monitoring, run time debugging and analysis of the coordination rules executions. To the best of the authors knowledge there exist no equivalent set of development tools for tuple space programming environment. This paper introduces several tools tailored to LINC but that can be of interest, at least partially, to other coordination environments, under some assumptions.

This paper is organised as follows. Section 2 briefly introduces the LINC model. Section 3 details the modelling and analysis tools that are available to developers of LINC applications. Then Sect. 4 presents a short summary of several applications built with LINC and these tools. Section 5 presents related works. Finally, Sect. 6 concludes the paper and presents future works.

2 LINC Model

To make this paper self-contained, this section presents an overview of the coordination environment LINC. More details on LINC can be found in [23]. Technical information can also be found on the LINC wiki[1].

2.1 Tuple Space Implementation

Bags: LINC uses a distributed tuple space [7] implemented as a set of bags. In a bag all the tuples have the same number of fields. Bags are accessed through three operations:

- rd(): takes a partially instantiated tuple as input parameter and returns a stream of fully instantiated tuples matching the input pattern;
- put(): takes a fully instantiated tuple as input parameter and inserts it in the bag;
- get(): takes a fully instantiated tuple as input parameter, verifies if a matching tuple exists in the bag and consumes it.

---

[1] http://linc.middlewares.info/.

Objects: LINC objects, or simply objects, are the deployment units of LINC. An object contains one or more bags. An object has a type that defines its bags and its internal implementation. For instance a Sensor object has a Sensor bag (with the last sensors' values) and a thread that periodically polls the sensors and puts their values in the Sensor bag. Objects' type can be inherited to include new bags or to modify the object implementation. Bags are grouped within objects according to application logic. For instance, all the bags managing a set of devices that communicate with the same communication technology can be grouped in the same object. Any object may execute coordination rules that manipulate tuples in its own bags or in the bags of any other objects. From a functional point of view, it makes no difference which object manipulates the tuples of a bag. However from a run-time performance point of view, this may have a strong impact on CPU, memory or network resources.

2.2 Coordination Rules

The three operations rd(), get() and put() are used within production rules [9]. A production rule is composed of a precondition phase and a performance phase.

The precondition phase is a sequence of rd() operations which detect or wait for the presence of tuples in several given bags. The tuples are, for instance, values from sensors, external events, or results of service calls. The output fields of a rd() operation can be used to define input fields of subsequent rd() operations. The precondition builds an inference tree with right propagation. A rd() is blocked until at least one tuple corresponding to the input pattern is available. In addition to read in the tuple spaces it is possible to call ASSERT and COMPUTE functions. Both can execute any Python code. ASSERT functions return a boolean value that stops the inference tree if false and triggers the subsequent token (rd, ASSERT or COMPUTE) if true. COMPUTE functions can take as input any previously instantiated variables; they return a tuple of variables. These variables can be used by subsequent tokens or in the performance phase. When the last token of the precondition is reached, the performance is triggered.

The performance phase combines the three rd(), get() and put() operations to respectively verify that some tuples are present (e.g. the one(s) found in the precondition phase), consume some tuples, and insert new tuples. In this phase, the operations are embedded in one or multiple distributed transactions [4], executed in sequence. Each transaction contains a set of operations that are performed in an atomic manner. Hence, LINC guarantees that for operations belonging to the same transaction, either all are executed successfully or none.

A LINC rule example is given in Listing 1.1. The precondition (before the symbol ::) first checks that "c1" is "*true*" (rd at line 1 on bag Condition belonging to object O2). Then it waits for events (line 2). Then it reads the parameters associated to the event (rd in line 3 with evt variable instantiated with the value return by the previous rd). For every branch of the inference tree reaching the last **rd**, a performance is triggered. This performance contains 1 transaction (between curly brackets). It first checks that the condition is still valid (i.e. (*"c1"*, *"true"*) is in the bag **Condition**), then it consumes the event (line 6 with variables instantiated in the precondition), then it adds this event in the bag **Stats** of the object **O1** (line 7) and puts the command *"cmd1"* with the parameters *p1* and *p2* in the bag **Cmd** of the object **O3** (line 8). Note that the performance does not read again the **Param** bag, because the rule assumes that this value does not change.

```
[ "O2", "Condition"].rd("c1", "true")&                        1
[ "O1", "Event"].rd(evt, time)&
[ "O3", "Params"].rd(evt, p1, p2)&                            3
::
{ [ "O2", "Condition"].rd("c1", "true")&                      5
  [ "O1", "Event"].get("evt1", p1, p2)&
  [ "O1", "Stats"].put("evt1", time, p1, p2)&                 7
  [ "O3", "Cmd"].put("cmd1", p1, p2)& }.
```

Listing 1.1. Example of LINC rule

Linda - LINC: **read** and **out** operations of Linda are respectively implemented in LINC by **rd** in precondition and **put** in performance. The **in** operation of Linda takes partially instantiated tuples and removes the matching tuples from the tuple space. If no tuple matches, the **in** is blocked. In LINC, this is implemented by a **rd** in the precondition and a **get** in the performance. In the precondition, the **rd** uses a partially instantiated tuple and blocks when no tuple matches. A performance is triggered for every matching tuple. In each performance, a **get** is done with the fully instantiated tuples created by the precondition **rd**.

3   Coordination Rules Development and Debugging

Being based on the tuple spaces paradigm LINC has a very small API (rd, get and put). Most of the complexity thus resides in how to use them best, or in other words how to write coordination rules. Two sets of tools are now presented, first to generate rules and second to analyse and debug them.

3.1   Rules Generation Tools

Two kinds of tools are available to developers. The first one consists in building domain specific tools, the second one relies on formal languages to ensure the correctness of the system. In both cases, rules are automatically validated and generated from the models built by the developers. Hence the developers can focus on the application logic and not the writing of rules. This paper presents a synthesis of several tools, how they are related and how they can help developers. Details on each tools can be found in papers cited in this section.

Domain Specific Tools. One solution to help developers is to provide them a domain specific design tool. Such tool limits the expressiveness offered by the coordination language to a valid subset. In addition, the tool uses knowledge on the domain to build advanced validation of the rules written by developers. The latter need only to be experts of their domains and not experts in coordination models or distributed systems.

An example of such tool is the Coordination Scheme Editor (CSE) [24] to design scenarios in building automation systems. CSE provides a drag an drop interface to design rules for sensors and actuators. The precondition is a set of rd on sensors and thresholds or ranges checks. The performance is a set of action on actuators. Examples of verification done when generating rules are: valid ranges in sensors, valid types of commands sent to actuators or invalid thresholds.

High-Level Reactive Language Support for Behavioural Specification

Motivation: As explained above, LINC provides applications with transactional guarantees that ensure their reliability at run-time. But, although LINC ensures the consistent execution of individual rules, it does not prevent from writing erroneous rules. Individual rules can present bugs, as in all programming languages, but more importantly, because more difficult to detect and avoid, the set of rules may contain design errors such as conflicts between rules, and violations of applicative constraints that can bring the system in unsafe or undesirable states. More precisely, a rule, written to achieve a given objective, can violate one or several other objectives of other rules. An example of conflict is between rule A which opens the window to decrease the CO_2 level in the room and rule B which closes the window and turns on the AC to decrease the room temperature. Moreover, the execution of a sequence of rules can bring the system in an undesirable state or into an undesired circularity or endless loop of rules having the effect of firing each other.

Therefore, when writing rules one has to control their resulting behaviours. Developers have to manually avoid conflicts and violations of constraints by adding the testing of numerous additional conditions on specific rules, and adding new rules. For large applications, programmed by large sets of rules, manually controlling the rules is a difficult combinatorial problem and is error prone.

Our Approach: To tackle this problem, we adopt the direction of high-level language support for behavioural specification. We consider high-level languages from the domain of reactive systems, related to transition systems, because they can be equipped with formal verification or synthesis tools, based on models for the behaviours of programs. On the other hand, we want them to be implemented in such a way as to be concretely executable in the LINC environment. We propose to combine the two reactive programming approaches in order to support the safe design and execution of control systems, in the application domain of smart environments. As illustrated in Fig. 1, data is gathered from the controlled environment through the tuple spaces. A transition system takes the correct decision and produces the commands executed by LINC transactions. LINC transactions update both the actual system and the state of the transition system. Hence if an action on the actual system fails (e.g. due to a communication error or a hardware failure), the state of the transition system is not updated and stays consistent with the actual system. For instance if a window failed to open due to a communication error, the transition system will not wrongly assume that it has been opened.

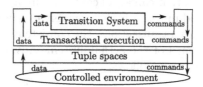

Fig. 1.

One approach, presented in [34], first models the application logic using coloured Petri nets. Then, it verifies the designed model using a model-checker [33], and finally, it generates the corresponding LINC rules. This approach enables the verification of several properties (e.g. absence of conflicts and violations of constraints) before execution. When generating LINC rules from the coloured Petri nets specification, the state of the system is embedded in a LINC bag. The transition and update of the state is performed in a transaction together with the actions on the system. However, modelling the application logic also requires to manually specify how to avoid conflicts and violations of constraints, in the model. Moreover, when a target property is not satisfied, the model has to be manually modified and verified again.

To overcome these limitations, we explore the use of a high-level language based on transition systems to access another formal technique: Discrete Controller Synthesis (DCS) [35]. Similarly to model-checking, DCS is an algorithmic technique that performs an exploration of the reachable state-space of a transition system. However, whereas model-checking verifies the satisfaction of a property in a programmed solution, DCS produces a solution from a more declarative specification. This specification contains the possible behaviours and properties to be enforced by control. More precisely, DCS takes (i) a transition system modelling possible behaviours of a system, (ii) a partition of the set of variables between controllable and uncontrollable ones, and (iii) a property to be enforced (e.g. invariance of a predicate). Given this, DCS synthesises, if it exists, the constraint on controllable variables in function of current values of state and uncontrollable variables, so that the resulting constrained transition system satisfies the property. This constitutes a controller that will avoid transitions leading to incorrect states (i.e. violating the property), or to correct states from which a sequence of uncontrollable conditions and transitions could lead to an incorrect state. Concretely, LINC has been combined with the automata-based language Heptagon/BZR [11]. Heptagon/BZR enables the verification and the control of the system behaviour at compilation time. The generated executable code is called from the execution of LINC rules. A related approach was used in the context of ECA rules [6], different from tuple spaces, but with a similar goal as a mean to coordinate the execution of rules so as to avoid inconsistencies, circularities, and environment and application related constraints.

This way designers are provided for a support for both design-time and run-time reliability. At design time the developers have language support and DCS to generate a control function that can avoid conflicts, circularities and violations of constraints. The generated function is then reliably executed using LINC which enforces, through distributed transactions, the consistency between the states of the automata and the states of the actual system. Advantages of our reactive language-based approach are as follows:

- high-level language support for controller specification, less tedious and error-prone than at lower level;
- correctness of the controller, w.r.t. specified properties, hard to enforce manually, obtained by using formal methods and algorithms like model checking;
- automated synthesis of controllers, using DCS with declarative objectives, which is more constructive than classical verification of a hard to write solution; our approach also ensures that developers need only to be expert of their domain and not expert in formal models;
- automated generation of executable code compatible with LINC.

Extension to Other Coordination Languages. The tools presented in this section generate LINC rules. Generating code or rules for other tuple spaces based coordination languages is possible under certain conditions. Most of the tuple spaces based languages will allow a level of abstraction similar to LINC. However the tools presented above assume the following:

- the consistency between the state of the actual system and the state of the transition system will be ensured only if a distributed consensus mechanism (transactions in LINC) is available;
- a reactive environment that calls the transition system when necessary;
- LINC combines tuple spaces, production rules and transactions. This allows to only consider the important states. For instance, consider a rule consuming events A and B and producing C and D. The state where only A is consumed or only C is produced is not possible in LINC. This simplifies the generation of LINC rules and might not be directly available in other environments.

3.2   Analysis and Debugging Tools

The tools developed for rules generation are naturally not meant to completely replace the hand writing of rules, but as a complement. The domain specific tools provide a solution limited to a domain and a subset of the coordination model.

The tools based on formal models help to ensure the correctness of the coordination in the system. They can avoid conflict between rules, within the parts of the systems modelled in the high-level languages. Moreover, advanced features of LINC such as guards, alternative transactions, graceful degradation (see [23] for more details) are not always available to developers. Hence a set of tools are now described to monitor, analyse and debug applications. Note that these tools can be used in combination with the modelling tools. Indeed, the latter produce correct rules according to the assumptions made in the formal model or the domain hypothesis. However, if an error occurs outside these assumptions, the rules generated from the modelling tool will behave incorrectly. Therefore rules have to be validated by analysis and debugging tools. This section now presents tools to monitor, modify and analyse the execution of an application.

Monitor. When developing and debugging a distributed application, it is not always easy to access the information of all the elements. Indeed they are spread out, possibly in different networks. Furthermore, it is possible that they move (e.g. due to load balancing, system update or failure). Hence the developer has to keep track of what is where and how to access it. Then another challenge is to know what to observe and how. In tuple spaces based models, the important information is stored in the tuple spaces. It is thus fundamental to be able to access them easily.

To answer these challenges, every object in LINC provides a web interface to monitor its content and access the monitor interface of the other objects in the application. The interface can be accessed from any web browser. It allows to observe the content of any bags of any objects. This is particularly useful when a rule is blocked. The developer can connect to the monitor and check if the required tuples are there or not. In addition, the monitor interface allows to modify the content of the bags of the object. Hence a developer can unlock an application by adding a missing tuple. At the development stage, this can help to move forward if a bug occurred. At the production stage, this allows the maintenance to unlock the application while tracking the cause of the missing tuple. Rules in LINC are also modelled as tuples. Hence it is possible, from the monitor, to start, stop or update rules or group of rules by adding or removing the corresponding tuples.

Debugging and Information Traces. In a distributed application it might be a daunting task to gather all the traces generated in one application. To help developers, a tracer is built for every LINC object. Instead of using print on various files, the developer simply calls the tracer to add a trace. The tracer contains all the traces that might be useful for the application (e.g. communication error, debug traces or traces defined by developers when writing new LINC objects). For instance, when a developer creates an object to support a new sensor protocol he/she will use traces to debug his/her own code. The traces are saved to disk. The trace files are accessible through the Monitor interface of each object; they can also be accessed offline, e.g. by downloading them in a development computer. Trace files are generated incrementally. Hence they can be periodically archived, possibly remotely, if needed.

Traces may have an important cost, in CPU and disk usage. To limit this, several levels of traces are available, from −1 (error) to 3 (debug information). The level of trace is set when starting an object. Then every trace with a level higher than the trace level are ignored. This is actually very efficient because the actual trace string is passed via a dictionary and is not evaluated if the trace is ignored. This mechanism allows to leave traces in the code and activate them only when necessary. Traces level can be dynamically changed. For instance the level can be increased when an error occurred. If the application behaviour is periodic or event based, the next loop or event handling will be traced with a higher level. Once the problem is understood, the trace level can be decreased again.

In the monitor, the traces are presented in a HTML table, sorted by date. The last line contains the most recent trace. Inside the LINC object, the tracer can either be used directly or cloned. All the clones of the tracer share the same file. Two filters criteria are provided to find specific traces in the table. The *tracer clone* displays traces of the selected clones only. The *Level* displays traces with a level lower or equal to the filter. The tracer clones allow to filter on functionality (e.g. communication traces or traces related to specific actions). Both filters can be combined to display the traces of one or more clones which are lower than a given level. It is possible to search within the traces. This creates a new filter that can be combined with the clone or level filters. A second level of search is provided to filter again the traces.

Exploring Coordination Rules Executions. A LINC application is composed of a set of rules defining the behaviour of the application. When executing these rules, the LINC objects build inference trees (precondition) and execute performances. All the preconditions and performances are logged in several log files. Logs are organised by rule: for each rule there is one log. These log files are then explored to help the developer understand the behaviour of its application. The logs are dedicated to rules executions and capture the application behaviour. They are complementary to traces.

Logger Interface. For each rule, the inference tree built can be walked through a web interface. Three types of elements are presented for the precondition:

- rd: contains the precondition rd() executed (e.g. rd("evt-a", ts) to read all the events "evt-a";
- result of rd, COMPUTE: contains the tuples returned (e.g. rd("evt-a", "X32");
- result of ASSERT: successful calls are shown as a specific tuple, failed calls are presented in red because they stop the inference tree.

When a performance is reached, successful transactions are displayed in green without details. If the transaction failed, it is automatically expended to see which operation caused the failure (displayed in red). Hence the developer can understand why this performance did not execute.

The logger may help the developer to see where an execution is blocked. Typically, when a rd has not returned matching tuples. From the logger interface, the developer can be redirected to the monitor of the object and inspect the bags' content. From there the developer can see for instance that the error comes from:

- an erroneous spelling and add the missing tuple to continue the execution;
- a missing tuple, meaning that another transaction (in the same rule or in another rule) consumed the tuple or that it has never been produced.

Filters. Looking at all the inference tree might not be possible when its size increases. However, most of the time the developer is only interested in some particular tuples. Hence, the logger interface allows developer to search the logs of interest. The search can be done in object, bag and/or tuple name. The search can be done on one or more rules. If matching logs are found, they are displayed in the interface. The developer can then browse them. For instance if it filters on tuples matching "evt-a" only the actions including matching tuples will be displayed (branches of the inference tree and transactions). If a rule handles all the events (rd(evt, ts)), only the interesting ones (i.e. handling evt-a) will be displayed. Figure 2a shows an example of log search on tuples containing "alice". This example contains only preconditions for this tuple, i.e. no performance with a tuple containing "alice" has been triggered. The problem here can be that a tuple is not added as expected by the rule.

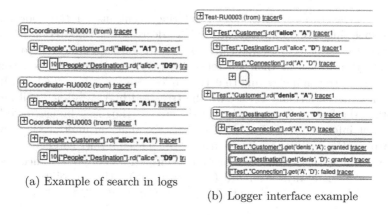

(a) Example of search in logs

(b) Logger interface example

Fig. 2. Logger interface and search (Color figure online)

Logger Interface Example. To illustrate the use of the logger interface, let's consider an application which models people travelling with a metro. This application has one object (Test) containing three bags. The bag Customer for customer locations (containing the tuples ("alice", "A"), ("denis", "A")); the bag `Arrival` for customer destinations (containing (`"alice"`, `"D"`), (`"denis"`, `"D"`)) and the bag `Connection` for metro connections (containing (`"A"`, `"D"`)). The precondition of the rule Listing 1.2 reads the customer location and arrival of each person and checks that a connection exists between the two stations. The performance then gets the customer, its destination, the connection and puts the customer in its arrival station. After executing the rule, the developer notices that only alice reached its destination, denis is still in its initial location.

```
[ "Test" ,"Customer"] . rd( name, departure) &
[ "Test" ,"Destination"] . rd( name, arrival) &                          2
[ "Test" ,"Connection"] . rd( departure, arrival)&
::                                                                       4
{ [ "Test" ,"Customer"] . get( name, departure) ;
  [ "Test" ,"Destination"] . get( name, arrival) ;                       6
  [ "Test" ,"Connection"] . get( departure, arrival) ;
  [ "Test" ,"Customer"] . put( name, arrival) ; }.                       8
```

Listing 1.2. Travel LINC rule

Figure 2b shows the log of the rule. The rule is executed twice (one starting with the tuple (`"alice"`,`"A"`) and the other starting with the tuple (`"denis"`,`"A"`)). In this example, the two people make the same journey, and the same connection tuple is used. The first transaction that executes succeeds and gets the tuple (`"A"`,`"D"`) which makes the second transaction fail because the tuple seen in the precondition is not there anymore. In Fig. 2b, the third action of the transaction (line 7 of Listing 1.2) for the second transaction (`get("A","D")`) has failed which is shown in the log displayed. The solution here is to use a `rd()` instead of a `get()` on the connection to avoid removing the tuple.

Current Inference Tree. The Logger interface contains all the coordination actions done since the application started. To decrease the resources used (CPU, memory), LINC objects periodically execute a garbage collector to remove unnecessary branches in their inference tree. The garbage collection consists in walking the tree and checking that the tuples seen are still in the bags. If not, this means the performances that will be triggered by this branch will fail. To avoid this, the branch is removed from the tree. It thus may be useful to know the current inference tree of a LINC object. For that, an interface is provided that displays the current tree in a textual form. This interface can help to understand why the garbage collection has not been performed, for instance because the same tuple is always produced (e.g. (`"evt-a"`)). Here a solution is to use different tuples to model different events (e.g. (`"evt-a"`, `"XX..."`)).

Analysing Coordination Rules Executions. The logger interface allows to understand what has been done by the rule. This can solve functional errors or highlight some performances issues. However it is not easy to draw high level conclusion by looking at all the coordination actions. For that, two analysis tools are provided; the first one focuses on data flow observations; the second one focuses on a global view of the logs.

Data Flow. This tool provides a data flow view of the coordination actions done. The information comes from the log files but is presented differently. This tool gives a picture of the rules' executions to link the data (tuples contained in bags) to the control flow (coordination actions done by the LINC objects). Two kinds of pictures are built, one for the preconditions and one for the performances. Figure 3a and b respectively show the preconditions and the performances for the execution of the rule in Listing 1.2. These pictures show the data flow between rules and bags (rd, get and put). The size of the line is proportional (logarithmic) to the number of actions done. The number of actions is also added in small on the line. By comparing the two pictures, one can see that there are more preconditions operations ($\sum_{prec\ op} = 1775$) than performances operations ($\sum_{perf\ op} = 46$). This means lots of preconditions never reach the performance phase, in other words big inference trees are built for nothing.

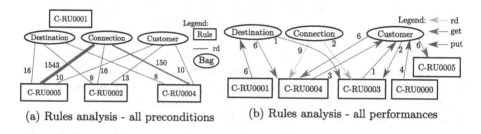

(a) Rules analysis - all preconditions   (b) Rules analysis - all performances

Fig. 3. Rules analysis

It is also possible to build a bag centred picture. This time only one bag is displayed with all the rules accessing this bag. This is particularly useful to find out which rule gets or puts tuples in a bag. For all analysis, it is possible to display only the successful performances, only the failed performances or both. Figure 4a is centred on the bag Customer. Here one can see that rule RU0001 is missing (compare to Fig. 3b) and that RU0002 does not access the bag. RU0002 is shown in the picture because it is connected to the Customer bag in the precondition. Figure 4b shows only the successful performances. Here only RU0003 and RU0004 update tuples in the bag Customer. Finally, Fig. 4c shows a picture of a rule that only copies data from a bag to another one.

All representations are also available in a table format with numbers instead of arrows of different size. Both views can be interesting depending on the type of patterns to observe, the number of bags, rules or tuples.

Error prone patterns that may be found with this tool are typically:

- overloading bags (a bag where more **put** than **get** are done);
- unused bags;
- performances which fail most of the time (meaning a lot of coordination is done just to fail afterwards).

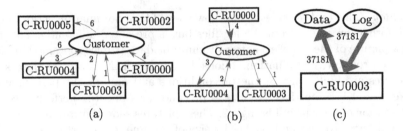

Fig. 4. Rules analysis - bag centered

This tool might also be useful to find or check some patterns such as a producer/consumer relationship between two or several rules. Hence better choices can be made for the deployment decision. Indeed, nothing prevents a rule to access only bags physically far from the object executing the rule. However, from a run-time performance point of view this may have a strong impact.

Global View on the Logs. The second tool for log analysis provides a global view of the logs. For that, the tool relies on the D3JS javascript framework[2]. This framework allows to easily build data driven document and to display them in a web browser. Several interesting points may be analysed with this tool. For instance, it is possible to view the size of the inference tree, if all the branches of the tree lead to a performance, or the ratio of successful performances over the number of performances tried. This tool can help developers to understand how the rules they wrote perform in the system. The goal is to optimise the rules in order to decrease the CPU and memory used by the LINC object executing them. Such optimisation may be achieved by reducing the size of the inference tree, the number of failing performances or the number of branches that lead to no performance.

Figure 5 shows the overview of three rules with a radial tree display[3]. At the centre is found the root node of the inference tree. The nodes of the inference tree leading nowhere are displayed in grey, the nodes leading to successful (resp. failing) performances are displayed in green (resp. red) and the nodes leading to both successful and failing performances are displayed in orange. Failing ASSERT in the precondition are displayed as failing performances. It is possible to click on each node to have the information of the action done (e.g. rd("evt-a"), put("action-b")). Figure 5 contains examples of log analysis for several rules. Here we can see that rule Fig. 5a is more efficient with a smaller inference tree and more green nodes than rule Fig. 5b which does a lot of work for nothing. Rule Fig. 5c shows a rule that simply copies data from a bag to another one; hence it is mainly green. The few orange points are failing ASSERT for tuples that should not be processed by this rule.

---

[2] https://d3js.org/.
[3] https://bl.ocks.org/mbostock/4063550.

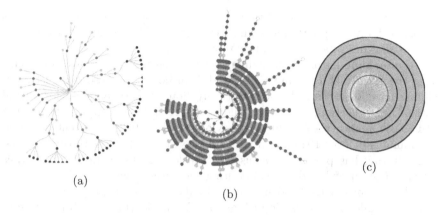

Fig. 5. Examples of global views (Color figure omline)

It is possible to filter the global view of the logs on tuples, objects or bag names and on time interval. This can help developers understand when a rule did more or less work, or if some tuples (e.g. modelling events) triggered a lot of work or none.

Extension to Other Coordination Languages. The tools presented in this section help to design, analyse and debug LINC rules. They could be adapted to other coordination environments with some assumptions.

The monitor is well suited for any tuple space environment because important information is stored in tuple spaces. This tool provides a central point of view to access all the information of the coordination entities (objects in LINC). To be as useful as in LINC, the monitor requires full introspection and intersession capacities of the coordination entities and tuple spaces. For the tracer tool, its main interest is to provide relevant filters and being accessible from the monitor.

The analysing tools require to log all the coordination actions. This requires to instrument the code of the coordination entities to log all relevant actions. This is of particular interest for exogenous coordination languages [1] that do not mix the coordination code within the computation code. For these languages it seems possible to extract, as in LINC, the relevant coordination actions to analyse them. Indeed the application state is stored in the tuple spaces and the application logic is done by the coordination entities.

The interfaces of the analyses tools are relevant if an inference tree is used. Some display are specific to LINC that uses rules with precondition and transactions in performances (typically the logger interface). The data flow and global view of the log could be adapted even if the rules execution paradigm is different.

4   Applications Developed with LINC

More than a dozen of demonstrators have been developed with LINC, within European or national projects, with industrial partners, in several domains.

LINC is now transferred to industry through the start-up Bag-Era[4] which is responsible for its support and commercialisation. This section details a few examples showing what LINC and its tools can be used for.

In the building automation domain, several demonstrators have been built during the H2020 TOPAs and FP7 SCUBA projects. In these demonstrators buildings have been controlled automatically. Some experiments ran for several months. Data collection, on several buildings in Ireland and France, is ongoing to continuously analyse the buildings' behaviour (with ≈1000 data points updated every minutes or ever 10 min). In such applications, with remote components, the monitoring has proven really useful. The logger observation and analysis tools have been useful to developers during the development stage.

In the Artemis Arrowhead project, a LINC application has been deployed across three different and remote Local Area Networks [14]. A web interface to control the application has been developed and used across Europe. Some of the LAN provide no external access. The monitor was available on some parts of the application. For the rest, the traces and log files were downloaded and analysed locally, with the same tools executed by local objects.

In the frame of French project IRT Nanoelec, a smart parking has been developed [13]. LINC allowed to coordinate a dozen of independent products, some off-the-shelf, some still under development. In this demonstrator, approximately one hundred rules were written. Part of them have been generated from Coloured Petri Nets [34]. The monitoring and log analysing tools, with their filtering and search features have proven useful to developers.

Finally, LINC has been used by control scientists to develop advanced control strategies [36]. In this work, LINC bridged the gap between the control scientists assumption and devices of wireless sensor networks.

5   Related Works

In [21] the authors propose the Peer Model, a design tool for parallel and distributed applications. The model assumes a tuple space middleware. The authors focus on some specific patterns commonly used in distributed applications such as split or join of data flow. This approach is extended in [20] where the author introduces design patterns dedicated to coordination. Similarly to our design tools, this helps developer using coordination models. However, no help is provided at run time. In addition, our design tools offer verification at design time. REO [2] is a coordination model focusing on the interaction between components. A lot of efforts have been put to provide a formal model of REO and connections with formal languages [12]. This is similar to our design tool based on formal languages. However, REO focuses only on the interaction between components whereas our approach provides developers with a complete model of the environment and the application.

---

[4] http://www.bag-era.fr/.

ReSpecT nets [38] is a language to map ReSpecT programs to Petri nets. ReSpecT is a reactive language based on TuCSoN [29] and tuple spaces. However, this fails to bridge the gap between (i) the large expression capabilities of tuple space coordination languages and (ii) the set of Petri nets on which interesting formal analysis can be done. Whereas, in our approach verification are done on the model and then the coordination code is generated. It is thus possible to limit in the model the expressiveness to provided formal guarantees. However this language could be a good target for our rule generation tools.

Finally, in [26] the authors propose a software engineering methodology to develop multiagent systems in the SAPERE project which target self awareness in pervasive systems. The developers use an API and a development methodology. However it is not clear if the authors provide any tools to help developers understand how their applications are evolving and how to debug them.

6   Conclusion

Design and debugging tools are essential to make coordination models and languages accepted by a broader range of developers. This paper has presented the development tools put in place with LINC, a coordination environment based on tuple spaces and implementing the chemical machine paradigm. The design tools detailed in this paper allow developers to generate rules that are validated with domain specific knowledge or by the use of formal methods. In addition several tools allow developers to monitor, analyse and update a distributed application.

To the best of the authors knowledge, there exists no other tuple space coordination environment providing an equivalent set of tools. The tools developed for LINC could be useful for other tuple spaces based coordination environments. The paper initiates the analysis of what might be reused and what assumptions, on the coordination environment, are made by the different tools.

Future works will focus on extending analysis tools to allow to re-execute an application with the same scheduling as the original execution. This is not guaranteed by default because most of the rules executions are not deterministic. We means that the same result may be achieved with different histories if we consider elementary actions (rd, get and put) order. In case of bug it could be possible that a particular history is the cause of the bug. Thus restarting the application is not enough to ensure that we will have the same sequence during the second execution and thus the bug is not reproducible. By forcing at the replay the order of the rd, get and put we can ensure that the order of the different event is kept and thus this helps in reproducing the bug. Regarding modelling tools, perspectives involve generalising the approach by integrating the potentials of having multiple controllers and control loops. These loops will require to be coordinated themselves, following a related approach involving coordination controllers for autonomic loops [18].

Acknowledgment. This work is funded by the H2020 TOPAs (grant 676760).

References

1. Arbab, F.: What do you mean, coordination. Bull. Dutch Assoc. Theor. Comput. Sci. NVTI **1122**, 1–18 (1998)
2. Arbab, F.: Reo: a channel-based coordination model for component composition. Math. Struct. Comput. Sci. **14**(3), 329–366 (2004)
3. Banătre, J.-P., Fradet, P., Métayer, D.: Gamma and the chemical reaction model: fifteen years after. In: Calude, C.S., PĂun, G., Rozenberg, G., Salomaa, A. (eds.) WMC 2000. LNCS, vol. 2235, pp. 17–44. Springer, Heidelberg (2001). doi:10.1007/3-540-45523-X_2
4. Bernstein, P.A., Hadzilacos, V., Goodman, N.: Concurrency Control and Recovery in Database Systems, vol. 370. Addison-Wesley, New York (1987)
5. Cabri, G., Leonardi, L., Zambonelli, F.: Mars: a programmable coordination architecture for mobile agents. IEEE Internet Comput. **4**(4), 26–35 (2000)
6. Cano, J., Delaval, G., Rutten, E.: Coordination of ECA rules by verification and control. In: Kühn, E., Pugliese, R. (eds.) COORDINATION 2014. LNCS, vol. 8459, pp. 33–48. Springer, Heidelberg (2014). doi:10.1007/978-3-662-43376-8_3
7. Carriero, N., Gelernter, D.: Linda in context. Commun. ACM **32**, 444–458 (1989)
8. Collins, J., Bagrodia, R.: Mobile application development with MELON. In: Guo, S., Lloret, J., Manzoni, P., Ruehrup, S. (eds.) ADHOC-NOW 2014. LNCS, vol. 8487, pp. 265–278. Springer, Cham (2014). doi:10.1007/978-3-319-07425-2_20
9. Cooper, T., Wogrin, N.: Rule-based Programming with OPS5, vol. 988. Morgan Kaufmann, San Fransisco (1988)
10. Costa, P., Mottola, L., Murphy, A.L., Picco, G.P.: Teenylime: transiently shared tuple space middleware for wireless sensor networks. In: Proceedings of the International Workshop on Middleware for Sensor Networks, pp. 43–48. ACM (2006)
11. Delaval, G., Marchand, H., Rutten, E.: Contracts for modular discrete controller synthesis. SIGPLAN Not. **45**(4), 57–66 (2010)
12. Dokter, K., Jongmans, S.-S., Arbab, F., Bliudze, S.: Combine and conquer: relating BIP and Reo. J. Logical Algebr. Methods Program. **86**(Ice), 3–20 (2016)
13. Ducreux, L.F., Guyon-Gardeux, C., Louvel, M., Pacull, F., Thior, S.R., Vergara-Gallego, M.I.: Rapid prototyping of complete systems, the case study of a smart parking. In: 2015 International Symposium on Rapid System Prototyping (RSP), vol. 2016, February, pp. 133–139, Amsterdam (2015)
14. Boutin, V., et al.: Energy optimisation using analytics and coordination, the example of lifts. In 19th IEEE Conference on Emerging Technologies and Factory Automation (2014)
15. Fernandez, H., Tedeschi, C., Priol, T.: Rule-driven service coordination middleware for scientific applications. Future Gener. Comput. Syst. **35**, 1–13 (2014)
16. Garnock-Jones, T., Felleisen, M.: Coordinated concurrent programming in syndicate. In: Thiemann, P. (ed.) ESOP 2016. LNCS, vol. 9632, pp. 310–336. Springer, Heidelberg (2016). doi:10.1007/978-3-662-49498-1_13
17. Gelernter, D.: Generative communication in linda. ACM Trans. Program. Lang. Syst. (TOPLAS) **7**(1), 80–112 (1985)
18. Gueye, S.M.K., Palma, N., Rutten, E.: Component-based autonomic managers for coordination control. In: Nicola, R., Julien, C. (eds.) COORDINATION 2013. LNCS, vol. 7890, pp. 75–89. Springer, Heidelberg (2013). doi:10.1007/978-3-642-38493-6_6

19. Julien, C., Roman, G.-C.: Egospaces: facilitating rapid development of context-aware mobile applications. IEEE Trans. Softw. Eng. **32**(5), 281–298 (2006)
20. Kühn, E.: Reusable coordination components: reliable development of cooperative information systems. Int. Jo. Cooper. Inf. Syst. **25**(4), 1740001 (2017)
21. Kühn, E., Craß, S., Joskowicz, G., Marek, A., Scheller, T.: Peer-based programming model for coordination patterns. In: Nicola, R., Julien, C. (eds.) COORDINATION 2013. LNCS, vol. 7890, pp. 121–135. Springer, Heidelberg (2013). doi:10.1007/978-3-642-38493-6_9
22. Kuhn, E., Riemer, J., Mordinyi, R., Lechner, L.: Integration of XVSM spaces with the web to meet the challenging interaction demands in pervasive scenarios. Ubiquit. Comput. Commun. J. CPE, 20–31 (2008). SI (Special issue of Coordination in Pervasive Environments)
23. Louvel, M., Pacull, F.: LINC: a compact yet powerful coordination environment. In: Kühn, E., Pugliese, R. (eds.) COORDINATION 2014. LNCS, vol. 8459, pp. 83–98. Springer, Heidelberg (2014). doi:10.1007/978-3-662-43376-8_6
24. Louvel, M., Pacull, F., Vergara-Gallego, M.I.: Coordination scheme editor for building management systems. In: IECON 2016 42nd Annual Conference of the IEEE, pp. 7052–7057. IEEE (2016)
25. Mamei, M., Zambonelli, F.: Programming pervasive and mobile computing applications: the TOTA approach. ACM Trans. Softw. Eng. Methodol. **18**(4), 15 (2009)
26. Molesini, A., Omicini, A., Viroli, M., Zambonelli, F.: Engineering pervasive multi-agent systems in SAPERE. In: Cossentino, M., Fallah Seghrouchni, A., Winikoff, M. (eds.) EMAS 2013. LNCS, vol. 8245, pp. 196–214. Springer, Heidelberg (2013). doi:10.1007/978-3-642-45343-4_11
27. Murphy, A.L., Picco, G.P., Roman, G.-C.: Lime: a coordination model and middleware supporting mobility of hosts and agents. ACM Trans. Softw. Eng. Methodol. **15**(3), 279–328 (2006)
28. Omicini, A., Viroli, M.: Coordination models and languages: from parallel computing to self-organisation. Knowl. Eng. Rev. **26**(01), 53–59 (2011)
29. Omicini, A., Zambonelli, F.: TuCSon: a coordination model for mobile information agents. In: Proceedings of the 1st Workshop on Innovative Internet Information Systems, vol. 138 (1998)
30. Omicini, A., Zambonelli, F.: Coordination for internet application development. Auton. Agents Multiagent Syst. **2**(3), 251–269 (1999)
31. Papadopoulos, G.A., Arbab, F.: Coordination models and languages. Adv. Comput. **46**, 329–400 (1998)
32. Pianini, D., Montagna, S., Viroli, M.: Chemical-oriented simulation of computational systems with alchemist. J. Simul. **7**(3), 202–215 (2013)
33. Schmidt, K.: LoLA a low level analyser. In: Nielsen, M., Simpson, D. (eds.) ICATPN 2000. LNCS, vol. 1825, pp. 465–474. Springer, Heidelberg (2000). doi:10.1007/3-540-44988-4_27
34. Sylla, A.N., Louvel, M., Pacull, F.: Coordination rules generation from coloured petri net models. In: PNSE@ Petri Nets, pp. 325–326 (2015)
35. Sylla, A.N., Louvel, M., Rutten, E.: Combining transactional and behavioural reliability in adaptive middleware. In: Proceedings of the 15th International Workshop on Adaptive and Reflective Middleware, p. 5. ACM (2016)

36. Vergara-Gallego, M.I., Mokrenko, O., Louvel, M., Lesecq, S., Pacull, F.: Implementation of an energy management control strategy for WSNs using the LINC middleware. In: Proceedings of the 2016 International Conference on Embedded Wireless Systems and Networks, pp. 53–58 (2016)
37. Viroli, M., Casadei, M., Montagna, S., Zambonelli, F.: Spatial coordination of pervasive services through chemical-inspired tuple spaces. CM Trans. Auton. Adapt. Syst. **6**(2), 14:1–14:24 (2011)
38. Viroli, M., Omicini, A.: Respect nets: towards an analysis methodology for respect specifications. Electron. Notes Theor. Comput. Sci. **180**(2), 123–144 (2007)

Types

Session-ocaml: A Session-Based Library with Polarities and Lenses

Keigo Imai[1]([✉]), Nobuko Yoshida[2], and Shoji Yuen[3]

[1] Gifu University, Gifu, Japan
keigoi@gifu-u.ac.jp
[2] Imperial College London, London, UK
[3] Nagoya University, Nagoya, Japan

Abstract. We propose session-ocaml, a novel library for session-typed concurrent/distributed programming in OCaml. Our technique solely relies on parametric polymorphism, which can encode core session type structures with strong static guarantees. Our key ideas are: (1) *polarised session types*, which give an alternative formulation of duality enabling OCaml to automatically infer an appropriate session type in a session with a reasonable notational overhead; and (2) a *parameterised monad* with a data structure called '*slots*' manipulated with *lenses*, which can statically enforce session linearity and delegations. We show applications of session-ocaml including a travel agency usecase and an SMTP protocol.

1   Introduction

Session types [5], from their origins in the π-calculus [17], serve as rigorous specifications for coordinating *link mobility* in the sense that a communication link can move among participants, while ensuring type safety. In session type systems such mobility is called *delegation*. Once the ownership of a session is delegated (transferred) to another participant, it cannot be used anymore at the sender side. This property is called *linearity* of sessions and appears indispensable for all session type systems.

Linearity of session channels, however, is a major obstacle to adopt session type disciplines in mainstream languages, as it requires special syntax extensions for session communications [9], or depends on specific language features, such as type-level functions in Haskell [11,16,20,26], and affine types in Rust [13], or even falling back on run-time and dynamic checking [7,8,22,27]. For instance, a common way in Haskell implementations is to track linear channels using an extra *symbol table* which denotes types of each resource conveyed by a *parameterised monad*. A Haskell type for a session-typed function is roughly of the form:

$$t_1 \to \cdots \to \mathsf{M}\{c_1 \mapsto s_1, c_2 \mapsto s_2, \cdots\}\{c_1 \mapsto s_1', c_2 \mapsto s_2', \cdots\}\alpha$$

J.-M. Jacquet and M. Massink (Eds.): COORDINATION 2017, LNCS 10319, pp. 99–118, 2017.
DOI: 10.1007/978-3-319-59746-1_6

where M is a monad type constructor of arity three, α is a result type and the two $\{\cdots\}$ are symbol tables before (and after) evaluation which assign each channel c_i to its session type s_i (and s'_i respectively). This symbol table is represented at the *type level*, hence the channel c_i is not a value, but a *type* which reflects an identity of a channel. Since this static encoding is Haskell-specific using type-level functions, it is not directly extendable to other languages.

This paper proposes the session-ocaml library, which provides a fully static implementation of session types in OCaml without any extra mechanisms or tools (i.e. sessions are checked at compile-time). We extend the technique posted to the OCaml mailing list by Garrigue [4] where linear usage of resources is enforced solely by the parametric polymorphism mechanism. According to [4], the type of a *file handle* guarantees linear access to *multiple resources* using a symbol table in a monad-like structures. Adapting this technique to session types, in session-ocaml, *multiple simultaneous sessions* are statically encoded in a parameterised monad. More specifically, we extend the monad structure to a *slot monad* and the file handles to *lenses*. The slot monad is based on a type (p, q, a) monad (hereafter we use postfix type constructor of OCaml) where p and q are called *slots* which act like a symbol table. Slots are represented as a sequence of types represented by nested pair types $s_1 * (s_2 * \cdots)$. Lenses [15] are combinators that provide access to a particular element in nested tuples and are used to manipulate a symbol table in the slot monad. These mechanisms can provide an *idiomatic way* (i.e. code does not require interposing combinators to replace standard syntactic elements of functional languages) to declare session delegations and labelled session branching/selections with the static guarantee of type safety and linearity (unlike FuSe [22] which combines static and dynamic checking for linearity, see Sect. 5).

To enable *session-type inference* solely by unification in OCaml, session-ocaml is equipped with *polarised session types* which give an alternative formulation of *duality* (binary relation over types which ensures reciprocal use of sessions). In a polarised session type (p, q) sess, the *polarity* q is either serv (server) or cli (client). The usage of a session is prescribed in the *protocol type* p which provides an *objective* view of a communication based on a *communication direction* of req (request; client to server) and resp (response; server to client). For example, the protocol type for sending of a message type 'v from client to server is [`msg of req * 'v * 's] and the opposite is [`msg of resp * 'v * 's]. Duality is not necessary for protocol types as it shows a protocol common to both ends of a session rather than biased by either end. Then the session type inference can be driven solely by type unification which checks whether a protocol matches its counterpart or not. For instance, the dual of (p, cli)sess is (p, serv)sess and vice versa. When a session is being initiated, polarities are assigned to each end of a session according to the primitives used, namely cli for the proactive peer and serv for the passive peer. The protocol types also provide a usual prefixing declaration of session types, which is more human-readable than FuSe types [22] (see Sect. 5).

Listing 1 The xor server and its client

```
1  open Session0                          7      close ()))  ();;
2  let xor_ch = new_channel ();;          8  connect_ xor_ch (fun () ->
3  Thread.create (fun () ->               9    send (false,true) >>
4    accept_ xor_ch (fun () ->           10    let%s b = recv () in
5      let%s x,y = recv () in            11    print_bool b;
6        send (xor x y) >>               12    close ()) ()
```

The rest of the paper is as follows. Section 2 outlines programming with session-ocaml. Section 3 shows the library design with the polarised session type and the slot monads. In Sect. 4, we present two examples, a travel agency usecase and SMTP protocol implementations. Section 5 discusses comparisons with session type implementations in functional languages. Section 6 concludes and discusses further application of our technique. Technical report [10] includes the implementation of session-ocaml modules and additional examples. Session-ocaml is available at https://github.com/keigoi/session-ocaml.

2   Programming with session-ocaml

In this section, we overview session-typed programming with session-ocaml and summarise communication primitives in the library.

Send and receive primitives. Listing 1 shows a server and client which communicate boolean values. The module Session0[1] introduces functions of session-ocaml in the scope. xor_ch (line 2) is a *service channel* (or *shared* channel) that is used to start communication by a client connecting (connect_) to the server waiting (accept_) at it.[2] The server (lines 3–7) receives (recv) a pair of booleans, then calculates the exclusive-or of these values, transmits (send) back the resulting boolean, and finishes the session (close). These communication primitives communicate on an implicit *session endpoint* (or *session channel*) which is connected to the other endpoint. For inferring session types by OCaml, communication primitives are concatenated by the *bind* operations >> and >>= of a parameterised monad [1] which conveys session endpoints. The syntax let% *pat* = e_1 in e_2 binds the value returned by e_1 to the pattern *pat* and executes e_2, which is shorthand for e_1 >>= fun *pat* -> e_2 (the % symbol indicates a syntax extension point in an OCaml program). The client (lines 8–12) sends a pair of boolean, receives from the server and finishes the session, as prescribed in the following type. These server and client behaviours are captured by the *protocol type* argument of the channel type inferred at xor_ch as follows:

```
[`msg of req * (bool * bool) * [`msg of resp * bool * [`close]]] channel
```

---

[1] The suffix 0 means that it only uses the slot 0 (see later in this section).

[2] The suffixed underscore means that they run immediately instead of returning a monadic action (see later).

Listing 2 A logical operation server

```
1   open Session0                         14   | `fin -> close ();;
2   type binop = And | Or | Xor | Imp     15
3   let log_ch = new_channel ()           16   Thread.create
4   let eval_op = function                17     (accept_ log_ch logic_server) ();;
5   | And -> (&&)    | Or -> (||)          18   connect_ log_ch (fun () ->
6   | Xor -> xor                           19     [%select0 `bin] >>
7   | Imp -> (fun a b -> not a || b)       20     send And >>
8   let rec logic_server () =              21     send (true, false) >>
9     match%branch0 () with               22     let%s ans = recv () in
10    | `bin -> let%s op = recv () in      23     (print_bool ans;
11             let%s x,y = recv () in      24     [%select0 `fin] >>
12             send (eval_op op x y) >>=   25     close ())) ()
13             logic_server
```

The protocol type is the primary language of communication specification in session-ocaml. Here, [`msg of $r * v * p$] is a protocol that represents communication of a message of type $v$ before continuing to $p$. $r \in$ {req,resp} indicates a *communication direction* from client to server and vice versa, respectively. [`close] is the end of a session. Thus the above type indicates that by a session established at xor_ch, (1) the server receives a request of type bool * bool and then (2) sends a response of type bool back to the client.

Branching and recursion. A combination of branching and recursion provides various useful idioms such as exception handling. As an example, Listing 2 shows a logical operation server. The protocol type inferred for log_ch is:

```
[`branch of req * [`bin of [`msg of req * binop *
    [`msg of req * (bool * bool) * [`msg of resp * bool * 'a]]]
    |`fin of [`close]]] as 'a
```

[`branch of $r * [\cdots | $ `lab_i of $p_i | \cdots]$] represents a protocol that branches to p_i when label lab_i is communicated. Here r is a communication direction. t as 'a is an equi-recursive type [24] of OCaml that represents recursive structure of a session where 'a in t is instantiated by t as 'a. Lines 8–14 describe the body of the server. It receives one of the labels bin or fin, and branches to a different protocol. match%branch0 () with $|\cdots|$ `lab_i -> $e_i|\cdots$ is the syntax for branching to the expression e_i after label lab_i is received. Upon receipt of bin, the server receives requests for a logical operation from the client (type binop and bool * bool), sends back a response and returns to the branch (note that the server is recursively defined by let rec). In the case of fin, the session is terminated. [%select0 `lab] is a syntax to select one of branches with a label lab.[3] A client using selection is shown in lines 18–25: it selects the label bin, requests conjunction, and selects fin; then the session ends.

---

[3] Here the bracket is another form of a syntax extension point applied to an expression (see the OCaml manual).

Listing 3 A highly responsive server using delegation (log_ch is from Listing 2.)

```
1  open SessionN                              10    deleg_recv _1 ~bindto:_0 >>
2  let worker_ch = new_channel ()             11    close _1 >>
3  let rec main () =                           12    logic_server () >>= worker;;
4    accept log_ch ~bindto:_0 >>              13
5    connect worker_ch ~bindto:_1 >>          14  for i = 0 to 5 do
6    deleg_send _1 ~release:_0 >>             15    Thread.create (run worker) ()
7    close _1 >>= main                        16  done;;
8  let rec worker () =                         17  run main ()
9    accept worker_ch ~bindto:_1 >>
```

For the branching primitive on arbitrary labels, session-ocaml uses OCaml polymorphic variants and syntax extensions. By using equi-recursive types, recursive protocols are also directly encoded into OCaml types.

Link mobility with delegation. Link mobility with *session delegation* enables one to describe a protocol where the communication counterpart dynamically changes during a session. A typical pattern utilising delegation incorporates a main thread accepting a connection and worker threads doing the actual work to increase responsiveness of a service.

In session-ocaml, a program using delegation handles *multiple sessions* simultaneously. We explicitly assign each session endpoint to a *slot* using *slot specifier*s _0, _1, ··· which gives an idiomatic way to use linear channels. Listing 3 shows an example of a highly responsive server using delegation. The server receives repeated connection requests on channel log_ch consisting of the main thread and six worker threads. The module SessionN provides slot specifiers and accompanying communication primitives, where the suffix N means that it can handle on arbitrary number of sessions. The main thread (lines 3–7) accepts a connection from a client (accept) with log_ch and assigns the established session to slot 0 (~bindto:_0).[4] Next, it connects (connect) to a worker waiting for delegation at channel worker_ch (line 2) and assigns the session to slot 1 (~bindto:_1). Finally it delegates the session with the client to the worker (deleg_send), then ends the session with the worker and accepts the next connection. The worker thread (lines 8–12) receives the delegated session from the main thread (deleg_recv) and assigns the session to slot 0, then continues to logic_server (Listing 2). Here, Session0 module used by logic_server implicitly allocates the session type to slot 0, hence can be used with SessionN module. Line 14 starts the main thread and workers. Here run is a function that executes session-ocaml threads.

The protocol type of worker_ch is inferred as follows:

```
[`deleg of req * (logic_p, serv) sess * [`close]]
```

Here logic_p is the protocol type of log_ch and [`deleg of $r * s * p$] is the delegation type. r is a communication direction, s is a polarised session type (a type with protocol and polarity which we explain next) for the delegated session and p is a continuation. By inferring the protocol types, session-ocaml can statically guarantee safety of higher-order protocols including delegations.

---

[4] ~arg:e is a *labelled argument* e for a named parameter arg.

The polarised session types. Communication safety is checked by matching each protocol type inferred at both ends. The *polarised session type* (p,q) sess given to each endpoint plays a key role for protocol type inference. Here p is a protocol type, and $q \in$ {serv,cli} is the *polarity* determined at session initiation. serv is assigned to the accept side and cli to the connect side. serv and cli are *dual* to each other.

The polarised session type gives a simple way to let the type checker infer a uniform protocol type according to a communication direction and a polarity assigned to the endpoint. For example, as we have seen, we deduce resp (response) from server transmission (send) and client reception (recv). Table 1 shows correspondences between polarities and communication directions.

Table 1. Correspondence between polarities and communication directions

	send	select	deleg_send	recv	branch	deleg_recv
cli	req	req	req	resp	resp	resp
serv	resp	resp	resp	req	req	req

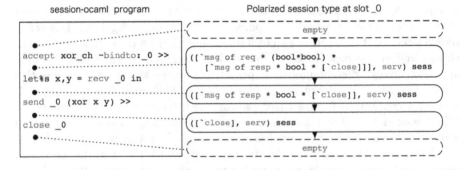

Fig. 1. Session type changes in xor_server

To track the entire session, a polarised session type changes in its protocol part as a session progresses. Figure 1 shows changes of the session type in slot 0 of the xor server (here we use the SessionN module). The server first accepts a connection and assigns the session type to slot 0, where the type before acceptance is empty. After the subsequent reception of the pair of booleans and transmission of the xor values of those booleans, req and resp are consumed, and becomes empty again at the end of the session. Similar type changes occur on both main and worker and their types would be:

```
unit -> (empty * (empty * 'ss), 'tt, 'a) session
```

Here the type $(s,\ t,\ a)$ session specifies that it expects slot sequence s at the beginning, and returns another slot sequence t and a value of type a. The type empty * (empty * 'ss) denotes that slot 0 and 1 are empty at the beginning, and since they never return the answer (i.e. the recursion runs infinitely), the rest of types `'tt` and `'a` are left as variables.

The type of `logic_server` in Listing 2 has a `session` type:

```
((logic_p, serv) sess * 'ss, empty * 'ss, unit) session
```

Here `logic_server` expects a session assigned at slot 0 before it is called, hence it expects the session type `(logic_p, serv)sess` in its pre-type. A difference from `main` and `worker` above is that since each of them establishes or receives sessions by their own (by using `accept`, `connect` or `deleg_recv`), they expect that slots 0 and 1 are `empty`.

Table 2 shows the type and communication behaviour before and after the execution of each `session-ocaml` communication primitive. Each row has a *pre-type* (the type required before execution) and *post-type* (the type guaranteed after execution). The protocol type at `serv` is obtained by replacing `req` with `resp` and `resp` with `req`. For example, the session `send _n e` has pre-type `([`msg of req * v * p], cli)sess` at `cli` and `([`msg of resp * v * p], serv)sess` at `serv` where `_n` is a slot specifier, e is an expression, v is a value type and p is a

Table 2. `session-ocaml` primitives and protocol types

Primitive	Pre-type (at `cli`[*1])	Post-type	Synopsis
`send _n e`	`[`msg of req * v * p]`	p	sending $e : v$ at slot n
`let%s pat = recv _n` `in ···`	`[`msg of resp * v * p]`	p	Reception at slot n, binding to pattern $pat : v$
`[%select _n `lab`$_i$`]`	`[`branch of req *` `[> `lab`$_i$` of p`$_i$`]]`	p_i	Select label lab_i at slot n
`match%branch _n with` `| `lab`$_0$` -> e`$_0$ `| ···` `| `lab`$_m$` -> e`$_m$	`[`branch of resp *` `[`lab`$_0$` of p`$_0$ `| ···` `| `lab`$_m$` of p`$_m$`]]`	t	Branch at n with labels lab_i (protocol type p_i is that of pre-type of e_i; t is a post-type of all e_i)
`deleg_send _n` `~release:_m`	`n:[`deleg of req * s * p]`[*2] `m:s`[*2]	$n{:}p$ $m{:}$empty [*3]	Delegate session at m with type s along n
`deleg_recv _n` `~bindto:_m`	`n:[`deleg of resp * s * p]`[*2] `m:`empty [*3]	$n{:}p$ $m{:}s$ [*2]	Reception of delegation along n and assign it to m
`close _n`	`[`close]`	empty [*3]	Close session at slot n

s is a polarised session type, `_n` and `_m` are slot specifiers, e is an expression of a base type, ch is a service channel, ``lab` is a polymorphic variant and pat is a binding pattern.

*1: At `serv`, `req` and `resp` are exchanged;   *2: s is a session type (not a protocol type); *3: Slot type changes to `empty`.

Primitive	Pre-type	Post-type	Synopsis
`accept ch ~bindto:_n`	empty	$(p,$ serv$)$ sess	Accept a connection at channel ch; assign a new session of polarity serv to n
`connect ch ~bindto:_n`	empty	$(p,$ cli$)$ sess	Connect to channel ch; assign a new session of polarity cli to n

protocol type. Selection [%select _n] has *open* polymorphic variant type [>...] in pre-type to simulate *subtyping* of the labelled branches.

3   Design and Implementation of session-ocaml

In this section, we first show the design of polarised session types associated with communication primitives (Sect. 3.1); then introduce the *slot monad* which conveys multiple session endpoints in a sequence of slots and constructs the whole session type for a session (Sect. 3.2). In Sect. 3.3, we introduce the *slot specifier* to look up a particular slot in a slot sequence with *lenses* which are a polymorphic data manipulation technique known in functional programming languages. We present the syntax extension for branching and selection, and explain a restriction on the polarised session types. This section mainly explains the *type signatures* of the communication primitives. Implementation of the communication *behaviours* is left to [10].

3.1   Polarity Polymorphism

The *polarity polymorphism* is accompanied within all session primitives in that the appropriate direction type is assigned according to the polarity. This resolves a trade-off of having two polarised session types for one transmission. For instance, a transmission of a value could have two candidates, [`msg of req * 'v * 's] and [`msg of resp * 'v * 's] but they are chosen according to the polarity from which the message is sent. In order to relate the polarities to the directions, cli and serv are defined by type aliases as follows:

$$\text{type cli = req * resp} \qquad \text{type serv = resp * req}$$

For each communication primitive, we introduce fresh type variables r_{req} and r_{resp} representing the communication direction, and put $r_{req} * r_{resp}$ as the polarity in its session type. When its polarity is cli, we put r_{req} for req and r_{resp} for resp, while when it is serv, we put r_{req} for resp and r_{resp} for req. For example, the pre-type of send is ([`msg of 'r1*'v*'p],'r1*'r2)sess and that of recv is ([`msg of 'r2*'v*'p],'r1*'r2)sess. The same discipline applies to branching and delegation. The actual typing is deferred to the following subsections.

3.2   The Slot Monad Carrying Multiple Sessions

The key factor to achieve linearity is to keep session endpoints securely inside a monad. In session-ocaml, multiple sessions are conveyed in slots using the *slot monad* of type

$$(s_0 * (s_1 * \cdots), t_0 * (t_1 * \cdots), \alpha) \text{ session}$$

Listing 4 The slot monad

```
1  type ('p,'q,'a) session and empty and all_empty = empty * 'a as 'a
2  val return : 'a -> ('p,'p,'a) session
3  val (>>=) : ('p,'q,'a) session -> ('a -> ('q,'r,'b) session) -> ('p,'r,'b) session
4  val (>>) : ('p,'q,'a) session -> ('q,'r,'b) session -> ('p,'r,'b) session
5  val run : (all_empty,all_empty,unit) session -> unit
```

---

which denotes a computation of a value of type α, turning each pre-type s_i of slot i to post-type t_i. We refer to slots before and after computation as *pre-* and *post-slots*, respectively. The type signature of the slot monad is shown in Listing 4. The operators >>= and >> (lines 3–4) compose computation sequentially while propagating type changes on each slot by demanding the same type 'q in the post-slots on the left-hand side and the pre-slots on the right-hand side. Usually they construct compound session types via *unification*. For example, in send And >> send (true, false) (from Listing 2 the left hand side (send Add) has the following type:

```
(([`msg of req*binop*'p1],cli) sess * 'ss1, ('p1,cli) sess * 'ss1, unit) session
```

While the type of the right hand side (send (true, false)) is:

```
(([`msg of req*(bool*bool)*'p2],cli) sess*'ss2, ('p2,cli) sess*'ss2, unit) session
```

By unifying the post-type in the preceding monad with the pre-type in the following monad (and the rest of slots 'ss1 with 'ss2), the bind operation produces a chain of protocol type in the pre-slots as follows:

```
(([`msg of req*binop*[`msg of req*(bool*bool)*'p2]],cli) sess*'ss2,
    ('p2,cli) sess*'ss2, unit) session
```

In line 5, run executes the slot monad and requires all slots being empty before and after execution, thus it precludes use of unallocated slots, and mandates that all sessions are finally closed (which corresponds to the absence of *contraction* in linear type systems). The type all_empty (line 1) is a type alias for OCaml equi-recursive type empty * 'a as 'a,[5] enabling use of *arbitrarily* many slots.

Table 3. Types for slot specifiers

Specifier	Type		
_0	('a, 'b, 'a * 'ss,	'b * 'ss	) slot
_1	('a, 'b, 's0 * ('a * 'ss),	's0 * ('b * 'ss)	) slot
_2	('a, 'b, 's0 * ('s1 * ('a * 'ss)),	's0 * ('s1 * ('b * 'ss))) slot	
_n	('a, 'b, 's0*($\cdots$*('s$_{n-1}$*('a*'ss))$\cdots$),	's0*($\cdots$*('s$_{n-1}$*('b*'ss))$\cdots$)) slot	

---

[5] In order to have such a type, we compile the code with the -rectypes option. If we chose types for slots using objects or polymorphic variants, there is no need to use this option.

Listing 5 Signatures for communication primitives in `session-ocaml`

```
1  val accept : 'p channel -> bindto:(empty, ('p, serv) sess, 'pre, 'post) slot
2        -> ('pre, 'post, unit) session
3  val connect : 'p channel -> bindto:(empty, ('p, cli) sess, 'pre, 'post) slot
4        -> ('pre, 'post, unit) session
5  val close : (([`close],'r1*'r2) sess, empty, 'pre, 'post) slot
6        -> ('pre, 'post, unit) session
7  val send : (([`msg of 'r1*'v*'p],'r1*'r2) sess, ('p,'r1*'r2) sess, 'pre, 'post) slot
8        -> 'v -> ('pre, 'post, unit) session
9  val recv : (([`msg of 'r2*'v*'p],'r1*'r2) sess, ('p,'r1*'r2) sess, 'pre, 'post) slot
10        -> ('pre, 'post, 'v) session
11 val deleg_send :
12        (([`deleg of 'r1*'s*'p],'r1*'r2) sess, ('p,'r1*'r2) sess, 'pre, 'mid) slot
13        -> release:('s, empty, 'mid, 'post) slot -> ('pre, 'post, 'v) session
14 val deleg_recv :
15        (([`deleg of 'r2*'s*'p],'r1*'r2) sess, ('p,'r1*'r2) sess, 'pre, 'mid) slot
16        -> bindto:(empty, 's, 'mid, 'post) slot -> ('pre, 'post, 'v) session
17 val select_left : (([`branch of 'r1 * [>`left of 's1]],'r1*'r2) sess,
18                ('s1,'r1*'r2) sess, 'pre, 'post) slot -> ('pre, 'post, unit) session
19 val select_right : (([`branch of 'r1 * [>`right of 's2]],'r1*'r2) sess,
20                ('s2,'r1*'r2) sess, 'pre, 'post) slot -> ('pre, 'post, unit) session
21 val branch2 : (([`branch of 'r2 * [`left of 's1 | `right of 's2]],'r1*'r2) sess,
22        ('s1,'r1*'r2) sess, 'pre, 'mid1) slot * (unit -> ('mid1, 'post, 'a) session)
23    -> (([`branch of 'r2 * [`left of 's1 | `right of 's2]],'r1*'r2) sess,
24        ('s2,'r1*'r2) sess, 'pre, 'mid2) slot * (unit -> ('mid2, 'post, 'a) session)
25    -> ('pre, 'post, 'a) session
```

3.3   Lenses Focusing on Linear Channels

In order to provide access to session endpoints conveyed inside a slot monad, we apply *lenses* [15] to slot specifiers $\_0, \_1, \cdots$ which are combinators to manipulate a polymorphic data structure. The following shows the type of a slot specifier which modifies slot n of a slot sequence:

```
type ('a, 'b, 's0*(···('s_{n-1}*('a*'ss))···), 's0*(···('s_{n-1}*('b*'ss))···)) slot
```

The type says that it replaces the type `'a` of slot n in the slot sequence `'s0*(···('s_{n-1}*('a*'ss))···)` with `'b` and the resulting sequence type becomes to `'s0*(···('s_{n-1}*('b*'ss))···)`. The type of each slot specifier ($\_0, \_1, \cdots$) is shown in Table 3.

Listing 5 exhibits type signatures of `accept`, `connect`, `close`, `send`, `recv`, `deleg_send` and `deleg_recv` which are compiled from lenses, the polarised session types (Sect. 3.1), slot monads (Sect. 3.2), and pre- and post-types in Table 2 (Sect. 2). Note that `bindto:` and `release:` are named parameters of a primitive.

`accept` and `connect` (lines 1–4) assign a new session channel to the `empty` slot, whereas `close` (lines 5–6) finishes the session and leave the slot `empty` again. `send` and `recv` (lines 7–10) proceed the protocol type by removing a `msg` prefix.

`deleg_send` and `deleg_recv` (lines 11–16) update a pair of slots; one is for the transmission/reception and the other is for the delegated session. To update the slots twice, they take a pair of slot specifiers which share an intermediate slot sequence `'mid`. They embody an aspect of linearity: `deleg_send` releases the ownership of the delegated session by replacing the slot type to `empty`, while `deleg_recv` allocates another `empty` slot to the acquired session.

The primitives for binary selection select_left, select_right and branching branch2 (lines 17–25) communicate left and right labels. branch2 takes a pair of continuations as well as a pair of slot specifiers. According to the received label, one of the continuations is invoked after the pre-type of the invoked continuation is assigned to the corresponding slot.

Finally, we present how to embed slot type changes into a pair of slot sequences in a slot monad where the position of the slot is specified by applying a slot specifier. In each type signature, the first and second type arguments of type slot prescribes *how* a slot type changes. The third and fourth arguments do not specify a slot in the slot sequence conveyed by the slot monad. For example, the type of function application close _1 is given by the following type substitution:

(change of the slot type specified by close)
```
'a ↦ (['`close],'r1*'r2) sess, 'b ↦ empty,
```
(change of the slot sequence type specified by _1)
```
'pre ↦ 's0 * (['`close],'r1*'r2) sess * 'ss, 'post ↦ 's0 * (empty * 'ss)
```
And the type completing the session at slot 1 is:
```
close _1: ('s0 * (['`close],'r1*'r2) sess * 'ss), 's0 * (empty * 'ss), unit) session
```

A note on delegation and slot assignment. The delegation [`deleg of $r * s * p$] distinguishes polarity in the delegated session s. This results in a situation where two sessions exhibiting the same communicating behaviour cannot be delegated at a single point in a protocol, if they have different polarities from each other. It is illustrated by the following (untypeable) example.
```
if b then connect ch1 ~bindto:_1 >> deleg_send _0 ~release:_1
else       accept ch2 ~bindto:_1 >> deleg_send _0 ~release:_1
```
Recall that connect yields a cli endpoint while accept gives a serv. Due to the different polarities in the delegated session types, the types of then and else clause conflict with each other, even if they have the identical behaviour. In [32], where polarity is not a type but a syntactic construct, such a restriction does not exist. A similar restriction exists in GV [30] which has polarity in end (end$_!$ and end$_?$).

In principle, it is possible to automatically assign numbers to slot specifiers *locally* in a function instead of writing them explicitly. However, since sequential composition of the session monad requires each post- and pre-type to match with each other, the *global* assignment of slot specifiers would require a considerable amount of work and can be hard to predict its behaviour. As shown in Listing 3, one can handle two sessions by just using two slot specifiers.

Listing 6 The helper functions for branching/selection with arbitrary labels

```
1  val _select :
2      (([`branch of 'r2 * 'br],'r1*'r2) sess, ('p,'r1*'r2) sess, 'pre, 'post) slot
3      -> ('p -> 'br) -> ('pre, 'post, unit) session
4  val _branch_start : (([`branch of 'r1 * 'br], 'r1*'r2) sess, 'x, 'pre, 'dummy) slot
5      -> ('br * ('r1*'r2) -> ('pre, 'post,'v) session) -> ('pre, 'post, 'v) session
6  val _branch :
7      (([`branch of 'r1 * 'br], 'r1*'r2) sess, ('p,'r1*'r2) sess, 'pre, 'mid) slot
8      -> 'p * ('r1*'r2) -> ('mid,'post,'v) session -> ('pre, 'post, 'v) session
```

Listing 7 Travel agency

```
1  let customer cst_ch =                    19      match%branch _0 with
2    connect cst_ch ~bindto:_0 >>           20      | `quote ->
3    [%select _0 `quote] >>                 21        let%s dest = recv _0 in
4    send _0 "London to Paris" >>           22        send _0 80.00 >>
5    let%s cost = recv _0 in                23        loop ()
6    if cost > 100. then                    24      | `reject -> close _0
7      [%select _0 `reject] >>              25      | `agree ->
8      close _0                             26        connect svc_ch ~bindto:_1 >>
9    else                                   27        deleg_send _1 ~release:_0 >>
10     [%select _0 `agree] >>               28        close _1
11     send _0 (Address("London")) >>       29    in loop ()
12     let%s d : date = recv _0 in          30  let service svc_ch =
13     close _0 >>                          31    accept svc_ch ~bindto:_1 >>
14     (Printf.printf "cost: %f\n" cost;    32    deleg_recv _1 ~bindto:_0 >>
15      return ())                          33    let%s (Address(addr)) = recv _1 in
16  let agency cst_ch svc_ch =              34    send _0 (now()) >>
17    accept cst_ch ~bindto:_0 >>           35    close _0 >> close _1
18    let rec loop () =
```

Syntax extension for arbitrarily labelled branch. Since the OCaml type system does not allow to parameterise type labels (polymorphic variants), we provide macros for arbitrarily-labelled branching. Listing 6 provides helper functions for the macros. For selection, the macro [%select _n`$lab_i$] is expanded to _select _n(fun x -> `lab_i(x)), where the helper function _select transmits label lab_i on the slot n. match%branch _n with | `$lab_1$ -> $e_1$|···| `lab_k -> e_k is expanded to:

```
_branch_start _n ((function |`lab₁(p1),q -> _branch _n (p1,q) (e₁) | ···
                  |`labₖ(pk),q -> _branch _n (pk,q) (eₖ))
                : [`labᵢ of 'p1|···|`labₖ of 'pk]*'x -> 'y)
```

The helper functions _branch_start and _branch have the type shown in Listing 6. The anonymous function will have type

$$[`lab_1 \text{ of } p_1 \mid \cdots \mid `lab_k \text{ of } p_k] * q \rightarrow (pre, post, v) \text{ session}$$

where q is the polarity and p_i is the protocol type in the pre-type at slot n in e_i. When a label lab_i ($i \in \{1 \ldots k\}$) is received, _branch_start _n f passes a pair of *witness* `$lab_i$(pi) and q of a polarised session type (pi, q) sess to the function $f$. The anonymous function extracts the witness and by _branch it rebuilds the session type ('pi,'q)sess and passes the session to the continuation $e_i$ as the pre-type. The type annotation [`lab_i of 'p1|···|`lab_k of 'pk]*'x -> 'y erases the row type variable [<···] generated by the anonymous function. The annotation is necessary because the row type variable turns into a useless *monomorphic* row type variable [_<···] in the inferred protocol type. This may cause a problem while compiling since the compiler requires monomorphic type variables to not escape from compilation units.

4   Applications

4.1   Travel Agency

We demonstrate programming in session-ocaml using the Travel agency scenario from [9], which consists of typical patterns found in business and financial protocols. The scenario is played by three participants: customer, agency and service (Listing 7). customer and service initially do not know each other, and agency mediates a deal between them by session delegation.

customer begins an order session with agency and binds it to their own slot 0 (each process has a separate slot sequence). Then customer requests and receives the price for the desired journey after sending the quote label. In our scenario, customer requests "London to Paris" and agency replies with a fixed price 80.0.

Then customer might send the **agree** label to proceed the transaction with the current price. Or if customer does not agree with the price, customer can cancel the transaction by sending the **reject** label. Or, customer can send quote again and this will be repeated an arbitrary number of times for different journeys (we omit this branch from the code). In our program, customer agrees with agency at a price less than 100.0, or otherwise rejects it and terminates the transaction.

Next, if customer agrees with the price, agency opens the session with service and binds it to slot 1. Then it delegates to service, through slot 1, the interactions with customer remaining for slot 0. customer then sends the billing address (unaware that he/she is now talking to service), and service replies with the dispatch date (now()) for the purchased tickets. The transaction is complete.

The protocol type between customer and agency is inferred as:

```
[`branch of req *
  [`quote of [`msg of req * string * [`msg of resp * float * 'a]]
  |`reject of [`close]
  |`agree of [`msg of req * addr * [`msg of resp * date * [`close]]]]] as 'a
```

Delegation from agency to service is inferred in the channel of service as:

```
[`deleg of req *
  (([`msg of 'r1 * addr * [`msg of 'r2 * date * [`close]]], 'r1*'r2) sess * [`close]]
```

The delegated type is polymorphic on the polarity and communication directions (Sect. 3.1), hence the service can handle both polarities. It reflects the part after agree in the protocol above where 'r1 is req and 'r2 is resp. Thus delegation with the polarised session types and slots effectively gives a way to coordinate *higher order* communication incurred by link mobility.

Listing 8 The protocol type of SMTP

```
1  type smtp =
2     [`msg of resp * r200 * [`msg of req * ehlo * [`msg of resp * r200 * mail_loop]]]
3  and mail_loop =
4     [`branch of req *
5        [`left of [`msg of req * mail * [`msg of resp * r200 * rcpt_loop]]
6       |`right of [`msg of req * quit * [`close]]]]
7  and rcpt_loop =
8     [`branch of req *
9        [`left of [`msg of req * rcpt *
10          [`branch of resp * [`left of [`msg of resp * r200 * rcpt_loop]
11            |`right of [`msg of resp * r500 * [`msg of req * quit * [`close]]]]]]
12       |`right of body]]
13 and body =
14    [`msg of req * data * [`msg of resp * r354 * [`msg of req * string list *
15       [`msg of resp * r200 * mail_loop]]]]
```

Listing 9 Types for SMTP commands and replies

```
1  (* EHLO example.com *)              (* MAIL FROM: alice@example.com *)
2  type ehlo = EHLO of string          type mail = MAIL of string
3  (* RCPT TO: bob@example.com *)       (* DATA *)
4  type rcpt = RCPT of string          type data = DATA
5  (* QUIT *)                          (* Success e.g. 250 Ok *)
6  type quit = QUIT                    type r200 = R200 of string list
7  (* Error e.g. 554 Relay denied *)   (* 354 Start mail input *)
8  type r500 = R500 of string list     type r354 = R354 of string list
```

Static checking of delegation makes it easier to find errors otherwise hard to analyse due to the indirect nature of delegation. Consider a case that service changes its behaviour to receive addr * paymeth. Now the inferred protocol type at service would be:

```
[`deleg of req* ([`msg of 'r1*(addr * paymeth)*[`msg of 'r2*date*[`close
    ]]], 'r1*'r2) sess * [`close]]
```

Whereas that of agency remains same as before, it results in a type error at the moment when a service channel is passed. Without static typing, the run-time error would be deferred until the beginning of actual client-service communication.

4.2   An SMTP Protocol

This section shows an SMTP client implementation by session-ocaml. Listings 8 and 9 shows the protocol type of SMTP and message types representing SMTP commands and replies; and Listing 10 shows the client implementation. Line 2 in Listing 10 generates a service channel for connecting to the SMTP server. Here smtp_adapter is an *adapter* that converts a sequence of session messages to a TCP stream. Its definition is shown in Listing 11 and built using the combinators shown in Listing 12. The functions req and resp accept a function to convert between a message of type 'v and a command string and construct an adapter. bra and sel are branching and selection respectively, and cls is the end of the session. The function with the same name as the message type is a function for converting to a string (or vice versa) and is responsible for actual stream processing. In OCaml, `f @@ g` means function composition `fun x -> f (g x)`, and begin `e` end means (`e`). Since OCaml evaluates eagerly, each function is η-expanded with a parameter `ch` so that it does not recurse infinitely.

Listing 10 An implementation of SMTP client

```
1  open Session0
2  let ch = TcpSession.new_channel smtp_adapter "smtp.example.com:25"
3  let smtp_client () = connect_ ch begin fun () -> let%s R200 s = recv () in
4      send (EHLO("me.example.com"))    >> let%s R200 _ = recv () in
5      select_left () >> (* enter into the main loop *)
6      send (MAIL("alice@example.com")) >> let%s R200 _ = recv () in
7      select_left () >> (* enter into recipient loop *)
8      send (RCPT("bob@example.com"))   >>
9      branch2 (fun () -> let%s R200 _ = recv () in (* recipient Ok *)
10                     select_right () >> (* proceed to sending the mail body *)
11                     send DATA              >> let%s R354 _ = recv () in
12                     send (escape mailbody) >> let%s R200 _ = recv () in
13                     select_right () >> send QUIT >> close ())
14             (fun () -> let%s R500 msg = recv () in (* a recipient is rejected *)
15                     (List.iter print_endline msg; send QUIT) >> close ()) end ()
```

Listing 11 The TCP adapter for a SMTP client

```
1  let rec smtp_adapter ch = (resp r200 @@ req ehlo @@ resp r200 @@ ml_p) ch
2  and ml_p ch = sel ~left:(req mail @@ resp r200 @@ rp_p) ~right:(req quit @@ cls) ch
3  and rp_p ch = sel ~left:(req rcpt @@ bra ~left:(r200, rp_p)
4                                       ~right:(resp r500 @@ req quit @@ cls))
5                    ~right:bd_p ch
6  and bd_p ch = (req data @@ resp r354 @@ req string_list @@ resp r200 @@ ml_p) ch
```

The adapter for branch `bra` is asymmetric in its parameters [18]. `bra` has a parser of type `string -> 'v option` on the `left` side since the adapter determines a continuation in a branch according to the parsed result of a received string. The adapter chooses `left` if the parser succeeds (returns `Some(x)`), and `right` if it fails (`None`). By nesting `bra`, any nesting of branch can be constructed.

Comparing to the existing Haskell implementation in [11], an advantage is that our OCaml version enjoys equi-recursive session types, so we avoid the manual annotation of repeated `unwind` operations needed to unfold iso-recursive types in Haskell. A shortcoming of the OCaml version is the explicit nature of adapter. However, since the adapter and the protocol type have the same structure, it can be generated semi-automatically from the type declaration in Listing 8 when OCaml gains ad hoc polymorphism such as type classes. We expect this to be possible with modular-implicits [31], which will be introduced in a future version of OCaml. On the other hand, it is also possible to omit the protocol type declaration in Listing 8 by inferring the type of the adapter.

Listing 12 Combinators for TCP adapters

```
1  type 'p net = raw_chan -> (('p, serv) sess * all_empty, all_empty, unit) monad
2  val req : ('v -> string) -> 'p net -> [`msg of req * 'v * 'p] net
3  val resp : (string -> 'v parse_result) -> 'p net -> [`msg of resp * 'v * 'p] net
4  val sel : left:'p1 net -> right:'p2 net ->
5          [`branch of req * [`left of 'p1|`right of 'p2]] net
6  val bra : left:((string -> 'v1 parse_result) * 'p1 net) -> right:'p2 net ->
7          [`branch of resp * [`left of [`msg of resp * 'v1 * 'p1] |`right of 'p2]] net
8  val cls : [`close] net
```

---

5 Related Work

We discuss related work focusing on the functional programming languages. For other related work, see Sect. 1.

Implementations in Haskell. The first work done by Neubauer and Thiemann [18] implements the first-order single-channel session types with recursions. Using parameterised monads, Pucella and Tov [26] provide multiple sessions, but manual reordering of symbol tables is required. Imai et al. [11] extend [26] with delegation, handling multiple sessions in a user-friendly manner by using type-level functions. Orchard and Yoshida [20] use an embedding of effect systems in Haskell via graded monads based on a formal encoding of session-typed π-calculus into PCF with an effect system. Lindley and Morris [16] provide an embedding of the GV session-typed functional calculus [30] into Haskell, building on a linear λ-calculus embedding by Polakow [25]. Duality inference is mostly represented by a multi-parameter type class with functional dependencies [14]; For instance, `class Dual t t'| t -> t', t' -> t` declares that t can be inferred from its dual `t'` and vice versa. However, all of the above works depend on type-level features in Haskell, hence they are not directly applicable to other programming languages including OCaml. See [21] for a detailed survey. `session-ocaml` generalises the authors' previous work in Haskell [11] by replacing type-level functions with lenses, leading to wider applicability to other programming languages.

Implementations in OCaml. Padovani [22] introduces FuSe, which implements multiple sessions with dynamic linearity checking and its single-session version with static checking in OCaml. Our `session-ocaml` achieves static typing for multiple sessions with delegation by introducing session manipulations based on lenses; and provides an idiomatic way to declare branching with arbitrary labels; while FuSe combines static and dynamic approach to achieve them.

The following example shows that `session-ocaml` can avoid linearity violation, while FuSe dynamically checks it at the runtime.

```
let rec loop () = let s = send "*" s in
                  match branch s with `stop s -> close s |`cont _ -> loop ()
```

`loop` sends `"*"` repeatedly until it receives label `stop`. Although the endpoint s should be used linearly, the condition is violated at the beginning of the second iteration since the endpoint is disposed by using the wildcard _ at the end of the loop. In FuSe 0.7, loop is well-typed and terminates in error InvalidEndpoint at runtime. In session-ocaml, this error inherently does not occur since each endpoint is implicit inside the monad and indirectly accessed by lenses.

[22] gives a micro-benchmark which measures run-time performance between the static and dynamic versions of FuSe. Based on the benchmark, it is shown that the overhead incurred by dynamic checking is negligible when implemented with a fast communication library such as Core [12], and concludes that the static version of FuSe performs well enough in spite of numerous closure creations in a monad. The FuSe implementation has been recently extended to *context free session types* [29] by adding an *endpoint* attribute to session types [23].

On duality inference, a simple approach in OCaml is firstly introduced by Pucella and Tov [26]. The idea in [26] is to keep a pair of the current session and its dual at every step; therefore the notational size of a session type is twice as big as that in [5]. FuSe [22] reduces its size by almost half using the encoding technique in [3] by modelling binary session types as a chain of linear channel types as follows. A session type in FuSe ('a, 'b) t prescribes input ('a) and output ('b) capabilities. A transmission and a reception of a value 'v followed by a session ('a, 'b) t are represented as (_0, 'v*('a, 'b) t) t and ('v*('a, 'b) t, _0) t respectively, where _0 means "no message"; then the dual of a session type is obtained by swapping the top pair of the type. A drawback of these FuSe notations is it becomes less readable when multiple nestings are present. For example, in a simplified variant of the logic operation server in Listing 2 with no recursion nor branch, the protocol type of log_ch becomes:

```
[`msg of req*binop*[`msg of req*(bool*bool)*[`msg of resp*bool*[`close]]]]
```

In FuSe, at server's side, the channel should be inferred as:

```
(binop*((bool*bool)*(_0, bool*(_0,_0) t) t, _0) t, _0) t
```

Due to a sequence of flipping capability pairs, more effort is needed to understand the protocol. To recover the readability, FuSe supplies the translator *Rosetta* which compiles FuSe types into session type notation with the prefixing style and vice versa. Our polarised session types are directly represented in a *prefixing* manner with the slight restriction shown in Sect. 3.3.

6   Conclusion

We have shown session-ocaml, a library for session-typed communication which supports multiple simultaneous sessions with delegation in OCaml. The contributions of this paper are summarised as follows. (1) Based on lenses and the slot monad, we achieved a fully static checking of session types by the OCaml type system without adding any substantial extension to the language. Previously, a few implementations were known for a single session [22,26], but the one that allows statically-checked multiple sessions is new and shown to be useful. To the authors' knowledge, this is the first implementation which combines lenses and a parameterised monad. (2) On top of (1), we proposed macros for arbitrarily labelled branches. The macros "patch up" only the branching and selection parts where linear variables are inevitably exposed due to limitation on polymorphic variants. (3) We proposed a session type inference framework solely based on the OCaml built-in type unification. Communication safety is guaranteed by checking equivalence of protocol types inferred at both ends with different polarities.

Type inference plays a key role in using lenses without the burden of writing any type annotations. Functional programming languages such as Standard ML, F# and Haskell have a nearly complete type inference, hence it is relatively easy to apply the method presented in this paper. On the other hand, languages such as Scala, Java and C# have a limited type inference system. However, by a recent extension with Lambda expressions in Java 8, lenses became available without type annotations in many cases (see a proof-of-concept at https://github.com/keigoi/slotjava). The main difficulty for implementing session types is selection primitives since they require type annotations for non-selected branches. Development of such techniques is future work.

Our approach which uses slots for simultaneous multiple sessions resembles parameterised session types [2,19], and it is smoothly extendable to the multiparty session type framework [6]. We plan to investigate code generations from Scribble [28] (a protocol description language for the multiparty session types) along the line of [7,8] integrating with parameterised features [2,19].

Acknowledgments. We thank Raymond Hu and Dominic Orchard for their comments on an early version of the paper. The third author thanks the JSPS bilateral research with NFSC for fruitful discussion. This work is partially supported by EPSRC projects EP/K034413/1, EP/K011715/1, EP/L00058X/1, EP/N027833/1 and EP/N028201/1; by EU FP7 612985 (UPSCALE), and COST Action IC1405 (RC); by JSPS International Fellowships (S15051), and KAKENHI JP17K12662, JP25280023 and JP17H01722 from JSPS, Japan.

References

1. Atkey, R.: Parameterized notions of computation. J. Funct. Program. **13**(3–4), 355–376 (2009)
2. Charalambides, M., Dinges, P., Agha, G.A.: Parameterized, concurrent session types for asynchronous multi-actor interactions. Sci. Comput. Program. **115–116**, 100–126 (2016)
3. Dardha, O., Giachino, E., Sangiorgi, D.: Session types revisited. In: Proceedings of the 14th Symposium on Principles and Practice of Declarative Programming (PPDP 2012), pp. 139–150. ACM, New York (2012)
4. Garrigue, J.: A mailing-list post (2006). https://groups.google.com/d/msg/fa.caml/GWWtHOP35dI/IsrOze-qVLwJ
5. Honda, K., Vasconcelos, V.T., Kubo, M.: Language primitives and type discipline for structured communication-based programming. In: Hankin, C. (ed.) ESOP 1998. LNCS, vol. 1381, pp. 122–138. Springer, Heidelberg (1998). doi:10.1007/BFb0053567
6. Honda, K., Yoshida, N., Carbone, M.: Multiparty asynchronous session types. In: POPL, pp. 273–284. ACM (2008). A full version, JACM, **63**(1), No. 9, 67 pages, 2016

7. Hu, R., Yoshida, N.: Hybrid session verification through endpoint API generation. In: Stevens, P., Wąsowski, A. (eds.) FASE 2016. LNCS, vol. 9633, pp. 401–418. Springer, Heidelberg (2016). doi:10.1007/978-3-662-49665-7_24

8. Hu, R., Yoshida, N.: Explicit connection actions in multiparty session types. In: Huisman, M., Rubin, J. (eds.) FASE 2017. LNCS, vol. 10202, pp. 116–133. Springer, Heidelberg (2017). doi:10.1007/978-3-662-54494-5_7

9. Hu, R., Yoshida, N., Honda, K.: Session-based distributed programming in Java. In: Vitek, J. (ed.) ECOOP 2008. LNCS, vol. 5142, pp. 516–541. Springer, Heidelberg (2008). doi:10.1007/978-3-540-70592-5_22

10. Imai, K., Yoshida, N., Yuen, S.: Session-ocaml: a session-based library with polarities and lenses. Technical report, Imperial College London (2017, to appear)

11. Imai, K., Yuen, S., Agusa, K.: Session type inference in Haskell. In: Postproceedings of Thrid Workshop on Programming Language Approaches to Concurrency and Communication-cEntric Software (PLACES 2010), vol. 69, pp. 74–91, March 2010

12. Jane Street Developers: Core library documentation (2016). https://ocaml.janestreet.com/ocaml-core/latest/doc/core/

13. Jespersen, T.B.L., Munksgaard, P., Larsen, K.F.: Session types for rust. In: Proceedings of the 11th ACM SIGPLAN Workshop on Generic Programming (WGP 2015), pp. 13–22. ACM (2015)

14. Jones, M.P.: Type classes with functional dependencies. In: Smolka, G. (ed.) ESOP 2000. LNCS, vol. 1782, pp. 230–244. Springer, Heidelberg (2000). doi:10.1007/3-540-46425-5_15

15. Kmett, E.: Lenses, folds and traversals (2012). http://lens.github.io/

16. Lindley, S., Morris, J.G.: Embedding session types in Haskell. In: Proceedings of the 9th International Symposium on Haskell (Haskell 2016), pp. 133–145. ACM (2016)

17. Milner, R.: Communicating and Mobile Systems: The π-Calculus. Cambridge University Press, Cambridge (1999)

18. Neubauer, M., Thiemann, P.: An implementation of session types. In: Jayaraman, B. (ed.) PADL 2004. LNCS, vol. 3057, pp. 56–70. Springer, Heidelberg (2004). doi:10.1007/978-3-540-24836-1_5

19. Ng, N., Figueiredo Coutinho, J.G., Yoshida, N.: Protocols by default. In: Franke, B. (ed.) CC 2015. LNCS, vol. 9031, pp. 212–232. Springer, Heidelberg (2015). doi:10.1007/978-3-662-46663-6_11

20. Orchard, D., Yoshida, N.: Effects as sessions, sessions as effects. In: 43th Annual ACM SIGPLAN-SIGACT Symposium on Principles of Programming Languages (POPL 2016), pp. 568–581. ACM (2016)

21. Orchard, D., Yoshida, N.: Sessions types with linearity in Haskell. In: Gay, S.J., Ravara, A. (eds.) Behavioural Types: From Theory to Tools. River Publishers (2017)

22. Padovani, L.: A simple library implementation of binary sessions. J. Funct. Program. **27**, e4 (2016)

23. Padovani, L.: Context-free session type inference. In: Yang, H. (ed.) ESOP 2017. LNCS, vol. 10201, pp. 804–830. Springer, Heidelberg (2017). doi:10.1007/978-3-662-54434-1_30

24. Pierce, B.C.: Recursive types. In: Types and Programming Languages, Chap. 20, pp. 267–280. MIT Press (2002)

25. Polakow, J.: Embedding a full linear lambda calculus in Haskell. In: Proceedings of the 2015 ACM SIGPLAN Symposium on Haskell (Haskell 2015), pp. 177–188. ACM (2015)

26. Pucella, R., Tov, J.A.: Haskell session types with (almost) no class. In: Proceedings of the First ACM SIGPLAN Symposium on Haskell (Haskell 2008), pp. 25–36. ACM (2008)
27. Scalas, A., Yoshida, N.: Lightweight session programming in scala. In: 30th European Conference on Object-Oriented Programming (ECOOP 2016). LIPIcs, vol. 56, pp. 21:1–21:28. Dagstuhl (2016)
28. Scribble Project homepage. www.scribble.org
29. Thiemann, P., Vasconcelos, V.T.: Context-free session types. In: Proceedings of the 21st ACM SIGPLAN International Conference on Functional Programming (ICFP 2016), pp. 462–475 (2016)
30. Wadler, P.: Propositions as sessions. In: Proceedings of the 17th ACM SIGPLAN International Conference on Functional Programming (ICFP 2012), pp. 273–286. ACM (2012)
31. White, L., Bour, F., Yallop, J.: Modular implicits. In: ACM SIGPLAN ML Family Workshop (ML 2014), vol. 198, pp. 22–63. Electronic Proceedings in Theoretical Computer Science (2015)
32. Yoshida, N., Vasconcelos, V.T.: Language primitives and type discipline for structured communication-based programming revisited: two systems for higher-order session communication. Electron. Notes Theor. Comput. Sci. **171**(4), 73–93 (2007)

Retractable and Speculative Contracts

Franco Barbanera[1]([⊠]), Ivan Lanese[2], and Ugo de'Liguoro[3]

[1] University of Catania, Catania, Italy
barba@dmi.unict.it
[2] Dipartimento di Informatica - Scienza e Ingegneria,
University of Bologna/INRIA, Bologna, Italy
ivan.lanese@gmail.com
[3] Dipartimento di Informatica, University of Torino, Torino, Italy
ugo.deliguoro@unito.it

Abstract. *Behavioral contracts* are abstract descriptions of the communications that clients and servers perform. Behavioral contracts come naturally equipped with a notion of *compliance*: when a client and a server follow compliant contracts, their interaction is guaranteed to progress or successfully complete. We study two extensions of contracts, dealing respectively with *backtracking* and with *speculative execution*. We show that the two extensions give rise to *the same notion of compliance*. As a consequence, they also give rise to the same *subcontract relation*, which determines when one server can be replaced by another preserving compliance. Moreover, compliance and subcontract relation are both decidable in polynomial time.

1 Introduction

Binary behavioral contracts [14,15,27] and binary session types [22] are abstractions of programs used to statically ensure that a client and a server interact successfully (see the survey in [24]). Along the years, the basic theory has been extended to deal with many features of clients and servers, such as exceptions [12], time [9], and so on. We consider here two new features: *backtracking*, allowing one to go back to previous stages of the interaction, and *speculative execution* [30], allowing one to try different alternatives concurrently. These two features have quite different origin and aims. Backtracking is used to avoid failures due to wrong past decisions in a wide range of settings, from the undo button

---

This work was partially supported by the COST Action IC1405 on "Reversible computation - extending horizons of computing". The first and third authors were partially supported also by the COST Action EUTYPES CA-15123 and, respectively, Project FIR 1B8C1 of the University of Catania and Project FORMS 2015 of Turin. We thank Mariangiola Dezani-Ciancaglini for interesting discussions and useful suggestions.

Published by Springer International Publishing AG 2017. All Rights Reserved
J.-M. Jacquet and M. Massink (Eds.): COORDINATION 2017, LNCS 10319, pp. 119–137, 2017.
DOI: 10.1007/978-3-319-59746-1_7

in web browsers, to the execution model of Prolog, to techniques for rollback-recovery [1]. Speculative execution is used for efficiency reasons in different areas, from simulation [13], to thread-level optimization [31], to web services [16].

We present two extensions of binary contracts (Sect. 2): *retractable contracts* capturing backtracking, and *speculative contracts* capturing speculative execution. The two extensions are based on the same syntax, but naturally have different semantics. Essentially, they add to the session contracts of [3,10] (called first-order session behaviors in [3]) an operator of *external choice among output* operations. The most interesting case is when an external choice among outputs and an external choice among inputs interact. In the retractable semantics, the client and the server agree on which option to explore, but they rollback and try a different possibility if the computation gets stuck. In the speculative semantics all the possibilities are explored concurrently, and it is enough for one of them to succeed to guarantee the success of the whole computation.

This paper defines retractable and speculative contracts, and studies the related theory, considering the notions of *compliance* (Sect. 3), guaranteeing that the interaction progresses or successfully completes, *subcontract relation* (Sect. 4), determining when a server (resp. client) can be replaced by another server (resp. client) preserving compliance, and *dual contract* (Sect. 4), that is the most general contract (in terms of the subcontract relation) compliant with a given contract. Our analysis provides two main insights:

- Even if retractable contracts and speculative contracts have different semantics and give rise to different client-server interactions, the relations of compliance, subcontract and duality in the two settings do coincide. While surprising at first sight, this can be explained by noticing that in both the cases different alternatives are explored (sequentially for retractable contracts, in parallel for speculative contracts) and the success of one of them guarantees the success of the whole computation. In other terms, the two semantics provide different implementations of *angelic nondeterminism*, first described by Hoare [21].
- While retractable/speculative contracts are strictly more expressive than session contracts (indeed they are a conservative extension, see Sect. 3.1), their theory preserves the main good properties of the theory of session contracts. In particular, compliance and subcontract relations are both decidable (Sect. 3) in polynomial time (Sect. 5), and the dual of a contract always exists and has a simple syntactic characterization (Sect. 4).

A natural way to ensure the existence of the dual contract is to introduce an operator of internal choice among inputs. While this operator has limited practical impact, it makes the model more symmetric and the mathematical treatment simpler.

A few preliminary results on the topic of this paper have been presented in a workshop paper [7], which considers *retractable session contracts*, i.e., retractable contracts without internal choice among inputs. The main result of [7] is the decidability of the compliance relation (while we study here also the complexity), which was obtained via an algorithm that we now know to be exponential. Here we present a more refined, polynomial one (Fig. 7). In [7] the subcontract relation and the dual contract were not studied, and indeed the dual contract did not exist due to the absence of internal choice among inputs.

Proofs, additional examples and additional background material are available in a companion technical report [8].

2   Contracts for Retractable and Speculative Interactions

We present below a uniform syntax for retractable and speculative contracts, with two semantics. It can be obtained from the syntax of session contracts of [3,10] (called first-order session behaviors in [3]), that we dub here SC, just adding external retractable/speculative choice among outputs and internal choice among inputs. As a matter of fact our contracts can also be seen as an extension of the retractable session contracts of [7], that we dub here rC, simply adding internal choice among inputs. Basics of session contracts and retractable session contracts are recalled in the companion technical report [8].

Definition 1 (Retractable/Speculative Contracts). *Let* $\mathcal{N}$ *(set of names) be some countable set of symbols and let* $\overline{\mathcal{N}}$ *(set of conames) be* $\{\overline{a} \mid a \in \mathcal{N}\}$, *with* $\mathcal{N} \cap \overline{\mathcal{N}} = \emptyset$. *The set* **rsC** *of* retractable/speculative contracts *is defined as the set of the* closed *expressions generated by the following grammar,*

$$
\sigma, \rho := \mid \; \mathbf{1} \qquad\qquad\qquad \text{SUCCESS}
$$
$$
\mid \; \textstyle\sum_{i \in I} a_i.\sigma_i \qquad \text{EXTERNAL INPUT CHOICE}
$$
$$
\mid \; \textstyle\sum_{i \in I} \overline{a}_i.\sigma_i \qquad \text{EXTERNAL OUTPUT CHOICE}
$$
$$
\mid \; \textstyle\bigoplus_{i \in I} a_i.\sigma_i \qquad \text{INTERNAL INPUT CHOICE}
$$
$$
\mid \; \textstyle\bigoplus_{i \in I} \overline{a}_i.\sigma_i \qquad \text{INTERNAL OUTPUT CHOICE}
$$
$$
\mid \; x \qquad\qquad\qquad \text{VARIABLE}
$$
$$
\mid \; \mathsf{rec}\, x.\sigma \qquad\qquad \text{RECURSION}
$$

where I *is non-empty and finite, the names and the conames in choices are pairwise distinct and* σ *is not a variable in* $\mathsf{rec}\, x.\sigma$.

Recursion in **rsC** is guarded and hence contractive in the usual sense. We take an equi-recursive view of recursion by equating $\mathsf{rec}\, x.\sigma$ with $\sigma[\mathsf{rec}\, x.\sigma/x]$. We use α to range over $\mathcal{N} \cup \overline{\mathcal{N}}$, with the convention $\overline{\alpha} = \overline{a}$ if $\alpha = a$, and $\overline{\alpha} = a$ if $\alpha = \overline{a}$. We write $\alpha_1.\sigma_1 + \alpha_2.\sigma_2$ for binary external input/output choice and $\alpha_1.\sigma_1 \oplus \alpha_2.\sigma_2$ for binary internal input/output choice. They are both commutative by definition. Also, $\alpha.\sigma$ denotes both internal and external unary choice. This is not a source of confusion since internal and external choices do coincide in the unary case. We also write $\alpha_k.\sigma_k + \sigma'$ for $\sum_{i \in I} \alpha_i.\sigma_i$ where $k \in I$ and $\sigma' = \sum_{i \in (I \setminus \{k\})} \alpha_i.\sigma_i$ (and similarly for internal choices). When no ambiguity can arise, we call just *contracts* the expressions in **rsC**. They are written by omitting all trailing **1**'s.

We discuss below the two interpretations and the two semantics for our contracts: the retractable one, and the speculative one.

2.1   Retractable Semantics

The main novelty of the retractable semantics is that when an external choice among outputs and an external choice among inputs interact, the client and the server agree on which option to explore, but they rollback and try a different possibility if the computation gets stuck.

In order to deal with rollbacks, we decorate contracts with their history, which memorizes, for past choices, the alternatives that have been discharged and that can be tried upon rollback. We use 'o' to stand for no-remaining-alternatives.

Definition 2 (Contracts with History). *Let* Histories *be the expressions generated by the grammar* $H ::= \langle \rangle \mid H:\sigma$, *where* $\sigma \in$ rsC$\cup \{o\}$ *and* $o \notin$ rsC. *Histories are hence stacks of contracts and* o. *Then the set of contracts with history is defined by:*   rsCH $= \{H \ltimes \sigma \mid H \in$ Histories, $\sigma \in$ rsC $\cup \{o\}\}$.

We write just $\sigma_1 : \cdots : \sigma_k$ for the stack $(\cdots (\langle \rangle : \sigma_1) : \cdots) : \sigma_k$.

As standard for contracts, the definition of the retractable semantics is in two stages: we first define a labeled transition system (LTS) for contracts with history (Definition 3), and then we use it to define a reduction semantics for pairs of contracts representing one client and one server (Definition 4).

Definition 3 (Semantics of Contracts with History).

$$(+) \ H \ltimes \alpha.\sigma + \sigma' \xrightarrow{\alpha} H:\sigma' \ltimes \sigma \qquad (\oplus) \ H \ltimes \alpha.\sigma \oplus \sigma' \xrightarrow{\tau} H \ltimes \alpha.\sigma$$

$$(\alpha) \ H \ltimes \alpha.\sigma \xrightarrow{\alpha} H:o \ltimes \sigma \qquad (rb) \ H:\sigma' \ltimes \sigma \xrightarrow{rb} H \ltimes \sigma'$$

In the transition rule for external choice $(+)$, the action α is executed, and the discharged branches in σ' are memorized. In internal choice $(\oplus)$, instead, the selection of one branch is represented by a label τ, and the history H is unchanged. When a single action is executed (α), a 'o' is added to the history, meaning that the only possible branch has been tried and no alternative is left. Rule (rb) pops the contract at the top of the stack, replacing the current one with it.

The client/server interaction is modeled by the reduction of their parallel composition, that can be either *forward*, consisting of CCS-style synchronizations and single internal choices, or *backward*, only when there is no possible forward reduction, and the client is not satisfied, i.e., it is different from **1**.

Definition 4 (Semantics of Retractable Client/Server Pairs).
The following rules, plus the rule symmetric to (τ) *w.r.t.* $\|$, *define the relation* $\longrightarrow$ *over pairs of contracts with history:*

(comm)

$$\frac{H_1 \ltimes \rho \xrightarrow{\alpha} H_1' \ltimes \rho' \qquad H_2 \ltimes \sigma \xrightarrow{\overline{\alpha}} H_2' \ltimes \sigma'}{H_1 \ltimes \rho \parallel H_2 \ltimes \sigma \longrightarrow H_1' \ltimes \rho' \parallel H_2' \ltimes \sigma'}$$

(τ)

$$\frac{H_1 \ltimes \rho \xrightarrow{\tau} H_1 \ltimes \rho'}{H_1 \ltimes \rho \parallel H_2 \ltimes \sigma \longrightarrow H_1 \ltimes \rho' \parallel H_2 \ltimes \sigma}$$

(rbk)

$$\frac{H_1 \ltimes \rho \xrightarrow{rb} H_1' \ltimes \rho' \qquad H_2 \ltimes \sigma \xrightarrow{rb} H_2' \ltimes \sigma' \qquad \rho \neq \mathbf{1}}{H_1 \ltimes \rho \parallel H_2 \ltimes \sigma \longrightarrow H_1' \ltimes \rho' \parallel H_2' \ltimes \sigma'}$$

Rule (rbk) *applies only if neither* (comm) *nor* (τ) *do.*

The *forward reduction* $\longrightarrow_f$ is the relation generated by rules (τ) and (comm).

Remark 1. The semantics defined above for retractable client/server pairs can be seen as an instantiation on contracts of the standard reversible semantics for process calculi, see, e.g., [17,25,26,29]. In particular, the semantics would become a classic uncontrolled semantics (according to the terminology in [26]) by removing the four control mechanisms below:

1. the fact that only external choices are retractable;
2. the side condition $\rho \neq 1$ in rule (*rbk*), which disallows backtrack after success;
3. the fact that rule (*rbk*) can be applied only if no other rule applies, ensuring that backtrack is enabled only when no forward reduction is possible;
4. the fact that in external choices the selected path is not stored in the history, so that each path can be tried at most once.

These mechanisms provide a semantic control of reversibility [26], specifying which rollback steps are allowed, and when. We discuss in Remark 2 the impact that removing the above control mechanisms would have on retractable contracts and on their theory.

Example 1. Retractable contracts allow one to first try a preferred alternative, but to accept also another alternative if the first one proves to be impossible to obtain. In cloud computing settings, companies may hire virtual machines and storing facilities from cloud providers with some agreed Quality of Service (QoS). A company is willing to hire at some medium or low price a certain amount of machines for online elaboration during day time, but, if the price is too high, it is also willing to switch to offline night elaboration. In this last case it is only willing to pay a low price.

A retractable contract with this behavior may be written as:

$$\text{cloudClient} = \overline{\text{QoSday}}.(\text{priceMed}.\overline{\text{ok}} + \text{priceLow}.\overline{\text{ok}}) + \overline{\text{QoSnight}}.\text{priceLow}.\overline{\text{ok}}$$

Notice that the contract does not specify which alternative the client prefers: this aspect of the client behavior is abstracted away. A sample server is:

$$\text{cloudServer} = \textstyle\sum_{\text{QoS} \in \{\text{QoSday}, \text{QoSnight}, \dots\}} \text{QoS}.\overline{\text{price}_{\text{QoS}}}.\text{ok}$$

A sample interaction is described in Fig. 1, where we assume that

$$\text{price}_{\text{QoSday}} = \text{priceHigh} \quad \text{and} \quad \text{price}_{\text{QoSnight}} = \text{priceLow}.$$

2.2   Speculative Semantics

The main idea of the speculative semantics is that in an external output choice all the options are tried concurrently: if at least one of them succeeds, then the whole computation succeeds. In order to represent concurrent trials we need runtime contracts featuring multiple threads.

$$
\begin{array}{ccc}
& \langle\,\rangle \ltimes \begin{array}{l} \overline{\text{QoSday}}.(\text{priceMed}.\overline{\text{ok}} \\ \quad\quad + \text{priceLow}.\overline{\text{ok}}) \\ + \overline{\text{QoSnight}}.\text{priceLow}.\overline{\text{ok}} \end{array} & \| & \langle\,\rangle \ltimes \sum_{\text{QoS}} \text{QoS}.\overline{\text{price}}_{\text{QoS}}.\text{ok}
\end{array}
$$

$$
\longrightarrow \quad \begin{array}{l} \langle\,\rangle : \overline{\text{QoSnight}}.\text{priceLow}.\overline{\text{ok}} \\ \ltimes \text{priceMed}.\overline{\text{ok}} + \text{priceLow}.\overline{\text{ok}} \end{array} \quad \| \quad \begin{array}{l} \langle\,\rangle : \sum_{\text{QoS}\neq\text{QoSday}} \text{QoS}.\overline{\text{price}}_{\text{QoS}}.\text{ok} \\ \ltimes \quad \text{priceHigh}.\text{ok} \end{array}
$$

$$
\longrightarrow \quad \langle\,\rangle \ltimes \overline{\text{QoSnight}}.\text{priceLow}.\overline{\text{ok}} \quad \| \quad \langle\,\rangle \ltimes \sum_{\text{QoS}\neq\text{QoSday}} \text{QoS}.\overline{\text{price}}_{\text{QoS}}.\text{ok}
$$

$$
\longrightarrow \quad \langle\,\rangle : \circ \ltimes \text{priceLow}.\overline{\text{ok}} \quad \| \quad \begin{array}{l} \langle\,\rangle : \sum_{\text{QoS}\neq\text{QoSday,QoSnight}} \text{QoS}.\overline{\text{price}}_{\text{QoS}}.\text{ok} \\ \ltimes \quad \text{priceLow}.\text{ok} \end{array}
$$

$$
\longrightarrow \quad \langle\,\rangle : \circ : \circ \ltimes \overline{\text{ok}} \quad \| \quad \begin{array}{l} \langle\,\rangle : \sum_{\text{QoS}\neq\text{QoSday,QoSnight}} \text{QoS}.\overline{\text{price}}_{\text{QoS}}.\text{ok} : \circ \\ \ltimes \quad \text{ok} \end{array}
$$

$$
\longrightarrow \quad \langle\,\rangle : \circ : \circ : \circ \ltimes \mathbf{1} \quad \| \quad \begin{array}{l} \langle\,\rangle : \sum_{\text{QoS}\neq\text{QoSday,QoSnight}} \text{QoS}.\overline{\text{price}}_{\text{QoS}}.\text{ok} : \circ : \circ \\ \ltimes \quad \mathbf{1} \end{array}
$$

Fig. 1. An example of retractable interaction

Definition 5 (Contracts with Threads). Contracts with threads **C**, *used as runtime syntax for contracts, are parallel compositions of* threads **T**. *Each thread is a contract prefixed by a sequence (possibly empty) of actions uniquely identifying it.*

$$
\mathbf{C} ::= \mathbf{T} \mid (\mathbf{C} \mid \mathbf{T}) \mid (\mathbf{T} \mid \mathbf{C}) \qquad \mathbf{T} ::= \sigma \mid \alpha @ \mathbf{T}
$$

We assume the operator '|' to be associative and commutative.

As for the retractable semantics, the definition of the speculative semantics is in two stages: we first define an LTS for contracts with threads (Definition 6), and then we use it to define a reduction semantics for pairs of contracts with threads representing one client and one server (Definition 7).

Definition 6 (Semantics of Contracts with Threads).
In the LTS below, we use as labels actions $\alpha ::= a \mid \overline{a}$, *sequences of actions* $\beta ::= \alpha \mid \alpha\beta$, *and complex labels* $\beta_\tau ::= \tau \mid \beta \mid \beta, \mathbf{T}$.

$$
\begin{array}{lll}
\text{(Fork)} & \text{($\oplus$)} & \text{(α)} \\[4pt]
\alpha.\sigma + \sigma' \xrightarrow{\alpha,\sigma'} \alpha @ \sigma & \alpha.\sigma \oplus \sigma' \xrightarrow{\tau} \alpha.\sigma & \alpha.\sigma \xrightarrow{\alpha} \alpha @ \sigma
\end{array}
$$

$$
\begin{array}{ll}
\text{(@-α)} & \text{(@-α-T)} \\[4pt]
\dfrac{\mathbf{T} \xrightarrow{\beta} \mathbf{T}'}{\alpha @ \mathbf{T} \xrightarrow{\alpha\beta} \alpha @ \mathbf{T}'} & \dfrac{\mathbf{T} \xrightarrow{\beta,\mathbf{T}''} \mathbf{T}'}{\alpha @ \mathbf{T} \xrightarrow{\alpha\beta,\alpha @ \mathbf{T}''} \alpha @ \mathbf{T}'}
\end{array}
$$

$$
\begin{array}{ll}
\text{(@-τ)} & \text{(ParL)} \\[4pt]
\dfrac{\mathbf{T} \xrightarrow{\tau} \mathbf{T}'}{\alpha @ \mathbf{T} \xrightarrow{\tau} \alpha @ \mathbf{T}'} & \dfrac{\mathbf{T} \xrightarrow{\beta_\tau} \mathbf{T}'}{\mathbf{T} \mid \mathbf{C} \xrightarrow{\beta_\tau} \mathbf{T}' \mid \mathbf{C}}
\end{array}
$$

In the rule for external choice $(Fork)$, when an action α is executed, its continuation σ is prefixed by it. The other branches σ' need to be executed in a freshly spawned thread. Since such thread needs to be installed at top level, σ' is added to the label, and the actual installation is performed at the level of speculative client/server pairs (see rule $(comm)$ in Definition 7). The rule for internal choice ($\oplus$) simply selects one of the available options. A unary choice (α) executes the action α and prefixes with it the continuation σ.

Because of rules $(@-\alpha)$, $(@-\alpha-T)$, and $(@-\tau)$, execution is allowed below an @ prefix. In rule $(@-\alpha)$, the prefix itself is added to the label β. Prefixes uniquely identify threads, and ensure that each thread interacts only with the one with dual prefix which is running on the communication partner. This is specified in Definition 7 below. Rule $(@-\alpha-T)$ is analogous to rule $(@-\alpha)$, but the label also contains a thread $\mathbf{T}''$, and the prefix α is added to both β and $\mathbf{T}''$. No prefix is added to τ actions, propagated by rule $(@-\tau)$. Rule $(ParL)$ simply allows components of a parallel composition to execute (a symmetric rule is not needed thanks to the commutativity of $|$).

The interaction of a client with a server is modeled by the reduction of their parallel composition.

Definition 7 (Semantics of Speculative Client/Server Pairs).

The following rules, plus the rule symmetric to (τ) w.r.t. $\|$, define the relation $\longrightarrow$ over pairs of contracts with threads. In the LTS below, $?\mathbf{T}$ denotes either the thread $\mathbf{T}$ or nothing. Hence, $\beta, ?\mathbf{T}$ and $\mathbf{C} | ?\mathbf{T}$ are respectively β and $\mathbf{C}$ if $?\mathbf{T}$ is nothing, and $\beta, \mathbf{T}$ and $\mathbf{C} | \mathbf{T}$ otherwise. Also, the duality operator extends from actions to sequences: $\overline{\alpha\beta} = \overline{\alpha}\,\overline{\beta}$.

$(comm)$

$$\frac{\mathbf{C} \xrightarrow{\beta, ?\mathbf{T}} \mathbf{C}' \quad \mathbf{C}'' \xrightarrow{\overline{\beta}, ?\mathbf{T}''} \mathbf{C}'''}{\mathbf{C} \parallel \mathbf{C}'' \longrightarrow \mathbf{C}' \, |?\mathbf{T} \parallel \mathbf{C}''' \, |?\mathbf{T}''}$$

(τ)

$$\frac{\mathbf{C} \xrightarrow{\tau} \mathbf{C}'}{\mathbf{C} \parallel \mathbf{C}'' \longrightarrow \mathbf{C}' \parallel \mathbf{C}''}$$

Rule $(comm)$ allows threads performing dual sequences of actions to interact. This implies that both the actual actions and the prefixes of the threads performing them should be dual. Threads in the labels, if present, are installed in parallel. Rule (τ) simply propagates the τ action.

Example 2. A server provides access to multiple algorithms for SAT solving [35]. A client first sends the problem instance to be solved, then selects the algorithm, and finally sends the relevant parameters. The server computes the solution according to the received commands, and sends it back. Since the most efficient technique depends on the problem instance [34], the server supports speculative execution, to allow one to try different algorithms at the same time (this is called the portfolio approach). The server contract is described by:

$$\mathsf{SATserver} = \mathtt{inst}.\sum_i \mathtt{alg}_i.\sum_j \mathtt{par}_j.\overline{\mathtt{sol}}$$

A simple client that tries both the DPLL approach and the walksat approach can be modeled as follows:

$$\mathsf{SATclient} = \overline{\mathtt{inst}}.(\overline{\mathtt{DPLL}}.\overline{\mathtt{par}}.\mathtt{sol} + \overline{\mathtt{walksat}}.\overline{\mathtt{par}}.\mathtt{sol})$$

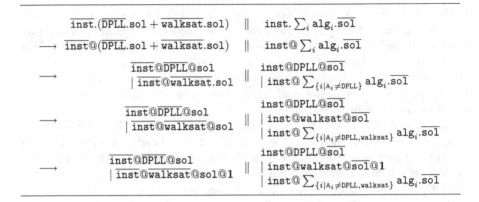

Fig. 2. An example of speculative interaction

A sample computation proceeds as described in Fig. 2, assuming that the server supports both DPLL and walksat. To keep the example simple we drop the choice of parameters. Let us see in more details how the creation of threads is managed. The first reduction in Fig. 2 is due to rule (*comm*), since

$$\overline{\text{inst}}.(\overline{\text{DPLL}}.\text{sol} + \overline{\text{walksat}}.\text{sol}) \xrightarrow{\overline{\text{inst}}} \overline{\text{inst}}@(\overline{\text{DPLL}}.\text{sol} + \overline{\text{walksat}}.\text{sol})$$

and

$$\text{inst}.\sum_i \text{alg}_i.\overline{\text{sol}} \xrightarrow{\text{inst}} \text{inst}@\sum_i \text{alg}_i.\overline{\text{sol}}.$$

The second reduction is also due to rule (*comm*), since, on the client side

$$\frac{\overline{\overline{\text{DPLL}}.\text{sol} + \overline{\text{walksat}}.\text{sol}} \xrightarrow{\overline{\text{DPLL}}, \overline{\text{walksat}}.\text{sol}} \overline{\text{DPLL}}@\text{sol}}{\overline{\text{inst}}@(\overline{\text{DPLL}}.\text{sol} + \overline{\text{walksat}}.\text{sol}) \xrightarrow{\overline{\text{inst}\,\text{DPLL}}, \overline{\text{inst}@\text{walksat}}.\text{sol}} \overline{\text{inst}}@\overline{\text{DPLL}}@\text{sol}} \text{(@-α-T)}$$
(Fork)

whereas, on the server side,

$$\frac{\sum_i \text{alg}_i.\overline{\text{sol}} \xrightarrow{\text{DPLL}, \sum_{\{i\,|\,A_i \neq \text{DPLL}\}} \text{alg}_i.\overline{\text{sol}}} \text{DPLL}@\overline{\text{sol}}}{\text{inst}@\sum_i \text{alg}_i.\overline{\text{sol}} \xrightarrow{\text{inst}\,\text{DPLL}, \text{inst}@\sum_{\{i\,|\,A_i \neq \text{DPLL}\}} \text{alg}_i.\overline{\text{sol}}} \text{inst}@\text{DPLL}@\overline{\text{sol}}} \text{(@-α-T)}$$
(Fork)

3 Compliance

The compliance relation for session contracts [3,10] consists in requiring that, whenever no reduction is possible, all client's requests and offers have been satisfied, i.e. the client is in the success state **1**. For retractable contracts, thanks to the retractable operational semantics taking care of forward and backward reductions, we can adopt the same definition. We use $\overset{*}{\longrightarrow}$ to denote the reflexive and transitive closure of $\longrightarrow$, and $\not\longrightarrow$ to specify that no $\longrightarrow$ reduction exists.

Definition 8 (Retractable Compliance Relation $\dashv\vdash^R$).

(i) The relation $\dashv\vdash^R$ on contracts with history is defined by:
$$H_1 \ltimes \rho \dashv\vdash^R H_2 \ltimes \sigma \quad \text{if, for each } H_1', H_2', \rho', \sigma' \text{ such that}$$
$$H_1 \ltimes \rho \parallel H_2 \ltimes \sigma \overset{*}{\longrightarrow} H_1' \ltimes \rho' \parallel H_2' \ltimes \sigma' \not\longrightarrow, \quad \text{we have} \quad \rho' = 1$$
(ii) The relation $\dashv\vdash^R$ on contracts is defined by: $\rho \dashv\vdash^R \sigma$ *if* $\langle\,\rangle\ltimes\rho \dashv\vdash^R \langle\,\rangle\ltimes\sigma$.

For speculative contracts we need to take into account the fact that the whole computation succeeds if at least one of its branches succeeds.

Definition 9 (Speculative Compliance Relation $\dashv\vdash^S$).
The relation $\dashv\vdash^S$ on contracts is defined by:

$$\rho \dashv\vdash^S \sigma \quad \text{if} \quad \text{for each } \mathbf{C}_\rho, \mathbf{C}_\sigma \text{ such that } \rho \parallel \sigma \overset{*}{\longrightarrow} \mathbf{C}_\rho \parallel \mathbf{C}_\sigma \not\longrightarrow$$
$$\text{there exist } \mathbf{C}, n, \alpha_1, \ldots, \alpha_n \text{ such that } \mathbf{C}_\rho = \mathbf{C} \mid \alpha_1 @ \ldots @ \alpha_n @ \mathbf{1}$$

We now provide a formal system characterizing compliance on both retractable and speculative contracts.

Definition 10 (Formal System for Compliance ▷).
Judgments in the formal system ▷ are expressions of the form $\Gamma \rhd \rho \dashv \sigma$, where the environment Γ is a finite set of expressions of the form $\delta \dashv \gamma$, with $\rho, \sigma, \delta, \gamma \in$ rsC. Axioms and rules are as in Fig. 3.

$(\textsc{Ax})$
$$\Gamma \rhd \mathbf{1} \dashv \sigma$$

$(\textsc{Hyp})$
$$\Gamma, \rho \dashv \sigma \rhd \rho \dashv \sigma$$

$(+\cdot+)$
$$\frac{\Gamma, \alpha.\rho + \rho' \dashv \overline{\alpha}.\sigma + \sigma' \ \rhd \ \rho \dashv \sigma}{\Gamma \ \rhd \ \alpha.\rho + \rho' \dashv \overline{\alpha}.\sigma + \sigma'}$$

$(\oplus \cdot +)$
$$\frac{\forall h \in I. \ \Gamma, \bigoplus_{i\in I}\overline{\alpha}_i.\rho_i \dashv \sum_{j\in I\cup J}\alpha_j.\sigma_j \ \rhd \ \rho_h \dashv \sigma_h}{\Gamma \ \rhd \ \bigoplus_{i\in I}\overline{\alpha}_i.\rho_i \dashv \sum_{j\in I\cup J}\alpha_j.\sigma_j}$$

$(+\cdot \oplus)$
$$\frac{\forall h \in I. \ \Gamma, \sum_{j\in I\cup J}\overline{\alpha}_j.\rho_j \dashv \bigoplus_{i\in I}\alpha_i.\sigma_i \ \rhd \ \rho_h \dashv \sigma_h}{\Gamma \ \rhd \ \sum_{j\in I\cup J}\overline{\alpha}_j.\rho_j \dashv \bigoplus_{i\in I}\alpha_i.\sigma_i}$$

Fig. 3. System ▷

The only non standard rule of system ▷ is $(+\cdot+)$, which ensures compliance of two external choices when they contain respectively (at least) *one* α and the corresponding $\overline{\alpha}$, followed by compliant contracts. This contrasts with the rules $(\oplus \cdot +)$ and $(+ \cdot \oplus)$, where *each* α in an internal choice must have a corresponding $\overline{\alpha}$ in the external choice, followed by compliant contracts. No rule is provided for the case $(\oplus \cdot \oplus)$ since two internal choices are compliant only if both of them are unary choices (otherwise they may always get stuck by choosing incompatible actions). Since unary internal choice coincides with unary external choice, this case is taken into account by the rules we already have. Notice that rule $(+ \cdot +)$ implicitly represents the fact that, in the decision procedure for two contracts made of external choices, the possible synchronizing branches have to be tried, until either a successful one is found or all fail. Looking at a derivation bottom-up, at each application of a rule, the considered pair of contracts is added to the environment Γ. In this way, if the same pair is reached again due to the equi-recursive view of contracts, the derivation can be closed using rule (Hyp). Rule (Ax) instead closes the derivation when the client reaches the success state 1. We write $\rhd \rho \dashv \sigma$ instead of $\Gamma \rhd \rho \dashv \sigma$ when Γ is empty.

Derivability in system $\rhd$ is decidable, since it is syntax-directed and proof reconstruction does terminate.

Theorem 1. *Derivability in the formal system $\rhd$ is decidable.*

We can prove the soundness and the completeness of the formal system $\rhd$ w.r.t. both the retractable and the speculative semantics (see [8] for the proofs).

Theorem 2 (Retractable Soundness and Completeness).

$$\rhd \rho \dashv \sigma \quad \text{iff} \quad \rho \dashv^R \sigma$$

Theorem 3 (Speculative Soundness and Completeness).

$$\rhd \rho \dashv \sigma \quad \text{iff} \quad \rho \dashv^S \sigma$$

By the soundness and completeness of system $\rhd$ w.r.t. both the relations of retractable and speculative compliance, we immediately get that the two compliance relations do coincide.

Corollary 1 (Retractable and Speculative Compliances Coincide).

$$\dashv^R \quad = \quad \dashv^S$$

By the above, from now on we write $\dashv$ instead of $\dashv^R$ or $\dashv^S$. So the following also easily follows.

Corollary 2 (Compliance Decidability). *The relation $\dashv$ is decidable.*

Remark 2 We now discuss the impact on the compliance relation of the four mechanisms for controlling reversibility in the semantics of retractable client/server pairs (see Remark 1). In particular, we analyze what would happen by dropping each one of them in isolation:

Drop "Not all reductions are retractable": each reduction could be undone. From the compliance point of view, all the choices would be retractable. Hence, retractable contracts would not be a conservative extension (see Subsect. 3.1) of session contracts any more. The case we consider is strictly more general, since we allow for both retractable and unretractable choices.

Drop the side condition $\rho \neq 1$ in rule (rbk) of Definition 4: any forward finite interaction would be followed by a rollback. In particular, most of the client/server pairs without recursion (except a few trivial ones, like $\langle\,\rangle\ltimes 1 \parallel \langle\,\rangle\ltimes\sigma$) would end into $\langle\,\rangle\ltimes \circ \parallel \langle\,\rangle\ltimes\circ$. Thus all these pairs of contracts would not be compliant.

Drop "rule (rbk) can be applied only if no other rule applies": interactions could rollback before succeeding. As in the case above, most client/server pairs (except a few trivial ones, but including recursive ones) could reduce to $\langle\,\rangle\ltimes \circ \parallel \langle\,\rangle\ltimes\circ$. Again all these pairs of contracts would not be compliant.

Drop "in choices the chosen path is not memorized": any client/server pair that would not normally succeed with at least one retractable choice could diverge by undoing and redoing the choice forever, thus trivially ensuring compliance.

None of the last three scenarios provides a reasonable setting. The first one would be reasonable, but the case we consider is strictly more general.

3.1 Conservativity Results

It is possible to show that all the relations on our retractable and speculative contracts (**rsC**) are conservative extensions of corresponding notions on (first-order) session contracts (**SC**) as defined in [3,10], and on the retractable session contracts (**rC**) as defined in [7].

As previously said, it is not difficult to check that session contracts **SC** are a subset of retractable session contracts **rC**, which, in turn, are a subset of the contracts **rsC** we are presently investigating, namely: $\mathsf{SC} \subsetneq \mathsf{rC} \subsetneq \mathsf{rsC}$. Obviously the strict inclusion $\mathsf{SC} \subsetneq \mathsf{rsC}$ is not enough, by itself, to guarantee the retractable and speculative operational semantics for **rsC** to be conservative extensions of the operational semantics of **SC**. We prove that it is so in the following Proposition 1. Informally, it states that both the forward retractable semantics $\longrightarrow_f$ and the speculative semantics $\longrightarrow$ of pairs of contracts in **SC** are annotated versions of their semantics in **SC** (recalled in the companion technical report [8]).

Proposition 1 (Operational Semantics Conservativity). *Let $\rho, \sigma \in \mathsf{SC}$.*

(i) $\rho \parallel \sigma \xrightarrow{*}_{\mathsf{SC}} \rho' \parallel \sigma'$ *iff* $H_1 \ltimes \rho \parallel H_2 \ltimes \sigma \xrightarrow{*}_f H_1' \ltimes \rho' \parallel H_2' \ltimes \sigma'$
for some H_1, H_2, H_1' *and* H_2'

(ii) $\rho \parallel \sigma \xrightarrow{*}_{\mathsf{SC}} \rho' \parallel \sigma'$ *iff* $\rho \parallel \sigma \xrightarrow{*} \alpha_1@\ldots\alpha_n@\rho' \mid \mathbf{C}_\rho \parallel \overline{\alpha_1}@\ldots\overline{\alpha_n}@\sigma' \mid \mathbf{C}_\sigma$
for some $n, \alpha_1, \ldots, \alpha_n, \mathbf{C}_\rho$ *and* $\mathbf{C}_\sigma$

where $\longrightarrow_{SC}$ *denotes the reduction relation on* SC *pairs in the theory of session contracts.*

We do not take into account conservativity of the retractable operational semantics for rsC over the one for rC because it is quite trivial, since the rules in the two semantics are essentially the same. A conservativity result of the speculative operational semantics for rsC over the one for rC would instead consist in a rather cumbersome and uninteresting statement.

The conservativity result for the operational semantics is not enough, in itself, to guarantee the theory of retractable compliance for rsC to be a conservative extension of both the theory of compliance for rC and for SC. Also in this case, however, we can prove it to be so, that is, the compliance relation for session contracts SC is the restriction of the compliance relation $\dashv\vdash$ for our contracts to pairs of session contracts SC, and similarly for the restriction of $\dashv\vdash$ to retractable session contracts rC.

Proposition 2 (Compliances Conservativity).

(i) *Let* $\rho, \sigma \in$ SC: $\quad \rho \dashv\vdash_{SC} \sigma \quad$ iff $\quad \rho \dashv\vdash \sigma$
(ii) *Let* $\rho, \sigma \in$ rC: $\quad \rho \dashv\vdash_{rC} \sigma \quad$ iff $\quad \rho \dashv\vdash \sigma$

4   Duality and the Subcontract Relation

Unlike the retractable session contracts of [7], in the present setting it is possible to get a natural notion of *duality*. The dual $\overline{\sigma}$ of an element σ of rsC is obtained, as for session contracts, by interchanging any name a with $\overline{a}$ and $+$ with $\oplus$.

The notion of dual contract allows one to combine pairs of contracts in the compliance relation, as follows:

Proposition 3. *For any* $\rho, \sigma, \sigma' \in$ rsC, $\rho \dashv\vdash \sigma$ *and* $\overline{\sigma} \dashv\vdash \sigma'$ *imply* $\rho \dashv\vdash \sigma'$

We will provide further properties of duality using the notion of subcontract relation. Indeed, the notion of compliance naturally induces a substitutability relation on servers, denoted $\preccurlyeq_s$, that we call *subcontract relation for servers*. Such a relation may be used for implementing contract-based query engines (see [28] for a detailed discussion). An analogous subcontract relation, denoted $\preccurlyeq_c$, can be defined for clients.

Definition 11 (Subcontract Relations for Servers and for Clients). *Let* $\sigma, \sigma' \in$ rsC. *We define*

(i) $\sigma \preccurlyeq_s \sigma' \triangleq \forall \rho \in$ rsC $[\rho \dashv\vdash \sigma$ *implies* $\rho \dashv\vdash \sigma']$
(ii) $\sigma \preccurlyeq_c \sigma' \triangleq \forall \rho \in$ rsC $[\sigma \dashv\vdash \rho$ *implies* $\sigma' \dashv\vdash \rho]$

Using Proposition 3 we can characterize both $\preccurlyeq_s$ and $\preccurlyeq_c$ in terms of duality and compliance, relate them and get their decidability.

Theorem 4. *For any* $\sigma, \sigma' \in$ rsC:

(i) $\sigma \preccurlyeq_s \sigma'$ iff $\overline{\sigma} \dashv\vdash \sigma'$
(ii) $\sigma \preccurlyeq_c \sigma'$ iff $\sigma' \dashv\vdash \overline{\sigma}$
(iii) $\sigma \preccurlyeq_s \sigma'$ iff $\overline{\sigma'} \preccurlyeq_c \overline{\sigma}$
(iv) $\sigma \preccurlyeq_s \sigma'$ and $\sigma \preccurlyeq_c \sigma'$ are decidable.

By item (iii) above, from now on we can simply concentrate on the relation $\preccurlyeq_s$.

We can now characterize duality in terms of the subcontract relation for servers: given a client ρ, its dual $\overline{\rho}$ is a least element among all its possible servers, that is it is a possible server, and it is smaller than all the other possible servers.

Proposition 4 (Dual as a Least Element w.r.t. $\preccurlyeq_s$).
Let $\rho \in \mathbf{rsC}$. *Then* $\overline{\rho}$ *is a server for* ρ, *namely* $\rho \dashv\vdash \overline{\rho}$, *and more precisely it is a least element in the set of the servers of* ρ, *that is,*
$$\forall \sigma \in \mathbf{rsC}: \ \rho \dashv\vdash \sigma \ \text{implies} \ \overline{\rho} \preccurlyeq_s \sigma$$

Since we have not yet proved that the subcontract relation is a partial order, we do not know yet whether $\overline{\rho}$ is also a minimal, i.e. there is no smaller element, neither whether other least elements or minimal elements exist. These questions will be answered by Proposition 5.

As done for the compliance relation, we characterize now the subcontract relation for servers in terms of derivability in the following formal system, where the symbol $\ll$ is used as syntactical counterpart of the relation $\preccurlyeq_s$.

Definition 12 (Formal System for Subcontract $\blacktriangleright$). *Judgments in the formal system* $\blacktriangleright$ *are expressions of the form* $\Gamma \blacktriangleright \rho \ll \sigma$, *where the environment* Γ *is a finite set of expressions of the form* $\delta \ll \gamma$, *with* $\rho, \sigma, \delta, \gamma \in \mathbf{rsC}$. *Axioms and rules are as in Fig. 4.*

$(\text{Ax-}\preccurlyeq_s)$
$\Gamma \blacktriangleright \mathbf{1} \ll \sigma'$

$(\text{Hyp-}\preccurlyeq_s)$
$\Gamma, \sigma \ll \sigma' \blacktriangleright \sigma \ll \sigma'$

$(\oplus \cdot + \text{-}\preccurlyeq_s)$
$$\frac{\Gamma, \alpha.\sigma_1 \oplus \sigma_2 \ll \alpha.\sigma_1' + \sigma_2' \blacktriangleright \sigma_1 \ll \sigma_1'}{\Gamma \blacktriangleright \alpha.\sigma_1 \oplus \sigma_2 \ll \alpha.\sigma_1' + \sigma_2'}$$

$(+ \cdot + \text{-}\preccurlyeq_s)$
$$\frac{\forall h \in I. \ \Gamma, \sum_{i \in I} \alpha_i.\sigma_i \ll \sum_{j \in I \cup J} \alpha_j.\sigma_j' \blacktriangleright \sigma_h \ll \sigma_h'}{\Gamma \blacktriangleright \sum_{i \in I} \alpha_i.\sigma_i \ll \sum_{j \in I \cup J} \alpha_j.\sigma_j'}$$

$(\oplus \cdot \oplus \text{-}\preccurlyeq_s)$
$$\frac{\forall h \in I. \ \Gamma, \bigoplus_{j \in I \cup J} \alpha_j.\sigma_j \ll \bigoplus_{i \in I} \alpha_i.\sigma_i' \blacktriangleright \sigma_h \ll \sigma_h'}{\Gamma \blacktriangleright \bigoplus_{j \in I \cup J} \alpha_j.\sigma_j' \ll \bigoplus_{i \in I} \alpha_i.\sigma_i'}$$

Fig. 4. The formal system $\blacktriangleright$

The rules in system $\blacktriangleright$ can be read as a translation of the rules in system $\rhd$ via Theorem 4(i). As for $\rhd$, in $\Gamma \blacktriangleright \rho \ll \sigma$ we may drop Γ if empty.

System $\blacktriangleright$ is sound and complete for the subcontract relation $\preccurlyeq_s$.

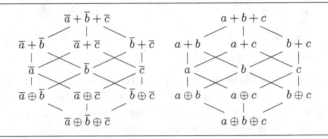

Fig. 5. Subcontract preorder: a sample

Theorem 5 (Soundness and Completeness of ►). ► $\sigma \ll \sigma'$ *iff* $\sigma \preccurlyeq_s \sigma'$

System ► can be used to show that $\preccurlyeq_s$ is a partial order and hence, by antisymmetry, $\overline{\rho}$ is also the minimum server of ρ: it is minimal, hence there is no smaller server, and there is a unique minimal.

Proposition 5. $\preccurlyeq_s$ *is a partial order* $\wedge$ $\forall \rho \in \mathbf{rsC}$, $\overline{\rho}$ *is the minimum server of* ρ.

The structure of the partial order is shown in Fig. 5, where the relations between terms with a unique choice among actions a, b, c, $\overline{a}$, $\overline{b}$ and $\overline{c}$ are pictured.

Remark 3. Analogously to what done in Subsect. 3.1, one can show the subcontract relation $\preccurlyeq_s$ to be a conservative extension of the corresponding notion in SC. Moreover, the restriction of $\preccurlyeq_s$ to $\mathbf{rC}$ provides a suitable notion of subcontract for $\mathbf{rC}$ (which has never been studied before).

5   Complexity Issues

One can define a decision procedure for compliance as the recursive proof-search algorithm obtained by reading *bottom-up* the rules of the formal system for compliance in Fig. 3. A similar algorithm is described in [7]. We show below that such an algorithm is strictly exponential.

To show it, roughly, it is possible to adapt the example presented in [20](Sect. 11) concerning the subtyping relation for recursive arrow and product types.

For each $n \in \mathbb{N}$ we define two contracts ρ_n and σ_n by induction, as follows.

$$\rho_0 = a + b \qquad \rho_{n+1} = \mathsf{rec}\, x.a.x + b.\rho_n$$
$$\sigma_0 = \mathsf{rec}\, x.\overline{a}.x \qquad \sigma_{n+1} = \overline{a}.\sigma_n \oplus \mathsf{rec}\, x.\overline{b}.x$$

As for the example in [20], the size of ρ_n and σ_n is linear in n, since ρ_n and σ_n appear just once in the definitions of ρ_{n+1} and σ_{n+1}, respectively. By complete induction over n it is possible to prove that, for any n, $\rho_n \dashv\mid \sigma_n$. By recursive breadth-first search, a derivation for $\triangleright \rho_n \dashv \sigma_n$ is built in an actual exponential

$$(\text{Ax}_\infty) \atop \rhd \mathbf{1} \dashv \sigma$$

$$(+\cdot+_\infty) \atop \dfrac{\rho \dashv \sigma}{\alpha.\rho + \rho' \dashv \overline{\alpha}.\sigma + \sigma'}$$

$$(\oplus \cdot +_\infty) \atop \dfrac{\forall h \in I.\ \rho_h \dashv \sigma_h}{\bigoplus_{i \in I} \overline{\alpha}_i.\rho_i \dashv \sum_{j \in I \cup J} \alpha_j.\sigma_j}$$

$$(+\cdot \oplus_\infty) \atop \dfrac{\forall h \in I.\ \rho_h \dashv \sigma_h}{\sum_{j \in I \cup J} \overline{\alpha}_j.\rho_j \dashv \bigoplus_{i \in I} \alpha_i.\sigma_i}$$

Fig. 6. The non-well founded system $\lessapprox$

number of calls. Given n, the first part of the recursive-call tree looks as follows (where we denote by "**Ps**" the **P**roof-search algorithm)

$$\text{Prove}(\emptyset \rhd \rho_n \dashv \sigma_n)$$
$$\underline{\text{Prove}(\Gamma_1 \rhd \rho_n \dashv \sigma_{n-1})} \quad \text{Prove}(\Gamma_2 \rhd \rho_{n-1} \dashv \sigma_n)$$
$$\text{Prove}(\Gamma_3 \rhd \rho_n \dashv \sigma_{n-2}) \quad \underline{\text{Prove}(\Gamma_4 \rhd \rho_{n-1} \dashv \sigma_{n-1})} \quad \underline{\text{Prove}(\Gamma_5 \rhd \rho_{n-1} \dashv \sigma_{n-1})} \quad \text{Prove}(\Gamma_6 \rhd \rho_{n-2} \dashv \sigma_n)$$
$$\cdots \cdots \text{ etc.}$$

where $\Gamma_4 = \{\rho_n \dashv \sigma_n, \rho_n \dashv \sigma_{n-1}\} \neq \{\rho_n \dashv \sigma_n, \rho_{n-1} \dashv \sigma_n\} = \Gamma_5$. So, any call of the shape $\text{Prove}(\Gamma \rhd \rho_k \dashv \sigma_k)$ produces two calls $\text{Prove}(\Gamma' \rhd \rho_{k-1} \dashv \sigma_{k-1})$ and $\text{Prove}(\Gamma'' \rhd \rho_{k-1} \dashv \sigma_{k-1})$ with $\Gamma' \neq \Gamma''$; overall there are at least 2^n calls.

However, the complexity of the compliance decision procedure can be drastically reduced down to a polynomial complexity as detailed below.

A polynomial decision algorithm.
We first define a non-well founded, but equivalent version of system $\rhd$.

Definition 13 (The *non-well founded* system $\lessapprox$). *We write $\lessapprox \rho \dashv \sigma$ whenever there exists a finite or infinite derivation tree formed by the rules in Fig. 6 having $\rho \dashv \sigma$ as conclusion, and such that each finite branch ends with an instance of axiom* (Ax_∞).

Lemma 1 (Systems $\rhd$ and $\lessapprox$ are equivalent). $\rhd \rho \dashv \sigma$ *iff* $\lessapprox \rho \dashv \sigma$

In Fig. 7 we present a decision algorithm **Decide**$_{\dashv}$, based on the procedures **P** and **P**$^+$. A run of the algorithm resembles a computation tree of an alternating Turing machine, where nodes corresponding to rules $(\oplus \cdot +_\infty)$ and $(+\cdot \oplus_\infty)$ are universal, and nodes corresponding to $(+\cdot+_\infty)$ are existential; $\mathbf{P}(\mathsf{A}, \mathsf{F}, \mathsf{L}, b)$ attempts to prove all statements in its goal list L, while $\mathbf{P}^+(\mathsf{A}, \mathsf{F}, \mathsf{L}, b)$ succeeds if at least one goal in L is satisfiable.

The **P**rovability procedure **P** is an adaptation of the concrete subtyping algorithm for recursive arrow and product types of [20](Sect. 10) to the present, more complex context. It consists of a proof reconstruction procedure for $\lessapprox$ using a depth-first technique. **P** accumulates in its first argument A all the judgments it encounters during the search, in order to avoid looping over the same judgments (a role similar to Γ in system $\rhd$). With respect to the algorithm in [20](Sect. 10) we have two further parameters, F and b. The argument F accumulates the judgments for which it has been found that no derivation exists. When a rule $(+\cdot+)$ is encountered, the algorithm proceeds by calling the procedure $\mathbf{P}^+$ which, in case a premise is unprovable, goes on checking the other premises. The negative

$\mathbf{Decide}_{\dashv\parallel} (\rho \dashv \sigma) = \mathbf{let}\ \ (\mathsf{A},\mathsf{F},\mathsf{b}) = \mathbf{P}(\emptyset,\emptyset,[\rho \dashv \sigma],\mathbf{ok})\quad \mathbf{in}\ \ \mathsf{b} = \mathbf{ok}$
where

$\mathbf{P}(\mathsf{A},\mathsf{F},[\,],\mathsf{b}) = (\mathsf{A},\mathsf{F},\mathsf{b})$
$\mathbf{P}(\mathsf{A},\mathsf{F},(\rho \dashv \sigma):\mathsf{xs},\mathsf{b}) =$
-1- $\mathbf{if}\ \ \rho = 1\ \ \mathbf{then}\ \ \mathbf{P}(\mathsf{A},\mathsf{F},\mathsf{xs},\mathsf{b})$
-2- $\mathbf{else\ if}\ \ \rho \dashv \sigma \in \mathsf{A}\ \ \mathbf{then}\ \ \mathbf{P}(\mathsf{A},\mathsf{F},\mathsf{xs},\mathsf{b})$
-3- $\mathbf{else\ if}\ \ \rho \dashv \sigma \in \mathsf{F}\ \ \mathbf{then}\ \ \ \ (\mathsf{A},\mathsf{F},\mathbf{fail})$
-4- $\mathbf{else\ if}\ \ \rho = \sum_{i\in I}\alpha_i.\rho_i\ \ \mathbf{and}\ \ \sigma = \sum_{j\in J}\overline{\alpha}_j.\sigma_j\ \mathbf{and}\ I\cap J = \{i_1,\dots,i_n\}$
-5- $\mathbf{then}\ \ \mathbf{let}\ (\mathsf{A_0},\mathsf{F_0},\mathsf{b_0}) = \mathbf{P^+}(\mathsf{A}\cup\{\rho \dashv \sigma\},\mathsf{F},[\rho_{i_1} \dashv \sigma_{i_1} \dots \rho_{i_n} \dashv \sigma_{i_n}],\mathsf{b})$
-6- $\mathbf{in}\ \ \mathbf{if}\ \ \mathsf{b_0}=\mathbf{fail}\ \mathbf{then}\ \ (\mathsf{A_0},\mathsf{F_0},\mathbf{fail})$
-7- $\mathbf{else}\ \ \mathbf{P}(\mathsf{A_0},\mathsf{F_0},\mathsf{xs},\mathsf{b_0})$
-8- $\mathbf{else\ if}\ \ \rho = \bigoplus_{i\in I}\overline{\alpha}_i.\rho_i\ \ \mathbf{and}\ \ \sigma = \sum_{j\in J}\alpha_j.\sigma_j\ \mathbf{and}\ I\subseteq J\ \mathbf{and}\ \ I = \{i_1,\dots,i_n\}$
-9- $\mathbf{then}\ \ \mathbf{let}\ (\mathsf{A_0},\mathsf{F_0},\mathsf{b_0}) = \mathbf{P}(\mathsf{A}\cup\{\rho \dashv \sigma\},\mathsf{F},[\rho_{i_1} \dashv \sigma_{i_1} \dots \rho_{i_n} \dashv \sigma_{i_n}],\mathsf{b})$
-10- $\mathbf{in}\ \ \mathbf{if}\ \ \mathsf{b_0}=\mathbf{fail}\ \mathbf{then}\ \ (\mathsf{A_0},\mathsf{F_0},\mathbf{fail})$
-11- $\mathbf{else}\ \ \mathbf{P}(\mathsf{A_0},\mathsf{F_0},\mathsf{xs},\mathsf{b_0})$
-12- $\mathbf{else\ if}\ \ \rho = \sum_{i\in I}\overline{\alpha}_i.\rho_i\ \ \mathbf{and}\ \ \sigma = \bigoplus_{j\in J}\alpha_j.\sigma_j\ \mathbf{and}\ I\supseteq J\ \mathbf{and}\ \ J = \{j_1,\dots,j_n\}$
-13- $\mathbf{then}\ \ \mathbf{let}\ (\mathsf{A_0},\mathsf{F_0},\mathsf{b_0}) = \mathbf{P}(\mathsf{A}\cup\{\rho \dashv \sigma\},\mathsf{F},[\rho_{i_1} \dashv \sigma_{i_1} \dots \rho_{j_n} \dashv \sigma_{j_n}],\mathsf{b})$
-14- $\mathbf{in}\ \ \mathbf{if}\ \ \mathsf{b_0}=\mathbf{fail}\ \mathbf{then}\ \ (\mathsf{A_0},\mathsf{F_0},\mathbf{fail})$
-15- $\mathbf{else}\ \ \mathbf{P}(\mathsf{A_0},\mathsf{F_0},\mathsf{xs},\mathsf{b_0})$
-16- $\mathbf{else\ if}\ \ \rho = \mathsf{rec}\,x.\rho'\ \ \mathbf{then}\ \ \ \ \mathbf{P}(\mathsf{A},\mathsf{F},(\{\mathsf{rec}\,x.\rho'/x\}\rho' \dashv \sigma):\mathsf{xs},\mathsf{b})$
-17- $\mathbf{else\ if}\ \ \sigma = \mathsf{rec}\,x.\sigma'\ \ \mathbf{then}\ \ \ \ \mathbf{P}(\mathsf{A},\mathsf{F},(\rho \dashv \{\mathsf{rec}\,x.\sigma'/x\}\sigma'):\mathsf{xs},\mathsf{b})$
-18- $\mathbf{else}\ \ (\mathsf{A},\mathsf{F}\cup\{\rho \dashv \sigma\},\mathbf{fail})$

and where
$\mathbf{P^+}(\mathsf{A},\mathsf{F},[\rho \dashv \sigma],\mathsf{b}) = \mathbf{P}(\mathsf{A},\mathsf{F},[\rho \dashv \sigma],\mathsf{b})$
$\mathbf{P^+}(\mathsf{A},\mathsf{F},(\rho \dashv \sigma):\mathsf{xs},\mathsf{b})=$
-19- $\mathbf{let}\ \ (\mathsf{A_0},\mathsf{F_0},\mathsf{b_0}) = \mathbf{P}(\mathsf{A},\mathsf{F},[\rho \dashv \sigma],\mathsf{b})\ \ \mathbf{in}$
-20- $\mathbf{if}\ \ \mathsf{b_0} = \mathbf{fail}\ \ \mathbf{then}\ \ \mathbf{P^+}(\mathsf{A}\cup\mathsf{A_0},\mathsf{F}\cup\mathsf{F_0},\mathsf{xs},\mathbf{ok})\quad \mathbf{else}\ \ (\mathsf{A_0},\mathsf{F_0},\mathsf{b_0})$

Fig. 7. The polynomial decision procedure for compliance

information inferred about unprovable judgments is stored in F and it is carried along by the procedure $\mathbf{P^+}$ (as well as the positive information stored in A) in order not to duplicate work. The argument b, that can be either $\mathbf{ok}$ or $\mathbf{fail}$, is used to record whether the last call was successful or not, and it is used by $\mathbf{P^+}$ to know whether it has to stop with success, or to check a new premise.

Let us note that, contrary to the previous treatment, while studying the algorithm $\mathbf{Decide}_{\dashv\parallel}$, we abandon the equi-recursive view of recursion, and we represent a contract by a particular explicit (possibly) recursive expression.

Proposition 6 (Complexity of Deciding Compliance/Subcontract).
Given two contracts $\rho,\sigma \in \mathbf{rsC}$, deciding whether $\rho \dashv \parallel \sigma$ (or $\rho \preccurlyeq_s \sigma$) holds has a complexity $\mathcal{O}(n^5)$, where n is the maximum size of ρ and σ.

Remark 4. It is worth noticing that the polynomial decision procedure **Decide**$_{\dashv|}$ applies also to the formalism of retractable session contracts of [7] (in this case clauses at lines -8- and -12- are never used) and to the formalism of sessions contracts (some more clauses are never used).

6 Related Work and Conclusion

We have presented two conservative extensions of the session contracts of [2,3,10], a formalism interpreting session types [22] into a subset of contracts [14,15,27]. One extension deals with backtracking and one with speculative execution. We have shown that they both give rise to *the same* compliance relation, and, as a consequence, to the same subcontract (both for servers and for clients) and duality relations. For each of these relations we provided syntactic characterizations of the semantic concepts, allowing for efficient ways of checking them.

We discussed in the Introduction the improvements w.r.t. the preliminary results about retractable session contracts in [7]. Another closely related work is [5,6], where a different form of contracts with rollback is presented. Our retractable contracts depart from that model on three main aspects: (1) we use rollback in a disciplined way to tolerate failures in the interaction (in [5,6] it is an internal decision of a participant), thus improving compliance; (2) we embed checkpoints in the structure of contracts, avoiding explicit checkpoints; (3) we keep a stack of "pasts", instead of just a single past as in [5,6].

Reversibility, generalizing backtracking by allowing one to go back to any past state, has also been studied in the setting of binary session types [32,33]. There however the emphasis is on defining the reversible engine, based on causal-consistent reversibility [26], and not on studying compliance or subtyping (which would correspond to our subcontract relation).

Similarly to our retractable contracts, long running transactions with compensations, and in particular interacting transactions [18], allow one to undo past agreements. In interacting transactions, however, abort (which corresponds to our backtracking) can occur at any time, not only when an agreement cannot be found as in our case. Also, each transaction offers just two possibilities, and they are sorted: first the normal execution, then the compensation. Finally, compliance of interacting transactions has never been studied.

In [4] a game-theoretical interpretation of the retractable session contracts of [7] has been provided. Such an interpretation is likely to extend to the retractable contracts presented here.

We plan also to investigate whether our approach can be extended to multi-party sessions [23]. An investigation of multi-party sessions with rollbacks and named checkpoints has been already undertaken in [19]. In such a paper, however, the cause of a rollback is not a synchronization failure, but it is completely transparent to the calculus. Moreover, chosen branches are not discarded and can be retried upon rollback.

Because of the relevance of higher-order features in type systems, and of session delegation in type systems with sessions in particular, also higher-order session contracts, i.e. session contracts with delegation, have been investigated [3,11]. It is hence worth studying the integration of backtracking (or speculative execution) and session delegation.

A last line of future work is the study of how to extract retractable or speculative contracts from actual software based on backtracking or on speculative parallelism, and how to propagate the results on contracts to the original software.

References

1. Avizienis, A., Laprie, J.-C., Randell, B., Landwehr, C.E.: Basic concepts and taxonomy of dependable and secure computing. IEEE Trans. Dep. Sec. Comput. **1**(1), 11–33 (2004)
2. Barbanera, F., de'Liguoro, U.: Two notions of sub-behaviour for session-based client/server systems. In: PPDP, pp. 155–164. ACM Press (2010)
3. Barbanera, F., Liguoro, U.: Sub-behaviour relations for session-based client/server systems. MSCS **25**(6), 1339–1381 (2015)
4. Barbanera, F., de'Liguoro, U.: A game interpretation of retractable contracts. In: Lluch Lafuente, A., Proença, J. (eds.) COORDINATION 2016. LNCS, vol. 9686, pp. 18–34. Springer, Cham (2016). doi:10.1007/978-3-319-39519-7_2
5. Barbanera, F., Dezani-Ciancaglini, M., de'Liguoro, U.: Compliance for reversible client/server interactions. In: BEAT, EPTCS, vol. 162, pp. 35–42 (2014)
6. Barbanera, F., Dezani-Ciancaglini, M., de'Liguoro, U.: Reversible client/server interactions. Formal Asp. Comput. **28**(4), 697–722 (2016)
7. Barbanera, F., Dezani-Ciancaglini, M., Lanese, I., de'Liguoro, U.: Retractable contracts. In: PLACES 2015, EPTCS, vol. 203, pp. 61–72. Open Publishing Association (2016)
8. Barbanera, F., Lanese, I., de'Liguoro, U.: Retractable and speculative contracts (TR) (2017). http://www.cs.unibo.it/~lanese/tmp/TR-coord2017.pdf
9. Bartoletti, M., Cimoli, T., Murgia, M., Podda, A.S., Pompianu, L.: Compliance and subtyping in timed session types. In: Graf, S., Viswanathan, M. (eds.) FORTE 2015. LNCS, vol. 9039, pp. 161–177. Springer, Cham (2015). doi:10.1007/978-3-319-19195-9_11
10. Bernardi, G.T., Hennessy, M.: Modelling session types using contracts. Math. Struct. Comput. Sci. **26**(3), 510–560 (2016)
11. Bernardi, G.T., Hennessy, M.: Using higher-order contracts to model session types. Logical Methods Comput. Sci. **12**(2), 1–43 (2016)
12. Carbone, M., Honda, K., Yoshida, N.: Structured interactional exceptions in session types. In: Breugel, F., Chechik, M. (eds.) CONCUR 2008. LNCS, vol. 5201, pp. 402–417. Springer, Heidelberg (2008). doi:10.1007/978-3-540-85361-9_32
13. Carothers, C.D., Perumalla, K.S., Fujimoto, R.: Efficient optimistic parallel simulations using reverse computation. ACM Trans. Model. Comput. Simul. **9**(3), 224–253 (1999)
14. Carpineti, S., Castagna, G., Laneve, C., Padovani, L.: A formal account of contracts for web services. In: Bravetti, M., Núñez, M., Zavattaro, G. (eds.) WS-FM 2006. LNCS, vol. 4184, pp. 148–162. Springer, Heidelberg (2006). doi:10.1007/11841197_10
15. Castagna, G., Gesbert, N., Padovani, L.: A theory of contracts for web services. ACM Trans. Prog. Lang. Syst. **31**(5), 19:1–19:61 (2009)

16. Preda, M., Gabbrielli, M., Lanese, I., Mauro, J., Zavattaro, G.: Graceful interruption of request-response service interactions. In: Kappel, G., Maamar, Z., Motahari-Nezhad, H.R. (eds.) ICSOC 2011. LNCS, vol. 7084, pp. 590–600. Springer, Heidelberg (2011). doi:10.1007/978-3-642-25535-9_45

17. Danos, V., Krivine, J.: Reversible communicating systems. In: Gardner, P., Yoshida, N. (eds.) CONCUR 2004. LNCS, vol. 3170, pp. 292–307. Springer, Heidelberg (2004). doi:10.1007/978-3-540-28644-8_19

18. Vries, E., Koutavas, V., Hennessy, M.: Communicating transactions. In: Gastin, P., Laroussinie, F. (eds.) CONCUR 2010. LNCS, vol. 6269, pp. 569–583. Springer, Heidelberg (2010). doi:10.1007/978-3-642-15375-4_39

19. Dezani-Ciancaglini, M., Giannini, P.: Reversible multiparty sessions with checkpoints. In: EXPRESS/SOS 2016, EPTCS, vol. 222, pp. 60–74 (2016)

20. Gapeyev, V., Levin, M.Y., Pierce, B.C.: Recursive subtyping revealed. J. Funct. Program. **12**(6), 511–548 (2002)

21. Hoare, C.A.R.: Communicating Sequential Processes. Prentice-Hall, New York (1985)

22. Honda, K., Vasconcelos, V.T., Kubo, M.: Language primitives and type discipline for structured communication-based programming. In: Hankin, C. (ed.) ESOP 1998. LNCS, vol. 1381, pp. 122–138. Springer, Heidelberg (1998). doi:10.1007/BFb0053567

23. Honda, K., Yoshida, N., Carbone, M.: Multiparty asynchronous session types. In: POPL, pp. 273–284. ACM Press (2008)

24. Hüttel, H., et al.: Foundations of session types and behavioural contracts. ACM Comput. Surv. **49**(1), 3:1–3:36 (2016)

25. Lanese, I., Mezzina, C.A., Stefani, J.-B.: Reversibility in the higher-order π-calculus. Theor. Comput. Sci. **625**, 25–84 (2016)

26. Lanese, I., Mezzina, C.A., Tiezzi, F.: Causal-consistent reversibility. Bull. EATCS **114** (2014)

27. Laneve, C., Padovani, L.: The *must* preorder revisited. In: Caires, L., Vasconcelos, V.T. (eds.) CONCUR 2007. LNCS, vol. 4703, pp. 212–225. Springer, Heidelberg (2007). doi:10.1007/978-3-540-74407-8_15

28. Padovani, L.: Contract-based discovery of web services modulo simple orchestrators. Theoret. Comput. Sci. **411**, 3328–3347 (2010)

29. Phillips, I.C.C., Ulidowski, I.: Reversing algebraic process calculi. J. Logic Alg. Program. **73**(1–2), 70–96 (2007)

30. Prabhu, P., Ramalingam, G., Vaswani, K.: Safe programmable speculative parallelism. In: PLDI, pp. 50–61. ACM (2010)

31. Quiñones, C.G., et al.: Mitosis compiler: an infrastructure for speculative threading based on pre-computation slices. In: PLDI, pp. 269–279. ACM (2005)

32. Tiezzi, F., Yoshida, N.: Towards reversible sessions. In: PLACES, EPTCS, vol. 155. pp. 17–24 (2014)

33. Tiezzi, F., Yoshida, N.: Reversible session-based pi-calculus. J. Log. Algebr. Meth. Program. **84**(5), 684–707 (2015)

34. Xu, L., Hutter, F., Hoos, H.H., Leyton-Brown, K.: Satzilla: Portfolio-based algorithm selection for SAT. J. Artif. Intell. Res. (JAIR) **32**, 565–606 (2008)

35. Zhang, L., Malik, S.: The quest for efficient boolean satisfiability solvers. In: Brinksma, E., Larsen, K.G. (eds.) CAV 2002. LNCS, vol. 2404, pp. 17–36. Springer, Heidelberg (2002). doi:10.1007/3-540-45657-0_2

A Denotational View of Replicated Data Types

Fabio Gadducci[1], Hernán Melgratti[2,3], and Christian Roldán[2(✉)]

[1] Dipartimento di Informatica, Università di Pisa, Pisa, Italy
[2] Departamento de Computación, FCEyN,
Universidad de Buenos Aires, Buenos Aires, Argentina
croldan@dc.uba.ar
[3] CONICET, Buenos Aires, Argentina

Abstract. "Weak consistency" refers to a family of properties concerning the state of a distributed system. One of the key issues in their description is the way in which systems are specified. In this regard, a major advance is represented by the introduction of Replicated Data Types (RDTs), in which the meaning of operators is given in terms of two relations, namely, visibility and arbitration. Concretely, a data type operation is defined as a function that maps visibility and arbitration into a return value. In this paper we recast such standard approaches into a denotational framework in which a data type is seen as a function that maps visibility into admissible arbitrations. This characterisation provides a more abstract view of RDTs that (i) highlights some of the implicit assumptions shared in operational approaches to specification; (ii) accommodates underspecification and refinement; (iii) enables a categorical presentation of RDT and the development of composition operators for specifications.

1 Introduction

Distributed systems replicate their state over different nodes in order to satisfy several non-functional requirements, such as performance, availability, and reliability. It then becomes crucial to keep a consistent view of the replicated data. However, this is a challenging task because consistency is in conflict with two common requirements of distributed applications: *availability* (every request is eventually executed) and tolerance to network *partitions* (the system operates even in the presence of failures that prevent communication among components). In fact, it is impossible for a system to simultaneously achieve strong Consistency, Availability and Partition tolerance [6]. Since many domains cannot renounce to availability and network partitions, developers need to cope with weaker notions

The first author has been partially supported by CONICET International Cooperation Grant 995/15. Research partially supported by UBACyT project 2014–2017 20020130200092BA and CONICET project PIP 11220130100148CO.

J.-M. Jacquet and M. Massink (Eds.): COORDINATION 2017, LNCS 10319, pp. 138–156, 2017.
DOI: 10.1007/978-3-319-59746-1_8

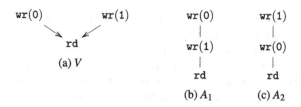

Fig. 1. A scenario for the replicated data type `Register`

of consistency by allowing, e.g., replicas to (temporarily) exhibit some discrepancies, as long as they eventually converge to the same state.

This setting challenges the way in which data are specified: states, state transitions and return values should account for the different views that a data item may simultaneously have. Consider a data type `Register` corresponding to a memory cell that is read and updated by using, respectively, operations `rd` and `wr`. In a replicated scenario, the value obtained when reading a register after two concurrent updates `wr(0)` and `wr(1)` (i.e., updates taking place over different replicas) is affected by the way in which updates propagate among the different replicas: it is perfectly possible that the result of the read is (i) undefined (when the read is performed over a third replica that has not received any of the updates), (ii) 0 or (iii) 1. Basically, the return value depends on the updates that are seen by that read operation. Choosing the return value is straightforward when a read sees just one update. This is less so if a read is performed over a replica that knows both updates, for allowing all replicas to (consistently) pick one of the available values. A common strategy for registers is that the *last-write wins*, i.e., the last update should be chosen when several concurrent updates are observed. This strategy implicitly assumes that all events in a system can be arranged in a total order. Several recent approaches focus on the operational specification of replicated data types [2–5,7,8,12,14]. Usually, the specification describes the meaning of an operation in terms of two different relations among events: *visibility*, which explains the causes for each result, and *arbitration*, which totally orders events. Consider the visibility relation V in Fig. 1a and the arbitrations A_1 and A_2 in Fig. 1b and c, respectively. The meaning of `rd` is defined such that $rd(V, A_1) = 1$ and $rd(V, A_2) = 0$. We remark that operational approaches require specifications to be *functional*, i.e., for every operation, visibility and arbitration relation, there exists exactly one return value. In this way operational specifications commit to concrete policies for resolving conflicts.

This work aims at putting on firm grounds the operational approaches for RDTs by giving them a purely functional description and, eventually, a categorical one. In our view, RDTs are functions that map visibility graphs (i.e., configurations) into sets of admissible arbitrations, i.e., all executions that generate a particular configuration. In this setting, a configuration mapped to an empty set of admissible arbitrations stands for an unreachable configuration. We rely on such an abstract view of RDTs to highlight some of the implicit assumptions shared by most of the operational approaches. In particular, we characterise operational approaches, such as [4,12], as those specifications that satisfy three properties: besides the evident requirement of being *functional* (i.e., deterministic and total), they must be *coherent* (i.e., larger states are explained as the composition of smaller ones), and *saturated* (e.g., an unobserved operation can be arbitrated in any position, even before the events that it sees). We show this inclusion to be strict and discuss some interesting cases that do not fall in this class. Moreover, we show that functional characterisation elegantly accounts for underspecification and refinement, which are standard notions in data type specification.

Then, we develop a categorical presentation for specifications. We focus on coherent specifications and show that there is a one-to-one correspondence between coherent specifications and a particular class of functors from the category $I(L)$ of labelled directed acyclic graphs and injective *past-reflecting morphism* (which are the dual notion of tp-morphisms [9]) to the category $P(L)$ of sets of paths and path-set morphisms preserving the initial object. As it is standard from classical results on algebraic specification theory, pullbacks and (a weak form of) pushouts in $I(L)$ provide basic operators for composing specifications, and thus our functorial presentation is the first step towards a denotational semantics of RDTs (see e.g. [1] and the references therein).

The paper has the following structure. Section 2 introduces the basic definitions concerning labelled directed acyclic graphs. Section 3 discusses our functional mechanism for the presentation of Replicated Data Types. Section 4 compares our proposal with the classical operational one [2]. Section 5 illustrates a categorical characterisation for our proposal. Finally, in the closing section we draw some conclusions and highlight further developments.

2   Labelled Directed Acyclic Graphs

In this section we recall the basics of labelled directed acyclic graphs, which are used for our description of replicated data types. We rely on countable sets $\mathcal{E}$ of events $e, e', \ldots, e_1, \ldots$ and L of labels $\ell, \ell', \ldots, \ell_1, \ldots$

Definition 1 (Labelled Directed Acyclic Graph). *A Labelled Directed Acyclic Graph (LDAG) over a set of labels L is a triple $G = \langle \mathcal{E}_G, \prec_G, \lambda_G \rangle$ such that $\mathcal{E}_G$ is a set of events, $\prec_G \subseteq \mathcal{E}_G \times \mathcal{E}_G$ is a binary relation whose transitive closure is a strict partial order, and $\lambda_G : \mathcal{E}_G \to L$ is a labeling function. An LDAG G is a path if $\prec_G$ is a strict total order.*

We write $\mathbb{G}(L)$ and $\mathbb{P}(L)$ to respectively denote the sets of all LDAGs and paths over L. We use G to range over $\mathbb{G}(L)$ and P to range over $\mathbb{P}(L)$. Moreover, we write $<_P$ instead of $\prec_P$ to make evident that paths are total orders. We say that P is a path over $\mathcal{E}$ if $\mathcal{E}_P = \mathcal{E}$ and write $\mathbb{P}(\mathcal{E}, \lambda)$ for $\{P \mid P$ is a path over $\mathcal{E}$ and $\lambda_P = \lambda\}$. We usually omit the subscript G (or P) when referring to the elements of G (of P, respectively) when no confusion arises. We write ϵ for the empty LDAG, i.e., such that $\mathcal{E}_\epsilon = \emptyset$.

Definition 2 (Morphism). *An* LDAG *morphism* f *from* G *to* G′, *written* f : G → G′, *is a mapping* f : $\mathcal{E}_G$ → $\mathcal{E}_{G'}$ *such that* λ_G = f; $\lambda_{G'}$ *and* e ≺$_G$ e′ *implies* f(e) ≺$_{G'}$ f(e′).

Hereafter we implicitly consider LDAGs up-to isomorphism, i.e., related by a bijective function that preserves and reflects the underlying relation.

Example 1. Consider the set $\mathcal{L}$ = {⟨rd, 0⟩, ⟨rd, 1⟩, ⟨wr(0), ok⟩, ⟨wr(1), ok⟩} of labels describing the operations of a 1-bit register. Each label is a tuple ⟨op, rv⟩ where op denotes an operation and rv its return value. For homogeneity, we associate the return value ok to every write operation. Now, take the LDAG over $\mathcal{L}$ defined as G_1 = ⟨{e_1, e_2, e_3}, ≺, λ⟩ where ≺= {(e_1, e_3), (e_2, e_3)} and λ is such that λ(e_1) = ⟨wr(0), ok⟩, λ(e_2) = ⟨wr(1), ok⟩, λ(e_3) = ⟨rd, 0⟩. A graphical representation of G_1 is in Fig. 2a. Since we consider LDAGs up-to isomorphism, we do not depict events and write instead the corresponding labels when no confusion arises. G_2 is an LDAG where ≺$_{G_2}$ is empty. Neither G_1 nor G_2 is a path, because they are not total orders. P_1 in Fig. 2c is an LDAG that is also a path. Hereinafter we use undirected arrows when depicting paths and avoid drawing transitions that are obtained by transitivity, as shown in Fig. 2d. All LDAGs in Fig. 2 belong to $\mathbb{G}(\mathcal{L})$, but only P_1 is in $\mathbb{P}(\mathcal{L})$.

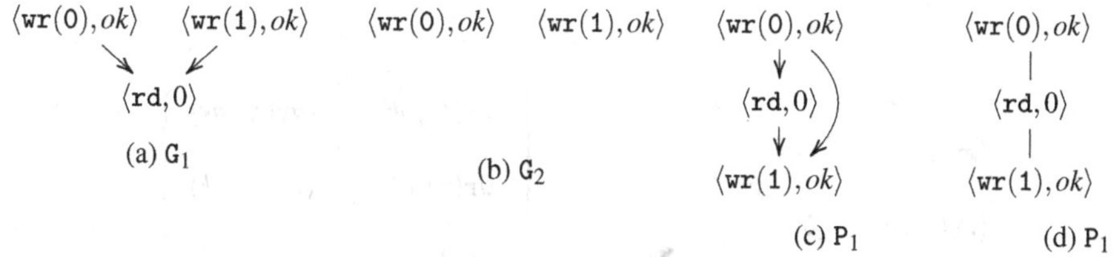

Fig. 2. Two simple LDAGs and two paths.

2.1 LDAG Operations

We now present a few operations on LDAGs, which will be used in the following sections. We start by introducing some notation for binary relations. We write ID for the identity relation over events and ≼ for ≺ ∪ ID. We write − ≺ e (and similarly − ≼ e) for the preimage of e, i.e., − ≺ e = {e′| e′ ≺ e}. We use ≺|$_{\mathcal{E}}$ for the restriction of ≺ to elements in $\mathcal{E}$, i.e. ≺|$_{\mathcal{E}}$ = ≺ ∩ ($\mathcal{E} \times \mathcal{E}$). Analogously, λ|$_{\mathcal{E}}$ is the domain restriction of λ to the elements in $\mathcal{E}$. We write $\mathcal{E}_T$ for the extension of the set $\mathcal{E}$ with a fresh element, i.e., $\mathcal{E}_T = \mathcal{E} \cup \{T\}$ such that T ∉ $\mathcal{E}$.

Definition 3 (Restriction and Extension). *Let* G = ⟨$\mathcal{E}$, ≺, λ⟩ *and* $\mathcal{E}' \subseteq \mathcal{E}$. *We define*

- G|$_{\mathcal{E}'}$ = ⟨$\mathcal{E}'$, ≺|$_{\mathcal{E}'}$, λ|$_{\mathcal{E}'}$⟩ *as the* restriction *of* G *to* $\mathcal{E}'$;
- G$^\ell_{\mathcal{E}'}$ = ⟨$\mathcal{E}_T$, ≺ ∪ ($\mathcal{E}' \times \{T\}$), λ[T ↦ ℓ]⟩ *as the* extension *of* G *over* $\mathcal{E}'$ *with* ℓ.

Restriction obviously lifts to sets X of LDAGs, i.e., $X|_{\mathcal{E}} = \{G|_{\mathcal{E}} \mid G \in X\}$. We omit the subscript $\mathcal{E}'$ in $G^{\ell}_{\mathcal{E}'}$ when $\mathcal{E}' = \mathcal{E}$.

Example 2. Consider the LDAGs G_1 and G_2 depicted in Fig. 2a and b, respectively. Then, $G_2 = G_1|_{\_\prec_{e_3}}$ and $G_1 = G_2^{\langle rd,0 \rangle}$.

The following operator allows for the combination of several paths and plays a central rol in our characterisation of replicated data types.

Definition 4 (Product). *Let* $X = \{\langle \mathcal{E}_i, <_i, \lambda_i \rangle\}_i$ *be a set of paths. The product of* X *is*

$$\bigotimes X = \{Q \mid Q \text{ is a path over } \bigcup_i \mathcal{E}_i \text{ and } Q|_{\mathcal{E}_i} \in X \}$$

Intuitively, the product of paths is analogous to the synchronous product of transition systems, in which common elements are identified and the remaining ones can be freely interleaved, as long as the original orders are respected.

Example 3. Consider the paths P_1 and P_2 in Fig. 3, and assume that they share the event labelled $\langle wr(2), ok \rangle$. Their product has two paths P_3 and P_4, each of them contains the elements of P_1 and P_2 and preserves the relative order of the elements in the original paths. We remark that the product is empty when the paths have incompatible orders. For instance, $P_3 \otimes P_4 = \emptyset$.

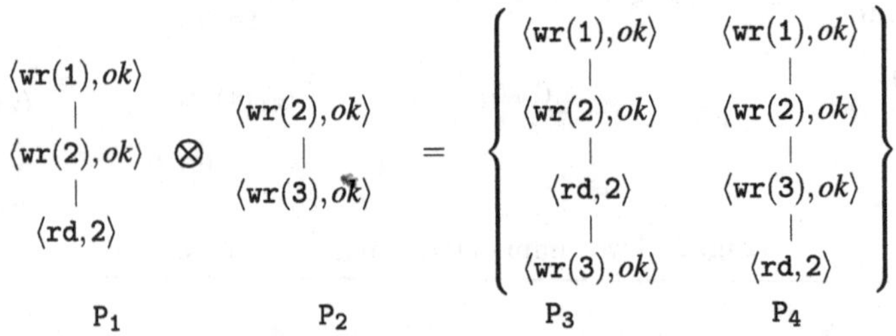

Fig. 3. Product between two paths.

It is straightforward to show that $\otimes$ is associative and commutative. Hence, we freely use $\otimes$ over sets of sets of paths.

3   Specifications

We introduce our notion of specification and applies it to some well-known data types.

Definition 5 (Specification). *A specification* S *is a function* $S : \mathbb{G}(L) \to 2^{\mathbb{P}(L)}$ *such that* $S(\epsilon) = \{\epsilon\}$ *and* $\forall G.\ S(G) \subseteq 2^{\mathbb{P}(\mathcal{E}_G, \lambda_G)}$.

A specification S maps an LDAG (i.e., a visibility relation) to a set of paths (i.e., its admissible arbitrations). Note that $P \in S(G)$ is a path over $\mathcal{E}_G$, and hence a total order of the events in G. However, we do not require P to be a topological ordering of G, i.e., $\prec_G \subseteq <_P$ may not hold. Although some specification approaches consider only arbitrations that include visibility [5,7], our definition accommodates also presentations, such as [2,4], in which arbitrations may not preserve visibility. We focus later on in a few subclasses, such as coherent specifications, in order to establish a precise correspondence with replicated data types. We also remark that it could be the case that $S(G) = \emptyset$, which means that S forbids the configuration G (more details in Example 4 below). For technical convenience, we impose $S(\epsilon) = \{\epsilon\}$ and disallow $S(\epsilon) = \emptyset$: S cannot forbid the empty configuration, which denotes the initial state of a data type.

We now illustrate the specification of some well-known replicated data types.

Example 4 (Counter). The data type `Counter` provides operations for incrementing and reading an integer register with initial value 0. A read operation returns the number of increments seen by that read. An increment is always successful and returns the value ok. Formally, we consider the set of labels $\mathcal{L} = \{\langle \text{inc}, ok \rangle\} \cup (\{\text{rd}\} \times \mathbb{N})$. Then, a `Counter` is specified by S_{Ctr} defined such that

$P \in S_{Ctr}(G)$ if $\forall e \in \mathcal{E}_G.\lambda(e) = \langle \text{rd}, k \rangle$ implies $k = \#\{e' \mid e' \prec_G e$ and $\lambda(e') = \langle \text{inc}, ok \rangle\}$

A visibility graph G has admissible arbitrations (i.e., $S_{Ctr}(G) \neq \emptyset$) only when each event e in G labelled by rd has a return value k that matches the number of increments anteceding e in G. We illustrate two cases for the definition of S_{Ctr} in Fig. 4. While the configuration in Fig. 4a has admissible arbitrations, the one in Fig. 4b has not, because the unique event labelled by rd returns 0 when it is actually preceded by an observed increment. In other words, an execution is not allowed to generate such a visibility graph. We remark that S_{Ctr} does not impose any constraint on the ordering $<_P$.

In fact, a path $P \in S_{Ctr}(G)$ does not need to be a topological ordering of G as, for instance, the rightmost path in the set of Fig. 4a.

$$S_{Ctr} \begin{pmatrix} \langle \text{inc}, ok \rangle \\ \downarrow \\ \langle \text{rd}, 1 \rangle \end{pmatrix} = \left\{ \begin{array}{cc} \langle \text{inc}, ok \rangle & \langle \text{rd}, 1 \rangle \\ | & | \\ \langle \text{rd}, 1 \rangle & \langle \text{inc}, ok \rangle \end{array} \right\} \qquad S_{Ctr} \begin{pmatrix} \langle \text{inc}, ok \rangle \\ \downarrow \\ \langle \text{rd}, 0 \rangle \end{pmatrix} = \emptyset$$

(a)   (b)

Fig. 4. Counter specification.

Example 5 (Last-write-wins Register). A `Register` stores a value that can be read and updated. We assume that the initial value of a register is undefined. We take $\mathcal{L} = \{\langle \mathtt{wr}(k), ok \rangle \mid k \in \mathbb{N}\} \cup (\{\mathtt{rd}\} \times \mathbb{N} \cup \{\bot\})$ as the set of labels. The specification $\mathcal{S}_{lwwR}$ gives the semantics of a register that adopts the last-write-wins strategy.

$$P \in \mathcal{S}_{lwwR}(\mathtt{G}) \text{ if } \forall e \in \mathcal{E}_G. \begin{cases} \lambda(e) = \langle \mathtt{rd}, \bot \rangle \text{ implies } \forall e' \prec_G e. \forall k. \lambda(e') \neq \langle \mathtt{wr}(k), ok \rangle \\ \lambda(e) = \langle \mathtt{rd}, k \rangle \text{ implies } \exists e' \prec_G e. \lambda(e') = \langle \mathtt{wr}(k), ok \rangle \text{ and} \\ \quad \forall e'' \prec_G e.\ e' <_P e'' \text{ implies } \forall k'. \lambda(e'') \neq \langle \mathtt{wr}(k'), ok \rangle \end{cases}$$

An LDAG G has admissible arbitrations only when each event associated with a read operation returns a previously written value. As per the first condition above, a read operation returns the undefined value $\bot$ when it does not see any write. By the second condition, a read e returns a natural number k when it sees an operation e' that writes that value k. In such case, any admissible arbitration P must order e' as the greatest (accordingly to $<_P$) of all write operations seen by e.

Example 6 (Generic Register). We now define a `Generic Register` that does no commit to a particular strategy for resolving conflicts. We specify this type as follows

$$P \in \mathcal{S}_{gR}(\mathtt{G}) \text{ if } \forall e \in \mathcal{E}_G. \begin{cases} \lambda(e) = \langle \mathtt{rd}, \bot \rangle \text{ implies } \forall e' \prec_G e. \forall k. \lambda(e') \neq \langle \mathtt{wr}(k), ok \rangle \\ \lambda(e) = \langle \mathtt{rd}, k \rangle \text{ implies } \exists e' \prec_G e. \lambda(e') = \langle \mathtt{wr}(k), ok \rangle \text{ and} \\ \quad \forall e''. \lambda(e'') = \langle \mathtt{rd}, k'' \rangle \text{ and } - \prec_G e = - \prec_G e'' \text{ implies } k = k'' \end{cases}$$

As in Example 5, the return value of a read corresponds to a written value seen by that read, but the specification does not determine which value should be chosen. We require instead that all read operations with the same causes (i.e., $- \prec_G e = - \prec_G e'$) have the same result. Since this condition is satisfied by any admissible configuration G, it ensures convergence. The fact that convergence is explicitly required contrasts with approaches like [2,4], where on the contrary convergence is ensured automatically by considering only deterministic specifications. We remark that for the deterministic cases, e.g., Examples 4 and 5, we do not need to explicitly require convergence.

3.1   Refinement

Refinement is a standard approach in data type specification, which allows for a hierarchical organisation that goes from abstract descriptions to concrete implementations. The main benefit of refinement relies on the fact that applications can be developed and reasoned about in terms of abstract types, which hide implementation details and leave some freedom for the implementation. Consider the specification $\mathcal{S}_{gR}$ of the `Generic Register` introduced in Example 6, which only requires a policy for conflict resolution that ensures convergence. On the contrary, the specification S_{lwwR} in Example 5 explicitly states that concurrent updates must be resolved by adopting the last-write-wins policy. Since the latter policy ensures convergence, we would like to think about S_{lwwR} as a refinement of S_{gR}. We characterise refinement in our setting as follows.

Definition 6 (Refinement). *Let* S_1, S_2 *be specifications. We say that* S_1 *refines* S_2 *and we write* $S_1 \sqsubseteq S_2$ *if* $\forall G.\ S_1(G) \subseteq S_2(G)$.

Example 7. It can be easily checked that $P \in S_{lwwR}(G)$ implies $P \in S_{gR}(G)$ for any G. Consequently, S_{lwwR} is a refinement of S_{gR}.

Example 8. Consider the data type Set, which provides (among others) the operations add, rem and lookup for respectively adding, removing and examining the elements within the set. Different alternatives have been proposed in the literature for resolving conflicts in the presence of concurrent additions and removals of elements (see [13] for a detailed discussion). We illustrate two possible alternatives by considering the execution scenario depicted in Fig. 5. A reasonable semantics for lookup over G and P would fix the result V as either $\emptyset$ or $\{1\}$. In fact, under the last-write-wins policy, the specification prescribes that lookup returns $\{1\}$ in this scenario. Differently, the strategy of 2P-Sets[1] establishes that the result is $\emptyset$.

The following definition provides a specification for an abstract data type Set that allows (among others) any of the above policies.

$$P \in S_{Set}(G) \text{ if } \forall e \in \mathcal{E}_G.\lambda(e) = \langle \text{lookup}, V \rangle \text{ implies } B_e \subseteq V \subseteq A_e \text{ and } \text{Conv}_{e,V}$$

where

$$A_e = \{k \mid e' \prec_G e \text{ and } \lambda(e') = \langle \text{add}(k), ok \rangle\}$$
$$B_e = A_e \setminus \{k \mid e' \prec_G e \text{ and } \lambda(e') = \langle \text{rem}(k), ok \rangle\}$$
$$\text{Conv}_{e,V} = \forall e'.\lambda(e') = \langle \text{lookup}, V' \rangle \text{ and } - \prec_G e = - \prec_G e' \text{ implies } V = V'$$

The set A_e contains the elements added to (and possibly removed from) the set seen by e while B_e contains those elements for which e sees no removal. Thus, the condition $B_e \subseteq V \subseteq A_e$ states that lookup returns a set that contains at least all the elements added but not removed (i.e., in B_e). However, the return value V may contain elements that have been added and removed (the choice is left unspecified). Condition Conv ensures convergence, similarly to the specification of S_{gR} in Example 6.

Then, a concrete resolution policy such as 2P-Sets can be specified as follows

$$P \in S_{2P\text{-}Sets}(G) \text{ if } \forall e \in \mathcal{E}_G.\lambda(e) = \langle \text{lookup}, V \rangle \text{ implies } V = B_e$$

Clearly, $S_{2P\text{-}Sets}$ is a refinement of S_{Sets}. Other policies can be specified analogously.

---

[1] In 2P-Sets, additions of elements that have been previously removed have no effect.

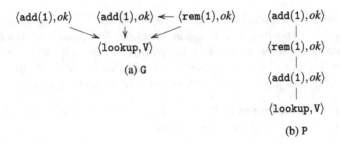

Fig. 5. A scenario for the replicated data type Set

3.2   Classes of Specifications

We now discuss two properties of specifications. Firstly, we look at specifications for which the behaviour of larger computations matches that of their shorter prefixes.

Definition 7 (Past-Coherent Specification). *Let S be a specification. We say that S is past-coherent (briefly, coherent) if*

$$\forall G.\ S(G) = \bigotimes_{e \in \mathcal{E}_G} S(G|_{-\preceq e})$$

Note that coherence implies that $S(G)|_{-\preceq e} \subseteq S(G|_{-\preceq e})$. Intuitively, sub-paths are obtained from the interleaving of the paths belonging to the associated sub-specifications.

Example 9. The specifications in Examples 4, 5 and 6 are all coherent, because their definitions are in terms of restrictions of the LDAGs. Now consider the specification S defined such that the equalities in Fig. 6 hold. S is not coherent

$$S\Big(\langle o_1, v_1 \rangle\Big) = \Big\{\langle o_1, v_1 \rangle\Big\}$$
$$S\Big(\langle o_2, v_2 \rangle\Big) = \Big\{\langle o_2, v_2 \rangle\Big\}$$

(a)

$$S\Big(\langle o_1, v_1 \rangle \quad \langle o_2, v_2 \rangle\Big) = \left\{\begin{array}{c}\langle o_1, v_1 \rangle \\ | \\ \langle o_2, v_2 \rangle\end{array}\right\}$$

(b)

$$S\left(\begin{array}{cc}\langle o_1, v_1 \rangle & \langle o_2, v_2 \rangle \\ \searrow & \swarrow \\ & \langle o_3, v_3 \rangle\end{array}\right) = \left\{\begin{array}{cc}\langle o_1, v_1 \rangle & \langle o_2, v_2 \rangle \\ | & | \\ \langle o_2, v_2 \rangle & \langle o_1, v_1 \rangle \\ | & | \\ \langle o_3, v_3 \rangle & \langle o_3, v_3 \rangle\end{array}\right\}$$

(c)

Fig. 6. A non-coherent specification.

because the arbitrations for the LDAG in Fig. 6b should contain all the interleavings for the paths associated with its sub-configurations, as depicted in Fig. 6a. Instead, note that the arbitration of $\langle o_2, v_2 \rangle$ before $\langle o_1, v_1 \rangle$ in the leftmost path on Fig. 6c would not hinder coherence by itself, even if it is not allowed by the sub-configuration in Fig. 6b.

A second class of specifications is concerned with saturation. Intuitively, a saturated specification allows every top element on the visibility to be arbitrated in any position. We first introduce the notion of saturation for a path.

Definition 8 (Path Saturation). *Let* P *be a path and* ℓ *a label. We write* $\mathtt{sat}(\mathsf{P}, \ell)$ *for the set of paths obtained by saturating* P *with respect to* ℓ, *defined as follows*

$$\mathtt{sat}(\mathsf{P}, \ell) = \{ \mathsf{Q} \mid \mathsf{Q} \in \mathbb{P}(\mathcal{E}_{\mathsf{P}\ell}, \lambda_{\mathsf{P}\ell}) \text{ and } \mathsf{Q}|_{\mathcal{E}_{\mathsf{P}}} = \mathsf{P} \}$$

A path P saturated with a label ℓ generates the set of all paths obtained by placing a new event labelled by ℓ in any position within P. A saturated specification thus extends a computation by adding a new operation that can be arbitrated in any position.

Definition 9 (Saturated Specification). *Let* S *be a specification. We say that* S *is saturated if*

$$\forall \langle \mathsf{G}, \mathsf{P} \rangle, \ell.\ \mathsf{P} \in S(\mathsf{G}^\ell)|_{\mathcal{E}_{\mathsf{G}}} \text{ implies } \mathtt{sat}(\mathsf{P}, \ell) \subseteq S(\mathsf{G}^\ell)$$

Example 10. The specifications in Examples 4, 5 and 6 are all saturated because a new event e can be arbitrated in any position. In fact, the specifications in Examples 4 and 6 do not use any information about arbitration, while the specification in Example 5 constrains arbitrations only for events that are not maximal. Figure 7 shows a specification that is not saturated because it does not allow to arbitrate the top event (the one labelled $\langle \mathtt{rd}, 1 \rangle$) as the first operation in the path. In a saturated specification, the equality in Fig. 4a should hold. We remark that the specification is coherent although it is not saturated.

$$S\left(\langle \mathtt{inc}, ok \rangle \right) = \left\{ \langle \mathtt{inc}, ok \rangle \right\}$$
$$S\left(\langle \mathtt{rd}, 1 \rangle \right) = \left\{ \langle \mathtt{rd}, 1 \rangle \right\}$$

$$S\left(\begin{array}{c} \langle \mathtt{inc}, ok \rangle \\ \downarrow \\ \langle \mathtt{rd}, 1 \rangle \end{array} \right) = \left\{ \begin{array}{c} \langle \mathtt{inc}, ok \rangle \\ | \\ \langle \mathtt{rd}, 1 \rangle \end{array} \right\}$$

Fig. 7. A non-saturated specification

4 Replicated Data Type

In this section we show that our proposal can be considered as (and it is actually more general than) a model for the operational description of RDTs as given in [2,4]. We start by recasting the original definition of RDT (as given in [2, Definition 4.5]) in terms of LDAGs. As hinted in the introduction, the meaning of each operation of an RDT is specified in terms of a context, written C, which is a pair $\langle G, P \rangle$ such that $P \in \mathbb{P}(\mathcal{E}_G, \lambda_G)$. We write $\mathbb{C}(\mathcal{L})$ for the set of contexts over $\mathcal{L}$, and fix a set O of operations and a set $\mathcal{V}$ of values. Then, the operational description of RDTs in [2,4] can be formulated as follows.

Definition 10 (Replicated Data Type). *A* Replicated Data Type *(RDT) is a function* $\mathcal{F} : O \times \mathbb{C}(O) \to \mathcal{V}$.

In words, for any visibility graph G and arbitration P, the specification $\mathcal{F}$ indicates the result of executing the operation op over G and P, which is $\mathcal{F}(\text{op}, \langle G, P \rangle)$.

Example 11. The data type `Counter` introduced in Example 4 is formally specified in [2,4] as follows

$$\mathcal{F}_{ctr}(\text{inc}, \langle G, P \rangle) = ok$$
$$\mathcal{F}_{ctr}(\text{rd}, \langle G, P \rangle) = \#\{e \mid e \in G \text{ and } \lambda(e) = \text{inc}\}$$

Given a context $\langle G, P \rangle$ in $\mathbb{C}(O \times \mathcal{V})$, we may check whether the value associated with each operation matches the definition of a particular RDT. This notion is known as *return value consistency* [2, Definition 4.8]. In order to relate contexts with and without return values, we use the following notation: given $G \in \mathbb{G}(O \times \mathcal{V})$, by $\overline{G} \in \mathbb{G}(O)$ we denote the LDAG obtained by projecting the labels of G in the obvious way.

Definition 11 (Return Value Consistent). *Let $\mathcal{F}$ be an* RDT *and* $\langle G, P \rangle \in \mathbb{C}(O \times \mathcal{V})$ *a context. We say that $\mathcal{F}$ is* Return Value Consistent *(RVAL) over* G *and* P *and we write* $\text{RVAL}(\mathcal{F}, G, P)$ *if* $\forall e \in \mathcal{E}_G . \lambda(e) = \langle op, v \rangle$ *implies* $\mathcal{F}(op, \overline{G}|_{-\preceq e}, \overline{P}|_{-\preceq e}) = v$. *Moreover, we define*

$$\text{PRVAL}(\mathcal{F}, G) = \{P \mid \text{RVAL}(\mathcal{F}, G, P)\}$$

Example 12. Consider the RDT $\mathcal{F}_{ctr}$ introduced in Example 11. The context in Fig. 8a is RVAL consistent while the one in Fig. 8b is not because $\mathcal{F}_{ctr}$ requires rd to return the number of inc operations seen by that read, which in this case should be 2.

The following result states that return value consistent paths are all coherent, in the sense that they match the behaviour allowed for any shorter configuration.

Lemma 1. *Let $\mathcal{F}$ be an* RDT *and* G *an* LDAG. *Then*

$$\text{PRVAL}(\mathcal{F}, G) = \bigotimes_{e \in \mathcal{E}_G} \text{PRVAL}(\mathcal{F}, G|_{-\preceq e}).$$

As for coherent specifications, the property $\text{PRVAL}(\mathcal{F}, G)|_{-\preceq e} \subseteq \text{PRVAL}(\mathcal{F}, G|_{-\preceq e})$ also holds for return value consistent paths.

$$\left\langle \begin{array}{ccc} & & \langle\mathrm{inc},ok\rangle \\ \langle\mathrm{inc},ok\rangle & \langle\mathrm{inc},ok\rangle & | \\ \searrow & \swarrow & , \quad \langle\mathrm{inc},ok\rangle \\ \langle\mathrm{rd},2\rangle & & | \\ & & \langle\mathrm{rd},2\rangle \end{array} \right\rangle \qquad \left\langle \begin{array}{ccc} & & \langle\mathrm{inc},ok\rangle \\ \langle\mathrm{inc},ok\rangle & \langle\mathrm{inc},ok\rangle & | \\ \searrow & \swarrow & , \quad \langle\mathrm{inc},ok\rangle \\ \langle\mathrm{rd},0\rangle & & | \\ & & \langle\mathrm{rd},0\rangle \end{array} \right\rangle$$

(a) Consistent.   (b) Non consistent.

Fig. 8. RVAL consistency for $\mathcal{F}_{ctr}$.

4.1   Deterministic Specifications

We now focus on the relation between our notion of specification, as introduced in Definition 5, and the operational description of RDTs, as introduced in [2,4] and formalised in Definition 10 in terms of LDAGs. Specifically, we characterise a proper subclass of specifications that precisely correspond to RDTs.

For this section we restrict our attention to specifications over the set of labels $O \times \mathcal{V}$, i.e., $S : \mathbb{G}(O \times \mathcal{V}) \to 2^{\mathbb{P}(O \times \mathcal{V})}$.

Definition 12 (Total Specification). *Let S be a specification. We say that S is total if*

$$\forall \langle \overline{G}, \overline{P} \rangle, \mathrm{op}. \ \exists G_1, v. \ \overline{G} = \overline{G_1} \ \wedge \ \overline{P} \in \overline{S(G_1^{\langle \mathrm{op},v \rangle})}\Big|_{\mathcal{L}_{G_1}}$$

Intuitively, a specification is total when every projection over O of a context in $\mathbb{C}(O \times \mathcal{V})$, as represented by $\langle \overline{G}, \overline{P} \rangle \in \mathbb{C}(O)$, can be extended with the execution of any operation of the data type. This is formalised by stating that for any operation op and any admissible arbitration (sequence of operations) $\overline{P}$ of a configuration $\overline{G}$ (once more, labelled only with operations), then $\overline{P}$ can be extended into an admissible arbitration of the configuration $G_1^{\langle \mathrm{op},v \rangle}$, where G_1 is just one of the possible configurations (the one labelled with the correct return values) whose projection corresponds to $\overline{G}$.

We remark that a total specification does not prevent the definition of an operation that admits more than one return value in certain configurations, i.e., v in Definition 12 does not need to be unique. For instance, consider the `Generic Register` in Example 6, in which operation rd may return any of the causally-independent, previously written values. Albeit being total, the specification for rd is not deterministic. On the contrary, a specification is deterministic if an operation executed over a configuration admits at most one return value, as formally stated below.

Definition 13 (Deterministic Specification). *Let S be a specification. We say that S is deterministic if*

$$\forall G, \mathrm{op}, v, v'. \ v \neq v' \ \textit{implies} \ \overline{S(G^{\langle \mathrm{op},v \rangle})}\Big|_{\mathcal{L}_G} \ \cap \ \overline{S(G^{\langle \mathrm{op},v' \rangle})}\Big|_{\mathcal{L}_G} = \emptyset$$

A weaker notion for determinism could allow the result for an added operation to depend also on the given admissible path. We say that a specification S is *value-deterministic* if

$$\forall G, op, v, v'. \ v \neq v' \wedge G \neq \epsilon \ \text{ implies } \ S(G^{\langle op, v \rangle})\big|_{\mathcal{E}_G} \cap S(G^{\langle op, v' \rangle})\big|_{\mathcal{E}_G} = \emptyset$$

Finally, we say that a specification is *functional* if it is both deterministic and total.

Example 13. Figure 9 shows a value-deterministic specification. Although a read operation that follows an increment may return two different values, such difference is explained by the previous computation: in one case the increment succeeds while in the other fails. The specification is however not deterministic because it admits a sequence of operations to be decorated with different return values.

$$S\left(\begin{array}{c}\langle \text{inc}, ok \rangle \\ \downarrow \\ \langle \text{rd}, 1 \rangle\end{array}\right) = \left\{\begin{array}{c}\langle \text{inc}, ok \rangle \\ | \\ \langle \text{rd}, 1 \rangle\end{array}\right\} \qquad S\left(\begin{array}{c}\langle \text{inc}, fail \rangle \\ \downarrow \\ \langle \text{rd}, \bot \rangle\end{array}\right) = \left\{\begin{array}{c}\langle \text{inc}, fail \rangle \\ | \\ \langle \text{rd}, \bot \rangle\end{array}\right\}$$

(a) \qquad\qquad (b)

Fig. 9. A value-deterministic and coherent specification.

Example 14. It is straightforward to check that the specifications in Examples 4 and 5 are deterministic. On the contrary, the specification of the Generic Register in Example 6 is not even value-deterministic. It suffices to consider a configuration in which a read operation sees two different written values. Similarly, Set in Example 8 is not deterministic.

The lemma below states a simple criterion for determinism.

Lemma 2. *Let S be a coherent and deterministic specification. Then*

$$\forall G_1, G_2. \ \overline{G_1} = \overline{G_2} \ \text{implies } G_1 = G_2 \vee \overline{S(G_1)} \cap \overline{S(G_2)} = \emptyset$$

So, if two configurations are annotated with the same operations yet with different values, then their admissible paths are already all different if we disregard return values.

4.2   Correspondence Between RDTs and Specifications

This section establishes the connection between RDTs and specifications. We first introduce a mapping from RDTs to specifications.

Definition 14. *Let $\mathcal{F}$ be an* RDT. *We write* $\mathbb{S}(\mathcal{F})$ *for the specification associated with* $\mathcal{F}$, *defined as follows*

$$\mathbb{S}(\mathcal{F})(\mathsf{G}) = \text{PRVAL}(\mathcal{F}, \mathsf{G})$$

Next result shows that RDTs correspond to specifications that are coherent, functional and saturated.

Lemma 3. *For every* RDT $\mathcal{F}$, $\mathbb{S}(\mathcal{F})$ *is coherent, functional, and saturated.*

The inverse mapping from specifications to RDTs is defined below.

Definition 15. *Let $\mathcal{S}$ be a specification. We write* $\mathbb{F}(\mathcal{S})$ *for the* RDT *associated with $\mathcal{S}$, defined as follows*

$$\mathbb{F}(\mathcal{S})(\mathsf{op}, \overline{\mathsf{G}}, \overline{\mathsf{P}}) = v \ \textit{if} \ \exists \mathsf{G}_1. \ \overline{\mathsf{G}} = \overline{\mathsf{G}_1} \ \wedge \ \overline{\mathsf{P}} \in \mathcal{S}(\overline{\mathsf{G}_1^{\langle \mathsf{op}, v \rangle}})\Big|_{\mathcal{I}_{\mathsf{G}_1}}$$

Note that $\mathbb{F}(\mathcal{S})$ may not be well-defined for some $\mathcal{S}$, e.g. when $\mathcal{S}$ is not deterministic. The following lemma states the conditions under which $\mathbb{F}(\mathcal{S})$ is well-defined.

Lemma 4. *For every coherent and functional specification $\mathcal{S}$,* $\mathbb{F}(\mathcal{S})$ *is well-defined.*

The following two results show that RDTs are a particular class of specifications, and hence, provide a fully abstract characterisation of operational RDTs.

Theorem 1. *For every coherent, functional, and saturated specification $\mathcal{S}$, $\mathcal{S} = \mathbb{S}(\mathbb{F}(\mathcal{S}))$.*

Theorem 2. *For every* RDT $\mathcal{F}$, $\mathcal{F} = \mathbb{F}(\mathbb{S}(\mathcal{F}))$.

The above characterisation implies that there are data types that cannot be specified as operational RDTs. Consider e.g. `Generic Register` and `Set`, as introduced respectively in Examples 6 and 8. As noted in Example 14, they are not deterministic. Hence, they cannot be translated as RDTs. We remark that a non-deterministic specification does not imply a non-deterministic conflict resolution, but it allows for underspecification.

5   A Categorical Account of Specifications

In the previous sections we provided a functional characterisation of RDTs. We now proceed on to a denotational account of our formalism by providing a categorical foundation which is amenable to the building of a family of operators on specifications.

5.1 Composing LDAGs

We start by considering a sub-class of morphisms between LDAGs, which account for the evolution of visibility relation by reflecting the information about observed events.

Definition 16 (Past-Reflecting Morphism). *Let* G_1 *and* G_2 *be* LDAGs *and* $f : G_1 \to G_2$ *an* LDAG *morphism. We say that* f *is past-reflecting if*

$$\forall e \in \mathcal{E}_{G_1}.\; f(-\prec e) = \bigcup_{e' \in -\prec f(e)} e'.$$

We can concisely write $f(-\prec e) = -\prec f(e)$ and spell out the definition as

$$\forall e \in \mathcal{E}_{G_1}.\; \forall e_2 \in G_2|_{-\prec f(e)}.\; \exists e_1 \in G_1|_{-\prec e}.\; f(e_1) = e_2$$

It is noteworthy that this requirement boils down to (the dual of) what are called *tp-morphisms* in the literature on algebraic specification theory, which are an instance of *open maps* [9]. As we will see, this property is going to be fundamental in obtaining a categorical characterisation of coherent specifications.

Now, let $G(L)$ be the category whose objects are LDAGs and arrows are past-reflecting morphisms, and $I(L)$ the sub-category whose arrows are injective morphisms.

Proposition 1 (LDAG **Pullbacks/Pushouts**). *The category* $G(L)$ *of* LDAGs *and past-reflecting morphisms has (strict) initial object, pullbacks and pushouts along monos.*

Note that pushout squares along monos are also pullback ones. As often the case, the property concerning pushouts does not hold in $I(L)$, even if a weak form does, since monos are stable under pushouts in $G(L)$. For the time being, we just remark that these properties guarantee a degree of modularity for our formalism.

We need a last definition before giving a categorical presentation.

Definition 17 (Downward closure). *Let* $G = \langle \mathcal{E}, \prec, \lambda \rangle$ *be an* LDAG *and* $\mathcal{E}' \subseteq \mathcal{E}$. *We say that* $\mathcal{E}'$ *is downward closed if*

$$\forall e \in \mathcal{E}'.\, -\prec e \subseteq \mathcal{E}'.$$

It is easy to show that for any past-reflecting morphism $f : G_1 \to G_2$ the image of $\mathcal{E}_{G_1}$ along f is downward closed. Should f be injective, we strengthen the relationship.

Lemma 5. *An injective morphism* $f : G_1 \to G_2$ *is past-reflecting if and only if*

1. $f(e_1) \prec_{G_2} f(e_2)$ *implies* $e_1 \prec_{G_1} e_2$;
2. $\bigcup_{e \in \mathcal{E}_{G_1}} f(e)$ *is downward closed.*

This result tells us that past-reflecting injective morphisms $\mathbf{f} : \mathsf{G}_1 \to \mathsf{G}_2$ are uniquely characterised as such by the properties of the image of $\mathcal{E}_1$ with respect to G_2.

Now, while the initial object of both $\mathcal{G}(L)$ and $\mathcal{I}(L)$ is the empty graph ϵ, the pullback in the latter has an easy characterisation, thanks to the previous lemma. Indeed, let $\mathbf{f}_i : \mathsf{G}_i \to \mathsf{G}$ be past-preserving injective morphisms, assuming the functions on elements to be identities for the sake of simplicity, and let $\mathcal{E} = \mathcal{E}_{\mathsf{G}_1} \cap \mathcal{E}_{\mathsf{G}_2}$. Then, $\mathsf{G}_1|_{\mathcal{E}} = \mathsf{G}_2|_{\mathcal{E}}$ and they correspond (with the obvious morphisms) to the pullback of $\mathbf{f}_1$ and $\mathbf{f}_2$.

5.2   The Model Category

We now move to define the model category.

Definition 18 (Morphism Saturation). *Let $\mathbb{P}(\mathcal{E}_1, \lambda_1)$ and $\mathbb{P}(\mathcal{E}_2, \lambda_2)$ be sets of paths and $\mathbf{f} : \mathcal{E}_1 \to \mathcal{E}_2$ an injective function such that $\lambda_1 = \mathbf{f}; \lambda_2$. The saturation function $\mathsf{sat}(-, \mathbf{f})$ is defined as follows*

$$\mathsf{sat}(\mathsf{P}, \mathbf{f}) = \{\mathsf{Q} \mid \mathsf{Q} \in \mathbb{P}(\mathcal{E}_2, \lambda_2) \text{ and } \mathsf{P} = \mathsf{Q}|_{\mathbf{f}(\mathcal{E}_1)}\}$$

That is, each Q is the image of P via a morphism with underlying function $\mathbf{f}$. We can exploit saturation in order to get a simple definition of our model category.

Definition 19 (Path-Set Morphism). *Let $X_1 \subseteq \mathbb{P}(\mathcal{E}_1, \lambda_1)$ and $X_2 \subseteq \mathbb{P}(\mathcal{E}_2, \lambda_2)$ be sets of paths. A* path-set morphism $f : X_1 \to X_2$ *is an injective function $f : \mathcal{E}_1 \to \mathcal{E}_2$ such that $\lambda_1 = f; \lambda_2$ and*

$$X_2 \subseteq \bigcup_{\mathsf{P} \in X_1} \mathsf{sat}(\mathsf{P}, \mathbf{f})$$

The property can be stated as

$$\forall \mathsf{P}_2 \in X_2. \ \exists \mathsf{P}_1 \in X_1. \ \mathsf{P}_2 \in \mathsf{sat}(\mathsf{P}_1, \mathbf{f})$$

thus each path in P_2 is related to a (unique) path in P_1 via a morphism induced by $\mathbf{f}$. Let $\mathcal{P}(L)$ be the category whose objects are sets of paths over the same elements and labelling (i.e., subsets of $\mathbb{P}(\mathcal{E}, \lambda)$ for some $\mathcal{E}$ and λ), and arrows are path-set morphisms.

Proposition 2 (Path Pullbacks/Pushouts). *The category $\mathcal{P}(L)$ of sets of paths and path-set morphisms has (strict) initial object and pullbacks.*

As for $\mathcal{I}(L)$, also $\mathcal{P}(L)$ admits a weak form of pushouts along monos.

Remark 1. The initial object is the set in $2^{\mathbb{P}(\emptyset, \lambda_\emptyset)}$ including only the empty path ϵ. As for pullbacks, let $\mathbf{f}_i : X_i \to X$ be path-set morphisms, assuming the functions on elements to be identities for the sake of simplicity, and let $\mathcal{E} = \mathcal{E}_1 \cap \mathcal{E}_2$. Then, the pullback is the set $X_1|_{\mathcal{E}} \cup X_2|_{\mathcal{E}}$ in $2^{\mathbb{P}(\mathcal{E}, \lambda)}$ with $\lambda = \lambda_1|_{\mathcal{E}} = \lambda_2|_{\mathcal{E}}$. As for pushouts, let $\mathbf{f} : X \to X_i$ be injective path-set morphisms, assuming the functions on elements to be identities for the sake of simplicity, and $\mathcal{E} = \mathcal{E}_1 \cup \mathcal{E}_2$. Then, the "weak" pushout is the set $X_1 \otimes X_2$ in $2^{\mathbb{P}(\mathcal{E}, \lambda)}$ with λ the extension of λ_1 and λ_2.

5.3   A Categorical Correspondence

It is now time to move towards our categorical characterisation of specifications.

First, let us restrict our attention to functors $F : I(L) \to \mathcal{P}(L)$ that preserve the underlying set of objects, i.e., such that the underlying function on objects Ob_F maps an LDAG G into a subset of $2^{\mathbb{P}(\mathcal{E}_G, \lambda_G)}$ (and preserves the underlring function on path-set morphisms). We also say that F is coherent if $F(G) = \bigotimes_{e \in \mathcal{E}_G} F(G|_{-\preceq e})$ for all LDAGs G. Thus, any such functor F that preserves the initial object (i.e., $F(\epsilon) = \{\epsilon\}$) gives raise to a specification: it just suffices to consider the object function $Ob_F : Ob_{I(L)} \to Ob_{\mathcal{P}(L)}$.

Proposition 3. *Let $F : I(L) \to \mathcal{P}(L)$ be a (coherent) functor preserving the initial object. Then Ob_F is a (coherent) specification.*

For the inverse we need an additional lemma.

Lemma 6. *Let S be a coherent specification and $\mathcal{E} \subseteq \mathcal{E}_G$ downward closed. Then $S(G)|_{\mathcal{E}} \subseteq S(G|_{\mathcal{E}})$.*

The lemma above immediately implies the following result.

Proposition 4. *A coherent specification S induces a coherent functor $\mathbb{M}(S) : I(L) \to \mathcal{P}(L)$ preserving the initial object such that $Ob_{\mathbb{M}(S)} = S$.*

By using Propositions 3 and 4 we can state the main result of this section.

Theorem 3. *There is a bijection between coherent specifications and coherent functors $I(L) \to \mathcal{P}(L)$ preserving the initial object.*

6   Conclusions and Future Works

Our contribution proposes a denotational view of replicated data types. While most of the traditional approaches are operational in flavour [4,7,8], we strived for a formalism for specifications which could exploit the classical tools of algebraic specification theory. More precisely, we associate to each configuration (i.e., visibility) a set of admissible arbitrations. Differently from those previous approaches, our presentation naturally accommodates non-deterministic specifications and enables abstract definitions allowing for different strategies in conflict resolution. Our formulation brings into light some properties held by mainstream specification formalisms: beside the obvious property of functionality, they also satisfy coherence and saturation. A coherent specification can neither prescribe an arbitration order between events that are unrelated by visibility nor allow for additional arbitrations over past events when a configuration is extended (i.e., a new top element is added to visibility). Instead, a saturated specification cannot impose any constraint to the arbitration of top elements. Note that saturation does not hold when requiring that admissible arbitrations should be also topological orderings of visibility. Hence, the approaches in [2,4] generate specifications that are not saturated. We remark that this relation between visibility and arbitration translates in a quite different property in our setting, and this suggests that consistency models defined as relations between visibility and arbitration (e.g., *monotonic* and *causal* consistency) could have alternative characterisations. We plan to explore these connections in future works.

Another question concerns coherence, which prevents a specification from choosing an arbitration order on events that are unrelated by visibility and forbids, e.g., the definition of strategies that arbitrate first the events coming from a particular replica. Consequently, it becomes natural to look for those RDTs and consistency models that are the counterpart of non-coherent specifications, still preserving some suitable notion of causality between events. We do believe that the weaker property $S(\mathsf{G})|_{-\prec e} \subseteq S(\mathsf{G}|_{-\prec e})$ (that is, no additional arbitration over past events when a configuration is extended) is a worthwhile alternative, accommodating for many examples that impose less restrictions on the set of admissible paths (hence, that may allow more freedom to the arbitration).

These issues might be further clarified by our categorical presentation. Our proposal is inspired by current work on the semantics of nominal calculi [11], and it shares similarities with [10], since our category $\mathcal{G}$ is the sub-category of their **FinSet**$^{\rightrightarrows}$ with past-reflecting morphisms. The results on Sect. 5 focus on a functorial characterisation of specifications. We chose an easy way out for establishing the bijection between functors and specifications by restricting the possible object functions and by defining coherence "on the nose", (i.e., by considering functors F such that $F(\mathsf{G}) \subseteq 2^{\mathbb{P}(E_\mathsf{G}, \lambda_\mathsf{G})}$ and $F(\mathsf{G}) = \bigotimes_{e \in E_\mathsf{G}} F(\mathsf{G}|_{-\prec e}))$, since requiring the specification to be coherent is needed in order to obtain the functor in Proposition 4. A proper characterisation should depend on the properties of F over the arrows of $\mathcal{G}$ (such as pullback/pushout preservation), instead of the properties of the objects in its image on $\mathcal{P}$.

The same categorical presentation may shed light on suitable operators on specifications. Indeed, this is the usual situation when providing a functorial semantics for a language (see e.g. [1], and the references therein, among many others), and intuitively we have already a freshness operator $F^\ell(\mathsf{G}) = F(\mathsf{G}^\ell)$, along the lines of edge allocation in [10]. We plan to extend these remarks into a full-fledged algebra for specifications.

References

1. Bonchi, F., Buscemi, M.G., Ciancia, V., Gadducci, F.: A presheaf environment for the explicit fusion calculus. J. Autom. Reasoning **49**(2), 161–183 (2012)
2. Burckhardt, S.: Principles of eventual consistency. Found. Trends Program. Lang. **1**(1–2), 1–150 (2014)
3. Burckhardt, S., Gotsman, A., Yang, H.: Understanding eventual consistency. Technical Report MSR-TR-2013-39, Microsoft Research (2013)
4. Burckhardt, S., Gotsman, A., Yang, H., Zawirski, M.: Replicated data types: specification, verification, optimality. In: Jagannathan, S., Sewell, P. (eds.) POPL 2014, pp. 271–284. ACM (2014)

5. Cerone, A., Bernardi, G., Gotsman, A.: A framework for transactional consistency models with atomic visibility. In: Aceto, L., de Frutos-Escrig, D. (eds.) CONCUR 2015. LIPIcs, vol. 42. Schloss Dagstuhl-Leibniz-Zentrum fuer Informatik (2015)

6. Gilbert, S., Lynch, N.: Brewer's conjecture and the feasibility of consistent, available, partition-tolerant web services. SIGACT News **33**(2), 51–59 (2002)

7. Gotsman, A., Yang, H.: Composite replicated data types. In: Vitek, J. (ed.) ESOP 2015. LNCS, vol. 9032, pp. 585–609. Springer, Heidelberg (2015). doi:10.1007/978-3-662-46669-8_24

8. Gotsman, A., Yang, H., Ferreira, C., Najafzadeh, M., Shapiro, M.: 'Cause i'm strong enough: reasoning about consistency choices in distributed systems. In: Bodík, R., Majumdar, R. (eds.) POPL 2016, pp. 371–384. ACM (2016)

9. Joyal, A., Nielson, M., Winskel, G.: Bisimulation and open maps. In: LICS 1993, pp. 418–427. IEEE (1993)

10. Montanari, U., Sammartino, M.: A network-conscious π-calculus and its coalgebraic semantics. Theor. Comput. Sci. **546**, 188–224 (2014)

11. Pitts, A.M.: Nominal Sets: Names and Symmetry in Computer Science. Cambridge University Press, Cambridge (2013)

12. Shapiro, M., Preguiça, N., Baquero, C., Zawirski, M.: Conflict-free replicated data types. In: Défago, X., Petit, F., Villain, V. (eds.) SSS 2011. LNCS, vol. 6976, pp. 386–400. Springer, Heidelberg (2011). doi:10.1007/978-3-642-24550-3_29

13. Shapiro, M., Preguiça, N., Baquero, C., Zawirski, M.: A comprehensive study of convergent and commutative replicated data types. Technical Report RR-7506, Inria-Centre Paris-Rocquencourt (2011)

14. Sivaramakrishnan, K.C., Kaki, G., Jagannathan, S.: Declarative programming over eventually consistent data stores. In: Grove, D., Blackburn, S. (eds.) PLDI 2015, pp. 413–424. ACM (2015)

Resource, Components and Information Flow

Many-to-Many Information Flow Policies

Paolo Baldan[1], Alessandro Beggiato[2], and Alberto Lluch Lafuente[3(✉)]

[1] Dipartimento di Matematica, Università di Padova, Padova, Italy
baldan@math.unipd.it
[2] IMT School for Advanced Studies Lucca, Lucca, Italy
alessandro.beggiato@imtlucca.it
[3] DTU Compute, Technical University of Denmark, Lyngby, Denmark
albl@dtu.dk

Abstract. Information flow techniques typically classify information according to suitable security levels and enforce policies that are based on binary relations between individual levels, e.g., stating that information is allowed to flow from one level to another. We argue that some information flow properties of interest naturally require coordination patterns that involve *sets* of security levels rather than individual levels: some secret information could be safely disclosed to a set of confidential channels of incomparable security levels, with individual leaks considered instead illegal; a group of competing agencies might agree to disclose their secrets, with individual disclosures being undesired, etc. Motivated by this we propose a simple language for expressing information flow policies where the usual admitted flow relation between individual security levels is replaced by a relation between sets of security levels, thus allowing to capture coordinated flows of information. The flow of information is expressed in terms of causal dependencies and the satisfaction of a policy is defined with respect to an event structure that is assumed to capture the causal structure of system computations. We suggest applications to secret exchange protocols, program security and security architectures, and discuss the relation to classic notions of information flow control.

Keywords: Information flow · Coordination · Concurrency · Declassification · Non-interference · Causality · Event structures

1   Introduction

As the number of interconnected devices increases, the focus on security-related aspects of coordinated computations gains more and more relevance and appeal. Techniques for controlling and enforcing the flow of information need to be applied, and possibly extended to deal with coordination aspects. Typically, the entities of a system are assigned a security level, and information flow policies prescribe which interactions are legal and which are forbidden. This is normally expressed via a relation that models the admitted flows between security levels.

J.-M. Jacquet and M. Massink (Eds.): COORDINATION 2017, LNCS 10319, pp. 159–177, 2017.
DOI: 10.1007/978-3-319-59746-1_9

Motivation and Problem Statement. The information flow relations used in the literature to model policies are almost invariably binary relations between individual security levels. This paper is motivated by the observation that some desired information flow properties naturally involve suitable coordinated *sets* of security levels rather than mere individual levels.

For example, some secret information (say, owned by a government agency E, cf. Fig. 1) could be safely disclosed to a set of confidential channels of incomparable security levels (say, corresponding to competing investors C and D) *simultaneously*, with individual leaks considered instead illegal or unfair. This is for instance, the spirit of U.S. security and exchange commission's *regulation fair disclosure* [22]. Dually, a group of competing companies (say A and B in Fig. 1) may agree to *collectively* disclose their secrets (say to the government agency E), with individual disclosures being undesired. This paper is motivated by such scenarios and, in general, by the following question: *what is a natural notion of information flow policies that regulate flows among sets of security levels?*

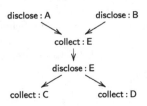

Fig. 1. Information flow example.

Contributions. We address the question by proposing a simple policy specification language that extends the usual security diagrams by allowing relations between *sets* of security levels instead of just *single* levels. The clauses in our policies are of the form $A_1, \ldots, A_m \rightsquigarrow B_1, \ldots, B_n$, intuitively meaning that the security levels $A_1, \ldots, A_m$ are allowed to coordinate in order to let information flow to security levels $B_1, \ldots, B_n$.

In our approach the flow of information between entities is captured in terms of the existence of causal dependencies between events representing occurrences of actions of such entities. In particular, we use event structures [16,25] as a reference semantic model. The idea is that causal dependencies between events represent the transfer of some information. Thus causal dependencies are required to obey to coordination patterns as prescribed by the information flow policy. For traditional intransitive binary policies any flow of information, i.e., any (direct) causality $a < b$ between events a and b needs to be allowed by the policy, i.e., if the level of a is A and the level of b is B then the policy has to include a clause $A \rightsquigarrow B$. We generalise this to many-to-many policies by requiring that any direct causality $a < b$ is part of a possibly more complex interaction that conforms to a coordination pattern allowed by the policy, i.e., if A_1 and B_1 are the security levels of a and b, respectively, there must exist a clause $A_1, A_2 \ldots A_n \rightsquigarrow B_1, B_2, \ldots, B_m$ in the policy and events $a_1, a_2, \ldots, a_n$, $b_1, b_2, \ldots, b_m$ (with b equal to some b_k) such that each event a_i has level A_i, each event b_j has level B_j, and events $a_1, \ldots a_n$ are (suitably coordinated) causes of the events $b_1, \ldots, b_m$.

As an example, consider the diagram of Fig. 1, where arrows represent direct causalities between events and the security levels coincide with the principals. For events we use the notation name : level. The direct causality from event disclose : A to event collect : E is allowed by the policy A, B $\rightsquigarrow$ E since collect : E is also causally dependent on disclose : B, thus providing some guarantee of the fact that A and B disclose their secrets collectively. Analogously, the direct causality from disclose : E to collect : C is allowed by the policy E $\rightsquigarrow$ A, B since there is a causality relation from disclose : E to collect : D as well, yielding some sort of simultaneity in the disclosure of the secrets from E to C, D.

We study several properties of our policy language. In particular, we observe that checking whether a system satisfies a policy is decidable for a general class of event structures, the so-called regular trace event structures [24]. As a matter of fact, policy satisfaction is expressible as a first-order property and the corresponding model checking problem is decidable [12]. We also discuss the relation with classical notions of information flow control, including non-interference and declassification, and suggest applications beyond secret exchange protocols, including program security and routing in security architectures.

Synopsis. Section 2 introduces several motivating examples, including a running example that is used throughout the paper. Section 3 provides some technical background on event structures. Section 4 presents the policy language, the notion of policy satisfaction and a decidability result. Section 5 compares with notions of information flow based on interleaving semantics, in particular with trace- and bisimulation-based non-interference. Section 6 discusses other related works. Section 7 concludes our paper and outlines future research.

2   Motivating Examples

We introduce here some examples that have motivated our work and that we envisage as application domains for many-to-many information flow analysis.

Simultaneous Secret Exchange. Consider first the problem of exchanging a secret between two parties, say Alice and Bob. We shall use this as a running example throughout the paper. A way to solve the problem would be to proceed according to the protocol in Fig. 2a, where Alice starts sending her secret to Bob, which then replies with his own secret. The graphical representation (technically a security-labelled event structure) will be explained later. Here it suffices to understand

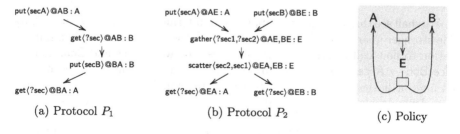

Fig. 2. Two secret exchange protocols and a security policy.

that the figure represents the structure of the communication in an execution, where an event put⟨m⟩@C : P, represents party P sending m on channel C, and an event get⟨t⟩@C : P, represents party P receiving a message from channel C to be saved according to the pattern t (binding/formal fields being denoted with a leading question mark "?"). Arrows represent (direct) causal dependencies between events. The protocol has essentially the same structure of classical key exchange protocols [14] and does not solve one of the main concerns of the so-called *simultaneous secret exchange problem*, which is to avoid or minimise competitive advantage among the parties exchanging the secrets (see e.g. [17]). If we assume to deal with information of two security levels (one for each party), a standard approach to information flow does not help much in this scenario, as we can just allow flows between Alice and Bob (and thus accept any protocol with no guarantee) or forbid them (and thus reject all protocols).

One standard solution to the simultaneous secret exchange problem is to use an intermediary (say Eve). Many-to-many information flow policies can be used to specify some desired properties of intermediary-based protocols. For example, we may require that the intermediary forwards information to Alice and Bob simultaneously (denoted by an information flow policy Eve ⇝ Alice, Bob), and that the intermediary accepts information from Alice and Bob only if collectively disclosed (denoted by an information flow policy by Alice, Bob ⇝ Eve). A graphical representation for this security policy, that will be refined and explained in detail later, can be found in Fig. 2c. The protocol sketched in Fig. 2b, which uses multi-party interactions, satisfies the desired information flow properties. The protocol uses in particular an MPI-like gather operation to point-wise collect a list messages from different sources, and MPI-like scatter operation to point-wise broadcast the list of secrets.

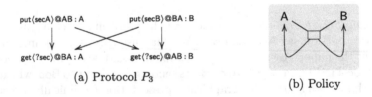

(a) Protocol P_3

(b) Policy

Fig. 3. A secret exchange protocol satisfying a policy without intermediary.

We shall see that the causality approach to information flow allows one to provide stronger guarantees on secret exchange protocols, by only admitting information to flow collectively and simultaneously between Alice and Bob, namely, Alice, Bob ⇝ Alice, Bob (see Fig. 3b, for a graphical representation), even without intermediaries. This is realised by the protocol in Fig. 3a, where vertical and cross dependencies are control and data dependencies, respectively.

Language-Based Security and Declassification. We use a classic problem of declassification in access control to illustrate how our approach can be used to check information flow properties in the traditional sense [20], and how our policies can be used to specify several useful forms of declassification [13,21]. The access control program below, on the left, written in a simple imperative programming language in the style of [20], is checking a **password** and preparing a reply to the **user** in a variable **display**. A causal semantics to the program can be given based on the following idea: (i) events correspond to variable updates or initialisations, (ii) an update $x := e$ causally depends on previous updates of all variables in e or their initialisation, (iii) if a control point is conditioned by y then all updates in all branches of the control causally depend on the latest update of y (or its initialisation), and (iv) conflict relations (represented as dotted lines) capture branching. For the program at hand, the resulting event structure can be found on the right.

```
if downgrade then
    if check(user,password) then
        display := "ok";
        log := log , ⟨user, "ok"⟩;
    else
        display := "ko";
        log := log , ⟨user, "ko"⟩;
```

Disregarding whether the password is correct or not, there is a flow of information concerning the password to the user, represented as a causality relation from the latest update of the password to the updates of variable **display**.

For simplicity assume that each variable has its own security level, coinciding with the variable name. A standard security type system would consider the program to be insecure and our approach would agree on that in absence of a policy **password** ⤳ **display** allowing the leaks. Of course, such a policy is not desirable in general (e.g. the user may be malicious). However, the program provides some guarantees that make it acceptable from the security point of view. First, the reply is also influenced by a check on variable **downgrade**, which may be used to disable login (e.g. after several unsuccessful attempts). This provides a standard form of controlled declassification. Requiring that the declassification is controlled as desired can be done through a policy **password, downgrade** ⤳ **display**. In addition, the program above is using a **log** to keep track of logging attempts. This provides the additional desirable property that password leaks are only possible when the information concerning the access attempt also flows to the **log** (denoted **user, password** ⤳ **display, log**).

Security Architectures. A third motivating case are systems where information of different security levels needs to traverse shared resources, like a routing network. An archetypal example is the *Multiple Independent Levels of Security* (MILS) architecture [19]. The diagram on the left of the figure below depicts a simplified version of such an architecture, inspired by the case study of [11]. Information from security level A (resp. B) should be allowed to flow into C (resp. D) only. Messages are routed through a common network made of a multiplexer component (M) that accepts messages from both A and B and forwards it to a demultiplexer component (W), which dispatches the messages either to C or to D, according to routing information.

The diagram on the left of the figure can be also seen as an information flow policy (isomorphic to the architecture) aiming at enforcing the desired flows. The problem of this naive policy is that it allows also for undesired flows, e.g., from A to D and from B to C, indirectly through the network: a protocol wrongly routing the information would be admitted by the policy. Consider instead a policy where individual flows from W to C and D are not allowed, and instead, they need to be collectively produced with A and B, respectively (denoted A, W ⤳ C and B, W ⤳ D). The new policy (sketched on the right of the figure) would reject protocols wrongly routing the messages.

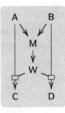

3   Event Structures

We model the causal behaviour of a system with prime event structures [16, 25], a well-studied semantic model of concurrency where causality is a primitive notion. The way in which an event structure is associated to a specific formalism will depend on the system features one intends to capture (data/control flow, etc.).

Definition 1 (event structure). *An* event structure $\mathcal{E} = \langle E, \leq, \# \rangle$ *consists of a set E of* events, *a partial order relation $\leq \subseteq E \times E$ called* causality, *and an irreflexive symmetric relation $\# \subseteq E \times E$ called* conflict *such that:*

(i) for all $e \in E$ the set of causes $[e] = \{e' \in E \mid e' \leq e\}$ is finite (finitariness);
(ii) for all $e, e', e'' \in E$, if $e \# e'$ and $e' \leq e''$ then $e \# e''$ (conflict inheritance).

For $e, e' \in E$ we write $e < e'$ (e is a proper cause of e') if $e \leq e'$ and $e \neq e'$. We say that e is a direct cause of e' (denoted $e \lessdot e'$) if $e < e'$ and for all $e'' \in E$ if $e \leq e'' \leq e'$ either $e'' = e$ or $e'' = e'$. The causes of a set of events $X \subseteq E$ are defined as $[X] = \bigcup_{e \in X}[e]$. We lift causality to sets of events, with a universal interpretation, i.e., for $X, Y \subseteq E$, we write $X < Y$ (resp. $X \lessdot Y$) if for all $e \in X$ and $e' \in Y$ we have $e < e'$ (resp. $e \lessdot e'$). For $e \in E$ we define the set of its *proper causes* as $[e) = [e] \backslash \{e\}$. We say that $e, e' \in E$ are in *direct conflict*, written $e \#_\mu e'$, when $e \# e'$ and for all $e'' \in [e)$ it holds $\neg(e'' \# e')$ and for all $e''' \in [e')$ it holds $\neg(e \# e''')$, i.e., the conflict is not inherited.

Figures 2a and 3a show three event structures corresponding to different protocols in our running example. The set of events correspond to communication operations, and are annotated with the initials of the principal executing the action (which is actually the security level assigned to the event, as we shall explain later). Causality is represented graphically by directed arrows, while conflict (to be seen in subsequent examples) is represented by dotted undirected lines. For the sake of a lighter notation, we follow the tradition of depicting direct causalities and conflicts only.

Event structures describe the possible events in computations and their mutual relations. When $e < e'$ then e must necessarily occur before e', while if $e\#e'$ then the occurrence of e excludes e' (and vice versa). Computations are characterised as conflict-free sets of events, containing the causes of all events.

Definition 2 (configuration). *Let $\mathcal{E} = \langle E, \leq, \# \rangle$ be an event structure.*
A configuration *of $\mathcal{E}$ is a subset $C \subseteq E$ such that $\neg(e\#e')$ for all $e, e' \in C$ and $[C] = C$. The set of configurations of $\mathcal{E}$ is denoted $\mathcal{C}(\mathcal{E})$.*

For any event e, the causes $[e]$ and the proper causes $[e)$ are configurations.

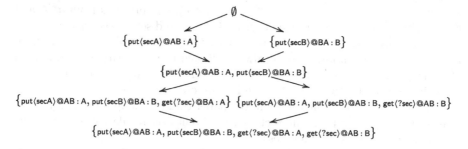

Fig. 4. Configurations of the event structure in Fig. 3a.

Figure 4 depicts all the configurations of the event structure of Fig. 3a. They are related by arrows that represent transitions, i.e., how a configuration can be extended to another configuration by adding an event.

Definition 3 (extension). *Let $\mathcal{E} = \langle E, \leq, \# \rangle$ be an event structure, and let $C \in \mathcal{C}(\mathcal{E})$. We say that an event e* extends *C when $e \notin C$ and $C \cup \{e\} \in \mathcal{C}(\mathcal{E})$. In this situation we write $C \oplus e$ for $C \cup \{e\}$. The set of possible extensions of a configuration C is $\mathsf{PE}(C) = \{e \in E \mid C \oplus e \in \mathcal{C}(\mathcal{E})\}$.*

The transition system semantics of an event structure is obtained considering configurations as states and extensions as transitions.

Definition 4 (transition system). *The* transition system *of an event structure $\mathcal{E} = \langle E, \leq, \# \rangle$ is the tuple $TS(\mathcal{E}) = \langle \mathcal{C}(\mathcal{E}), \{C \rightarrow C \oplus e \mid C \in \mathcal{C}(\mathcal{E}) \wedge e \in E\} \rangle$.*

The diagram of Fig. 4 represents the transition system of the event structure in Fig. 3a. When events carry a label, the above definition yields labelled transition systems with transitions $C \xrightarrow{a} C \oplus e$, where a is the label of e.

4 Many-to-Many Information Flow Policies

We introduce here our notion of many-to-many information flow policies, which describe the legal interactions among sets of security levels. Section 4.1 presents the policy language, Sect. 4.2 defines the semantics, Sect. 4.3 studies some of its properties, and Sect. 4.4 provides a decidability result.

4.1   A Policy Language for Many-to-Many Information Flows

We start by introducing the syntax of many-to-many information flow policies.

Definition 5 (many-to-many information flow policy). *Let $\mathscr{L}$ be a finite set of security levels and $\mathscr{C} = \{d, f\}$ be a set of coordination constraints. A many-to-many multi-level information flow policy is a pair $\Pi = \langle \mathscr{L}, \leadsto \rangle$ where $\leadsto \subseteq 2^{\mathscr{L}} \times 2^{\mathscr{C}} \times 2^{\mathscr{L}}$ and $(A, \emptyset, A) \in \leadsto$ for all $A \in \mathscr{L}$. We denote by $\mathcal{P}$ the set of all policies.*

We will write $A \overset{\sigma}{\leadsto} B$ for $(A, \sigma, B) \in \leadsto$, often dropping brackets from σ, A and B. Security levels in $\mathscr{L}$ are ranged over by $A, B, \ldots$ and sets of security levels are ranged over by $A, B, \ldots$. The requirement that $A \leadsto A$ for all $A \in \mathscr{L}$ is natural in information flow: information is always allowed to flow within the same level of security. Finiteness of the set of security levels $\mathscr{L}$ is a natural assumption. It could be meaningful to allow $\mathscr{L}$ to be infinite only when security levels can be generated dynamically. The theory in the paper could be adapted trivially apart from the decidability result in Sect. 4.4, that relies on regularity of the model which in turn implies the finiteness of $\mathscr{L}$.

Note that an information flow policy can be seen as a directed hyper-graph whose hyper-arcs are labelled by (possibly empty) subsets of the alphabet of coordination constraints $\mathscr{C}$ (to be explained later). This analogy is exploited in the visual representation of security policies.

Informally, a clause $A \overset{\sigma}{\leadsto} B$ specifies that a group of entities whose set of security levels is A is allowed to influence a group of entities whose set of security levels is B, subject to the coordination constraints in σ. E.g., a policy

$$\text{Alice, Bob} \leadsto \text{Eve} \tag{1}$$

allows Alice and Bob to influence Eve, while the policy

$$\text{Eve} \leadsto \text{Alice, Bob} \tag{2}$$

allows Eve to influence Alice and Bob. We will see that the above two policies can be combined to allow Alice and Bob to exchange their secrets using Eve as an intermediary, and providing some fairness guarantees. A different policy that would allow a similar flow of information is

$$\begin{aligned} \text{Alice,Bob,Eve} &\leadsto \text{Alice,Bob} \\ \text{Alice} &\leadsto \text{Eve} \\ \text{Bob} &\leadsto \text{Eve} \end{aligned} \tag{3}$$

that allows Alice, Bob and Eve to influence Alice and Bob, Alice to influence Eve, and Bob to influence Eve. Intuitively, this can be used to specify that both Alice and Bob can talk individually to the intermediary Eve, which in turn can talk to Alice and Bob in coordination with them.

For a clause in $A \overset{\sigma}{\leadsto} B$ the superscript $\sigma \subseteq \mathscr{C}$ allows one to specify some additional coordination constraints on the interaction pattern among the levels

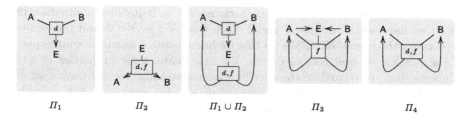

Fig. 5. Security policies, graphically.

in $\mathbb{A}$ and $\mathbb{B}$. The superscript d requires all entities in $\mathbb{A}$ to influence all the entities in $\mathbb{B}$ *directly*. For instance, for the policy (1) we might want Alice and Bob to influence Eve directly, with no delegation among them or to another intermediary. This leads to the policy $\Pi_1 \triangleq$ Alice, Bob $\overset{d}{\rightsquigarrow}$ Eve depicted in Fig. 5.

In general the flow of information to all of the entities in $\mathbb{B}$ is just potential, i.e., the information is made available to entities in $\mathbb{B}$ simultaneously, but it could happen that after one entity in $\mathbb{B}$ acquired the information (some of) the others get disabled. The superscript f, that stands for "fair" disclosure, prevents the above to happen: whenever information flows to one of the entities in $\mathbb{B}$, then it must eventually flow to all other entities in $\mathbb{B}$.

It is worth to remark that the information flowing to the entities in $\mathbb{B}$ need not be the same since causality in our approach represents in general the transfer of *some* information. Ensuring that the *same* information is being transferred depends on the actual causal semantics under consideration.

In our previous examples, for policies (2) and (3) it is natural to require fairness to forbid competition among Alice and Bob. This leads to the policies Π_2 and Π_3 in Fig. 5. Observe that fairness constraints are superfluous when there is only one security level in the target, like Eve in Π_1. Notice that in policy Π_3, the absence of the "direct" constraint allows Eve to act as an intermediary. A variant of Π_3 without intermediary is $\Pi_4 \triangleq$ Alice, Bob $\overset{d,f}{\rightsquigarrow}$ Alice, Bob, which specifies a direct exchange of information between Alice and Bob.

4.2 Semantics of Many-to-Many Policies

In our setting, a *security model* is an event structure used to capture the structure of computations and flows. Events correspond to actions of some security level.

Definition 6 (causal security model). *Let $\mathscr{L}$ be a set of security levels. A (causal) security model in $\mathscr{L}$ is a pair $\langle \mathcal{E}, \lambda \rangle$ where $\mathcal{E} = \langle E, \leq, \# \rangle$ is an event structure and $\lambda : E \to \mathscr{L}$ is a security assignment.*

The security assignment λ maps each event to a security level and can be lifted to sets of events: given $X \subseteq E$ we let $\lambda X = \{ \mathsf{A} \in \mathscr{L} \mid \exists e \in X . \lambda(e) = \mathsf{A} \}$. For $X \subseteq E$ and $\mathbb{A} \subseteq \mathscr{L}$ we write $X : \mathbb{A}$ if $|X| = |\mathbb{A}|$ and $\lambda X = \mathbb{A}$. We write $e : \mathsf{A}$ instead of $\{e\} : \{\mathsf{A}\}$. The event structures of Figs. 1, 2 and 3a are security models, where the security assignment corresponds to the principal annotations.

We next formalise in which sense a clause $\mathbb{A} \stackrel{\sigma}{\leadsto} \mathbb{B}$ justifies a situation in which we have sets of events X and Y such that $X : \mathbb{A}$, $Y : \mathbb{B}$ and the events in X cause the events in Y. We do this by introducing a semantic counterpart of the relation $\stackrel{\sigma}{\leadsto}$ over sets of events. We first define some properties of sets of events that are related to the coordination constraints. We say that a set of events $X \subseteq E$ is *flat* if $[X)$ is a configuration and for every $e, e' \in X$ it holds $e \not< e'$. Notice that when X is flat, all events in X are enabled at $[X)$. The events in a flat set X may disable each other or there can be future events that disable some of them but not the others. We say that X is *fair* if for all events $e, e' \in X$ and event $e'' \in E$, we have $e\#e''$ iff $e'\#e''$. Note that in this case, since the events in X have the same conflicts and conflict is irreflexive, either all or none of them is executable.

Definition 7 (relation $\stackrel{\sigma}{\to}$). *Let $\mathcal{E} = \langle E, \leq, \# \rangle$ be an event structure and let $X, Y \subseteq E$. We write*

(i) $X \twoheadrightarrow Y$ *if $X < Y$, and Y is flat;*

(ii) $X \stackrel{d}{\twoheadrightarrow} Y$ *if $X \twoheadrightarrow Y$ and $X \lessdot Y$;*

(iii) $X \stackrel{f}{\twoheadrightarrow} Y$ *if $X \twoheadrightarrow Y$ and Y is fair;*

(iv) $X \stackrel{d,f}{\twoheadrightarrow} Y$ *if $X \stackrel{d}{\twoheadrightarrow} Y$ and $X \stackrel{f}{\twoheadrightarrow} Y$.*

In words, we write $X \twoheadrightarrow Y$ whenever each event in X is a cause for each event in Y, and the set Y is flat, ensuring that $[Y)$ is a configuration enabling all events in Y.

We write $X \stackrel{d}{\twoheadrightarrow} Y$ when additionally $X \lessdot Y$, i.e., causality is direct, meaning that delegation is not permitted.

Notice that when $X \twoheadrightarrow Y$ events in Y are all enabled at configuration $[Y)$, so that the possibility of getting information from X is granted to all elements of Y, but once an event in Y is executed other events in Y could get disabled: it may be the case that the events in Y disable each other or, more generally, they could be in conflict with different events. The constraint $X \stackrel{f}{\twoheadrightarrow} Y$, asking that Y is fair, guarantees, instead, that if the information reaches one of the events in Y it will eventually reach all of them, or, more formally, that any configuration intersecting Y extends to a configuration including Y. Note that, in absence of conflicts, the fairness constraint becomes inessential since it is always trivially satisfied.

We can now define what it means for a security model to satisfy a policy.

Definition 8 (security). *Let $\Pi = \langle \mathcal{L}, \leadsto \rangle$ be an information flow policy, $\mathcal{E} = \langle E, \leq, \# \rangle$ be an event structure, let $\langle \mathcal{E}, \lambda \rangle$ be a security model in $\mathcal{L}$. Given $X, Y \subseteq E$ and $\sigma \subseteq \mathcal{C}$, we say that the clause $\mathbb{A} \stackrel{\sigma}{\leadsto} \mathbb{B} \in \Pi$ allows $X \stackrel{\sigma}{\twoheadrightarrow} Y$, written $\mathbb{A} \stackrel{\sigma}{\leadsto} \mathbb{B} \models X \stackrel{\sigma}{\twoheadrightarrow} Y$ if $X : \mathbb{A}$, $Y : \mathbb{B}$.*

We say that $\langle \mathcal{E}, \lambda \rangle$ satisfies Π or that $\langle \mathcal{E}, \lambda \rangle$ is Π-secure, denoted $\langle \mathcal{E}, \lambda \rangle \models \Pi$, if for all $e, e' \in E$ such that $e \lessdot e'$ there exist $X, Y \subseteq E$ with $e' \in Y$ such that $X \stackrel{\sigma}{\twoheadrightarrow} Y$ and $\mathbb{A} \stackrel{\sigma}{\leadsto} \mathbb{B} \models X \stackrel{\sigma}{\twoheadrightarrow} Y$ for some $\mathbb{A} \stackrel{\sigma}{\leadsto} \mathbb{B} \in \Pi$ such that $\lambda(e) \in \mathbb{A}$.

When λ is clear from the context we sometimes write $\mathcal{E} \models \Pi$.

Intuitively, a security model satisfies a policy if any direct causality $e \lessdot e'$ is part of a (possibly larger) interaction $X \xrightarrow{\sigma} Y$ justified by some clause $\mathbb{A} \xrightarrow{\cdot} \mathbb{B}$ of the policy. We require $e' \in Y$ in order to ensure that the flow to e' is influenced by $X : \mathbb{A}$ (recall that $X < Y$) and thus by all levels in $\mathbb{A}$. On the other hand, event e is not necessarily in X since the information of level $\lambda(e)$ that is required to flow to all levels in $\mathbb{B}$ might have been provided by another cause of e'. Still, since e is a cause of e', it will be part of any computation involving e', hence it will coordinate with the events in X to enable e'. This is fundamental, e.g., to implement a simultaneous disclosure asynchronously as we shall explain later.

Table 1. Models versus policies.

	$\Pi_1 \cup \Pi_2$	Π_3	Π_4
P_1			
P_3			✓
P_2	✓	✓	
P_4			
P_5		✓	
P_6		✓	

Table 1 summarizes the satisfaction of policies by the protocols of our running example. The double horizontal lines separate protocols without intermediaries (P_1, P_3) from those with intermediaries (P_2, P_4, P_5, P_6), and the vertical double lines separates policies with intermediaries $(\Pi_1 \cup \Pi_2$ and $\Pi_3)$ from policies without intermediaries (Π_4). We start discussing the scenarios with intermediaries.

The security model of Fig. 2b (Protocol P_2) satisfies the policies $\Pi_1 \cup \Pi_2$ and Π_3 of Fig. 5. For example, the direct causality $\mathsf{put}\langle \mathsf{secA}\rangle@\mathsf{AE} : \mathsf{A} \lessdot \mathsf{gather}\langle ?\mathsf{sec1}, ?\mathsf{sec2}\rangle@\mathsf{AE}, \mathsf{BE} : \mathsf{E}$ is justified by clause $\mathsf{Alice}, \mathsf{Bob} \xrightarrow{d} \mathsf{Eve}$ of policy Π_1, by choosing $X = \{\mathsf{put}\langle \mathsf{secA}\rangle@\mathsf{AE} : \mathsf{A}, \mathsf{put}\langle \mathsf{secB}\rangle@\mathsf{BE} : \mathsf{B}\}$ and $Y = \{\mathsf{gather}\langle ?\mathsf{sec1}, ?\mathsf{sec2}\rangle@\mathsf{AE}, \mathsf{BE} : \mathsf{E}\}$. In words, the disclosure to Eve is allowed since it is collectively made by Alice and Bob. The direct causalities between the multicast of Eve and the receptions by Alice and Bob are justified by the clauses in policies Π_2 or Π_3. In order to see this for the only clause of Π_2, observe that we can choose $X = \{\mathsf{scatter}\langle \mathsf{sec2}, \mathsf{sec1}\rangle@\mathsf{EA}, \mathsf{EB} : \mathsf{E}\}$ and $Y = \{\mathsf{get}\langle ?\mathsf{sec}\rangle@\mathsf{EA} : \mathsf{A}, \mathsf{get}\langle ?\mathsf{sec}\rangle@\mathsf{EB} : \mathsf{B}\}$. In words, both message receptions of Alice and Bob depend on Eve sending the secrets, and they cannot be disabled, hence they have the same (i.e., no) conflicts. For the only clause of Π_3 the situation is a bit more involved: the idea is to select Y as before and X to be the rest of the events. Intuitively, Eve acts as a delegated intermediary: the submission of the secrets by Alice and Bob influence their final receptions, indirectly through the events of Eve.

Consider now the event structures in Fig. 6, which represent variants of the protocols of our running example where Eve is used as an intermediary. They can be seen as alternatives to the protocol P_2 in Fig. 2b. Protocol P_4 is like P_2

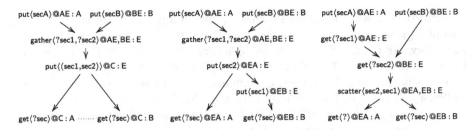

Fig. 6. Secret exchange protocols P_4 (left), P_5 (center) and P_6 (right).

but the intermediary does not scatter the secrets; these are instead combined in a composite message and sent to a channel C thus creating a conflict between Alice and Bob since both expect to extract the (combined) secrets from C. In protocol P_5, Eve sends the messages asynchronously with point-to-point operations, first to Alice and then to Bob. Finally, in P_6, the reception of the secrets is asynchronous, with point-to-point operations.

None of these variants satisfies policy $\Pi_1 \cup \Pi_2$. For instance, no clause in $\Pi_1 \cup \Pi_2$ justifies the direct causality put$\langle(\text{sec1}, \text{sec2})\rangle$@C : E < get$\langle?\text{sec}\rangle$@C : A in P_4 due to the conflict between get$\langle?\text{sec}\rangle$@C : A and get$\langle?\text{sec}\rangle$@C : B. In P_5 the direct causalities from Eve's put events to the get events of Alice and Bob cannot be justified since there is no Eve-labelled event that is a direct cause for both get events. Notice that such causalities could be justified if we drop the directness constraints from the clauses since the reception of the messages by Bob and Alice are causally dependent by the first put of Eve. Similarly, the direct causalities from Alice and Bob's put events to Eve's get events in P_6 cannot be justified.

The situation is different for Π_3. Indeed, both P_5 and P_6 satisfy the policy. Intuitively, the asynchronous collection of the secrets in P_6 that could not be justified in Π_2 can now be justified since Alice and Bob are allowed to talk to Eve independently. On the other hand, the asynchronous disclosure by Eve in P_5 is justified since it also depends on both Alice and Bob without directness constraint.

Similarly, it can be seen that among the protocols not using intermediaries, namely P_1 (Fig. 2a) and P_3 (Fig. 3a), only P_3 satisfies the policy Π_4. Protocol P_3 is indeed the only one that guarantees that Alice and Bob collectively make their secrets available to Alice and Bob simultaneously. Indeed, protocol P_3 has a unique advantage over P_1: when Alice (resp. Bob) gets the secrets, (s)he is not ensured to be in competitive advantage. Clearly, protocol P_1 does not have this property. Therefore, P_3 offers a solution to the simultaneous secret exchange problem with guarantees based on causality rather than on bounds on the amount of different information obtained by the parties (as e.g. in [8]).

4.3   Semantic Properties

We next present some properties of security policies. We first observe that aggregating security levels preserves the satisfaction of policies.

Proposition 1 (soundness of level aggregation). *Let $\langle \mathcal{E}, \lambda \rangle$ be a security model in $\mathcal{L}$ and $\rho : \mathcal{L} \to \mathcal{L}$, a total mapping between security levels (possibly merging some of them). If $\langle \mathcal{E}, \lambda \rangle \models \Pi$ then $\langle \mathcal{E}, \rho \circ \lambda \rangle \models \rho(\Pi)$.*

In the above definition $\rho(\Pi)$ is the homomorphic lifting of ρ to policies, i.e., $\rho(\Pi \cup \Pi') = \rho(\Pi) \cup \rho(\Pi')$, $\rho(\mathbb{A} \overset{\sigma}{\rightsquigarrow} \mathbb{B}) = \rho(\mathbb{A}) \overset{\sigma}{\rightsquigarrow} \rho(\mathbb{B})$ and $\rho(\emptyset) = \emptyset$.

Secondly, we discuss how policies can be related according to their strictness.

Definition 9 (strictness relation). *The strictness relation $\sqsubseteq \subseteq \mathcal{P} \times \mathcal{P}$ is defined as the least transitive and reflexive relation among policies closed under*

$$\frac{\Pi \sqsubseteq \Pi' \quad \Pi'_1 \sqsubseteq \Pi_1}{\Pi \cup \Pi_1 \sqsubseteq \Pi' \cup \Pi'_1} \text{ (CTX)} \qquad \frac{\sigma' \subseteq \sigma}{\mathbb{A} \overset{\sigma'}{\rightsquigarrow} \mathbb{B} \sqsubseteq \mathbb{A} \overset{\sigma}{\rightsquigarrow} \mathbb{B}} \text{ (CONSTR)}$$

$$\frac{\mathbb{A} = \mathbb{A}' \cup \mathbb{A}''}{\{\mathbb{A}' \overset{\sigma}{\rightsquigarrow} \mathbb{B}, \mathbb{A}'' \overset{\sigma}{\rightsquigarrow} \mathbb{B}\} \sqsubseteq \mathbb{A} \overset{\sigma}{\rightsquigarrow} \mathbb{B}} \text{ (SPLITL)} \qquad \frac{|\mathbb{B}| = 1}{\mathbb{A} \overset{\sigma \cup \{f\}}{\rightsquigarrow} \mathbb{B} \sqsubseteq \mathbb{A} \overset{\sigma}{\rightsquigarrow} \mathbb{B}} \text{ (CONSTRF)}$$

$$\frac{\mathbb{B} = \mathbb{B}' \cup \mathbb{B}''}{\{\mathbb{A} \overset{\sigma}{\rightsquigarrow} \mathbb{B}', \mathbb{A} \overset{\sigma}{\rightsquigarrow} \mathbb{B}''\} \sqsubseteq \mathbb{A} \overset{\sigma}{\rightsquigarrow} \mathbb{B}} \text{ (SPLITR)} \qquad \frac{|\mathbb{A}| = |\mathbb{B}| = 1}{\mathbb{A} \overset{\sigma \cup \{d\}}{\rightsquigarrow} \mathbb{B} \sqsubseteq \mathbb{A} \overset{\sigma}{\rightsquigarrow} \mathbb{B}} \text{ (CONSTRD)}$$

The intuition is the following. Rule CTX says that the strictness relation is preserved under context closure (i.e., if $\Pi \sqsubseteq \Pi'$ then $\Pi \cup \Pi'' \sqsubseteq \Pi' \cup \Pi''$). In addition, the relation is preserved even if the weaker policy Π is embedded in a larger context since the addition of clauses to a policy makes it more permissive. By rule SPLITL if the source $\mathbb{A}$ of a clause is split as $\mathbb{A}' \cup \mathbb{A}''$ then the clause can be relaxed by replacing it with two clauses having the same coordination constraints, the same targets and $\mathbb{A}'$ and $\mathbb{A}''$, respectively, as sources. This weakens the policy since any direct causality from an event of level $\mathbb{A} \in \mathbb{A}$ to an event of level $\mathbb{B} \in \mathbb{B}$ that is justified by $\mathbb{A} \overset{\sigma}{\rightsquigarrow} \mathbb{B}$ can be justified by $\mathbb{A}' \overset{\sigma}{\rightsquigarrow} \mathbb{B}$ or by $\mathbb{A}' \overset{\sigma}{\rightsquigarrow} \mathbb{B}$. Rule SPLITR is analogous, but with the split performed on the target. Rule CONSTR says that a clause can be relaxed by removing coordination constraints in σ. The last two rules CONSTRF and CONSTRD capture the fact that some constraints are trivially satisfied when clauses have a special shape. More precisely, given a clause $\mathbb{A} \overset{\sigma}{\rightsquigarrow} \mathbb{B}$ with $|\mathbb{B}| = 1$ the fairness constraint is vacuously satisfied and this motivates rule CONSTRF. If, additionally, $|\mathbb{A}| = 1$ the same applies to the directness constraint and this leads to rule CONSTRD.

When $\Pi \sqsubseteq \Pi'$ we say that Π is less restrictive than Π'. For instance, the policies Π_1 and Π_2 of our example are less restrictive than $\Pi_1 \cup \Pi_2$, and $\Pi_1 \cup \Pi_2$ and Π_3 are incomparable.

An interesting result is that the strictness relation $\sqsubseteq$ is sound and complete with respect to policy satisfaction.

Proposition 2 ($\sqsubseteq$ is sound and complete). *Let $\Pi = \langle \mathcal{L}, \rightsquigarrow \rangle, \Pi' = \langle \mathcal{L}, \rightsquigarrow' \rangle$ be two policies. The following holds*

(i) if $\Pi' \sqsubseteq \Pi$ then, for all models $\langle \mathcal{E}, \lambda \rangle$ in $\mathcal{L}$, $\langle \mathcal{E}, \lambda \rangle \models \Pi$ implies $\langle \mathcal{E}, \lambda \rangle \models \Pi'$;
(ii) if for all models $\langle \mathcal{E}, \lambda \rangle$ in $\mathcal{L}$, $\langle \mathcal{E}, \lambda \rangle \models \Pi$ implies $\langle \mathcal{E}, \lambda \rangle \models \Pi'$, then $\Pi' \sqsubseteq \Pi$.

By soundness, whenever $\Pi \sqsubseteq \Pi' \sqsubseteq \Pi$, the policies Π and Π' are equivalent, i.e., they are satisfied by exactly the same models. Syntactically different policies can be equivalent because they have clauses that differ for constraints which are vacuously satisfied (see rules CONSTRF and CONSTRD). Moreover, equivalent policies can differ for the presence of clauses which are useless because they are subsumed by others (e.g., if a policy includes the clauses $A \overset{\mathscr{C}}{\rightsquigarrow} B$, and $A' \overset{\mathscr{C}}{\rightsquigarrow} B$, the addition of a clause $A \cup A' \overset{\mathscr{C}}{\rightsquigarrow} B$ produces an equivalent policy).

It can be proved that the partial order induced by the preorder $(\mathcal{P}, \sqsubseteq)$ is a complete lattice. The (equivalence class of the) policy $\{(A, \mathscr{C}, A) \mid A \in \mathcal{L}\}$ is the top element (the most restrictive policy, which admits flows within individual security levels only), and (the equivalence class of) $\mathcal{L} \times \emptyset \times \mathcal{L}$ is the bottom element (the most permissive policy, which accepts all flows).

It is interesting to observe that the most restrictive policy satisfied by a security model does not exist in general. In fact, in order to determine such policy the idea could be to start with the most permissive policy, allowing for all binary flows, and keep using the rules (by joining or removing clauses, or adding coordination constraints) in order to restrict it until no more rules can be applied. This works, but the policy obtained is not uniquely determined, not even up to equivalence. For example, consider the security model $\mathcal{M}$ on the left of the figure below.

and the policies $\Pi_1 = (A, B \rightsquigarrow C), (A \rightsquigarrow B)$ and $\Pi_2 = (A \rightsquigarrow B), (B \rightsquigarrow C)$. Clearly, $\mathcal{M}$ satisfies both Π_1 and Π_2. Such policies are incomparable with respect to $\sqsubseteq$ (none of them can be obtained from the other by removing or joining classes, and indeed event structures can be found that satisfy one of them but not the other like those at the middle and the right of the figure above). Hence Π_1 and Π_2 are distinct minimal policies satisfied by model $\mathcal{M}$: the most restrictive policy satisfied by $\mathcal{M}$ does not exist.

4.4 Decidability on Regular Trace Event Structures

The event structure associated with a system exhibiting a cyclic behaviour is infinite, since events represent "occurrences" of computational steps. Nevertheless, we can show that policy satisfaction is decidable once we focus on regular trace event structures [24], a class of "effectively represented" event structures enjoying suitable regularity properties. This result relies on the observation that policy satisfaction can be expressed as a first order property and first order logic (FOL) is known to be decidable on regular trace event structures [12].

Roughly speaking, for regular trace event structures dependencies are required to be induced by a finite labelling, endowed with an independence relation. More precisely, recall that a *trace alphabet* consists of a pair $M = \langle \Sigma, I \rangle$ where Σ is a finite label alphabet and $I \subseteq \Sigma \times \Sigma$ is an irreflexive relation called the independence relation. An M-labelled event structure is an event structure $\mathcal{E}$, with a labelling function $\xi : E \to \Sigma$ satisfying (1) if $e \#_\mu e'$ then $\xi(e) \neq \xi(e')$; (2) if $e \lessdot e'$ or $e \#_\mu e'$ then $(\xi(e), \xi(e')) \notin I$; and (3) if $(\xi(e), \xi(e')) \notin I$ then $e \leq e'$ or $e \# e$. Conditions (2) and (3) ensure that the concurrency relation of the event structure (unordered events that are not in conflict) conforms to the independence relation of M. Condition (1) asks that the Σ-labelled transition system associated with $\mathcal{E}$ is deterministic. In addition, as in [12], we require the regularity of the set of (labelled) sequences of execution from the empty configuration in the event structure, i.e., of the set $seq(\mathcal{E}) = \{\sigma \in \Sigma^* \mid \emptyset \xrightarrow{\sigma}^* C \text{ in } TS(\mathcal{E})\}$.

Definition 10 (regular trace event structure). *An event structure $\mathcal{E}$ is regular trace if it is M-labelled for some trace alphabet $M = \langle \Sigma, I \rangle$ and $seq(\mathcal{E}) \subseteq \Sigma^*$ is a regular language.*

When we need to make the trace alphabet explicit, we say that the event structure $\mathcal{E}$ is M-regular trace. The class of regular trace event structures is quite general. In [23] it has been shown to coincide with the class of event structures associated with finite safe Petri nets by the unfolding construction [16]. We first instantiate the notion of regularity in the setting of security models.

Definition 11 (regular trace model). *A security model $\langle \mathcal{E}, \lambda \rangle$ in $\mathscr{L}$ is regular trace if there exists a trace alphabet $M = \langle \Sigma, I \rangle$ such that $\mathcal{E}$ is M-regular trace via the labelling $\xi : E \to \Sigma$ and $\lambda = \lambda' \circ \xi$ for some $\lambda' : \Sigma \to \mathcal{L}$.*

The encoding of policy satisfaction as a FOL sentence crucially relies on the fact that, in order to check whether a causal dependency $a \lessdot b$ is justified by some clause $\mathbb{A} \xrightarrow{} \mathbb{B}$, we need to find sets of events $X : \mathbb{A}$, $Y : \mathbb{B}$ with bounded cardinality $|X| = |\mathbb{A}|$ and $|Y| = |\mathbb{B}|$. Then decidability follows from [12].

Proposition 3 (decidability on regular trace security models). *Let $\Pi = \langle \mathscr{L}, \leadsto \rangle$ be an information flow policy and let $\langle \mathcal{E}, \lambda \rangle$ be a regular trace security model in $\mathscr{L}$. The decision problem $\langle \mathcal{E}, \lambda \rangle \models \Pi$ is decidable.*

5   Non-interference

We discuss in this section how our causality-based notion of information flow compares with notions of information flow based on non-interference for concurrent systems. The key differentiating factor resides in the semantic model: causal semantics are normally finer than interleaving semantics. The paradigmatic example is given by processes $a \mid b$ and $a.b + b.a$ which are equated in an interleaving world but are different from a causal point of view. Hence we would expect our notion of security, when confined to binary policies, to be more restrictive than those based on interleaving semantics. However, this is not always the case mainly because observational non-interference approaches capture flows of information due to conflicts (i.e., branching), which are instead not considered in our notion of security. We will also briefly discuss how our approach could be amended to consider conflict-related flows.

Consider, for example *Strong Non-deterministic Non-Interference* (SNNI) [3, 6,7]. Informally, a system S is SNNI whenever $S\backslash H$ (i.e., the low level system in isolation) and S/H (i.e., the entire system where high H actions are unobservable) are weak trace equivalent. Let us say that an event structure $\mathcal{E}$ is SNNI whenever its transition system $TS(\mathcal{E})$ is SNNI. Then it is easy to see that $\{L \rightsquigarrow H\}$-security is strictly finer than SNNI. The easiest case is to show that SNNI does not imply $\{L \rightsquigarrow H\}$-security. The counterexample is the event structure $\mathcal{E}_0$ below:

Clearly $\mathcal{E}_0$ is SNNI since the set of traces of both $\mathcal{E}_0\backslash H$ and $\mathcal{E}_0/H$ is $\{\epsilon, l\}$, but $\mathcal{E}_0$ is not $\{L \rightsquigarrow H\}$-secure since the direct causality $h < l'$ cannot be justified.

On the other hand, $\{L \rightsquigarrow H\}$-security implies SNNI: if $\mathcal{E}_0$ is $\{L \rightsquigarrow H\}$-secure then it contains no direct causality $e < e'$ with $e : L$ and $e' : H$, and hence all traces are such that high transitions are never necessarily followed by low transitions. Hence, the traces of $\mathcal{E}_0\backslash H$ and the traces of $\mathcal{E}_0/H$ coincide.

Observational non-interference properties are expressive enough to capture information leakages arising from deadlocks and divergence. Particularly popular in this tradition are notions based on weak bisimulation, like the Bisimulation-based SNNI (BSNNI) and the finer Bisimulation-based Non-Deducibility on Compositions (BNDC) [6,7]. BSNNI is like SNNI but with weak bisimulation equivalence instead of trace equivalence. Note that BSNNI and $\{L \rightsquigarrow H\}$-security are incomparable. First, it is easily seen that $\{L \rightsquigarrow H\}$-security does not imply BSNNI.

The event structure $\mathcal{E}_1$ above is $\{L \rightsquigarrow H\}$-secure (since there is no direct causality between l and h) but is not BSNNI, since $TS(\mathcal{E}_1)\backslash H$ and $TS(\mathcal{E}_1)/H$ are not weak bisimilar. Informally, the low part of the system can deduce that h occurred by observing that l is not executable. Vice versa, one can show that BSNNI does not imply $\{L \rightsquigarrow H\}$-security. Consider the event structure $\mathcal{E}_2$ below.

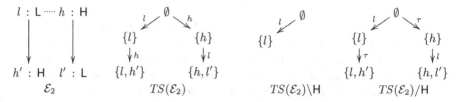

Clearly, $\mathcal{E}_2$ is not $\{L \rightsquigarrow H\}$-secure since the direct causality $h \lessdot l'$ is not allowed. On the other hand, $\mathcal{E}_2$ is BNNI since $TS(\mathcal{E}_2)\backslash H$ and $TS(\mathcal{E}_2)/H$ are weak bisimilar.

For similar reasons, our notion of security is also incomparable to other observational notions of non-interference based on transition systems such as BNDC and those that extend [18] by requiring the source and the target states of every high transition to be (low) trace equivalent [1,7,9].

6   Related Work

Logic-based languages have been investigated as flexible formalisms to express security properties. We mention, e.g., *hyperproperties* [5] and their logics (e.g. [4, 15]). Our policies can be easily integrated in logic-based languages to obtain a richer policy language. For instance, the simplest solution is to combine our policies by using standard propositional operators.

Another example is Paralocks [2], a language for specifying role-based information flow policies. In Paralocks a data item x can be annotated with clauses of the form $\Sigma \to a$, specifying the conditions Σ under which x can flow into actor a. Such policies can be related to many-to-one policies in our approach, i.e., of the form $A_1 \ldots A_m \rightsquigarrow B_1$. It less clear how many-to-many policies, i.e., policies stating that data can flow to an agent a if it also flows to an agent b, could be expressed in Paralocks.

In addition to FOL and MSO for event structures [12], our work can be related to other logics motivated by causality. An example is *Event Order Logic* (EOL) of [10], a logic based language used to specify boolean conditions on the occurrence of events, with applications to safety analysis. EOL is inspired by Linear-time Temporal Logic (LTL) and introduces ad-hoc operators to specify the order of events. The more relevant operator is $\psi_1 \wedge \psi_2$ which allows one to express that the events described by ψ_1 occur before those described by ψ_2. Hence, a policy $A_1 \ldots A_m \rightsquigarrow B_1 \ldots B_n$ can be related to an EOL formula $A_1 \vee \ldots \vee A_m \wedge B_1 \vee \ldots \vee B_n$. However, EOL does not feature operators to express some of our coordination constraints.

7   Conclusion

We have presented a novel approach to many-to-many information flow policies that allows one to specify patterns of coordination among several security levels. In particular, each clause in a policy can specify that a certain set of levels is allowed to cooperate to provide the flow *collectively*, and possibly *simultaneously* to another set of security levels. We believe that the approach can turn useful in several scenarios including secret exchange protocols, security architectures and systems with controlled forms of declassification. We have provided decidability results and discussed the relation to some traditional notions of security, including observational non-interference and language-based security. We are currently investigating the development of verification and enforcement mechanisms for concrete specification languages, like programming languages and Petri nets. We are also investigating extensions of our work in several directions, including how to suitably deal with indirect flows of information due to conflicts, and how to deal with the transfer of specific values.

References

1. Bossi, A., Piazza, C., Rossi, S.: Modelling downgrading in information flow security. In: Proceedings of CSFW 2004, p. 187. IEEE Computer Society (2004)
2. Broberg, N., Sands, D.: Paralocks: role-based information flow control and beyond. In: Hermenegildo, M.V., Palsberg, J. (eds.) Proceedings of POPL 2010, pp. 431–444. ACM (2010)
3. Busi, N., Gorrieri, R.: Structural non-interference in elementary and trace nets. Math. Struct. Comput. Sci. **19**(6), 1065–1090 (2009)
4. Clarkson, M.R., Finkbeiner, B., Koleini, M., Micinski, K.K., Rabe, M.N., Sánchez, C.: Temporal logics for hyperproperties. In: Abadi, M., Kremer, S. (eds.) POST 2014. LNCS, vol. 8414, pp. 265–284. Springer, Heidelberg (2014). doi:10.1007/978-3-642-54792-8_15
5. Clarkson, M.R., Schneider, F.B.: Hyperproperties. J. Comput. Secur. **18**(6), 1157–1210 (2010)
6. Focardi, R., Gorrieri, R.: A taxonomy of security properties for process algebras. J. Comput. Secur. **3**(1), 5–34 (1995)
7. Focardi, R., Gorrieri, R.: Classification of security properties. In: Focardi, R., Gorrieri, R. (eds.) FOSAD 2000. LNCS, vol. 2171, pp. 331–396. Springer, Heidelberg (2001). doi:10.1007/3-540-45608-2_6
8. Fujisaki, E., Okamoto, T.: How to enhance the security of public-key encryption at minimum cost. In: Imai, H., Zheng, Y. (eds.) PKC 1999. LNCS, vol. 1560, pp. 53–68. Springer, Heidelberg (1999). doi:10.1007/3-540-49162-7_5
9. Gorrieri, R., Vernali, M.: On intransitive non-interference in some models of concurrency. In: Aldini, A., Gorrieri, R. (eds.) FOSAD 2011. LNCS, vol. 6858, pp. 125–151. Springer, Heidelberg (2011). doi:10.1007/978-3-642-23082-0_5
10. Leitner-Fischer, F., Leue, S.: Probabilistic fault tree synthesis using causality computation. IJCCBS **4**(2), 119–143 (2013)
11. Li, X., Nielson, F., Nielson, H.R., Feng, X.: Disjunctive information flow for communicating processes. In: Ganty, P., Loreti, M. (eds.) TGC 2015. LNCS, vol. 9533, pp. 95–111. Springer, Cham (2016). doi:10.1007/978-3-319-28766-9_7
12. Madhusudan, P.: Model-checking trace event structures. In: Proceedings of LICS 2013, pp. 371–380. IEEE Computer Society (2003)
13. Mantel, H., Sands, D.: Controlled declassification based on intransitive noninterference. In: Chin, W.-N. (ed.) APLAS 2004. LNCS, vol. 3302, pp. 129–145. Springer, Heidelberg (2004). doi:10.1007/978-3-540-30477-7_9

14. Merkle, R.C.: Secure communications over insecure channels. Commun. ACM **21**(4), 294–299 (1978)

15. Milushev, D., Clarke, D.: Towards incrementalization of holistic hyperproperties. In: Degano, P., Guttman, J.D. (eds.) POST 2012. LNCS, vol. 7215, pp. 329–348. Springer, Heidelberg (2012). doi:10.1007/978-3-642-28641-4_18

16. Nielsen, M., Plotkin, G., Winskel, G.: Petri nets, event structures and domains. In: Kahn, G. (ed.) Semantics of Concurrent Computation. LNCS, vol. 70, pp. 266–284. Springer, Heidelberg (1979). doi:10.1007/BFb0022474

17. Okamoto, T., Ohta, K.: How to simultaneously exchange secrets by general assumptions. In: Denning, D.E., Pyle, R., Ganesan, R., Sandhu, R.S., (eds.), CCS 1994, Proceedings of the 2nd ACM Conference on Computer and Communications Security, pp. 184–192. ACM (1994)

18. Rushby, J.: Noninterference, transitivity, and channel-control security policies. Technical report, Stanford Research Institute (1992)

19. Rushby, J.: Separation and integration in MILS (the MILS constitution). Technical report, Computer Science Laboratory SRI International (2008)

20. Sabelfeld, A., Myers, A.C.: Language-based information-flow security. IEEE J. Sel. Areas Commun. **21**(1), 5–19 (2003)

21. Sabelfeld, A., Sands, D.: Declassification: dimensions and principles. J. Comput. Secur. **17**(5), 517–548 (2009)

22. Selective disclosure and insider trading. Technical report. U.S. Securities and Exchange Commission (SEC), August 2000

23. Thiagarajan, P.: Regular trace event structures. Technical Report RS-96-32, BRICS (1996)

24. Thiagarajan, P.S.: Regular event structures and finite petri nets: a conjecture. In: Brauer, W., Ehrig, H., Karhumäki, J., Salomaa, A. (eds.) Formal and Natural Computing. LNCS, vol. 2300, pp. 244–253. Springer, Heidelberg (2002). doi:10.1007/3-540-45711-9_14

25. Winskel, G.: Event structures. In: Brauer, W., Reisig, W., Rozenberg, G. (eds.) ACPN 1986. LNCS, vol. 255, pp. 325–392. Springer, Heidelberg (1987). doi:10.1007/3-540-17906-2_31

Modelling the Dynamic Reconfiguration of Application Topologies, Faults Included

Antonio Brogi, Andrea Canciani, and Jacopo Soldani[✉]

Department of Computer Science, University of Pisa, Pisa, Italy
`soldani@di.unipi.it`

Abstract. Fault-aware management protocols permit modelling the management of application components (including potential faults) and analysing the management behaviour of a multi-component application. The analysis is driven by the application topology, and it assumes many-to-1 dependencies among application components, i.e. each requirement of a component can be satisfied by exactly one other component.

In this paper we extend fault-aware management protocols to account for many-to-many dependencies among components, i.e. different application components can be used to satisfy a requirement of another component. The extension also accounts for dynamic changes in the topology, hence enabling the analysis of the management behaviour of dynamically reconfigurable multi-component applications.

1 Introduction

How to automatically manage composite applications is currently one of the major concerns in enterprise IT [4,20]. Composite applications typically integrate various heterogeneous components, like in microservice-based applications [15], and the deployment, configuration, enactment, and termination of the components forming a composite application must be suitably coordinated, by taking into account all dependencies occurring among application components.

It is worth noting that, while coordinating the management of a composite application, we must "enable failure" [19]. Namely, we must be aware that the components forming a composite application may fail, and we should be able to react to such failures by restoring the desired application configuration.

A convenient way to represent the structure of a composite application is a topology graph [5], whose nodes represent the application components, and whose arcs represent the dependencies occurring among such components. Each topology node can be associated with the requirements of a component, the capabilities it features, and the operations to manage it. Inter-node dependencies associate the requirements of a node with capabilities featured by other nodes.

In [7] we showed how the management behaviour of topology nodes can be modelled by *fault-aware management protocols*, specified as finite state machines

© IFIP International Federation for Information Processing 2017
Published by Springer International Publishing AG 2017. All Rights Reserved
J.-M. Jacquet and M. Massink (Eds.): COORDINATION 2017, LNCS 10319, pp. 178–196, 2017.
DOI: 10.1007/978-3-319-59746-1_10

whose states and transitions are associated with conditions defining the consistency of a node's states and constraining the executability of its management operations. Such conditions are defined on the requirements of a node, and each requirement of a node has to be fulfilled by a capability of another node. Fault-aware management protocols also permit modelling how a node behaves when a fault occurs (viz., when a node is assuming a requirement to be satisfied by a capability, and such capability stops being provided by the corresponding node). The management behaviour of a composite application can then be easily derived by composing the management protocols of its nodes according to the dependencies defined in its topology.

Fault-aware management protocols (as per their definition in [7]) assume many-to-1 dependencies among components. Namely, while a capability can be used to satisfy multiple requirements, a requirement can be satisfied only by one capability. This is a quite strict assumption, which impedes modelling and analysing applications where a requirement of a node can be satisfied by different capabilities offered by different nodes (e.g., a microservice-based application where a microservice requires a certain API, and alternative implementations of such an API are offered by different microservices).

In this paper we present a proper extension of fault-aware management protocols that relaxes the above mentioned assumption, allowing application topologies to have many-to-many dependencies among components. More precisely, we not only allow a capability to be connected to multiple requirements (viz., the set of requirements it can satisfy), but also a requirement to be connected to multiple capabilities (viz., the set of capabilities that can be used to satisfy such requirement). Whenever a node needs one of its requirements, any capability connected to such requirement can be used to satisfy it, and faults are raised whenever a node stops providing a capability actually satisfying a requirement. The extension also permits indicating whether the actual binding of a requirement can be dynamically changed while executing a management operation or while handling a pending fault, hence allowing to dynamically reconfigure the topology of an application.

We then illustrate how the management behaviour of a composite application can be derived by composing the management protocols of its nodes according to the static dependencies defined in its topology. We also show how this permits automating various useful analyses, like determining whether a plan orchestrating the management of a composite application is "valid", which are its effects (e.g., which capabilities are available after executing it, or whether it can dynamically reconfigure an application), and finding management plans achieving specific goals (e.g., reaching a desired application configuration, or dynamically reconfiguring an application to recover it from a fault).

The rest of the paper is organised as follows. Section 2 illustrates a scenario motivating the need for extending fault-aware management protocols to account for many-to-many dependencies in application topologies. Such extension is then formalised in Sect. 3. Section 4 shows how to automatically compose management protocols to analyse and automate the management of a composite application in presence of faults. Finally, Sects. 5 and 6 discuss related work and draw some concluding remarks, respectively.

2   Motivating Scenario

Consider the (toy) microservice-based application in Fig. 1, which is composed by a JavaScript-based microservice acting as web-based frontend of the application, two alternative and interchangeable implementations of a backend microservice, and a microservice hosting a Mongo database. The frontend microservice exposes a requirement endp, as it needs to know which is the endpoint where to invoke the RESTful api offered by the backend microservices. These in turn expose a requirement db, as they need to set up a persistent connection to the microservice hosting a Mongo database.

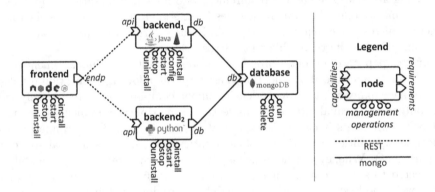

Fig. 1. Motivating example.

Suppose that we wish to orchestrate the deployment of the whole application with a dedicated management plan. Since the represented application topology does not include any management protocol, one may produce invalid management plans. For instance, while Fig. 2 illustrates three seemingly valid plans, only (a) is a valid plan. Plan (b) is not valid since the operation config of $backend_1$ must be executed before actually starting the node (to provide $backend_1$ with the necessary information to set up the connection with the Mongo database). Plan (c) is not valid either, since database must be running before $backend_1$ and $backend_2$ can start (as this also results in connecting them to the database).

Suppose now that all microservices have been deployed, started, and properly connected (e.g., by executing plan (a) in Fig. 2), with frontend being configured to invoke the api offered by $backend_2$. What happens if the operation stop of $backend_2$ is executed? The microservice $backend_2$ is stopped, and this may generate a fault in frontend, as it becomes unable to serve its clients simply because the api that it remotely invokes is not offered anymore by $backend_2$. A simple yet effective solution would be to dynamically reconfigure the microservice frontend

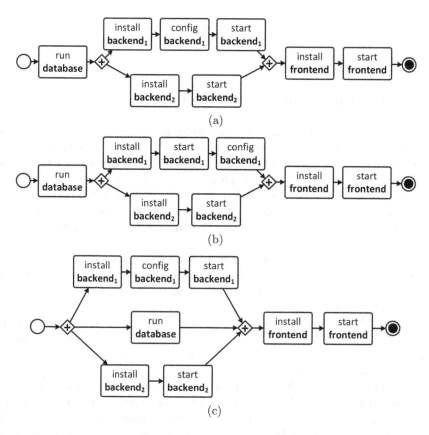

Fig. 2. Example of deployment plans. Empty circles denote the start of plans, boxes represent the execution of management operations, "plus" operators are used to start and terminate parallel flows, and filled circles denote the end of plans.

to invoke the api offered by backend$_1$. Even worse is the case when database is stopped, as this causes a fault in backend$_1$ and backend$_2$, which become unable to serve their clients, and this in turn causes a fault also in frontend.

Both the above mentioned cases fail because a microservice stops providing its capabilities while other microservices are relying on them to continue to work. In both cases we would like to recover our microservice-based application, by automatically determining a valid reconfiguration plan capable of restoring the desired application configuration.

In summary, while the validity of management plans can be manually verified, this is a time-consuming and error-prone process, especially in microservice-based applications [19]. In order to enable the automated verification of the validity of plans, as well as the automated generation of valid plans reaching desired application configurations, we need an explicit representation of the management protocols of the nodes appearing in the topology of a composite application. Such management protocols have to take into account the possibility of faults to occur, and should permit reacting to them to recover the desired configuration of an application, e.g., by dynamically reconfiguring the inter-connections among the components of an application.

3   Fault-Aware Management Protocols

Most of the available languages for modelling composite applications permit describing the states, requirements, capabilities, and management operations of the nodes building the topology of a composite application (e.g., enterprise topology graphs [5], TOSCA [24]). Fault-aware management protocols [7] permit specifying the management behaviour of the nodes composing an application, i.e. the behaviour of a node's management operations, their relations with states, requirements, and capabilities, and how a node reacts to the occurrence of a fault.

However, fault-aware management protocols assume many-to-1 dependencies among the nodes forming a topology (i.e., each requirement of a node is connected to exactly one capability of another node, while each capability of a node can be connected to multiple requirements of other nodes). We hereby present an extension of fault-aware management protocols that relaxes such assumption, by also allowing to specify whether the capability used to satisfy a requirement may be dynamically changed (by choosing another capability connected to it in the application topology).

Let N be a node modelling an application component, whose finite sets of its states, requirements, capabilities, and management operations are denoted by S_N, R_N, C_N, and O_N, respectively. Fault-aware management protocols permit modelling the management behaviour of N by describing (i) the order in which the management operations of N can be executed, (ii–iii) whether and how N depends on other nodes providing the capabilities that satisfy its requirements, and (iv) how N reacts when a fault occurs. More precisely:

(i) The order in which the operations of N can be executed is described by a transition relation τ_N specifying whether an operation $o \in O_N$ can be executed in a state $s \in S_N$, and which state is reached by executing o in s.

(ii) The states and transitions of N can be associated with (possibly empty) sets of requirements to indicate that the capabilities satisfying them are assumed to be provided by the corresponding nodes.
   - The requirements associated with a state $s \in S_N$ specify that the capabilities satisfying them must (continue to) be offered by the corresponding nodes in order for N to (continue to) work properly.
   - The requirements associated with a transition $t \in \tau_N$ specify that the capabilities satisfying them must be provided by corresponding nodes to enable the execution of t.

(iii) Each state $s \in S_N$ is also associated with the (possibly empty) set of capabilities provided by N in s.

(iv) N is affected by a fault whenever it is in a state assuming some requirement(s) to be satisfied, and some other node stops providing the capabilities satisfying such requirement(s). The explicit fault handling of N is described by a transition relation φ_N specifying how N changes its state from s to s' (with $s, s' \in S_N$) when some of the requirements it assumes in s stop being satisfied.

Definition 1 (Fault-aware management protocols). *Let* $N = \langle S_N, R_N, C_N, O_N, \mathcal{M}_N \rangle$ *be a node, where* S_N, R_N, C_N, *and* O_N *are the finite sets of its states, requirements, capabilities, and management operations.* $\mathcal{M}_N = \langle \overline{s}_N, \rho_N, \chi_N, \tau_N, \varphi_N \rangle$ *is a finite state machine defining the* fault-aware *management protocol of* N, *where:*

- $\overline{s}_N \in S_N$ *is the initial state,*
- $\rho_N : S_N \to 2^{R_N}$ *is a function indicating which requirements must hold in each state* $s \in S_N$,
- $\chi_N : S_N \to 2^{C_N}$ *is a function indicating which capabilities of* N *are offered in each state* $s \in S_N$,
- $\tau_N \subseteq S_N \times 2^{R_N} \times 2^{R_N} \times O_N \times S_N$ *is a set of quintuples modelling the transition relation, i.e.* $\langle s, P, \Delta, o, s' \rangle \in \tau_N$ *denotes that in state* s, *and if the requirements in* P *are satisfied (with those in* $\Delta \subseteq P$ *potentially being satisfied by a different capability after the transition),* o *is executable and leads to state* s', *and*
- $\varphi_N \subseteq S_N \times 2^{R_N} \times S_N$ *is a set of triples modelling the explicit fault handling for a node, i.e.* $\langle s, \Delta, s' \rangle \in \varphi_N$ *denotes that the node will change its state from* s *to* s' *if a subset of the requirements in* $(\rho(s) - \rho(s')) \cup \Delta$ *stops being satisfied (with the requirements in* Δ *potentially being satisfied by a different capability after the transition)*[1].

Remark. Note that we permit specifying which requirements may be satisfied by different capabilities after a transition to enable dynamic reconfiguration (as we will see in Sect. 4). Intuitively, for each requirement r that is assumed to hold in a given application configuration, only one among the capabilities connected to r is actually used to satisfy r (provided that the corresponding node is actually offering such capability). A transition $\langle s, P, \Delta, o, s' \rangle \in \tau_N$ ensures that the capabilities used to satisfy the requirements in $P - \Delta$ continue to be the same after the transition, while the capabilities used to satisfy the requirements in Δ may be dynamically changed. Similarly, a transition $\langle s, \Delta, s' \rangle \in \varphi_N$ permits dynamically changing the capabilities used to satisfy the requirements in Δ. □

Example 1. Figure 3 shows the management protocols of the nodes composing our motivating scenario (thick arrows represent τ, dashed arrows represent φ).

Consider, for instance, the management protocol $\mathcal{M}_{\text{frontend}}$, which describes the management behaviour of the microservice frontend. In states uninstalled

---

[1] A transition $\langle s, \Delta, s' \rangle \in \varphi_N$ permits handling the fault of a requirement r either by leading to a state s' not assuming r any more (when $r \in \rho(s) - \rho(s')$), or by changing its actual binding (when $r \in \Delta$).

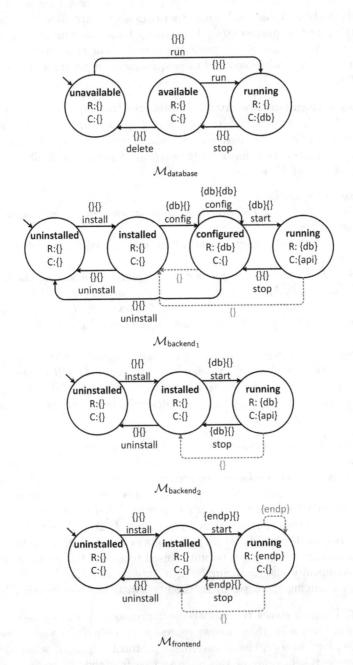

Fig. 3. Example of fault-aware management protocols.

(initial) and installed it does not require nor provide anything. The same does not hold in the running state, where frontend assumes the requirement endp to (continue to) be satisfied. If the requirement endp is faulted, and there exists a different capability (with respect to that currently bound to endp) that can satisfy it, it is possible to remain in state running by executing the fault-handling transition dynamically changing the actual binding of endp. If instead there is no capability capable of satisfying endp, then the microservice frontend goes back to its state installed. Finally, the protocol specifies that operations install, and uninstall do not need any requirement to be performed, while start and stop require endp to be satisfied.

$\mathcal{M}_{backend_1}$ is another example of management protocol worth looking at. It indeed includes a state offering a capability (viz., $backend_1$ is offering its capability api only in the state running), and a transition to dynamically reconfigure the actual binding of a requirement (viz., $backend_1$ can change the actual binding of the requirement db by executing the operation config in state configured).   □

In the following, we assume fault-aware management protocols to be well-formed, deterministic, and race-free [6,7]. Also, as the management protocol of a node may leave unspecified how it will behave in case some requirements stop being fulfilled in some states, we assume that management protocols have been automatically completed by adding transitions for all unhandled faults[2].

4   Analysing the Management of Composite Applications

In this section we illustrate how to analyse and automate the management of composite applications in a fault-resilient manner, by also taking that the application topology may be dynamically reconfigured while the application is managed. More precisely, we show how to automatically determine the management behaviour of an application by composing the protocols of its nodes according to the application topology (Sect. 4.1). We then describe how this permits automating various useful analyses, like checking the validity of a management plan, which are its effects, or how to automatically determine a valid management plan reaching a desired application configuration (Sect. 4.2).

4.1   Management Behaviour of an Application

We hereby show how to determine the fault-aware management behaviour of an application by composing the fault-aware management protocols of its components. In doing so, we exploit some shorthand notations to denote generic composite applications, the nodes in their topology, and the connections among the requirements and capabilities of such nodes.

---

[2] The procedure to automatically complete management protocols is discussed in [7]. Essentially, they are completed by adding transitions for all unhandled faults, all leading to a "sink" state that requires and provides nothing.

Definition 2 (Composite application). *We denote with* $A = \langle T, B \rangle$ *a generic composite application, where* T *is the finite set of nodes in the application topology*[3], *and where inter-node connections are described by a binding relation*

$$B \subseteq R_T \times C_T, \text{with } R_T = \bigcup_{N \in T} R_N \text{ and } C_T = \bigcup_{N \in T} C_N,$$

which associates each requirement of each node with the capabilities that can be used to satisfy it.

Formally, the semantics of the management protocols of a composite application $A = \langle T, B \rangle$ can be defined by a labelled transition system over configurations that denote the states of the nodes in T and the association between each requirement assumed by a node in T and the capability of another node in T that is actually used to satisfy such requirement. Intuitively, $\langle G, b \rangle \xrightarrow{o}_A \langle G', b' \rangle$ is a transition denoting that operation o can be executed (on a node) in A when the "global state" of A is G and the "actual binding" among requirements and capabilities is b, making A evolve into a new global state G' with a new actual binding b'. We next formally define the notions of *global state* and *actual binding* for a composite application.

The global state G of an application A stores the current state of each of its nodes, while the actual binding b of an application A stores the current association between the requirements assumed by the nodes in A and the capabilities used to satisfy them.

Definition 3 (Global state). *Let* $A = \langle T, B \rangle$ *be a composite application, and let* $N = \langle S_N, R_N, C_N, O_N, M_N \rangle$. *A global state* G *of* A *is a set of states such that:*

$$G \subseteq \bigcup_{N \in T} S_N \wedge \forall N \in T. \exists! s \in G : s \in S_N.$$

Notation 1. *Let* G *be a global state of a composite application* $A = \langle T, B \rangle$. *We denote with* $\rho(G)$ *the set of requirements that are assumed to hold by the nodes in* T *when* A *is in* G, *and with* $\chi(G)$ *the set of capabilities that are provided by such nodes in* G. *Formally:*

$$\rho(G) = \bigcup_{N \in T} \{\rho_N(s) \mid s \in G \wedge s \in S_N\}, \text{ and}$$

$$\chi(G) = \bigcup_{N \in T} \{\chi_N(s) \mid s \in G \wedge s \in S_N\}.$$

An actual binding is a partial function from the requirements R_T to the capabilities C_T of an application $A = \langle T, B \rangle$ which, informally speaking, defines a "subset" of the binding relation B.

---

[3] For simplicity, and without loss of generality, we assume that the names of states, requirements, capabilities, and operations of a node are all disjoint. We also assume that, given two different nodes in a topology, the names of their states, requirements, capabilities, and operations are disjoint.

Definition 4 (Actual binding). *Let $A = \langle T, B \rangle$ be a composite application. An* actual binding *b of A is a partial function from the requirements in T to the capabilities in T, which is defined as follows:*

$$b : R_T \rightarrow C_T \ \wedge \ \forall r \in R_T : (b(r) = \bot \ \vee \ \langle r, b(r) \rangle \in B).$$

We now define a function f to denote the set of *pending faults* in an application A when its global state is G and when its actual binding is b. Intuitively, the faults that are pending in A are the requirements assumed in G that (according to b) are bound to capabilities that are not provided in G or not bound at all.

Definition 5 (Pending faults). *Let $A = \langle T, B \rangle$ be a composite application. The function f denotes the set of* pending faults *in A:*

$$f(G, b) = \{ r \in \rho(G) \mid b(r) \notin \chi(G) \ \vee \ b(r) = \bot \}$$

where G is a global state of A, and b is an actual binding of A.

We also define a function h_N to denote the set of *settling handlers* for handling all the faulted requirements of a node N that are pending in $f(G, b)$. Such handlers are all fault handling transitions $\langle s, \Delta, s' \rangle \in \varphi_N$ such that:

- $s \in G$, i.e. $\langle s, \Delta, s' \rangle$ is executable from the current state s of N in G,
- $\rho_N(s') - \Delta \subseteq \rho_N(s) - f(G, b)$, i.e. $\langle s, \Delta, s' \rangle$ handles all faulted requirements of N (as its target state s' is not assuming any of the requirements faulted in $f(G, b)$ but those that can be dynamically rebound), and
- $\forall r \in \Delta.\exists c \in \chi(G) : \langle r, c \rangle \in B$, i.e. for each requirement r that can be dynamically rebound by $\langle s, \Delta, s' \rangle$, there exists a capability c that is actually offered in G and that is capable of satisfying r.

Definition 6 (Settling handlers). *Let $A = \langle T, B \rangle$ be a composite application, and let G and b be a global state and an actual binding of A, respectively. Let $N = \langle S_N, R_N, C_N, O_N, \mathcal{M}_N \rangle$ be a node in T, with $\mathcal{M}_N = \langle \overline{s}_N, \rho_N, \chi_N, \tau_N, \varphi_N \rangle$. The function h_N denotes the set of* settling handlers *for the faults pending in $f(G, b)$ and affecting N:*

$$h_N(G, b) = \{ \langle s, \Delta, s' \rangle \in \varphi_N \mid s \in G \ \wedge$$
$$\rho_N(s') - \Delta \subseteq \rho_N(s) - f(G, b) \ \wedge$$
$$\forall r \in \Delta.\exists c \in \chi(G) : \langle r, c \rangle \in B \ \}$$

The management behaviour of a composite application $A = \langle T, B \rangle$ is defined by a labelled transition system over pairs denoting the global state and actual binding of A. The transition system is characterised by two inference rules, *(op)* for operation execution and *(fault)* for fault propagation. The former permits executing a management operation o on a node $N \in T$ only if there are no pending faults and all the requirements needed by N to perform o are satisfied (by the capabilities provided by other nodes in T). The latter defines how to execute settling handlers when there are pending faults.

Example 2. Consider again the application in our motivating scenario (Sect. 2), and suppose that it is in the following *global state* G (Definition 3):

$$\text{frontend.running} \qquad\qquad \text{backend}_1.\text{configured}$$
$$\text{backend}_2.\text{running} \qquad\qquad \text{database.running}$$

Suppose also that the *actual binding* b of the application (Definition 4) is the following:

$$b(\text{frontend.endp}) = \text{backend}_1.\text{api}$$
$$b(\text{backend}_1.\text{db}) = \text{database.db}$$
$$b(\text{backend}_2.\text{db}) = \text{database.db}$$

In the above situation, the set of *pending faults* $f(G, b)$ (Definition 5) is the following:

$$\text{frontend.endp}$$

The set of *settling handlers* $h_{\text{frontend}}(G, b)$ (Definition 6) for the above pending fault is the following:

$$\langle \text{frontend.running}, \{\text{frontend.endp}\}, \text{frontend.running} \rangle$$
$$\langle \text{frontend.running}, \{\}, \text{frontend.installed} \rangle$$

$\square$

Definition 7 (Management behaviour of a composite application). *Let* $A = \langle T, B \rangle$ *be a composite application, and let* $N = \langle S_N, R_N, C_N, O_N, \mathcal{M}_N \rangle$ *with* $\mathcal{M}_N = \langle \overline{s}_N, \rho_N, \chi_N, \tau_N, \varphi_N \rangle$. *The* management behaviour *of* A *is modelled by a labelled transition system whose configurations are pairs* $\langle G, b \rangle$, *where* G *is a global state of* A *and* b *is an actual binding for* A, *and whose transition relation is defined by the following inference rules:*

$$\frac{\begin{array}{ccc} f(G,b) = \varnothing \quad s \in G \quad \langle s, P, \Delta, o, s' \rangle \in \tau_N \quad G' = G - \{s\} \cup \{s'\} \\ \forall r \in \rho(G) : r \notin \Delta \Rightarrow b'(r) = b(r) \qquad \forall r \in \rho(G') : \langle r, b'(r) \rangle \in B \\ \forall r \in P : b'(r) \in \chi(G) \wedge \langle r, b'(r) \rangle \in B \end{array}}{\langle G, b \rangle \xrightarrow{o} \langle G', b' \rangle} \quad (op)$$

$$\frac{\begin{array}{ccc} f(G,b) \neq \varnothing \quad s \in G \quad \langle s, \Delta, s' \rangle \in h_N(G,b) \quad G' = G - \{s\} \cup \{s'\} \\ \forall r \in \rho(G) : r \notin \Delta \Rightarrow b'(r) = b(r) \qquad \forall r \in \rho(G') : \langle r, b'(r) \rangle \in B \\ \forall r \in \Delta : b'(r) \in \chi(G) \wedge \langle r, b'(r) \rangle \in B \\ \forall \langle s, \_, s'' \rangle \in h_N(G,b) : \rho(s'') \subseteq \rho(s') \end{array}}{\langle G, b \rangle \xrightarrow{\perp} \langle G', b' \rangle} \quad (fault)$$

The *(op)* rule defines how the global state of a composite application is updated when a node N performs a transition $\langle s, P, \Delta, o, s' \rangle \in \tau_N$. Such transition can be performed if there are no pending faults (viz., $f(G, b) = \varnothing$), and if there exists a new actual binding b' such that:

- $\forall r \in \rho(G) : r \notin \Delta \Rightarrow b'(r) = b(r)$, i.e. b' preserves the actual binding of the requirements that are assumed in G and that cannot be dynamically changed by the transition,
- $\forall r \in \rho(G') : \langle r, b'(r) \rangle \in B$, i.e. all requirements assumed after the transition are bound to capabilities that can satisfy them (according to B), and
- $\forall r \in P : b'(r) \in \chi(G) \wedge \langle r, b'(r) \rangle \in B$, i.e. all requirements needed to perform the transition are bound to capabilities actually provided in the global state G and that can satisfy them (according to B).

As a result, the application configuration $\langle G, b \rangle$ is changed to $\langle G', b' \rangle$, where G' is obtained from G by updating the state of N (viz., $G' = G - \{s\} \cup \{s'\}$), and where b' is a new actual binding satisfying the above explained conditions.

The *(fault)* rule instead models fault propagation. It defines how the global state G of a composite application A is updated when executing a settling handler $\langle s, \Delta, s' \rangle$ for a node N. A settling handler $\langle s, \Delta, s' \rangle \in h_N$ can be executed if there are pending faults (viz., $f(G, b) \neq \varnothing$), and if there exists a new actual binding b' satisfying conditions analogous to those imposed by the *(op)* rule. Also, among all settling handlers, $\langle s, \Delta, s' \rangle$ is the handler whose target state s' assumes the biggest set of requirements[4] (viz., $\forall \langle s, \_, s'' \rangle \in h_N(G, b).\rho(s'') \subseteq \rho(s')$). As a result, the application configuration $\langle G, b \rangle$ is changed to $\langle G', b' \rangle$, where G' is obtained from G by updating the state of N (viz., $G' = G - \{s\} \cup \{s'\}$), and where b' is a new actual binding satisfying the above explained conditions.

4.2   Analysing the Management Behaviour of Applications

The management behaviour defined in Definition 7 permits analysing and automating the management of a composite application. For instance, we can easily determine which sequences (or, more in general, which workflows) of management operations can be considered valid in a given application configuration. To simplify definitions, we introduce some shorthand notations to observe only the (transitions corresponding to) management operations executed while managing a composite application.

Notation 2. *Let $A = \langle T, B \rangle$ be a composite application. The observable behaviour of A is denoted by a labelled transition system whose configurations are pairs $\langle G, b \rangle$ (where G is a global state of A and b is an actual binding for A), and whose transition relation is defined by the following inference rules:*

$$\frac{\langle G, b \rangle \xrightarrow{o} \langle G', b' \rangle}{\langle G, b \rangle \xmapsto{o} \langle G', b' \rangle} \qquad \frac{\langle G, b \rangle \xrightarrow{\perp} \langle G', b' \rangle \quad \langle G', b' \rangle \xmapsto{o} \langle G'', b'' \rangle}{\langle G, b \rangle \xmapsto{o} \langle G'', b'' \rangle}$$

---

[4] In this way, fault-handling transitions are guaranteed (to handle all the faults on a node and) to minimise the amount of requirements that stop being assumed.

Intuitively, a sequence of operations $o_1 o_2 \ldots o_n$ is *valid* in a given application configuration $\langle G, b \rangle$ if (i) o_1 is executable in $\langle G, b \rangle$, and (ii) whatever is the application configuration $\langle G', b' \rangle$ reached by executing o_1 in $\langle G, b \rangle$, the sequence $o_2 \ldots o_n$ can always be performed in $\langle G', b' \rangle$. Validity of plans follows from that of their sequential traces.

Definition 8 (Valid plan). *Let $A = \langle T, B \rangle$ be a composite application. Let also G and b be a global state and an actual binding of A, respectively. A sequence of management operations $o_1 o_2 \ldots o_n$ is valid in $\langle G, b \rangle$ iff it is empty or*

(i) $\exists \langle G', b' \rangle : \langle G, b \rangle \overset{o_1}{\mapsto} \langle G', b' \rangle$, and
(ii) $\forall \langle G', b' \rangle : \langle G, b \rangle \overset{o_1}{\mapsto} \langle G', b' \rangle \Rightarrow o_2 \ldots o_n$ is valid in $\langle G', b' \rangle$.

A workflow W orchestrating the management operations in A is a valid plan *in $\langle G, b \rangle$ iff all the sequential traces of W are valid in $\langle G, b \rangle$.*

The introduced modelling can be exploited for various other purposes besides checking plan validity. For instance, since different sequential traces of a valid plan may lead to different global states, it is interesting to characterise *deterministic* plans.

Definition 9 (Deterministic plan). *Let $A = \langle T, B \rangle$ be a composite application. Let also G and b be a global state and an actual binding of A, respectively. A sequence of management operations $o_1 \ldots o_n$ in $\langle G, b \rangle$ is deterministic iff*

$$o_1 \ldots o_n \text{ is valid in } \langle G, b \rangle \ \wedge \ \exists! G'. \langle G, b \rangle \overset{o_1}{\mapsto} \ldots \overset{o_n}{\mapsto} \langle G', \_ \rangle.$$

A workflow W orchestrating the management operations in A is a deterministic plan *in $\langle G, b \rangle$ iff all its sequential traces are deterministic in $\langle G, b \rangle$ and reach the same global state G'.*

Example 3. One can readily check that plan (a) in Fig. 2 is valid and deterministic. Indeed, all its sequential traces are valid in the initial application configuration (i.e., when database is unavailable, backend$_1$, backend$_2$ and frontend are uninstalled, and the actual binding is empty), and they all bring the application to the global state where all microservices are running. Note that the above holds independently from the fact that the requirement endp of frontend will be bound to the capability api offered by backend$_1$ or to that offered by backend$_2$.

Plan (b) is instead not valid in the initial application configuration. This is because all sequential traces starting with database.run $\cdot$ backend$_1$.install $\cdot$ backend$_1$.start are not valid (because the management protocol of backend$_1$ does not allow to execute start before config — see $\mathcal{M}_{\text{backend}_2}$ in Fig. 3).

Plan (c) is not valid either in the initial application configuration, because all the sequential traces starting with backend$_1$.install $\cdot$ backend$_1$.config are not valid. This is because the management protocol of backend$_1$ constrains the executability of config to the satisfaction the requirement endp of backend$_2$ (see $\mathcal{M}_{\text{backend}_2}$ in Fig. 3). The latter can only be satisfied by the capability db of database, which is however not provided by database in its starting state unavailable (see $\mathcal{M}_{\text{database}}$ in Fig. 3). $\qquad\square$

Checking whether a given plan is valid or deterministic corresponds to visiting the graph generated by the transition system of an application's management behaviour (Definition 7), which also models the non-determinism due to the choice of the new actual binding b'. It is worth noting that, thanks to the constraints on management protocols and to the way they are combined, both the possible global states and the possible actual bindings are *finite*, hence guaranteeing that the above mentioned visit of the graph eventually terminates.

It is also worth noting that the effects of a deterministic workflow W on the states of an application's components, as well as on the requirements and capabilities that are available, can be directly determined from the global state reached by performing any of the sequential traces of W.

Moreover, the problem of *finding* whether there is a deterministic plan that starts from an application configuration and achieves a specific goal (e.g., bringing some components of an application to specific states, or making some capabilities available) can also be solved with a visit of the graph associated with the transition system of an application's management behaviour. This is especially useful to automatically determine plans dynamically reconfiguring the topology of an application, or to restore a desired application configuration after some application components got stuck because of a fault[5] (as we discussed in our motivating scenario — Sect. 2).

Finally, it is worth characterising a weaker notion of validity, to denote those plans whose sequential traces may fail depending on the actual bindings chosen while executing them. Intuitively, a sequence of operations is weakly valid if *there exists* an application configuration $\langle G', b' \rangle$ reached by executing o_1 in $\langle G, b \rangle$ such that $o_2 \ldots o_n$ can all be performed. Weak validity of plans follows from that of their sequential traces.

Definition 10 (Weakly valid plan). *Let $A = \langle T, B \rangle$ be a composite application. Let also G and b be a global state and an actual binding of A, respectively. The sequence $o_1 o_2 \ldots o_n$ of management operations in A is weakly valid in $\langle G, b \rangle$ iff it is empty or*

$$\exists \langle G', b' \rangle : \langle G, b \rangle \overset{o_1}{\mapsto} \langle G', b' \rangle \ \wedge \ o_2 \ldots o_n \text{ is weakly valid in } \langle G', b' \rangle$$

A workflow W orchestrating the management operations in A is a weakly valid plan in $\langle G, b \rangle$ iff one of its sequential traces is weakly valid in $\langle G, b \rangle$.

A weakly valid plan warns that it may fail. By observing its sequential traces, it is possible to understand whether such a warning can be ignored when deploying and managing a concrete instance of the application (e.g., since a problematic actual binding will never be chosen because of security policies), or whether they

---

[5] In [7] we illustrate how to recover application that are stuck because a fault was not properly handled, or because of unforeseen faults (e.g., due to non-deterministic application bugs). The approach is based on the idea of automatically determining valid plans restoring a desired application configuration, and (despite [7] assumes many-to-1 dependencies among application components) it can be easily adapted to cope with the notion of validity presented in this paper.

can cause real issues at runtime. Notably, such issues can be avoided by exploiting the above explained planning techniques to find a deterministic plan (if any) reaching the same global state reached by the successful traces of a weakly valid plan.

5   Related Work

The problem of automating composite application management is one of the major trends in today's IT [20]. Management protocols [6,8], as well as Aeolus [12], permit automatically deploying and managing multi-component cloud applications. The underlying idea of both approaches is quite simple: Developers describe the behaviour of their components through finite-state machines, and such descriptions can be composed to model the management behaviour of a composite application. Engage [14] is another approach for processing application descriptions to automatically deploy applications. Fault-aware management protocols [7] extend management protocols [6], and differ from Aeolus [12] and Engage [14], since they permit explicitly modelling possible faults of components, as well as how to react when such faults occurs.

However, the fault-aware management protocols in [7] assume many-to-1 dependencies among the nodes forming a topology. The approach presented in this paper properly extends fault-aware management protocols by relaxing this assumption, and by also allowing to specify whether the capability used to satisfy a requirement may be dynamically changed (by choosing among the many available and connected to it in the application topology).

Other approaches worth mentioning are Rapide [22], Darwin [23] and π-ADL [25]. Rapide, Darwin and π-ADL are very close in the spirit to our approach, as they are languages for describing composite systems, whose components expose *require* and *provide* ports (corresponding to our notions of requirements and capabilities, respectively). The structure of a system is given by interconnecting such ports, and it can dynamically be changed while execution progresses. Rapide, Darwin and π-ADL however differ from our approach as they only permit many-to-1 interconnections among components, since they assume application components to be stateless (viz., once instantiated, a component assumes all its *require* ports to be satisfied, and it offers all its *provide* ports), and since they do not permit explicitly specifying how to handle the faults affecting a component (when one of the requirements it assumes stop being satisfied).

The rigorous engineering of fault-tolerant systems is a well-known problem in computer science [9], with many existing approaches targeting the design and analysis of such systems. For instance, [17] proposes a way to design object-oriented systems by starting from fault-free systems, and by subsequently refining such design by handling different types of faults. [3,26] instead focus on fault-localisation, thus permitting to redesign a system to avoid the occurrence of such a fault. These approaches differ from ours because they aim at obtaining applications that "never fail", since all potential faults have been identified and properly handled. Our approach is instead more recovery-oriented [10], since we focus on applications where faults possibly occur, and we permit designing applications capable of being recovered.

Similar considerations apply to [1,16,18], which however share with our approach the basic idea of modelling faults in single components and of composing the obtained models according to the dependencies between such components (i.e., according to the application topology).

[13] proposes a decentralised approach to deploy and reconfigure cloud applications in presence of failures. It models a composite application as a set of interconnected virtual machines, each equipped with a configurator managing its instantiation and destruction. The deployment and reconfiguration of the whole application is then orchestrated by a manager interacting with virtual machine configurators. [13] shares with our approach the objective of providing a decentralised and fault-aware management of a composite application, by specifying the management of each component separately. However, it differs from our approach since it focuses on recovering virtual machines that have been terminated only because of environment faults, while we also permit describing how components react to application-specific faults.

[21] proposes an approach to identify failures in a system whose components' behaviour is described by finite state machines. Even though the analyses are quite different, the modelling in [21] is quite similar to ours. It indeed relies on a sort of requirements and capabilities to model the interaction among components, and it permits "implicitly" modelling how components behave in presence of single/multiple faults. Our modelling is a strict generalisation of that in [21], since a component's state can evolve not only because of requirement unsatisfaction but also because of invoked operations, and since we permit "explicitly" handling faults (i.e., fault handling transitions are distinct from those modelling the normal behaviour of a component). Similar considerations apply to [11], whose modelling is also based on finite state machines with input and output channels (which permit fault communication and propagation by components).

In summary, to the best of our knowledge, the approach we propose in this paper is the first that permits automatically orchestrating the management of composite applications (i) accounting for many-to-many dependencies among application components, (ii) allowing to dynamically change/reconfigure application topologies, and (iii) assuming that faults possibly occur while managing composite applications.

6   Conclusions

Fault-aware management protocols [7] are a modular and reusable way to model the management behaviour of application components (including how they react to potential faults), and to analyse and automate the management of a complex application composed by multiple components. However, the fault-aware management protocols in [7] assume many-to-1 dependencies among the nodes in an application topology (viz., a capability can be used to satisfy multiple requirements, while a requirement can be satisfied only by a given capability), and this does not permit dealing with composite applications having multiple nodes that can satisfy a given requirement of another node (such as the microservice-based application in our motivating scenario — Sect. 2).

In this paper we have presented an extension of fault-aware management protocols, which permits modelling and analysing composite applications whose topologies have many-to-many dependencies among components. The proposed extension is such that any capability connected to a requirement can be used to satisfy such requirement when the latter is needed by the corresponding node. The proposed extension also permits specifying whether the capability used to satisfy a requirement of a node can be dynamically changed (when executing a management operation or handling a fault), hence allowing to dynamically reconfigure the topology of an application.

The proposed extension of fault-aware management protocols paves the way for their exploitation for modelling and analysing elasticity and live updates of the components forming a composite application. Both cases require to add/remove replicas of nodes, as well as of their ingoing and outgoing dependencies, to/from the topology of a composite application, hence requiring to support many-to-many dependencies and dynamic reconfiguration. The proposed extension of fault-aware management protocols includes such support, and it can hence be exploited to model the evolution of the states of node replicas. The formalisation of the above is in the scope of our immediate future work.

We believe that the proposed modelling and analysing techniques can also pave the way towards the development of self-adaptive composite applications. Self-adaptive applications are controlled by the so-called MAPE (*Monitor, Analyse, Plan* and *Execute*) loop [27]. Indeed, our techniques can be exploited during the *Analyse* and *Plan* steps of the MAPE loop controlling a composite application. The *Monitor* and *Execute* instead require to adapt and integrate existing approaches to work with fault-aware management protocols. Such adaptation and integration are left for future work.

It is also worth noting that, even if some of the analyses we presented in Sect. 4 have exponential time complexity in the worst case, they still constitute a significant improvement with respect to state-of-the-art, as currently the management of composite applications is coordinated manually (e.g., by developing ad-hoc scripts), and it is hardly reusable since it is tightly coupled to the application. We plan to further improve the support for the analyses in Sect. 4, by offering a tool capable of validating management plans and of automatically determining valid plans reaching desired goals (by extending the prototype[6] for the fault-aware management protocols of [7]).

Finally, it is worth noting that fault-aware management protocols do not take into account costs nor QoS, since their focus is on automatically coordinating the management of the components forming a composite application. Cost and QoS are however important factors [2], and they should be taken into account when modelling and analysing the management of composite applications. This could be solved by further extending management protocols by allowing to specify the

---

[6] https://github.com/di-unipi-socc/barrel.

amount of resources actually offered by a capability, and "how many" of such resources are needed to satisfy a requirement connected to such capability. The extension of fault-aware management protocols to include cost and QoS is in the scope of our future work.

References

1. Alhosban, A., Hashmi, K., Malik, Z., Medjahed, B., Benbernou, S.: Bottom-up fault management in service-based systems. ACM Trans. Internet Technol. **15**(2), 7:1–7:40 (2015)
2. Armbrust, M., Fox, A., Griffith, R., Joseph, A.D., Katz, R., Konwinski, A., Lee, G., Patterson, D., Rabkin, A., Stoica, I., Zaharia, M.: A view of cloud computing. Commun. ACM **53**(4), 50–58 (2010)
3. Betin Can, A., Bultan, T., Lindvall, M., Lux, B., Topp, S.: Eliminating synchronization faults in air traffic control software via design for verification with concurrency controllers. Autom. Softw. Eng. **14**(2), 129–178 (2007)
4. Binz, T., Breitenbücher, U., Kopp, O., Leymann, F.: TOSCA: portable automated deployment and management of cloud applications. In: Bouguettaya, A., Sheng, Q.Z., Daniel, F. (eds.) Advanced Web Services, pp. 527–549. Springer, New York (2014)
5. Binz, T., Fehling, C., Leymann, F., Nowak, A., Schumm, D.: Formalizing the cloud through enterprise topology graphs. In: 2012 IEEE 5th International Conference on Cloud Computing (CLOUD), pp. 742–749. IEEE (2012)
6. Brogi, A., Canciani, A., Soldani, J.: Modelling and analysing cloud application management. In: Dustdar, S., Leymann, F., Villari, M. (eds.) ESOCC 2015. LNCS, vol. 9306, pp. 19–33. Springer, Cham (2015). doi:10.1007/978-3-319-24072-5_2
7. Brogi, A., Canciani, A., Soldani, J.: Fault-aware application management protocols. In: Aiello, M., Johnsen, E.B., Dustdar, S., Georgievski, I. (eds.) ESOCC 2016. LNCS, vol. 9846, pp. 219–234. Springer, Cham (2016). doi:10.1007/978-3-319-44482-6_14
8. Brogi, A., Canciani, A., Soldani, J., Wang, P.W.: A petri net-based approach to model and analyze the management of cloud applications. In: Koutny, M., Desel, J., Kleijn, J. (eds.) ToPNoC XI. LNCS, vol. 9930, pp. 28–48. Springer, Heidelberg (2016). doi:10.1007/978-3-662-53401-4_2
9. Butler, M., Jones, C.B., Romanovsky, A., Troubitsyna, E. (eds.): Rigorous Development of Complex Fault-Tolerant Systems. LNCS, vol. 4157. Springer, Heidelberg (2006)
10. Candea, G., Brown, A.B., Fox, A., Patterson, D.: Recovery-oriented computing: building multitier dependability. Computer **37**(11), 60–67 (2004)
11. Chen, L., Jiao, J., Fan, J.: Fault propagation formal modeling based on stateflow. In: Proceedings of the 1st ICRSE, pp. 1–7. IEEE (2015)
12. Di Cosmo, R., Mauro, J., Zacchiroli, S., Zavattaro, G.: Aeolus: a component model for the cloud. Inform. Comput. **239**, 100–121 (2014)
13. Durán, F., Salaün, G.: Robust and reliable reconfiguration of cloud applications. J. Syst. Softw. **122**, 524–537 (2016)
14. Fischer, J., Majumdar, R., Esmaeilsabzali, S.: Engage: a deployment management system. In: Proceedings of the 33rd PLDI, pp. 263–274. ACM (2012)
15. Fowler, M., Lewis, J.: Microservices. ThoughtWorks (2016). https://www.thoughtworks.com/insights/blog/microservices-nutshell

16. Grunske, L., Kaiser, B., Papadopoulos, Y.: Model-driven safety evaluation with state-event-based component failure annotations. In: Heineman, G.T., Crnkovic, I., Schmidt, H.W., Stafford, J.A., Szyperski, C., Wallnau, K. (eds.) CBSE 2005. LNCS, vol. 3489, pp. 33–48. Springer, Heidelberg (2005). doi:10.1007/11424529_3
17. Johnsen, E., Owe, O., Munthe-Kaas, E., Vain, J.: Incremental fault-tolerant design in an object-oriented setting. In: Proceedings of 2nd APAQS, pp. 223–230 (2001)
18. Kaiser, B., Liggesmeyer, P., Mäckel, O.: A new component concept for fault trees. In: Proceedings of the 8th SCS, pp. 37–46. Australian Comp. Soc., Inc. (2003)
19. Killalea, T.: The hidden dividends of microservices. Commun. ACM **59**(8), 42–45 (2016)
20. Leymann, F.: Cloud computing. it. Inform. Technol. **53**(4), 163–164 (2011)
21. Liggesmeyer, P., Rothfelder, M.: Improving system reliability with automatic fault tree generation. In: Proceedings of the 28th FTCS, pp. 90–99. IEEE (1998)
22. Luckham, D.C., Kenney, J.J., Augustin, L.M., Vera, J., Bryan, D., Mann, W.: Specification and analysis of system architecture using rapide. IEEE Trans. Softw. Eng. **21**(4), 336–355 (1995)
23. Magee, J., Kramer, J.: Dynamic structure in software architectures. SIGSOFT Softw. Eng. Notes **21**(6), 3–14 (1996)
24. OASIS: Topology and Orchestration Specification for Cloud Applications (2013). http://docs.oasis-open.org/tosca/TOSCA/v1.0/TOSCA-v1.0.pdf
25. Oquendo, F.: π-adl: an architecture description language based on the higher-order typed π-calculus for specifying dynamic and mobile software architectures. SIGSOFT Softw. Eng. Notes **29**(3), 1–14 (2004)
26. Qiang, W., Yan, L., Bliudze, S., Xiaoguang, M.: Automatic fault localization for BIP. In: Li, X., Liu, Z., Yi, W. (eds.) SETTA 2015. LNCS, vol. 9409, pp. 277–283. Springer, Cham (2015). doi:10.1007/978-3-319-25942-0_18
27. Salehie, M., Tahvildari, L.: Self-adaptive software: landscape and research challenges. ACM Trans. Auton. Adapt. Syst. **4**(2), 14:1–14:42 (2009)

Constraint-Flow Nets: A Model for Building Constraints from Resource Dependencies

Simon Bliudze[1]([✉]), Alena Simalatsar[2], and Alina Zolotukhina[1]

[1] École Polytechnique Fédérale de Lausanne, Lausanne, Switzerland
{`simon.bliudze,alina.zolotukhina`}`@epfl.ch`
[2] University of Applied Sciences Western Switzerland, Sion, Switzerland
`alena.simalatsar@hevs.ch`

Abstract. The major research in the resource management literature focuses primarily on two complementary sub-problems: (1) specification languages for formulating resource requests and (2) constraint problems modelling allocation and scheduling. Both directions assume the knowledge of the underlying platform architecture and the dependencies it induces on the usage of the various resources. In this paper, we bridge this gap by introducing constraint-flow nets (cfNets). A cfNet is defined by a set of resources and dependencies between them, each dependency having an associated constraint schema. The model is inspired by Petri nets, with resources corresponding to places and dependencies—to transitions. Given an architecture of dependent resources, an initial resource request is propagated through the dependencies. The generated constraints are then conjuncted into the global allocation constraint. We study the notion of conflicts in cfNets and prove that for *conflict-free* cfNets the global allocation constraint can be constructed unambiguously. Furthermore, we provide an SMT-based algorithm for conflict detection and discuss the use of priorities to dynamically resolve conflicts at run-time. Finally, we illustrate the use of cfNets on a case study inspired by the Kalray MPPA architecture.

Keywords: Resource management · Resource dependencies · Constraint-flow nets · Petri nets · Marking reachability · Conflict detection

1 Introduction

Providing resource management is of key importance to many different areas, from embedded systems domain to distributed resource management in large-scale systems or in a cloud.

In the literature, two main complementary sub-problems are investigated: specification languages for formulating resource requests [8,13,20,31] and resource management architectures [10,11,17,19,24]. The former provides application developers with the means to specify application resource requirements, cation developers with the means to specify application resource requirements,

© IFIP International Federation for Information Processing 2017
Published by Springer International Publishing AG 2017. All Rights Reserved
J.-M. Jacquet and M. Massink (Eds.): COORDINATION 2017, LNCS 10319, pp. 197–216, 2017.
DOI: 10.1007/978-3-319-59746-1_11

whereas the latter is using the request information to build a constraint problem, which is then solved by a satisfiability modulo theories (SMT) [2,26] or a constraint solver [29] to find a satisfactory resource allocation. However, for non-trivial architectures, this approach presents a substantial gap. Indeed, on one hand, the resource manager assumes that an application completely specifies all its resource requirements. On the other hand, specification languages provide request primitives formulated in terms of ⟨required amount/resource type⟩ pairs, e.g. "5 Mb of memory" or "1 thread". Ignoring the physical nature of the resources and the dependencies among them makes it impossible for applications to define sufficiently complete resource requests. Furthermore, we argue that such completeness is not desirable. In order to avoid strong platform dependencies, applications should have the possibility to operate on a more abstract level. For a simple example, consider a multicore Network-on-Chip (NoC) platform (e.g. [16]), where each core has a dedicated local memory, but can also access that of the other cores through the NoC. Depending on the location of the requested memory and under the assumptions above, application developers must also explicitly request access to the NoC. Another example is provided by modular platforms, where resources, such as memory, channels or threads, can be created dynamically: applications should be allowed to specify requests for a certain type of resources without having the knowledge of their structure. While some advanced compilation tools, e.g. [15,26,27] provide ad-hoc solutions for specific target platforms, the objective of the work presented in this paper is to bridge this gap in a generic manner, sufficient to describe resource dependencies for a wide class of platforms.

We consider an environment with a global set of resources $\mathcal{R}$ and an entity (application) that makes a request for a subset of these resources. In general, the information contained in the request is not sufficient to find a satisfactory resource allocation, due to potential dependencies among the resources (in the above example, remote memory access requires the use of the NoC). To model such dependencies we introduce the notion of *Constraint-Flow Nets* (cfNets), inspired by Petri nets with inhibitor arcs. Inhibitor arcs are used to limit dependency applications (e.g. there is no need to repeat a request for a given resource, if it has already been requested). In order to specify relations between the amounts of the resources requested by the application and the necessary amounts of the resources introduced by dependencies, we associate *constraint schemata* to all transitions of a cfNet. These constraint schemata are then used to build the global constraint problem associated to the initial resource request. We prove that such global constraint problems can be unambiguously built for *conflict-free* cfNets. Furthermore, we provide a technique for detection of conflicts and their resolution by introducing priority relations among the conflicting transitions. Hence, given a cfNet with a *priority model*, the global constraint can always be built unambiguously.

The paper is structured as follows. Section 2 presents the motivating example that we use to illustrate our theory throughout the paper. Section 3 introduces cfNets and their semantics in terms of the process leading to constraint problems corresponding to resource requests. Section 4 focuses on the notion of conflict in cfNets, providing an algorithm for detecting conflicts and introducing priorities to resolve them. Section 5 provides a complete cfNet modelling the Kalray architecture described in Sect. 2. Section 6 provides a short overview of related work. Section 7 concludes the paper and discusses some future research directions.

Additional material and proofs of all results in this paper are provided as a technical report available online [7].

2 Motivating Example

Our running example is inspired by the many-core architecture of Kalray MPPA-256 [16], which consists of 256 processing elements (PE), i.e. cores, grouped into compute clusters of 16 cores each. Within a cluster, cores communicate through a shared memory, which consists of 16 independent memory banks grouped into two sides: *left* and *right*. In this paper, we will consider a simplified Kalray cluster composed of four cores and four memory banks as shown in Fig. 1.

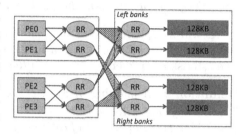

Fig. 1. Compute cluster reference architecture with arbitration points

Two cores cannot access the same memory bank at the same time. Cores are organised in pairs. Each pair shares two data-buses: one for each of the memory sides [12]. Therefore, the access to memory banks is arbitrated by two stages of arbiters implementing the Round Robin (RR) arbitration policy. Our goal in this paper will be to allocate cores, buses and memory banks, such that there will be at most one request for any arbiter queue, making the resource unavailable otherwise. Thus, we assume that two cores of one pair can access different memory sides simultaneously and two cores from different pairs may access different memory banks of the same side.

3 Modelling Resource Dependencies

3.1 Flow Nets

In this section, we introduce fNets, which we use to model resource dependencies. Syntactically, fNets are Petri nets with inhibitor arcs. The semantics of fNets can be compared to that of Coloured Petri nets with inhibitor arcs and capacities (each place has capacity 1 with respect to each token colour). The colour of a token in an fNet depends on the transition that has produced this token. The main difference between fNets and Petri nets is the following: *firing a transition does not remove tokens from its pre-places*. Therefore, the capacity restriction effectively prevents any transition from being fired more than once.

Definition 1. *Consider a tuple* $\mathcal{N} = (\mathcal{R}, T, F, I)$, *where* $\mathcal{R}$ *is a finite set of places (resources);* T *is a finite set of* transitions *(dependencies), such that* $\mathcal{R}$ *and* T *are disjoint;* $F \subseteq (\mathcal{R} \times T) \cup (T \times \mathcal{R})$ *is a set of arcs and* $I \subseteq \mathcal{R} \times T^a \times T$, *with* $T^a \stackrel{def}{=} T \cup \{*\}$, *for some fresh symbol* $* \notin T$, *is a set of* inhibitor arcs.

For $t \in T$, *we denote by* $R^-(t) \stackrel{def}{=} \{r \in \mathcal{R} \,|\, (r, t) \in F\}$ *the set of its* pre-places *and by* $R^+(t) \stackrel{def}{=} \{r \in \mathcal{R} \,|\, (t, r) \in F\}$ *the set of its* post-places. *Similarly, for* $r \in \mathcal{R}$, *we denote* $T^-(r) \stackrel{def}{=} \{t \in T \,|\, (t, r) \in F\}$ *the set of its* incoming *transitions. If* $(r, t', t) \in I$, *for some* $t' \in T^a$, *we say that* r *is an* inhibitor place *for* t. *Finally, we denote* $I(t) \stackrel{def}{=} \{(r, t') \in \mathcal{R} \times T^a \,|\, (r, t', t) \in I\}$.

$\mathcal{N}$ *is a* flow net *(fNet), if (1)* $R^-(t) \cap R^+(t) = \emptyset$, *for any* $t \in T$ *(i.e. there are no looping transitions), and (2)* $t' \in T^-(r)$, *for all* $(r, t', t) \in I$.

As will be apparent from the following definitions, an inhibitor arc (r, t', t) checks for the absence of a token in the place r produced by the transition t'. The asterisk $*$ represents a *virtual initial transition* (see Definition 2 below).

Definition 2. *A* marking *of an fNet* $(\mathcal{R}, T, F, I)$ *is a set of tokens* $M \subseteq \mathcal{R} \times T^a$. *We say that a token* $(r, t) \in \mathcal{R} \times T^a$, *has the* colour t *and denote* $T_M \stackrel{def}{=} \{t \in T^a \,|\, (r, t) \in M\}$ *the set of colours involved in the marking* M. *A marking* M *is* initial *if* $T_M = \{*\}$.

Below, we will identify a marking M with its characteristic function $M : \mathcal{R} \times T^a \to \mathbb{B}$, where $\mathbb{B} = \{\mathtt{tt}, \mathtt{ff}\}$. We now provide the formal semantics of fNets.

Definition 3. *A transition* $t \in T$ *of an fNet* $(\mathcal{R}, T, F, I)$ *is* enabled *with a marking* M *if the following three conditions hold: (1) for each* $r \in R^-(t)$, *there is a token* $(r, t') \in M$; *(2) for each* $r \in R^+(t)$, *the corresponding token is not in* M, *i.e.* $(r, t) \notin M$; *(3) for each* $(r, t', t) \in I$, *the corresponding token is not in* M, *i.e.* $(r, t') \notin M$. *A marking is* final *if it does not enable any transitions.*

The marking M' *obtained by firing a transition* $t \in T$ *enabled with* M *(denoted* $M \stackrel{t}{\rightarrow} M'$*) is defined by putting* $M' \stackrel{def}{=} M \cup \{(r, t) \,|\, r \in R^+(t)\}$.

Notice that each transition can consume any token regardless of its colour: colours are relevant only for post-places and inhibitor arcs of transitions. Furthermore, transitions do not remove tokens from their pre-places.

In the rest of the paper, we use the following convention for the graphical representation of fNets: transitions that have not been fired are shown in black, whereas transitions that have already been fired—and therefore cannot be fired again—are shown in white. Moreover, in all the illustrations in the paper, token colours can be unambiguously derived by considering which transitions have been fired (visible from the black or white colour of the transition in the diagram). Therefore, we use the usual graphical notation for tokens in Petri nets, i.e. a bullet within the corresponding place.

Example 1 (Memory and Bus). Whenever an application requires a core and a memory bank on a Kalray platform, access to the bus is required implicitly.

(a) Initial marking for the request $\{p, m\}$ (b) Final marking for the request $\{p, m\}$

Fig. 2. The cfNet modelling the dependency from Example 1

This dependency is modelled by the fNet shown in Fig. 2. The fNet has three places, p, m and b, corresponding to the processor, the memory and the bus. The resource dependency is modelled by the transition t with incoming arcs from p and m, and one outgoing arc to b.

Consider an initial resource request $R = \{p, m\}$. The corresponding initial marking M_0 of the fNet has two tokens: $(p, *)$ and $(m, *)$ (Fig. 2a). Transition t is enabled and can be fired, generating the token (b, t). Thus, we have $M_0 \xrightarrow{t} M$ with M shown in Fig. 2b. Since t is not enabled with M, this marking is final.

Definition 4. *A* run *of an fNet from a marking M_0 is a sequence $M_0 \xrightarrow{t_1} M_1 \xrightarrow{t_2} \ldots \xrightarrow{t_n} M_n$. When such a run exists, we say that M_n is* reachable *from M_0 and write $M_0 \xrightarrow{\langle t_1, \ldots, t_n \rangle} M_n$. We say that a marking is* reachable *if it is reachable from some initial marking.*

Notice that, for any marking M obtained by firing a sequence of transitions, T_M (see Definition 2) is the set comprising $*$ and these transitions (see Proposition 1 below).

Definition 5. *A marking M of an fNet $(\mathcal{R}, T, F, I)$ is* well-formed *if, for all $t \in T_M \setminus \{*\}$, the following three conditions hold:*

1. *for all $r \in R^-(t)$, there exists a token $(r, t') \in M$, for some $t' \in T^-(r) \cup \{*\}$;*
2. *for all $r \in R^+(t)$, $(r, t) \in M$;*
3. *for all $(r, *) \in I(t)$, $(r, *) \notin M$.*

In Definition 5, conditions 1 and 3 are necessary for the transition t to have been enabled. They are not sufficient, since, for the transition to be enabled, inhibitor tokens referring to colours other than $*$ must also be absent from the marking. However, we cannot include this stronger requirement in the definition of well-formedness. Indeed, such inhibitor tokens can appear once t has already been fired. Condition 2 requires that all the tokens generated by firing t be, indeed, present in the marking.

Proposition 1. *Let M' be a marking reachable from an initial marking M_0 with*
$M_0 \xrightarrow{\langle t_1,\dots,t_n \rangle} M'$. *Then M' is well-formed and $T_{M'} = \{*, t_1, \dots, t_n\}$.*

Marking well-formedness over-approximates reachability: all reachable markings are well-formed, but some well-formed markings are not reachable.

3.2 Constraints

For each resource $r \in \mathcal{R}$, we assume that possible amounts form an additive group $\langle D_r, +, 0 \rangle$. We extend the definition of fNets by associating to each transition a constraint schema, instantiated into a constraint for a given final marking.

Definition 6. *Consider an fNet $(\mathcal{R}, T, F, I)$. For any transition $t \in T$, denote $X_t \overset{def}{=} \{x_r \mid r \in R^-(t) \cup R^+(t)\}$, where each x_r is a variable ranging over D_r. A constraint schema c_t associated to t is a predicate over X_t.*

Definition 7. *A constraint-flow net (cfNet) is a tuple $(\mathcal{R}, T, F, I, \mathcal{C})$, where $(\mathcal{R}, T, F, I)$ is an fNet and $\mathcal{C} = \{c_t \mid t \in T\}$ is a set of constraint schemata associated to the transitions in T.*

We build global constraint problems encoding resource allocations compatible with the causal dependencies defined by a cfNet. A constraint problem is based on an initial resource request and the constraint schemata associated to the transitions constituting a run of the cfNet. To this end, we introduce, for each place-colour pair $(r, t) \in \mathcal{R} \times T^a$, a variable d_r^t with the domain value D_r.

Definition 8. *Let M be a well-formed marking of a cfNet $(\mathcal{R}, T, F, I, \mathcal{C})$. We define a platform constraint*

$$C[M] \overset{def}{=} \bigwedge_{t \in T_M} c_t \left[\left(\sum_{t':(r,t') \in M} d_r^{t'} \right) \middle/ x_r \,\middle|\, r \in R^-(t) \right] \left[d_r^t \middle/ x_r \,\middle|\, r \in R^+(t) \right], \quad (1)$$

where we denote by $E[x/y \mid C]$ the expression obtained by substituting in E all occurrences of y, which satisfy the condition C, by x. Thus, each conjunct in (1) is obtained by replacing, in the corresponding constraint schema c_t, (1) for each $r \in R^-(t)$, the variable x_r with the sum of all variables $d_r^{t'}$ corresponding to all the tokens $(r, t') \in M$; (2) for each $r \in R^+(t)$, the variable x_r with the corresponding variable d_r^t.

Notice that the conjuncts in (1) are unambiguously defined, since, by Definition 1, there are no looping transitions in the cfNet, i.e. $R^-(t) \cap R^+(t) = \emptyset$, for all $t \in T$. Hence the two substitutions operate on disjoint sets of variables.

Example 2 (Memory and Bus—continued). Building on Example 1, we introduce the constraint linking the actual resource requirements. Since any data to be written or read from the memory must transit through the bus, we associate to the transition t a constraint schema $c_t = (x_b \geq x_m)$, imposing that the required bus capacity be greater than or equal to the requested amount of memory.

Consider again the initial request $R = \{p, m\}$ with the corresponding initial marking in Fig. 2a. The variables corresponding to the initial tokens are d_p^* and d_m^*. Since the final marking M in Fig. 2b contains a token (b, t), we also introduce the corresponding variable d_b^t. Substituting these variables in the constraint schema for t, we obtain the platform constraint

$$C[M] = c_t\left[d_p^*/x_p, d_m^*/x_m, d_b^t/x_b\right] = (d_b^t \geq d_m^*).$$

(a) Initial marking for the request $\{r\}$ (b) Final marking for the request $\{r\}$

Fig. 3. The cfNet modelling the dependency from Example 3

Example 3 (Virtual resources). Recall that the architecture of our running example consists of four identical processing elements p_1, p_2, p_3 and p_4, two identical memory sides left L and right R, each consisting of pairs of identical memory banks (m_1, m_2) and (m_3, m_4). An application may request a processing element and some memory. This request can be for a specific processing element, e.g. p_1 and a specific memory bank, e.g. m_1. However, if one of the requested resources is unavailable, the request will not be satisfied. Alternatively, the request can be made without specifying which of p_i and m_i is needed, allowing for a more flexible resource allocation. This can be modelled by introducing a "virtual" resource p for processing elements, L and R for memory sides or even more generally m for memory sides and banks as shown in Sect. 5.

Let us abstract from our example architecture and consider a system with two physical resources of the same type, r_1 and r_2, and a virtual resource r representing this resource type, modelled with a cfNet shown in Fig. 3. These resources could be, for example, two processing cores, memory sides or banks.

When the virtual resource is requested, the actual allocation depends on the policy that the system implements, for instance:

- *Dispatching the request:* one of r_1 or r_2 must provide the requested amount;
- *Redundant allocation:* both r_1 and r_2 must provide the requested amount;
- *Joint allocation:* part of the requested amount is provided by one of the two physical resources and the rest is provided by the other.

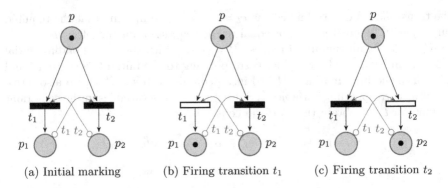

(a) Initial marking   (b) Firing transition t_1 (c) Firing transition t_2

Fig. 4. The cfNet modelling virtual processing cores using inhibitor arcs

The request for *dispatching* allocation, when only one of the resources is actually allocated, is suitable for modelling the request of a processing core, while *redundant* and *joint* allocation can be used for memory request.

The constraint scheme of the transition depends on the policy:

Dispatching the request: $c_t = (x_{r_1} = x_r \wedge x_{r_2} = 0) \vee (x_{r_1} = 0 \wedge x_{r_2} = x_r)$,

Redundant allocation: $c_t = (x_{r_1} = x_r \wedge x_{r_2} = x_r)$,

Joint allocation: $c_t = (x_{r_1} + x_{r_2} = x_r)$.

Consider the initial request $R = \{r\}$ with the joint allocation policy. The corresponding initial marking M_0 is shown in Fig. 3a. The variable corresponding to the initial token is d_r^*. Since the final marking M in Fig. 3b contains tokens (r_1, t) and (r_2, t), we also introduce the corresponding variables $d_{r_1}^t$ and $d_{r_2}^t$. Substituting these variables in the constraint schema for t for the joint allocation policy, we obtain the platform constraint

$$C[M] = c_t\left[d_r^*/x_r, d_{r_1}^t/x_{r_1}, d_{r_2}^t/x_{r_2}\right] = (d_{r_1}^t + d_{r_2}^t = d_r^*).$$

Example 4, below, presents an alternative approach for modelling virtual resources with the *dispatching* policy. This approach relies on *inhibitors* to generate simpler platform constraints involving less variables.

Example 4 (Virtual resources with inhibitors). Consider a different model of "virtual" resources, shown in Fig. 4 representing two processing cores of the Kalray architecture. The constraint schemata associated, respectively, to transitions t_1 and t_2 are $c_{t_1} = (x_p = x_{p_1})$ and $c_{t_2} = (x_p = x_{p_2})$.

In the dispatching allocation of Example 3, the constraint schemata ensured that only one core can be allocated for a single request. In the cfNet of Fig. 4, this is ensured by the inhibitor arcs (p_1, t_1, t_2) and (p_2, t_2, t_1). The initial marking for the request of a "virtual" processing core p is shown in Fig. 4a. Figures 4b and c show the two possible runs of the cfNet, where the firing of transition t_1 inhibits the firing of transition t_2 and vice versa.

Notice that the constraint schemata associated to the transitions t_1 and t_2 involve less variables than the dispatching schema in Example 3, simplifying the task of the constraint solver.

3.3   Allocation Constraint Problem

In the following, we assume that a partial cost function $cost_r : D_r \to \mathbb{R}$ is associated with each resource $r \in \mathcal{R}$. When defined, the value $cost_r(d)$ represents the cost of allocating the amount $d \in D_r$ of the resource r. When $cost_r(d)$ is undefined, this means that it is not possible to allocate the amount d of the resource r (e.g. d is greater than the resource capacity).

Definition 9. *Let $R \subseteq \mathcal{R}$ be a set of resources. A utility function over R is a partial function $u : \prod_{r\in\mathcal{R}} D_r \to \mathbb{R}$ such that u is constant on all D_r for $r \notin R$ (i.e. u depends only on resources belonging to R).*

Definition 10. *An allocation over a set of resources $R \subseteq \mathcal{R}$ is a value $d = (d_r)_{r\in\mathcal{R}} \in \prod_{r\in\mathcal{R}} D_r$, such that $d_r = 0$ for all $r \notin R$.*

Consider a system of resource dependencies defined by a cfNet N. Let $R_0 \subseteq \mathcal{R}$ be a set of resources corresponding to an initial request, and let u be a utility function over R_0. Let $M_0 = \{(r, *) \mid r \in R_0\}$ be the initial marking corresponding to R_0, and let M be a final marking obtained by running N. Let $C[M]$ be the corresponding platform constraint (see Definition 8). Finally, let $cost_r$, for all $r \in \mathcal{R}$, be the corresponding cost functions.

Definition 11. *An allocation $d = (d_r)_{r\in\mathcal{R}}$ over R is valid, if the predicate*

$$C_M(d) \overset{\text{def}}{=} C[M] \wedge \bigwedge_{r\in R} \left(d_r = \sum_{t:(r,t)\in M} d_r^t \right) \tag{2}$$

evaluates to true and if the following value is defined:

$$U_M(d) \overset{\text{def}}{=} u(d) - \sum_{r\in\mathcal{R}} cost_r(d_r). \tag{3}$$

We call the function $U_M(d)$ the global utility *of the allocation d.*

Finding an optimal resource allocation for a request R_0 is then formalised by the following constrained optimisation problem: $\text{argmax}_{\{d \mid C_M(d)\}} U_M(d)$.

Notice that both the notions of validity and global utility, and the optimisation problem above depend on the marking M obtained by running the cfNet. In the next section we characterise those cfNets, where this dependency does not hold and provide a disambiguating mechanism for the rest of cfNets.

4   Conflicting Dependencies

In the previous section, we have introduced the notion
of cfNets and shown how the constraint problem associated to a resource request is built by running one. In
particular, we have shown (Examples 3 and 4) that, in
cfNets, where only one among a set of alternative dependencies is to be activated, the use of inhibitors leads to
simpler constraint problems with fewer variables.

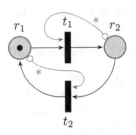

Figure 5 shows another example, where inhibitors
are useful. It models a system with two resources that
must be used together: if one is requested, the other one
should be included also; however, if both are requested
initially, there is no need to introduce additional con-

Fig. 5. Mutual depen-
dency

straints. This example cannot be realised without inhibitors.

Thus, inhibitor arcs increase the expressiveness of cfNets and are beneficial for the complexity of the resulting constraint problems. On the other hand,
inhibitors can introduce conflicts between transitions, thereby introducing potential ambiguity in the definition of a constraint problem associated to a given
initial marking. Below, we show that any cfNet that does not contain inhibitor
arcs referring to token colours other than $*$, is conflict-free. We then provide a
method for conflict detection in cfNets that do contain such inhibitors.

4.1   Conflicting Transitions

Definition 12. *A cfNet* $(\mathcal{R}, T, F, I, \mathcal{C})$ *under marking* M *has a conflict, if there
exist two distinct enabled transitions* $t_1, t_2 \in T$, *such that* $M \xrightarrow{t_1} M'$ *and* t_2 *is
disabled with* M'.

We also say that transitions $t_1, t_2 \in T$ *are in conflict under the marking* M.
A cfNet is conflict-free *if it does not have conflicts under any reachable marking.*

Proposition 2. *Any transition* t, *enabled with a marking* M *of a conflict-free
cfNet, is also enabled with any marking reachable from* M *without firing* t.

An important consequence of Proposition 2 is that a platform constraint
obtained by running a conflict-free cfNet depends only on the initial marking.
Indeed, for a given initial marking the runs of the cfNet can only differ in the
order of transition firing. However, the set of transitions is the same, generating
the same conjuncts contributing to the platform constraint (1).

Proposition 3. *Let* $(\mathcal{R}, T, F, I, \mathcal{C})$ *be a cfNet and* $t_1, t_2 \in T$ *(with* $t_1 \neq t_2$) *be
two transitions in conflict under some marking* M. *Then there exists a place
$r \in \mathcal{R}$, such that either* $(r, t_2, t_1) \in I$ *or* $(r, t_1, t_2) \in I$.

A simple corollary of Proposition 3 is that any cfNet that does not contain
inhibitor arcs referring to token colours other than $*$, is conflict-free. Notice,
however, that Proposition 3 does not rely on the reachability of markings. Indeed,

a conflict-free cfNet can still have conflicting transitions, provided that they are not enabled together under any reachable marking.

Definition 13. *Transitions t_1 and t_2 are* mutually exclusive *if no reachable marking enables them both.*

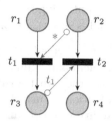

Fig. 6. A simple net with mutually exclusive transitions

Figure 6 shows an example of two mutually exclusive transitions. Transitions t_1 and t_2 cannot be enabled simultaneously, since the place r_2 has a regular arc to t_2 and an inhibitor arc to t_1, thus one transition requires a token in r_2 while the other requires the place to be empty.

Definition 14. *An inhibitor arc (r, t', t) (with $t' \neq *$) is called* non-conflicting *if t is mutually exclusive with t'.*

Theorem 1. *A cfNet is conflict-free if and only if all its inhibitor arcs refer to initial tokens or are non-conflicting.*

Lemma 1. *Let $(\mathcal{R}, T, F, I, C)$ be a conflict-free cfNet, M be a marking enabling two transitions $t_1 \neq t_2$ and $M \xrightarrow{t_1} M'_1 \xrightarrow{t_2} M'_2$ and $M \xrightarrow{t_2} M''_1 \xrightarrow{t_1} M''_2$ be two possible runs of N. Then $M'_2 = M''_2$.*

Theorem 2. *A conflict-free cfNet is terminating and confluent, i.e. for any initial marking M_0, there exists a unique final marking M reachable from M_0.*

Theorem 2 implies that in a conflict-free cfNet, the platform constraint (1) depends only on the initial marking M_0, given by a request R_0. Therefore, the problem of finding a resource allocation defined by Eqs. (2) and (3) in a conflict-free cfNet is defined uniquely.

4.2   Conflict Detection

Theorem 1 provides a criterion characterising conflict-free cfNets: all the inhibitor arcs must refer to initial tokens or be non-conflicting. In order to determine whether an inhibitor arc (r, t', t) is non-conflicting, we must check whether t and t' are mutually exclusive. Mutual exclusiveness of two transitions requires that there be no reachable marking enabling them simultaneously (Definition 13). However, checking the existence of such a reachable marking by direct exploration is complex: in the worst case, the number of possible markings is of the order of $2^{|T^a| \times |\mathcal{R}|}$, since each transition—including the initial request—can potentially generate a token in each of the places. Instead, we exploit the notion of marking well-formedness, which over-approximates reachability (Proposition 1). Given two conflicting transitions of a cfNet $(\mathcal{R}, T, F, I, \mathcal{C})$ (fixed for the remainder of this sub-section), we proceed in three steps:

1. We encode the existence of a well-formed marking enabling both transitions as a Boolean satisfiability problem and submit it to a SAT-solver.
2. If the problem is unsatisfiable, the two transitions are mutually exclusive. Otherwise, the satisfying valuation returned by the SAT-solver encodes a well-formed marking, reachability whereof can be efficiently checked.
3. If this marking is reachable, the two transitions are not mutually exclusive. Otherwise, we repeat step 1 with a refined encoding excluding this marking.

Boolean encoding of transition enabledness. With each place-colour pair (r, t) we associate a Boolean variable y_r^t, evaluating to tt iff the corresponding token is present in a given marking. For a transition $t \in T$, we define the following four predicates on markings ($\mathcal{T}$ stands for *tokens*, $\mathcal{I}$ stands for *inhibitors*):

$$\mathcal{T}_t^- \overset{def}{=} \bigwedge_{r \in R^-(t)} \left(\bigvee_{t \in T^-(r)} y_r^t \right), \qquad // \text{ tokens are present in pre-places of } t \quad (4)$$

$$\mathcal{T}_t^+ \overset{def}{=} \bigwedge_{r \in R^+(t)} y_r^t, \qquad // \text{ tokens are present in post-places of } t \quad (5)$$

$$\mathcal{I}_t^* \overset{def}{=} \bigwedge_{(r,*,t) \in I} \overline{y_r^*}, \qquad // \text{ tokens are absent from initial inhibitors of } t \quad (6)$$

$$\mathcal{I}_t^\circ \overset{def}{=} \bigwedge_{(r,t',t) \in I, \, t' \neq *} \overline{y_r^{t'}}. \quad // \text{ tokens are absent from non-initial inhibitors of } t \quad (7)$$

For a well-formed marking M, if the transition t has already been fired in the run leading to M, then $\mathcal{T}_t^+(M)$ evaluates to tt. Thus, t *is enabled* under M iff $\mathcal{E}_t(M) \overset{def}{=} \mathcal{T}_t^- \wedge \overline{\mathcal{T}_t^+} \wedge \mathcal{I}_t^* \wedge \mathcal{I}_t^\circ = $ tt.

Lemma 2. *If a transition t is enabled with a marking M, then holds the equality $\mathcal{E}_t(M) = $ tt. Conversely, if $\mathcal{E}_t(M) = $ tt and M is well-formed then t is enabled.*

Lemma 2 provides a characterisation of transition enabledness under well-formed markings. The following results provide a similar characterisation of the well-formedness of a marking.

Transition t *may have been enabled* in the run leading to a marking M only if $\mathcal{B}_t(M) \overset{def}{=} \mathcal{T}_t^- \wedge \mathcal{I}_t^* = $ tt. Notice that the stronger predicate $\mathcal{T}_t^- \wedge \mathcal{I}_t^* \wedge \mathcal{I}_t^\circ$ does not characterise the desired property, since some of the tokens inhibiting t may have been generated after t has been fired (clearly, this cannot be the case for the initial tokens). Notice also that once $\mathcal{B}_t(M)$ holds for some marking M, it will hold for all markings reachable from M.

The well-formedness of a marking essentially means that, for every non-initial token, there is a transition that could have generated it. Thus, a marking M is well-formed iff $\mathcal{W}(M) \stackrel{def}{=} \bigwedge_{r \in R} \bigwedge_{t \in T^-(r)} \left(y_r^t \Rightarrow \mathcal{B}_t \wedge \mathcal{T}_t^+ \right) = \mathsf{tt}$.

Thus, the fact that two transitions, t_1 and t_2 can be both enabled with the same well-formed marking is encoded by the predicate $\mathcal{E}_{t_1} \wedge \mathcal{E}_{t_2} \wedge \mathcal{W}$. If this predicate is not satisfiable then transitions t_1 and t_2 are mutually exclusive. Recall from Sect. 3.1 that well-formedness is an over-approximation of reachability. Therefore, the converse does not hold: given a marking M satisfying $\mathcal{E}_{t_1} \wedge \mathcal{E}_{t_2} \wedge \mathcal{W}$, one has to check whether M is reachable.

Marking reachability. Let $M \subseteq \mathcal{R} \times T^a$ be a well-formed marking of a cfNet $(\mathcal{R}, T, F, I, \mathcal{C})$. We associate to the marking M the corresponding *causality graph*, which is a directed hyper-graph $\mathcal{G}_M \stackrel{def}{=} (V, E)$ with vertices $V = T_M$ and the set $E \subseteq T_M \times 2^{T_M}$ of edges representing the "must be fired before" relation among the corresponding transitions: an edge (t, T) with $T \in 2^{T_M}$ means that, *for the transition t to be fired, at least one transition in T must be fired before t.*

We put $E = E_1 \cup E_2$ with E_1 and E_2 defined by (8) and (9) below.

For a place $r \in \mathcal{R}$, denote $T_r \stackrel{def}{=} \{t \in T_M \mid (r, t) \in M\}$ the set of colours of the tokens in r present in the marking M. We put

$$E_1 \stackrel{def}{=} \left\{ (t, T_r) \in T_M \times 2^{T_M} \mid t \in T_M, r \in R^-(t) \right\}. \tag{8}$$

By Definition 3, for any transition t to be fired, it is necessary that in each place $r \in R^-(t)$ there be at least one token. Hence, at least one of the transitions generating such tokens must be fired before t.

Furthermore, if firing a transition t' generates a token that inhibits some transition t, then firing of t cannot happen after that of t'. Thus, we put

$$E_2 \stackrel{def}{=} \left\{ (t', \{t\}) \in T_M \times 2^{T_M} \mid \exists r \in \mathcal{R} : (r, t', t) \in I \right\}. \tag{9}$$

Notice that, if such $(r, t', t) \in I$ actually exists, necessarily $(r, t') \in M$, since $t' \in T_M$. Thus, we do not have to state this condition explicitly in (9).

Definition 15. *Let $G = (V, E)$ with $E \subseteq V \times 2^V$ be a hyper-graph. A* path *in G is a sequence $(e_i)_{i=0}^n$, with $e_i = (v_i, S_i) \in E$, such that $v_{i+1} \in S_i$, for all $i < n$. When $n \in \mathbb{N}$, we say that the path is* finite, *otherwise, when $n = \infty$, it is* infinite. *We say that the path* starts with *the edge e_0.*

Definition 16. *A hyper-graph $G = (V, E)$ with $E \subseteq V \times 2^V$ has a* cycle *$C \subseteq V$, if there exists a set of finite paths $\{(e_i^j)_{i=0}^{n_j}\}_{j \in J}$, with $e_i^j = (v_i^j, S_i^j) \in E$, such that $C = \{v_i^j \mid j \in J, i \in [0, n_j]\}$ and, for all $j \in J$ and $i \in [0, n_j]$, we have $S_i^j \subseteq C$. Otherwise, G is said to be* free from cycles.

Theorem 3. *Let M be a well-formed marking and $\mathcal{G}_M$ its causality graph. The marking M is reachable iff $\mathcal{G}_M$ is free from cycles.*

Cycle-freedom of a hyper-graph can be checked in linear time [7].

Encoding refinement. Let $M \subseteq \mathcal{R} \times T^a$ be a well-formed marking of a cfNet $\mathcal{N}$, enabling two conflicting transitions t_1 and t_2. If M is reachable, $\mathcal{N}$ has a conflict. If it is not reachable, the encoding has to be refined to exclude M. Let Φ be the predicate used at the previous step of the process (initially $\Phi = \mathcal{E}_{t_1} \wedge \mathcal{E}_{t_2} \wedge \mathcal{W}$). We refine this predicate by taking $\Phi \wedge \overline{\Phi_M}$, where $\Phi_M = \bigwedge_{(r,t)\in M} y_r^t \wedge \bigwedge_{(r,t)\notin M} \overline{y_r^t}$ is the characteristic predicate of the marking M.

4.3 Priority

As shown in Sect. 4.1, conflict-free cfNets are confluent: the same platform constraint is obtained by any run of the cfNet, for a given initial marking. In other words, enabled transitions can be fired in arbitrary order. This is not the case for cfNets with conflicts: firing one of two conflicting transitions disables the other one, generating different platform constraints. Thus, for reachable conflicts, the choice of which of the two conflicting transitions should be fired, has to be resolved externally to the cfNet. This can be achieved by introducing priority among the conflicting transitions.

For a cfNet $N = (\mathcal{R}, T, F, I, \mathcal{C})$, a priority relation is a partial order $> \subseteq T \times T$ on its set of transitions. For two transitions t_1 and t_2, a priority $t_1 > t_2$ means that when both transitions are enabled, t_1 must be fired before t_2. Priorities can be defined statically or dynamically, depending, for example, on the availability of the resources corresponding to the post-places of the two transitions.

Example 5 (Virtual resources with inhibitors—continued). In Example 4 we have presented a cfNet modelling a "virtual" resource p (see Fig. 4) representing two processing cores p_1 and p_2. With the initial request p there can be two possible runs of the cfNet as shown in Fig. 4a and c.

The fact that a virtual resource is used to represent the two cores implies that they are functionally equivalent. However, we can consider a scenario, where the two cores differ in their non-functional properties. For instance, suppose that p_1 has better energy efficiency than p_2. Imposing the priority $t_1 > t_2$ for the cfNet in Fig. 4a, would ensure that p_1 is allocated rather than p_2.

Consider now the second scenario, where two applications are running on this platform, both requiring a processing core, but unaware of the platform architecture. In the first cycle, one of the applications requests p and p_1 is allocated as discussed above. In the next cycle, the second application also requests p. Since, p_1 is not available (indicated by its cost function being undefined for all values), we inverse the priority, setting $t_1 < t_2$. Thus, t_2 will be fired leading to an allocation of p_2 to the second application.

Finally, notice that, if none of p_1 and p_2 is available, the choice of priority is irrelevant, since the constraint problems generated from both markings in Fig. 4b and c will be unsatisfiable.

5 The Kalray Architecture Case Study

Figure 7 shows the complete cfNet modelling a single cluster of the Kalray architecture described in Sect. 2. For the sake of clarity, we group the resources in several boxes: one for each group of processors, one for each memory side and one for each bus. In order to further unclutter the figure, the smaller rectangles on the sides of each box allow us to group the arcs of the cfNet. For instance, the thicker red arc in the figure represents four arcs of the cfNet, going from places p_1 and p_2 to transitions t_{61} and t_{62}.

Each memory side box repeats the virtual resource pattern (Example 3). The arcs between a processor box, a memory box and a bus box reproduce the memory and bus example (Example 1).

The architectural constraints are modelled as follows: (1) transition t_1 ensures mutual exclusion among processors p_1, p_2, p_3 and p_4; (2) transition t_2 ensures the mutual exclusion among memory sides, and t_3, t_4—among memory banks of each side respectively; (3) transitions t_{51}, t_{52}, t_{61}, t_{62}, t_{71}, t_{72}, t_{81} and t_{82} ensure that only one of the processors from one group can have access to one memory side using a dedicated bus.

It is possible to request either a virtual processing core p or a specific one out of p_1, p_2, p_3 or p_4. Similarly, it is possible to request virtual memory m, a specific memory side L or R, or a specific memory bank m_1, m_2, m_3 or m_4.

The resource allocation constraints for the existing transitions implementing the dispatching policy are as follows (S_4 is the symmetric group on $\{1, 2, 3, 4\}$):

$$c_{t_1}(x_p, x_{p_1}, x_{p_2}, x_{p_3}, x_{p_4}) = \bigvee_{\sigma \in S_4} (x_{p_{\sigma(1)}} = x_p \wedge x_{p_{\sigma(2)}} = x_{p_{\sigma(3)}} = x_{p_{\sigma(4)}} = 0),$$

$$c_{t_2}(x_m, x_L, x_R) = (x_L = x_m \wedge x_R = 0) \vee (x_R = x_m \wedge x_L = 0),$$

$$c_{t_3}(x_L, x_{m_1}, x_{m_2}) = (x_{m_1} = x_L \wedge x_{m_2} = 0) \vee (x_{m_2} = x_L \wedge x_{m_1} = 0),$$

$$c_{t_{51}}(x_{m_1}, x_{p_3}, x_{p_4}, x_{bus_{L34}}) = \big(x_{bus_{L34}} > 0 \wedge x_{m_1} > 0 \wedge$$

$$((x_{p_3} = 0 \wedge x_{p_4} > 0) \vee (x_{p_4} = 0 \wedge x_{p_3} > 0)))$$

$$\vee \big(x_{bus_{L34}} = 0 \wedge ((x_{p_3} = 0 \wedge x_{p_4} = 0) \vee x_{m_1} = 0)\big),$$

c_{t_4} is similar to c_{t_3}, whereas $c_{t_{52}}$, $c_{t_{61}}$, $c_{t_{62}}$, $c_{t_{71}}$, $c_{t_{72}}$, $c_{t_{81}}$, $c_{t_{82}}$ are similar to $c_{t_{51}}$.

The initial cost functions for the resources are as follows: (1) for all $i \in [1, 4]$, $cost_{p_i}(d) = 0$, if $d \in \{0, 1\}$ and undefined otherwise; (2) for all $i \in [1, 4]$, $cost_{m_i}(d) = 0$, if $0 \leq d \leq 128$ and undefined otherwise; (3) for $i \in \{L, R\}$ and $j \in \{12, 34\}$, $cost_{bus_{ij}}(d) = 0$, if $d \in \{0, 1\}$ and undefined otherwise; (4) the cost function for p, m, L, R are defined everywhere as constant 0.

Here, the focus is on resource availability, rather than the actual cost. Hence, all cost functions are 0 when defined. Notice also, that we require the whole bus once a memory is requested, regardless of the amount of data to be passed.

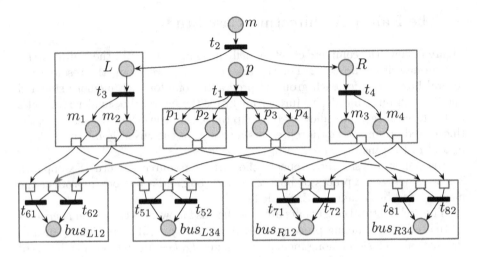

Fig. 7. A cfNet modelling a Kalray cluster

6 Related Work

The idea of using Petri nets for resource management is not novel. A number of works explore Resource Allocation Systems (RAS) in the context of Flexible Manufacturing Systems (FMS) [9] and introduce different subclasses of Petri nets to account for various allocation requirements [14,28]. In [21] the authors investigate how the methods used in FMS can be extended to software applications with concurrent processes competing for shared resources. They propose a new subclass of Petri nets, PC^2R, where the resources of different types, their availability and control flow of each process are represented as a unique system. A small change in the process flow or resources set will require a change of this model. In contrast, we are applying the separation of concerns principle by providing distinct models for systems of interdependent resources with their available capacities and for resource requests from abstract applications.

Numerous works study constraints and dependencies, such as temporal, causality and resource constraints, in various contexts by considering the underlying dependency graphs, e.g. [1,4,18,25]. Due to their syntactic structure inspired from Petri nets, cfNets generalise these approaches.

The term "constraint-flow net" can be confused with "network of constraints", a notion initially proposed in [22]. In fact, these two formalisms are very different. Constraint-flow nets consist of places and transitions, representing, respectively, resources and dependencies among them. Each transition has an associated constraint schema, whereof the arity is the total number of incoming and outgoing arcs of the transitions. These constraint schemata are used to generate constraints imposed on the possible resource allocations by the execution platform modelled by the cfNet. On the other hand, networks of constraints have been proposed in [22] to palliate the combinatorial explosion, when a given relation among

n variables (constraint) is represented by an n-dimensional $(0, 1)$-matrix. Instead, such n-ary constraint can be optimally approximated by a network of n binary ones, thereby considerably reducing the size of the representation.

Constraint-flow nets bear some similarity with event structures [23], in particular the more recent generalisations involving conflict [30] and dynamicity [3]. Event structures encode causality and conflict relations among concurrent events. The generalisation proposed in [30] matches the expressive power of arbitrary Petri nets. This suggests that it should be capable of encoding the flow part of cfNets: in our context, an event structure configuration would represent the set of transitions having been fired. However, since places—representing resources in cfNets—do not appear explicitly in event structures, it is not immediately clear how the initial requests and constraint schemata should be encoded. We leave a more detailed study of the correspondence between the various forms of event structures and cfNets for future work.

Constraint-flow nets are specifically tailored to provide a natural way of incorporating constraint schemata that allow expressing quantitative dependencies among amounts of allocated resources. To the best of our knowledge, such combinations of constraint schemata with an underlying graph structure have not been studied in existing literature.

7 Conclusion

In this paper, we have introduced constraint-flow nets (cfNets) that allow modelling resource dependencies, thereby bridging a gap in the current state-of-the-art approaches to the specification of requests for resources and resource allocation to applications: resource allocation commonly relies on the assumption that the requested resources are completely specified, whereas specification languages operate with high-level abstractions of resources, e.g. "memory" or "thread", leaving the resource manager to endow these with precise semantics.

The cfNet model provides a means to formally specify the structure of resources provided by the platform and the dependencies among them. This specification serves as an abstraction layer, which allows designers to focus on the resources immediately relevant to the application functionality, while taking care of low-level structure and dependencies inherent to the specific target platform. Thus, our approach simplifies application design and greatly enhances portability. This is particularly useful for platforms with complex resource architectures, such as the Massively Parallel Processor Arrays (MPPA) (e.g. Kalray), or cloud platforms, where the resource architecture can change dynamically at run time.

In this paper, we have defined the cfNet model and provided its semantics, defining a constraint problem for a given initial resource request. The cfNet model comprises inhibitor arcs. On one hand, these increase the expressiveness of the model and simplify certain constraint problems by reducing the number of variables involved. On the other hand, inhibitors can generate conflicts introducing ambiguity in the constraint problem definition. We have provided a sufficient condition—which can be easily checked syntactically—for the cfNet to be conflict-free. For cfNets that do not satisfy this condition, we have provided an efficient method for determining whether a given inhibitor induces a conflict. As shown by the virtual resources example, reachable conflicts can appear, for example, when the use of different instances of the same similar resource type are preferable in different situations. Such conflicts can be dynamically resolved by defining priorities between conflicting transitions.

In future work, we are planning to further improve the conflict detection algorithm: the encoding refinement presented in this paper excludes only one marking; by exploiting the causality hyper-graph, more unreachable markings could be excluded in one step. Similarly, the structure of a cfNet could be exploited for building concurrent or distributed resource allocators. We also consider implementing the cfNet model in the JavaBIP [5,6] component coordination framework in order to evaluate the practical performance, using various SMT and constraint solvers.

Acknowledgements. This paper has received a large number of very constructive comments. Although—mostly due to space and time limitations—we did not manage to address all of them, we are very grateful to the anonymous reviewers for their suggestions that we hope to implement in our future work.

References

1. Agarwal, M.K., Appleby, K., Gupta, M., Kar, G., Neogi, A., Sailer, A.: Problem determination using dependency graphs and run-time behavior models. In: Sahai, A., Wu, F. (eds.) DSOM 2004. LNCS, vol. 3278, pp. 171–182. Springer, Heidelberg (2004). doi:10.1007/978-3-540-30184-4_15
2. Ansótegui, C., Bofill, M., Palahí, M., Suy, J., Villaret, M.: Satisfiability modulo theories: an efficient approach for the resource-constrained project scheduling problem. In: Symposium on Abstraction, Reformulation, and Approximation (2011)
3. Arbach, Y., Karcher, D., Peters, K., Nestmann, U.: Dynamic causality in event structures. In: Graf, S., Viswanathan, M. (eds.) FORTE 2015. LNCS, vol. 9039, pp. 83–97. Springer, Cham (2015). doi:10.1007/978-3-319-19195-9_6
4. Berson, D.A., Gupta, R., Soffa, M.L.: GURRR: a global unified resource requirements representation. SIGPLAN Not. **30**(3), 23–34 (1995)
5. Bliudze, S., Mavridou, A., Szymanek, R., Zolotukhina, A.: Coordination of software components with BIP: application to OSGi. In: Proceedings of the 6th International Workshop on Modeling in Software Engineering, MiSE 2014, pp. 25–30. ACM, New York (2014)
6. Bliudze, S., Mavridou, A., Szymanek, R., Zolotukhina, A.: Exogenous coordination of concurrent software components with JavaBIP. Software: Practice and Experience (2017). Early view: http://dx.doi.org/10.1002/spe.2495
7. Bliudze, S., Simalatsar, A., Zolotukhina, A.: Modelling resource dependencies. Technical report 218599, EPFL. https://infoscience.epfl.ch/record/218599
8. Chien, A.A., Casanova, H., Kee, Y.-S., Huang, R.: The virtual grid description language: vgDL. Technical report CS2005-0817, Department of Computer Science and Engineering, University of California, San Diego (2004)

9. Colom, J.M.: The resource allocation problem in flexible manufacturing systems. In: Aalst, W.M.P., Best, E. (eds.) ICATPN 2003. LNCS, vol. 2679, pp. 23–35. Springer, Heidelberg (2003)

10. Cui, Y., Nahrstedt, K.: QoS-aware dependency management for component-based systems. In: Proceedings of the 10th IEEE International Symposium on High Performance Distributed Computing, pp. 127–138 (2001)

11. Czajkowski, K., Foster, I., Karonis, N., Kesselman, C., Martin, S., Smith, W., Tuecke, S.: A resource management architecture for metacomputing systems. In: Feitelson, D.G., Rudolph, L. (eds.) JSSp. 1998. LNCS, vol. 1459, pp. 62–82. Springer, Heidelberg (1998). doi:10.1007/BFb0053981

12. de Dinechin, B.D., van Amstel, D., Poulhiès, M., Lager, G.: Time-critical computing on a single-chip massively parallel processor. In: Proceedings of the Conference on Design, Automation & Test in Europe, DATE 2014, p. 97: 1–97: 6, 3001 Leuven, Belgium, Belgium, European Design and Automation Association (2014)

13. Ensel, C., Keller, A.: An approach for managing service dependencies with XML and the resource description framework. J. Netw. Syst. Manage. $10(2)$, 147–170 (2002)

14. Ezpeleta, J., Colom, J., Martínez, J.: A Petri net based deadlock prevention policy for flexible manufacturing systems. IEEE Trans. Robot. Autom. 11, 173–184 (1995)

15. Giannopoulou, G., Stoimenov, N., Huang, P., Thiele, L., de Dinechin, B.: Mixed-criticality scheduling on cluster-based manycores with shared communication and storage resources. Real-Time Syst. $51(4)$, 1–51 (2015)

16. Kalray. Kalray MPPA-256, March 2015. http://www.kalray.eu/IMG/pdf/FLYER_MPPA_MANYCORE.pdf

17. Kee, Y.-S., Logothetis, D., Huang, R.Y., Casanova, H., Chien, A.A.: Efficient resource description and high quality selection for virtual grids. In: CCGRID, pp. 598–606. IEEE Computer Society (2005)

18. Kountouris, A.A., Wolinski, C.: Hierarchical conditional dependency graphs for conditional resource sharing. In: Proceedings of the 24th Euromicro Conference, vol. 1, pp. 313–316,., August 1998

19. Krauter, K., Buyya, R., Maheswaran, M.: A taxonomy and survey of grid resource management systems for distributed computing. Softw. Pract. Experience $32(2)$, 135–164 (2002)

20. Lassila, O., Swick, R.R.: Resource description frame-work (RDF) model and syntax specification. Technical report REC-rdf-syntax-19990222, World Wide Web Consortium (W3C), February 1999

21. López-Grao, J.-P., Colom, J.-M.: A petri net perspective on the resource allocation problem in software engineering. In: Jensen, K., Donatelli, S., Kleijn, J. (eds.) ToPNoC V. LNCS, vol. 6900, pp. 181–200. Springer, Heidelberg (2012). doi:10.1007/978-3-642-29072-5_8

22. Montanari, U.: Networks of constraints: fundamental properties and applications to picture processing. Inf. Sci. 7, 95–132 (1974)

23. Nielsen, M., Plotkin, G., Winskel, G.: Petri nets, event structures and domains, part I. Theoret. Comput. Sci. $13(1)$, 85–108 (1981)

24. Raman, R., Livny, M., Solomon, M.: Matchmaking: an extensible framework for distributed resource management. Cluster Comput. $2(2)$, 129–138 (1999)

25. Senkul, P., Toroslu, I.H.: An architecture for workflow scheduling under resource allocation constraints. Inform. Syst. $30(5)$, 399–422 (2005)

26. Tendulkar, P., Poplavko, P., Galanommatis, I., Maler, O.: Many-core scheduling of data parallel applications using SMT solvers. In: 2014 17th Euromicro Conference on Digital System Design (DSD), pp. 615–622. IEEE (2014)

27. Tendulkar, P., Poplavko, P., Maselbas, J., Galanommatis, I., Maler, O.: A runtime environment for real-time streaming applications on clustered multi-cores. Technical report, Verimag (2015)
28. Tricas, F., Garcia-Valles, F., Colom, J.M., Ezpeleta, J.: A Petri net structure-based deadlock prevention solution for sequential resource allocation systems. In: Proceedings of the 2005 IEEE International Conference on Robotics and Automation, ICRA 2005, pp. 271–277, April 2005
29. Van, H.N., Tran, F.D., Menaud, J.M.: SLA-aware virtual resource management for cloud infrastructures. In: Ninth IEEE International Conference on Computer and Information Technology, CIT 2009, vol. 1, pp. 357–362,., October 2009
30. Glabbeek, R., Plotkin, G.: Event structures for resolvable conflict. In: Fiala, J., Koubek, V., Kratochvíl, J. (eds.) MFCS 2004. LNCS, vol. 3153, pp. 550–561. Springer, Heidelberg (2004). doi:10.1007/978-3-540-28629-5_42
31. Vanderham, J., Dijkstra, F., Travostino, F., Andree, H., Delaat, C.: Using RDF to describe networks. Future Gener. Comput. Syst. **22**(8), 862–867 (2006)

Verification

Verifying Timed BPMN Processes Using Maude

Francisco Durán[1($\boxtimes$)] and Gwen Salaün[2]

[1] University of Málaga, Málaga, Spain
duran@lcc.uma.es
[2] University of Grenoble Alpes, LIG, CNRS, Grenoble, France

Abstract. A business process is a collection of structured activities producing a particular product or software. BPMN is a workflow-based graphical notation for specifying business processes. Formally analyzing such processes is a crucial challenge in order to avoid erroneous executions of the corresponding software. In this paper, we focus on timed business processes where execution time can be associated to several BPMN constructs. We propose an encoding of timed business processes into the Maude language, which allows one to automatically verify several properties of interest on processes such as the maximum/minimum/average execution time or the timed degree of parallelism that provides a valuable guide for the problem of resource allocation. The analysis is achieved using the rewriting-based tools available in Maude, which also provides other techniques (*e.g.*, reachability analysis and model checking) for verifying BPMN specifications. We applied our approach on a large set of BPMN processes for evaluation purposes.

1 Introduction

Business Process Model and Notation (BPMN) [14] is a graphical modelling language for specifying business processes. A business process is a collection of structured activities or tasks that produce a specific product and fulfill a specific organizational goal for a customer or market. More precisely, a process aims at modelling activities, their causal and temporal relationships, and specific business rules that process executions have to comply with. Business process modelling is an important area in software engineering since it supports the development of workflow-based software, such as information and distributed systems. BPMN is the *de facto* notation for designing business processes and was published as an ISO standard in 2013.

When modelling processes using BPMN, many questions arise: is my workflow precisely modelling what I expect from it? Is my workflow free of errors and bugs? Are certain properties of interest preserved? What is the degree of parallelism of my process? What is the minimum execution time of my workflow? All these questions are meaningful, but they are not that simple to answer, particularly when modelling complex processes involving many tasks and intricate combinations of gateways. Some of these questions (and corresponding

© IFIP International Federation for Information Processing 2017
Published by Springer International Publishing AG 2017. All Rights Reserved
J.-M. Jacquet and M. Massink (Eds.): COORDINATION 2017, LNCS 10319, pp. 219–236, 2017.
DOI: 10.1007/978-3-319-59746-1_12

computations) may even turn out to be undecidable if the whole expressiveness of BPMN is considered (*e.g.*, cyclic behaviours, data aspects, or time).

In this paper, we focus on software development based on a subset of BPMN where we can model process behaviours (tasks, sequence flows, gateways) and time aspects (duration associated to tasks and flows). We propose automated analysis techniques for verifying that certain properties of interest are satisfied for timed business processes modelled with BPMN. In this work, we focus on properties that are application independent, which allows us to provide press-button verification techniques without requiring any input from the developer. Properties of interest are for instance the minimum/maximum/average execution time of a process and the timed degree of parallelism, which is a valuable information for resource allocation. Our approach also enables one to carry on other kinds of analysis such as reachability analysis to search, *e.g.*, for deadlock states, or state-based LTL model checking to verify the satisfaction of temporal properties (safety and liveness). In these cases, since the properties depend on the input process, they have to be provided by the developer, who can reuse well-known patterns for timed properties as those presented in [12,15].

Our approach relies on an encoding of the BPMN execution semantics into the rewriting-logic-based language Maude [7]. The three challenges of this encoding were to properly translate all gateways (including the inclusive merge gateway), to describe time durations and passing, and to support loops and unbalanced workflows. Unbalanced workflows are those processes that exhibit an unbalanced structure with no exact correspondence between split and merge gateways. The expressive power of the Maude language allowed us to model these features in a uniform way. Moreover, Maude is equipped with a large variety of analysis tools, which can be used for automatically verifying properties of interest such as the aforementioned execution time measures and the timed degree of parallelism. We applied our approach on many business processes for validation purposes and verification times turn out to be reasonable for real-size examples.

To sum up, the main contributions of this work with respect to existing results on this topic are the following: (i) an encoding into Maude of a subset of BPMN including time aspects, inclusive gateways, looping behaviours, and unbalanced workflows; (ii) automated analysis techniques for verifying properties of interest on timed BPMN models using reachability analysis and model checking tools; and (iii) tool support for automating the transformation to Maude and validation of the approach by application to many BPMN processes.

The organization of the rest of the paper is as follows. Section 2 introduces the BPMN notation and Maude. Section 3 explains our Maude encoding of the considered subset of BPMN, with emphasis on the handling of time. In Sect. 4, we present our techniques for automatically analyzing properties on BPMN processes. This section also presents experimental results. Section 5 surveys related work and Sect. 6 concludes the paper.

2   Preliminaries

In this section we provide a brief account of BPMN and Maude.

2.1   BPMN

BPMN is a graphical notation for modelling business processes as collections of related tasks that produce specific services or products for particular clients. BPMN is an ISO/IEC standard [14], and BPMN processes can be simulated by using different process interpretation engines (*e.g.*, Activiti, Bonita BPM, or jBPM). The semantics of BPMN is described informally in official documents (see, e.g., [14,23]), and some attempts have been made for giving a formal semantics to BPMN (see, *e.g.*, [9,17,19,24,29]).

In this paper, our goal is not to consider the whole expressiveness of the BPMN language, but to concentrate on the BPMN elements related to control-flow modelling and on time aspects that can be represented in BPMN constructs. This enables us to focus on those aspects and show how automated analysis is possible for them. Specifically, we consider the node types *event*, *task*, and *gateway*, and the edge type *sequence flow*. Start and end events are used, respectively, to initialize and terminate processes. A task represents an atomic activity that has exactly one incoming and one outgoing flow. A gateway is used to control the divergence and convergence of the execution flow. A sequence flow describes two nodes executed one after the other, *i.e.*, imposing the execution order.

Gateways are crucial since they are used to model control flow branching in BPMN and therefore influence the overall process execution. There are five types of gateways in BPMN: *exclusive*, *inclusive*, *parallel*, *event-based* and *complex* gateways. We consider all of them except complex gateways, because they are used to model complex synchronization behaviours especially based on data control, and we do not take data objects, nor conditions on flows outgoing of split gateways, into account.

Gateways with one incoming branch and multiple outgoing branches are called *splits*, *e.g.*, split inclusive gateway. Gateways with one outgoing branch and multiple incoming branches are called *merges*, *e.g.*, merge parallel gateway. An exclusive gateway chooses one out of a set of mutually exclusive alternative incoming or outgoing branches. For an inclusive gateway, any number of branches among all its incoming or outgoing branches may be taken. A parallel gateway creates concurrent flows for all its outgoing branches or synchronizes concurrent flows for all its incoming branches. For an event-based gateway, it takes one of its outgoing branches or accepts one of its incoming branches based on events. In the following, we call the branches that are taken by a gateway during an execution as *active* branches. In this work, we support unbalanced workflows, meaning that each merge gateway does not necessarily have a corresponding split gateway with an exact correspondence of the branches among outgoing and incoming flows. We also support workflows with looping behaviours.

The execution semantics of BPMN constructs can be described using tokens as depicted in Fig. 1. The start event node can be triggered once at any moment, which creates a token in its outgoing sequence flow. Whenever a token is present in the incoming sequence flow of an end event, this execution flow can terminate by consuming this token. If a token is in a sequence flow, then the destination node for this sequence flow can be triggered. The semantics of gateways is also given, emphasizing that specific care should be taken when considering inclusive split/merge gateways since all possible combinations should be generated and all triggered branches should be awaited for at the merge synchronization point. The inclusive merge is particularly problematic from a semantic point of view as discussed in [6]. We will show in the next section how our Maude executable semantics allows the encoding of these BPMN gateways.

In addition to these classic BPMN constructs, one can also specify notions of time. In this paper, we consider time as a duration, which can be associated to tasks or flows. When a flow has a duration d greater than zero, it means that the destination node is triggered after d units of time. If the duration is zero, that node is immediately triggered. Similarly, a task triggers its outgoing flow at once for a duration equal to zero and waits for d units of time when a duration d greater than zero is associated to that task.

In this paper, we assume that BPMN processes are syntactically correct. This can be enforced using existing works, *e.g.*, [11], or using a BPMN engine, *e.g.*, the Activiti BPM platform, Bonita BPM, or the Eclipse BPMN Designer.

Running example. The process we use as running example (Fig. 2) aims at monitoring the organization of a business trip. The process starts by reserving flight tickets and by completing the mission paperwork. Flight booking may take some time, because in many companies this task is subcontracted to a third party company. Once the flight tickets are issued, accommodation reservation and other additional services (insurance, vaccines, etc.) are tackled in parallel. Visa process is initiated only when all reservations (flights and hotel) are completed and when the paperwork is finished. Once all the aforementioned prerequisites of the trip are completed, the mission details are stored in a specific database.

2.2 Maude and Real-Time Maude

Real-Time Maude [22] is a rewriting-logic-based specification language and formal analysis tool that extends the Maude system [7] to support the formal specification and analysis of *real-time systems*. Real-Time Maude provides support for symbolic simulation through timed rewriting, and time-bounded temporal logic model checking and search for reachability analysis.

Rewriting logic [20] is a logic of change that can naturally deal with states and non-deterministic concurrent computations. A rewrite logic theory is a tuple $(\Sigma, E \cup A, R)$, where $(\Sigma, E \cup A)$ is a *membership equational logic* [3] theory with Σ its signature, E a set of conditional equations, A a set of equational axioms such as associativity, commutativity and identity, so that rewriting is performed *modulo* A, and R is a set of labeled conditional rules. In rewriting logic, a distributed system is axiomatized by an equational theory, describing its set of states as an algebraic data type, and a collection of conditional rewrite rules, specifying

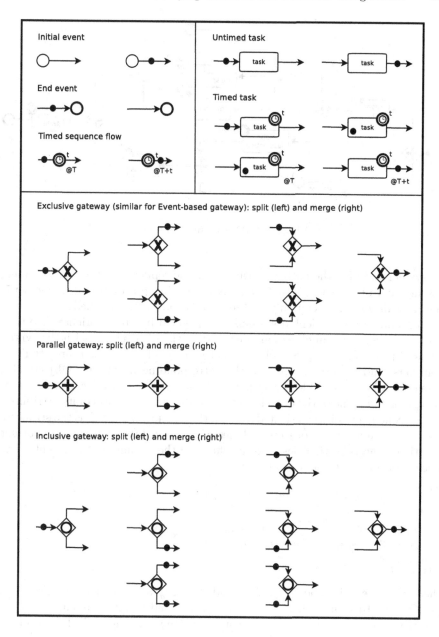

Fig. 1. BPMN execution semantics

its dynamics. Rewrite rules are written crl $[l] : t => t'$ if C, with l the rule label, t and t' terms, and C a condition. We may have rules without label or condition. An unlabelled unconditional rule would be written rl $t => t'$. Rules describe the local, concurrent transitions that are possible in the system, *i.e.*, when a part of

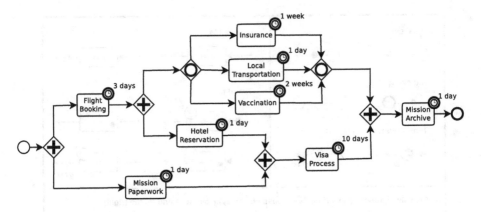

Fig. 2. BPMN running example

the system state fits the pattern t, then it can be replaced by the corresponding instantiation of t'. The guard C acts as a blocking precondition, in the sense that a conditional rule can only be fired if its condition is satisfied.

In Maude, object-oriented systems are specified by object-oriented modules in which classes and subclasses are declared. A class is declared with the syntax `class` $C \mid a_1 : S_1,\ \dots,\ a_n : S_n$, where C is the name of the class, a_i are attribute identifiers, and S_i are the sorts of the corresponding attributes. Objects of a class C are then record-like structures of the form $<O : C \mid a_1 : v_1,\ \dots,\ a_n : v_n>$, where O is the name of the object, and v_i are the current values of its attributes.

In a concurrent object-oriented system, the concurrent state has the structure of a multiset made up of objects and messages. Such state evolves by concurrent rewriting using rules that describe the effects of the communication events. The general form of such rewrite rules is:

```
crl [r] :
    < O₁ : C₁ | atts₁ > ... < Oₙ : Cₙ | attsₙ >
    M₁ ... Mₘ
    =>
    < Oᵢ₁ : C'ᵢ₁ | atts'ᵢ₁ > ... < Oᵢₖ : C'ᵢₖ | atts'ᵢₖ >
    < Q₁ : C''₁ | atts''₁ > ... < Qₚ : C''ₚ | atts''ₚ >
    M'₁ ... M'q
    if Cond .
```

where r is the rule label, $M_1...M_m$ and $M'_1...M'_q$ are messages, $O_1...O_n$ and $Q_1...Q_p$ are object identifiers, $C_1...C_n$, $C'_{i_1}...C'_{i_k}$ and $C''_1...C''_p$ are classes, $i_1...i_k$ is a subset of $1...n$, and $Cond$ is a condition (the rule's *guard*). The result of applying such a rule is that: (a) messages $M_1...M_m$ disappear, i.e., they are consumed; (b) the state, and possibly the classes of objects $O_{i_1}...O_{i_k}$ may change; (c) all the other objects O_j vanish; (d) new objects $Q_1...Q_p$ are created; and (e) new messages $M'_1...M'_q$ are created, i.e., they are posted.

Real-Time Maude provides a sort Time to model the time domain, which can be either discrete or dense time (we use discrete time in this paper).

Given a constructor {_,_} of sort GlobalSystem, time passing is modelled by rewrite rules known as *tick rules*:

```
crl [l] : {t, T} => {t', T + τ} if C .
```

where t is the state of the system, T is its global time, and τ is the *duration* of the rewrite. Since tick rules affect the global time, in Real-Time Maude time elapse is usually modeled by one single tick rule, and the system dynamic behaviour by instantaneous transitions [22]. Although there are other strategies, the most flexible one models time elapse by using two functions, namely, delta, which defines the effect of time elapse over every model element, and mte (maximal time elapse), which defines the maximum amount of time that can elapse before any action is performed.

```
crl [tick] : {t, T} => {delta(t), T + τ} if τ := mte(t) /\ τ > 0 /\ C .
```

In Maude, rule conditions may be given as a short-circuited conjunction of conditional terms using operator /\. In the previous rule, Boolean expressions and assignments are used as conjuncts (see [7] for further details).

3   The Encoding of BPMN Processes into Maude

In this section, we present our encoding of our subset of BPMN into Maude. This encoding consists of two parts: the syntactic encoding of a BPMN process into Maude and the set of rewrite rules encoding the BPMN execution semantics. The encoding of the BPMN process into Maude (Sect. 3.1) depends on the example, so the corresponding Maude code has to be generated for each new process. This transformation is fully automated by applying a Python script we implemented. The rewrite rules have been encoded once and for all, and we will present in Sect. 3.2 the rules corresponding to the handling of some of the constructs in our BPMN processes. The complete Maude specification with all the rules and examples of BPMN processes is available online [1].

3.1   Process Encoding

We represent a BPMN process as a set of flows and a set of nodes. A flow is represented as a term flow(sf_i, t), with sf_i an identifier and t a duration. If there is no duration associated to a flow, the duration value is zero. We distinguish different kinds of nodes: start, end, task, split, and merge. A start (end, resp.) node consists of an identifier and an output (input, resp.) flow identifier. A task node involves an identifier, a task description, two flow identifiers (input and output), and a duration (zero if no duration is associated to this task). A split node includes a node identifier, a gateway type (exclusive, parallel, inclusive, or event-based), an input flow identifier, and a set of output flow identifiers. A merge node includes a node identifier, a gateway type, a set of input flow identifiers, and an output flow identifier.

These constructs are illustrated in Fig. 3, which shows an excerpt of the representation of the running example. Constants fls and nds represent, respectively, its set of flows and its set of nodes.

```
1 eq fls = ( flow(sf1, 0), flow(sf2, 0), ... ) .          --- flows
2
3 eq nds = ( start(initial, sf1),                          --- nodes
4             end(final, sf13),
5             split(g1, parallel, sf1, (sf2, sf14)),
6             ...
7             task(t7, "transportation", sf6, sf9, 1),
8             task(t8, "vaccination", sf7, sf10, 14) ) .
9
10 eq initSystem
11   = < p : Process | nodes : nds, flows : fls >
12     < s : Simulation | tokens : token(initial, 0), gtime : 0 > .
```

Fig. 3. Running example in Maude

3.2   Execution Semantics

The execution of BPMN activities is modeled using tokens, which are associated to tasks and flows, and circulate along activities as the execution evolves (see Sect. 2.1). For instance, split gateways produce tokens for their outgoing flows, and merge gateways collect tokens from their incoming flows and produce one single token. This simple approach allows us to support unbalanced workflows where there is no strict correspondence between splits and merges, as well as looping behaviours.

The execution semantics of BPMN is defined using Maude rewrite rules, which operate on systems composed of a process object and a *simulation* object. The process object represents the BPMN process, and it does not change. The simulation object keeps information on the execution of the process.

```
class Process | nodes : Set{Node}, flows : Set{Flow} .
class Simulation | tokens : Set{Token}, gtime : Time .
```

A simulation involves a set of tokens and a global time (gtime) described using a natural number (discrete time). Tokens are used to represent the evolution of the workflow during its execution. These tokens correspond to flow or task identifiers, plus a time that express a delay, used to model duration of flows and tasks. Thus, a token token(t8, t) indicates that the task t8 has a token, and that such task will be completed in t time units. The operator initSystem in Fig. 3 represents the initial state for the process introduced in Fig. 2.

Tick rule. A *tick* rule is necessary to simulate the time evolution, which is modelled by the increase of the global time and the decrease of the tokens' timers. Given appropriate definitions of functions mte and delta, the tick rule is written as in Fig. 4. The delta function is straightforward, since it just increments the global time present in the simulation object of the indicated amount of time and decrements the timers of the tokens by the same amount. The mte function is more subtle. Although one could think that it is enough taking the smallest of the tokens' delays, notice that parallel and inclusive merges may require additional delays in the incoming branches, requiring a more intricate calculation. A parallel merge is not activated until all its incoming flows are active, meaning that there can be tokens with time zero that have to wait until all these flows get their

```
1  crl [tick] :
2    < PId : Process | nodes : Nodes , Atts >
3    < SId : Simulation | tokens : Tks , gtime : T >
4    =>
5    < PId : Process | nodes : Nodes , Atts >
6    < SId : Simulation |
7        tokens : delta(Tks, T1),           --- updates all tokens
8        gtime : (T + T1) >                  --- increments the global time
9    if T1 := mte(Nodes , Tks)
10   /\ 0 < T1 .
```

Fig. 4. Tick rule

tokens. The case of inclusive merges is similar, although in this case we do not know beforehand how many tokens are to be expected. Thus, each incoming flow must be traversed backwards to check whether that flow must be awaited for or discarded in the calculation of the mte function.

The semantics we choose for describing time obliges to execute actions and move tokens in the process as soon as possible. The time cannot elapse when there are timers to zero and thus possible actions to be triggered in the process.

Start/end events. We assume that the initial set of tokens includes a token token(initial, 0). Thus, the start rule (Fig. 5) is triggered when this token is available (line 6). When the startProc rule is applied, the initial token is consumed and another one is added to the set of current tokens (line 13), which indicates that the flow outgoing from the start event has been activated (FId). The time assigned to this new token is the delay of the flow FId (line 11).

```
1  rl [startProc] :
2    < PId : Process |
3        nodes : (start(NId, FId), Nodes),
4        flows : (flow(FId, T), Flows) >
5    < SId : Simulation |
6        tokens : (token(NId, 0), Tks),      --- init token available
7        Atts >
8    =>
9    < PId : Process |
10       nodes : (start(NId, FId), Nodes),
11       flows : (flow(FId, T), Flows) >
12   < SId : Simulation |                     --- token for FId with flow duration
13       tokens : (token(FId, T), Tks),
14       Atts > .
```

Fig. 5. Start event rule

The end event rule is triggered when there is a token for the incoming flow with zero time duration. In that case, the simulation consumes this token without generating new ones, which terminates this flow execution. Note that there is no specific rules for flows. It is enough to have tokens representing flow activations and the tick rule we have presented before in this section makes the time evolves for these tokens, thus for these flows once they are activated.

Tasks. A task execution is encoded with two rules to express the possibility that a task may take time if a duration is associated to it. An initiation rule

```
1  rl [execTask] :
2    < PId : Process |
3          nodes : (task(NId, TaskName, FId1, FId2, T), Nodes),
4          flows : Flows >
5    < SId : Simulation |
6          tokens : (token(NId, 0), Tks),      --- token available with 0 time
7          Atts >
8    =>
9    < PId : Process |
10         nodes : (task(NId, TaskName, FId1, FId2, T), Nodes),
11         flows : Flows >
12   < SId : Simulation |                --- new token for outgoing flow FId2
13         tokens : (token(FId2, retrieveTimeFlow(FId2, Flows)), Tks),
14         Atts > .
```

Fig. 6. Task completion rule

activates the task when a token representing the incoming flow is available. In that case, we generate a new token with the task identifier and the task duration. A second rule is used for representing the task completion. This rule is triggered when there is a token for that task with time zero. In that case, this token is consumed and a new one is generated for the outgoing flow (Fig. 6).

Gateways. The semantics of exclusive (event-based, resp.) gateways is encoded with two rules, one rule for the split gateway and one rule for the merge gateway. The rule for the exclusive split gateway fires when a token with time zero is available in the input flow and non-deterministically generates a token for one of the output branches. The exclusive merge gateway executes when there is one token for one of the incoming flows. In that case, the token is consumed and a token is generated for the merge outgoing flow.

The parallel split gateway rule is triggered when a token corresponding to the input flow is available. If so, the token is consumed and one token is added for each outgoing flow. The merge rule for the parallel gateway (Fig. 7) is executed when there is a token for each incoming branch (function allTokensParallel in Fig. 7, line 12). In that case, these tokens are removed (function removeTokensParallel, line 11) and a new token is generated for the outgoing flow.

The semantics of inclusive gateways is more intricate [6]. An inclusive split gateway can trigger any number of outgoing flows (at least one). To do so, we generate tokens for a non-deterministic number of outgoing flows to simulate the

```
1  crl [mergeParallelGateway] :
2    < PId : Process |
3          nodes : (merge(NId, parallel, FIds, FId), Nodes),
4          flows : (flow(FId, T), Flows) >
5    < SId : Simulation | tokens : Tks, Atts >
6    =>
7    < PId : Process |
8          nodes : (merge(NId, parallel, FIds, FId), Nodes),
9          flows : (flow(FId, T), Flows) >
10   < SId : Simulation |
11         tokens : (token(FId, T), removeTokensParallel(FIds, Tks)), Atts >
12   if allTokensParallel(FIds, Tks) .   ---- all incoming flows activated
```

Fig. 7. Parallel merge gateway rule

concurrent execution of those flows. The inclusive merge gateway is one of the most subtle parts of this encoding. This gateway is triggered when *all expected tokens* are available. However, we cannot know beforehand the number of active branches, and therefore, the only way is to traverse the process backwards and look for active branches (available tokens), similar to the procedure described for the mte function. Function allTokensInclusive (line 14, Fig. 8) explores the process upstream looking for active flows and deduces whether all the expected tokens are present in order to fire the merge gateway or if other tokens must be expected before executing this gateway. To avoid unnecessary computations, this checking is only performed when a token has reached the gateway (atLeastOneToken, line 13, Fig. 8). Once this rule is executed, all expected tokens are consumed and a fresh token is added for the outgoing flow.

```
1  crl [mergeInclusiveGateway] :
2    < PId : Process |
3        nodes : (merge(NId, inclusive, FIds, FId), Nodes),
4        flows : (flow(FId, T), Flows) >
5    < SId : Simulation | tokens : Tks, Atts >
6    =>
7    < PId : Process |
8        nodes : (merge(NId, inclusive, FIds, FId), Nodes),
9        flows : (flow(FId, T), Flows) >
10   < SId : Simulation |
11       tokens : (token(FId, T), removeTokensInclusive(FIds, Tks)),
12       Atts >
13   if atLeastOneToken(FIds, Tks)
14   /\ allTokensInclusive(FIds,Tks,(merge(NId,inclusive,FIds,FId),Nodes)).
```

Fig. 8. Inclusive merge gateway rule

4 Rewriting-Based Verification of Timed Processes

In this section, we successively present the verification of properties on timed processes, other kinds of analysis (simulation, reachability, model checking), and experimental results. It is worth stressing that by using an encoding into an existing framework (Maude here), we can reuse and take advantage of all the existing tools without having to develop new algorithms (*from scratch*) for computing execution times and checking timed properties.

Verification of timed properties. There are several properties of interest to be checked on timed processes. We focus on the minimum/maximum/average execution time and on the degree of parallelism in this work. These metrics are independent of any concrete BPMN process instance, which makes these checks generic and easily reusable.

Given a module M including a BPMN process to analyze and an initial system I (Process and Simulation objects), the function execTime(M, I) generates all solutions (states where an end node has been reached) and computes their minimum, maximum and average execution times. The calculation of these values relies on the search and meta-programming capabilities of Maude.

The search takes place following a breadth-first strategy. In order to avoid infinite runs of our system, which may happen when processes include infinite loops, one can either bound the search depth or the global time. By using Maude's facilities, solutions are considered one by one, making the computation more efficient and saving storage space.

As far as the parallelism degree is concerned, for a specific process, we traverse all reachable states (and not only the final solutions) to search the state with the maximum number of tokens, which corresponds to the degree of parallelism.

Simulation and reachability analysis. Simulation is very useful for exploring system executions. In Maude, simulation relies on rewriting, which consists in successively applying equations and rewrite rules on an initial term (a BPMN process here), with the possibility of using some strategy language to guide the execution. Since systems may be rewritten in many different ways, Maude also provides a *search* command, which allows us to explore the reachable state space up to a certain depth. Thus, we can perform analysis on the reachability of states satisfying certain conditions, *e.g.*, when searching for deadlock states or other undesired situations. For example, given our running example in Fig. 2, and its corresponding Maude representation InitSystem in Fig. 3, the following search command checks that there is no reachable final state with tokens in it, which shows that there is no deadlock.

```
> search InitSystem =>! Conf such that getNumberTokens(Conf) =/= 0 .
No solution.
```

Notice the use of '=>!' to limit the check to final states. Variants of this command allows us to carry on other types of search.

Model checking. We can also take advantage of our encoding for using other analysis tools available in the Maude system. For instance, Maude's Linear Temporal Logic (LTL) explicit-state model checker [10] can be used for analyzing all possible executions of a business process. Maude's model checker allows one to check whether every possible behaviour starting from a given initial state (the start node in BPMN) satisfies a given LTL property. It can be used to check safety and liveness properties of systems when the set of states reachable from an initial state is finite. Full verification of invariants in infinite-state systems can be accomplished by verifying them on finite-state abstractions [21] of the original infinite-state system, that is, on an appropriate quotient of the original system whose set of reachable states is finite. In our context, beyond classic properties such as deadlock-freeness, the properties that can be verified depend on the example and should be specified by the developer, *e.g.*, a certain task is always achieved after another specific task. In order to make the property writing easier, the developer can rely on well-known patterns as those presented in [12,15] for timed properties.

For instance, given propositions FlightBooking and VisaProcess, which are true in states in which the process is executing these respective tasks, *i.e.*, there is a token in the corresponding task, we can check that the visa request is always processed after a flight booking as follows:

```
> reduce modelCheck(InitSystem, []( FlightBooking -> <> VisaProcess )) .
result Bool: true
```

Experimental evaluation. We made experiments on about 100 examples, some of them taken from the literature on this topic, *e.g.*, [24,27,31], or hand-crafted for testing some special structures such as multiple nested gateways. Our main goal was to see how our verification approach scales in terms of time and explored state space depending on the size of the input process. We used a Mac OS laptop running on a 2.9 GHz Intel Core i5 processor with 16 GB of memory. We present in Table 1 some of these results. The table gives for each process the number of tasks, the number of sequence flows, and the number of gateways. The exploration is characterized giving the number of solutions and the total number of states. As for verification, for each example, we give the results for process execution times and for the degree of parallelism. The last column shows the analysis time for the parallelism degree calculation, which is the operation that takes longer.

Table 1. Experimental results

BPMN Proc.	Size					Exploration		Proc. exec. time			Parall. degree	Analysis time
	Tasks	Flows	⟨×⟩	⟨+⟩	⟨○⟩	Sol	States	Min	Max	Avg		
1	8	19	–	4	2	2	138	15	17	16	5	0.07 s
2	7	14	2	2	–	2	59	4,837	5,322	5,079	2	0.02 s
3	8	17	–	5	–	1	44	3,863	3,863	3,863	4	0.02 s
4	8	16	–	–	4	3	127	3,288	5,095	3,913	3	0.05 s
5	12	24	–	–	6	6	1,051	2,902	3,900	3,547	6	0.6 s
6	20	39	–	–	8	35	8,760	4,529	8,222	6,423	7	10.3 s
7	20	43	–	6	6	7	2,653	5,649	7,341	6,453	7	3.7 s
8	40	87	14	9	2	24	28,327	7,619	9,235	8,332	7	49.7 s
9	40	87	12	9	4	24	55,693	7,619	9,235	8,332	8	1 m 48 s
10	40	87	10	9	6	24	288,025	7,619	9,235	8,332	12	24 m 20 s
11	16	31	–	–	2	13	225,378	1,370	3,024	2,274	13	6 m 23 s
12	213	215	4	6	4	22	5,844	4,189	21,199	17,367	6	16.8 s

First of all, it is worth noting that we made experiments varying time durations (durations between 0 and 10 units of time, between 0 and 100, between 0 and 1000). This does not impact analysis times because the function mte avoids an execution where the time would elapse unit by unit. Therefore, this function speeds up the time passing whatever maximum time is considered for task and flow duration. Regarding the experimental results presented in Table 1, we set flow and task durations between 0 and 1000 units of time.

Example 1 is the running example. The minimum time (15 days) is obtained when the vaccination task is not executed in the inclusive gateway. When this task is required, we obtain the maximum time (17 days). The degree of parallelism (5) corresponds to the case where both hotel reservation and paperwork tasks are not yet completed, and the three tasks in the inclusive gateway are all triggered in parallel.

The analysis time is short for small and medium size examples, even when there are several nested inclusive or parallel gateways (see examples 5–7 in the table). Example 3 exhibits the same minimum, maximum, and average times because it involves only parallel gateways, and in that case, all behaviours are systematically executed. We made experiments with variants of the same example (rows 8–10) to observe how our approach scales. These examples are quite large, involving 40 tasks and more than 20 gateways (most of them nested). We can see how, by increasing the number of inclusive gateways and reducing the number of exclusive gateways, the analysis time goes from 52 s (example 8) to over 24 min (example 10). These times are long because the number of states to explore is rather large. Let us emphasize that we may encounter realistic processes larger than those ones in terms of number of tasks, but we have not seen yet a real example with as many nested gateways as in those examples (8–10). Example 12 shows an example with more than 200 tasks. This process mainly exhibits sequential behaviours. In that case, we can see that the number of states is lower and thus the analysis time is quite short (16 s).

5   Related Work

Several works focus on providing formal semantics and verification techniques for business processes using Petri nets. [16] proposes to formalize business processes and more specifically composition of Web services using Petri nets. Decker and Weske present in [8] an extension of BPMN 1.0 (iBPMN) in the direction of inter-action modelling. They also propose a formal semantics for iBPMN in terms of interaction Petri nets. [9] presents a mapping from BPMN to Petri nets that enables the static analysis of BPMN models. [26] presents a double transformation from BPMN to Petri nets and from Petri nets to mCRL2. This allows one to use both Petri nets based tools and the mCRL2 toolset for searching deadlocks, livelocks, or checking temporal properties. [2] describes how BPMN processes can be represented using the Reo coordination language, which admits formal analysis using model checking and bisimulation techniques. Compared to these results, our encoding also gives a semantics to BPMN by translation to Maude, yet it was not our primary goal. The main difference with respect to these related works is our focus on timed aspects.

Another line of works aimed at using process algebras for formalizing and verifying BPMN processes. The authors of [29] present a formal semantics for BPMN by encoding it into the CSP process algebra. They show in [30] how this semantic model can be used to verify compatibility between business participants in a collaboration. This work was extended in [31] to propose a timed semantics of BPMN with delays. [5,18,19] focus on the semantics formalized in [29,31] and propose an automated transformation from BPMN to timed CSP, as well as composition verification techniques for checking properties using the FDR2 model checker. In [25], the authors present an encoding of an untimed subset of BPMN into the LNT process algebra for supporting the analysis of process evolution. [13,24] address the issue of checking whether a BPMN choreography is realizable by computing participant implementations using projection. We go one step farther compared to these related works because we provide verification techniques for a timed version of BPMN including all main gateways (in particular inclusive gateways), loops, and unbalanced structures for workflows.

Another paper [11] attempted to translate BPMN to Maude for verification purposes. In this work, the authors focus on data objects semantics and data-based decision gateways, and provide new mechanisms to avoid structural issues in workflows such as flow divergence. To do so, they introduce the notion of well-formed BPMN processes, which allows one to guarantee structural properties of the workflows. This paper mainly handles syntactic issues and aims at avoiding incorrect syntactic patterns. The main difference compared to our contributions here is that the authors have a specific interest on data-centric workflows whereas we look at behavioural and timed features of processes. One can also take advantage of our Maude encoding and verification framework for checking other timed properties, such as those presented in [4,28] (sojourn time, synchronization time, waiting time).

[17] proposes a general approach for computing the degree of parallelism of BPMN processes using model checking techniques. To do so, the authors propose a transformation to process algebra and a low-level model for BPMN processes based on Labelled Transition Systems. However, the subset of BPMN considered in [17] makes abstraction of times and durations possibly associated to tasks and flows. [27] focuses on timed aspects and proposes several algorithms for directly calculating the degree of parallelism of a BPMN process. In this work, a duration constraint is associated to each task. They do not consider inclusive gateways and propose different algorithms for special cases of processes, *e.g.*, processes with only one type of gateways or acyclic processes with only parallel gateways. Our work focuses on BPMN processes with time constraints too, but we associate durations not only to tasks but also to flows. In addition, we consider any combination of gateways as well as cyclic processes.

6   Concluding Remarks

BPMN is now widely used by companies for supporting the workflow-based development of their information and management systems. However, we are still far from having press-button analysis techniques integrated in the existing modelling and development BPMN frameworks. This work is a contribution in that direction, that is, to provide automated techniques for analyzing BPMN processes. In this paper, we have focused on a subset of BPMN containing the main behavioural constructs (tasks, sequence flows, gateways) and time aspects associated to flows and tasks. We have proposed an encoding of this BPMN subset into the input language of the rewriting-based system Maude. Maude was expressive enough for representing unbalanced BPMN processes with moderate effort using a token-based semantics. The whole approach consisting of the translation to Maude and of the verification of several properties of interest on concrete BPMN processes is fully automated. In particular, we have showed how several measures of execution time (minimum, maximum, average) or the degree of parallelism can be computed with Maude. Several other tools can be used, such as simulation, reachability analysis, or LTL model checking. Our encoding and verification approach was validated through experiments we achieved on a significant number of BPMN processes, showing that these checks are completed in a reasonable time for real-size examples.

A first perspective of this work is to extend our approach with other BPMN constructs. We have focused in this paper on the behavioural part of BPMN, which allows us to formally analyze important properties, and we have discarded data aspects. Dataless models are over-approximations of the corresponding processes. This may generate false negative results, that is, our approach may return that a process has a deadlock for example whereas it is not the case because the blocking case actually never occurs. We plan to take data into account and in particular conditions that may be associated to outgoing flows for split gateways. As far as activities are concerned, we would like to support not only tasks but also interactions and message sending/reception. This extension would require to accept the description of distributed systems using BPMN collaboration diagrams. Finally, we intend to extend our time analysis capabilities by considering inter-activity and inter-process temporal constraints (*e.g.*, process deadline, timers, or time conflicts).

Acknowledgements. This work has been partially supported by MINECO/FEDER project TIN2014-52034-R and Universidad de Málaga, Campus de Excelencia Internacional Andalucía Tech.

References

1. http://maude.lcc.uma.es/MaudeBPMN/
2. Arbab, F., Kokash, N., Meng, S.: Towards using reo for compliance-aware business process modeling. In: Margaria, T., Steffen, B. (eds.) ISoLA 2008. CCIS, vol. 17, pp. 108–123. Springer, Heidelberg (2008). doi:10.1007/978-3-540-88479-8_9
3. Bouhoula, A., Jouannaud, J.-P., Meseguer, J.: Specification and proof in membership equational logic. Theor. Comput. Sci. **236**(1), 35–132 (2000)
4. Bruni, R., Corradini, A., Ferrari, G., Flagella, T., Guanciale, R., Spagnolo, G.: Applying process analysis to the Italian eGovernment enterprise architecture. In: Carbone, M., Petit, J.-M. (eds.) WS-FM 2011. LNCS, vol. 7176, pp. 111–127. Springer, Heidelberg (2012). doi:10.1007/978-3-642-29834-9_9
5. Capel Tuñón, M.I., Mendoza Morales, L.E.: Automating the transformation from BPMN models to CSP+T specifications. In: Proceedings of SEW 2012, pp. 100–109. IEEE Computer Society (2012)
6. Christiansen, D.R., Carbone, M., Hildebrandt, T.: Formal semantics and implementation of BPMN 2.0 inclusive gateways. In: Bravetti, M., Bultan, T. (eds.) WS-FM 2010. LNCS, vol. 6551, pp. 146–160. Springer, Heidelberg (2011). doi:10.1007/978-3-642-19589-1_10

7. Clavel, M., Durán, F., Eker, S., Lincoln, P., Martí-Oliet, N., Meseguer, J., Talcott, C.: All About Maude - A High-Performance Logical Framework, How to Specify, Program and Verify Systems in Rewriting Logic. LNCS, vol. 4350. Springer, Heidelberg (2007). doi:10.1007/978-3-540-71999-1

8. Decker, G., Weske, M.: Interaction-centric modeling of process choreographies. Inf. Syst. **36**(2), 292–312 (2011)

9. Dijkman, R., Dumas, M., Ouyang, C.: Semantics and analysis of business process models in BPMN. Inf. Softw. Technol. **50**(12), 1281–1294 (2008)

10. Eker, S., Meseguer, J., Sridharanarayanan, A.: The Maude LTL model checker. In: Proceedings of WRLA 2002. ENTCS, vol. 71, pp. 115–142. Elsevier (2002)

11. El-Saber, N., Boronat, A.: BPMN formalization and verification using Maude. In: Proceedings of BM-FA 2014, pp. 1–8. ACM (2014)

12. Gruhn, V., Laue, R.: Patterns for timed property specifications. Electr. Notes Theor. Comput. Sci. **153**(2), 117–133 (2006)

13. Güdemann, M., Poizat, P., Salaün, G., Ye, L.: VerChor: a framework for the design and verification of choreographies. IEEE Trans. Serv. Comput. **9**(4), 647–660 (2016)

14. ISO/IEC: International Standard 19510, Information technology - Business Process Model and Notation (2013)

15. Konrad, S., Cheng, B.H.C.: Real-time Specification Patterns. In: Proceedings of ICSE 2005, pp. 372–381. ACM (2005)

16. Martens, A.: Analyzing web service based business processes. In: Cerioli, M. (ed.) FASE 2005. LNCS, vol. 3442, pp. 19–33. Springer, Heidelberg (2005). doi:10.1007/978-3-540-31984-9_3

17. Mateescu, R., Salaün, G., Ye, L.: Quantifying the parallelism in BPMN processes using model checking. In: Proceedings of CBSE 2014, pp. 159–168. ACM (2014)

18. Morales, L.E.M., Tuñón, M.I.C., Pérez, M.A.: A formalization proposal of timed BPMN for compositional verification of business processes. In: Filipe, J., Cordeiro, J. (eds.) ICEIS 2010. LNBIP, vol. 73, pp. 388–403. Springer, Heidelberg (2011). doi:10.1007/978-3-642-19802-1_27

19. Mendoza Morales, L.E., Capel Tuñón, M.I., Pérez, M.A.: Conceptual framework for business processes compositional verification. Inf. Softw. Technol. **54**(2), 149–161 (2012)

20. Meseguer, J.: Conditional rewriting logic as a unified model of concurrency. Theor. Comput. Sci. **96**(1), 73–155 (1992)

21. Meseguer, J., Palomino, M., Martí-Oliet, N.: Equational abstractions. In: Baader, F. (ed.) CADE 2003. LNCS, vol. 2741, pp. 2–16. Springer, Heidelberg (2003). doi:10.1007/978-3-540-45085-6_2

22. Ölveczky, P.C., Meseguer, J.: Semantics and pragmatics of real-time Maude. High. Order Symb. Comput. **20**(1–2), 161–196 (2007)

23. OMG: Business Process Model and Notation (BPMN) - Version 2.0, January 2011

24. Poizat, P., Salaün, G.: Checking the realizability of BPMN 2.0 choreographies. In: Proceedings of SAC 2012, pp. 1927–1934. ACM Press (2012)

25. Poizat, P., Salaün, G., Krishna, A.: Checking business process evolution. In: Kouchnarenko, O., Khosravi, R. (eds.) FACS 2016. LNCS, vol. 10231, pp. 36–53. Springer, Cham (2017). doi:10.1007/978-3-319-57666-4_4

26. Raedts, I., Petkovic, M., Usenko, Y.S., van der Werf, J.M., Groote, J.F., Somers, L.: Transformation of BPMN models for behaviour analysis. In: Proceedings of MSVVEIS 2007, pp. 126–137 (2007)

27. Sun, Y., Su, J.: Computing degree of parallelism for BPMN processes. In: Kappel, G., Maamar, Z., Motahari-Nezhad, H.R. (eds.) ICSOC 2011. LNCS, vol. 7084, pp. 1–15. Springer, Heidelberg (2011). doi:10.1007/978-3-642-25535-9_1

28. van der Aalst, W.M.P., Adriansyah, A., van Dongen, B.F.: Replaying history on process models for conformance checking and performance analysis. Wiley Interdiscip. Rev. Data Min. Knowl. Discov. 2(2), 182–192 (2012)

29. Wong, P.Y.H., Gibbons, J.: A process semantics for BPMN. In: Liu, S., Maibaum, T., Araki, K. (eds.) ICFEM 2008. LNCS, vol. 5256, pp. 355–374. Springer, Heidelberg (2008). doi:10.1007/978-3-540-88194-0_22

30. Wong, P., Gibbons, J.: Verifying business process compatibility. In: Proceedings of QSIC 2008, pp. 126–131. IEEE (2008)

31. Wong, P.Y.H., Gibbons, J.: A relative timed semantics for BPMN. Electr. Notes Theor. Comput. Sci. 229(2), 59–75 (2009)

Full-Abstraction for Must Testing Preorders
(Extended Abstract)

Giovanni Bernardi[1(✉)] and Adrian Francalanza[2]

[1] IRIF, Université Paris-Diderot, Paris, France
gio@irif.fr
[2] University of Malta, Msida, Malta
adrian.francalanza@um.edu.mt

Abstract. The client must preorder relates tests (clients) instead of processes (servers). The existing characterisation of this preorder is unsatisfactory for it relies on the notion of *usable* clients which, in turn, are defined using an existential quantification over the servers that ensure client satisfaction. In this paper we characterise the set of usable clients for finite-branching LTSs, and give a sound and complete decision procedure for it. We also provide a novel coinductive characterisation of the client preorder, which we use to argue that the preorder is decidable, thus positively answering the question opened in [3,6].

1 Introduction

The standard testing theory of De Nicola–Hennessy [12,15] has recently been employed to provide theoretical foundations for web-services [9,25] (where processes denote servers). To better fit that setting, in [6] this theory has been enriched with preorders for clients (tests) and peers (where both interacting parties mutually satisfy one another). Client preorders also tie testing theory with session type theory, as is outlined in [2]: they are instrumental in defining semantic models of the Gay & Hole subtyping [14] for first-order session types [3, Theorem 6.3.4] and [5, Theorem 5.2].

The testing preorders for clients and peers are *contextual* preorders, defined by comparing the capacity of either being satisfied by servers or the capacity of peers to mutually satisfy one another. This paper focuses on the client preorder due to the must testing relation [12,15]: a client r_2 is better than a client r_1, denoted $r_1 \lesssim_{\mathsf{clt}} r_2$, whenever *every* server p that must pass r_1 also must pass r_2. Although this definition is easy to understand, it suffers from the endemic universal quantification over contexts (servers) and, by itself, does not give any effective proof method to determine pairs in the preorder. To solve this problem, contextual preorders usually come equipped with *behavioural characterisations* that avoid universal context quantification thereby facilitating reasoning. In [6] the authors develop such characterisations for the client and the peer must preorders; these preorders are however *not* fully-abstract, for they are defined modulo *usable* clients, i.e., clients that are satisfied by *some* server.

© IFIP International Federation for Information Processing 2017
Published by Springer International Publishing AG 2017. All Rights Reserved
J.-M. Jacquet and M. Massink (Eds.): COORDINATION 2017, LNCS 10319, pp. 237–255, 2017.
DOI: 10.1007/978-3-319-59746-1_13

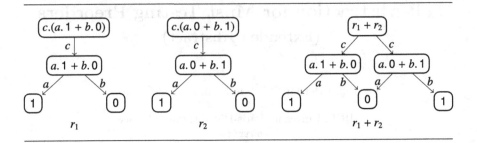

Fig. 1. LTS depictions of the behaviours described in Eq. (1)

Usability is a pivotal notion that appears frequently in the literature of process calculi and web-service foundations, *cf.* viability in [18,26] and controllability in [8,24], and has already been studied, albeit for restricted or different settings, in [6,7,18,25,26]. In general though, the characterisation of usability is problematic, for solving it requires finding the conditions under which one can either (a) construct a server p that satisfies a given client, or (b) show that every p does *not* satisfy a given client. Whereas proving (b) is complicated by the universal quantification over *all* servers, the proof of (a) is complicated by the non-deterministic behaviour of clients. In particular, the approach in (a) is complicated because client usability is *not* compositional. For instance consider the following clients, whose behaviours are depicted in Fig. 1:

$$r_1 = c.(a.1 + b.0) \qquad \text{and} \qquad r_2 = c.(a.0 + b.1) \tag{1}$$

where 1 denotes satisfaction (success). Both clients are usable, since r_1 is satisfied by the server $\bar{c}.\bar{a}.0$, and r_2 is satisfied by server $\bar{c}.\bar{b}.0$. However, their composition $r_1 + r_2$ is *not* a usable client, *i.e.*, p m̸u̸st $r_1 + r_2$ for every p; intuitively, this is because r_1 and r_2 impose opposite constraints on the processes that pass one or the other (*e.g.*, $\bar{c}.(\bar{a}.0 + \bar{b}.0)$) does not satisfy $r_1 + r_2$). A compositional analysis is even more unwieldy for recursive tests. For instance, the client $\mu x.(c.(a.1 + b.x) + c.(a.0 + b.1))$ is not usable because of the non-determinism analogous to $r_1 + r_2$, and the unsuccessful computations along the infinite trace of interactions $(c.b)^*$; this argument works because infinite unsuccessful computations are catastrophic *wrt.* must testing.

This paper presents a sound and complete characterisation for usable clients with finite-branching LTSs. Through the results of [6] — in particular, the equivalence of usability for clients and peers stated on [6, p. 11] — our characterisation directly yields a fully-abstract characterisation for the must preorder for clients and peers. We go a step further and use this characterisation to develop a novel *coinductive* and fully-abstract characterisation of ⊑clt, which we find easier to use than the one of [6] when proving inequalities involving recursive clients. This coinductive characterisation turns out to be informed by our study on usability, and differs from related coinductive characterisations for the server preorder [18,25] in a number of respects. Finally, our inductive definition for usable clients also provides deeper insights into the original client preorder of [6]: we show that limiting contexts to servers offering only *finite* interactions preserves the discriminating power of the original preorder. Our contributions are:

- a fully-abstract characterisation of usable clients, Theorem 2;
- a coinductive, fully-abstract characterisation of the client preorder $\lesssim_{\text{clt}}$, Theorem 5;
- a contextual preorder $\lesssim_{\text{clt}}^{f}$ that is equivalent to $\lesssim_{\text{clt}}$ but relies only on non-recursive contexts Theorem 6;
- decidability results for usable clients and the client preorder, Theorem 7.

The solutions devised here addressing client usability are directly relevant to controllability issues in service-oriented architectures [21,30]. Our techniques may also be extended beyond this remit. The ever growing sizes of test suites, together with the ubiquitous reliance on testing for the increasing quality-assurance requirements in software systems, has directed the attention to non-deterministic (or *flaky*) tests. Such tests arise frequently in practice and their impact on software development has been the subject of various studies [19,20,22]. By some measures, $\approx 4.56\%$ of test failures of the TAP (Test Anything Protocol) system at Google are caused by flaky tests [19]. We believe that our concepts, models and procedures can be extended to such testing methodologies to analyse detrimental non-deterministic behaviour arising in test suites, thereby reducing the gap between empirical practices and theory.

Structure of the paper: Sect. 2 outlines the preliminaries for client must testing. Section 3 tackles client usability and gives a fully-abstract definition for it. Section 4 uses this result to give a coinductive characterisation for client preorders. In Sect. 5 we present expressiveness results for servers with finite interactions together with decidability results for client usability and the client testing preorder. Section 6 concludes.

2   Preliminaries

Let $a, b, c, \ldots \in \mathsf{Act}$ be a set of actions, and let $\tau, \checkmark$ be two distinct actions *not* in Act; the first denotes *internal* unobservable activity whereas the second is used to *report success* of an experiment. To emphasise their distinctness, we use $\alpha \in \mathsf{Act}_\tau$ to denote $\mathsf{Act} \cup \{\tau\}$, and similarly for $\lambda \in \mathsf{Act}_{\tau\checkmark}$. We assume Act has an involution function, with $\bar{a}$ being the complement to a.

A *labelled transition system*, LTS, consists of a triple $\langle \mathsf{Proc}, \mathsf{Act}_{\tau\checkmark}, \longrightarrow \rangle$, where Proc is a set of processes and $\longrightarrow \subseteq (\mathsf{Proc} \times \mathsf{Act}_{\tau\checkmark} \times \mathsf{Proc})$ is a transition relation between processes decorated with labels drawn from the set $\mathsf{Act}_{\tau\checkmark}$; we write $p \xrightarrow{\lambda} q$ in lieu of $(p, \lambda, q) \in \longrightarrow$. An LTS is *finite-branching* if for all $p \in \mathsf{Proc}$ and for all $\lambda \in \mathsf{Act}_{\tau\checkmark}$, the set $\{ q \mid p \xrightarrow{\lambda} q \}$ is finite. For $s \in (\mathsf{Act}_{\checkmark})^{\star}$ we also have the standard weak transitions, $p \xRightarrow{s} q$, defined by *ignoring* the occurrences of τs.

Syntax $\quad\quad\quad p, q, r, o \in \mathsf{CCS}^\mu ::= 0 \ \mid \ 1 \ \mid \ \alpha.p \ \mid \ p + q \ \mid \ \mu x.p \ \mid \ x$

Semantics

$$\frac{}{1 \xrightarrow{\checkmark} 0} \text{(A-Ok)} \quad\quad\quad \frac{}{\alpha.p \xrightarrow{\alpha} p} \text{(A-Pre)} \quad\quad\quad \frac{}{\mu x.p \xrightarrow{\tau} p\{\mu x.p/x\}} \text{(A-Unfold)}$$

$$\frac{p \xrightarrow{\lambda} p'}{p + q \xrightarrow{\lambda} p'} \text{(R-Ext-L)} \quad\quad\quad \frac{q \xrightarrow{\lambda} q'}{p + q \xrightarrow{\lambda} q'} \text{(R-Ext-R)}$$

Contract Composition Semantics

$$\frac{p \xrightarrow{\lambda} p'}{p \parallel r \xrightarrow{\lambda} p' \parallel r} \text{(P-Srv)} \quad\quad \frac{r \xrightarrow{\lambda} r'}{p \parallel r \xrightarrow{\lambda} p \parallel r'} \text{(P-Cli)} \quad\quad \frac{p \xrightarrow{a} p' \quad r \xrightarrow{\bar{a}} r'}{p \parallel r \xrightarrow{\tau} p' \parallel r'} \text{(P-Syn)}$$

Fig. 2. Syntax and Semantics of recursive CCS^μ with 1.

We limit ourselves to finite-branching LTSs. Whenever sufficient, we describe such LTSs using a version of CCS with recursion [23] and augmented with a *success* operator, denoted as 1. The syntax of this language is depicted in Fig. 2 and assumes a denumerable set of variables $x, y, z \ldots \in \mathsf{Var}$. For finite I, we use the notation $\sum_{i \in I} p_i$ to denote the *resp.* sequence of summations $p_1 + \ldots + p_n$ where $I = 1..n$. Similarly, when I is a non-empty set, we define $\bigoplus_{i \in I} p_i = \sum_{i \in I} \tau.p_i$ to represent process *internal* choice. The transition relation $p \xrightarrow{\lambda} q$ between terms of the language is the least one determined by the (standard) rules in Fig. 2. As usual, $\mu x.p$ binds x in p and we identify terms up to alpha conversion of bound variables. The operation $p\{\mu x.p/x\}$ denotes the unfolding of the recursive process $\mu x.p$, by substituting the term $\mu x.p$ for the free occurrences of the variable x in p.

To model the interactions taking place between the server and the client contracts, we use the standard binary composition of contracts, $p \parallel r$, whose operational semantics is given in Fig. 2. A *computation* consists of sequence of τ actions of the form

$$p \parallel r = p_0 \parallel r_0 \xrightarrow{\tau} p_1 \parallel r_1 \xrightarrow{\tau} \ldots \xrightarrow{\tau} p_k \parallel r_k \xrightarrow{\tau} \ldots \quad\quad (2)$$

It is *maximal* if it is infinite, or whenever $p_n \parallel r_n$ is the last state then $p_n \parallel r_n \not\xrightarrow{\tau}$. We say (2) is *client-successful* if there exists some $k \geq 0$ such that $r_k \xrightarrow{\checkmark}$.

Definition 1 (Client Testing preorder [6]). We write p must r if every maximal computation from $p \parallel r$ is *client-successful*, and write $r_1 \lesssim_{\mathsf{clt}} r_2$ if, for every p, p must r_1 implies p must r_2. ∎

Although intuitive, the universal quantification on servers in Definition 1 complicates reasoning about $\lesssim_{\mathsf{clt}}$. One way of surmounting this is by defining alternative characterisations for $\lesssim_{\mathsf{clt}}$ of Definition 1, that come equipped with practical proof methods.

2.1   Characterising the Client Preorder

In [6, Definition 3.10, p. 9], an alternative characterisation for the preorder $\precsim_{\mathsf{clt}}$ is given and proven to be sound and complete. We recall this characterisation, restating the *resp.* notation. The alternative characterisation relies on *unsuccessful* traces: $r \stackrel{s}{\Longrightarrow}_{\not\checkmark} r'$ means that r may weakly perform the trace of external actions s reaching state r' *without* passing through *any* successful state; in particular neither r nor r' are successful. Formally, $r \stackrel{s}{\Longrightarrow}_{\not\checkmark} r'$ is the least relation satisfying (a) $r \stackrel{\checkmark}{\not\rightarrow}$ implies $r \stackrel{\epsilon}{\Longrightarrow}_{\not\checkmark} r$, and (b) if $r'' \stackrel{s}{\Longrightarrow}_{\not\checkmark} r'$ and $r \stackrel{\checkmark}{\not\rightarrow}$ then (i) $r \stackrel{a}{\longrightarrow} r''$ implies $r \stackrel{as}{\Longrightarrow}_{\not\checkmark} r'$, and (ii) $r \stackrel{\tau}{\longrightarrow} r''$ implies $r \stackrel{s}{\Longrightarrow}_{\not\checkmark} r'$. The *unsuccessful* acceptance set of r after s, are defined as

$$\mathsf{Acc}_{\not\checkmark}(r, s) = \{\, S(r') \mid r \stackrel{s}{\Longrightarrow}_{\not\checkmark} r' \stackrel{\tau}{\not\rightarrow} \,\} \tag{3}$$

where $S(r) = \{\, a \in \mathsf{Act} \mid r \stackrel{a}{\longrightarrow} \,\}$ denotes the strong actions of r. Intuitively, for the client r, the set $\mathsf{Acc}_{\not\checkmark}(r, s)$ records all the actions that lead r out of *potentially deadlocked* (i.e. stable) states that it reaches performing *unsuccessfully* the trace s. It turns out that these abstractions are fundamental to characterise must-testing preorders and also compliance preorders [3,6,25]. In the sequel, we shall also use $r \stackrel{\alpha}{\longrightarrow}_{\not\checkmark} r'$ whenever $r \stackrel{\alpha}{\longrightarrow} r'$, $r \stackrel{\checkmark}{\not\rightarrow}$ and $r' \stackrel{\checkmark}{\not\rightarrow}$ hold.

Example 1. For client $r_3 = \tau.(1 + \tau.0)$ we have $\mathsf{Acc}_{\not\checkmark}(r_3, \epsilon) = \emptyset$, but for $r_3' = r_3 + \tau.0$ we have $\mathsf{Acc}_{\not\checkmark}(r_3', \epsilon) = \{\emptyset\}$. We also have $\mathsf{Acc}_{\not\checkmark}(r_3'', \epsilon) = \emptyset$ for $r_3'' = r_3 + \mu x.x$.   ∎

Note that, whenever $\mathsf{Acc}_{\not\checkmark}(r, s) = \emptyset$, then any sequence of moves with trace s from r to a *stable* reduct r' must pass through a successful state, for otherwise we would have $S(r') \in \mathsf{Acc}_{\not\checkmark}(r, s)$ for some r'.

Definition 2 (Usable Clients). $\mathcal{U} = \{\, r \mid \text{there exists } p.\, p \text{ must } r \,\}$.   ∎

Example 2. Recall clients r_1 and r_2 from (1) in Sect. 1. We show that despite being individually usable, the sum of these clients is not: $p \not\!\text{must } r_1 + r_2$ for *every* p. Fix a process p. If p does not offer an interaction on $\bar{c}$, then, plainly, $p \not\!\text{must } r_1 + r_2$. Suppose that $p \stackrel{\bar{c}}{\longrightarrow} p'$; to prove $p \not\!\text{must } r_1 + r_2$, it suffices to show that there exists a client r reached by $r_1 + r_2$ by performing action c (i.e., $r \in \{\, a.1 + b.0, a.0 + b.1 \,\}$) such that $p' \not\!\text{must } r$. Indeed, for $r = a.1 + b.0$, if p' must r implies p' has to interact on a and *not* on b, but then such a p' does not satisfy the derivative $r = a.0 + b.1$, i.e., $p' \not\!\text{must } r$ (because the composition $p' \parallel r$ is stable but *not* client-successful). Using a symmetric argument we deduce that if p' must $a.0 + b.1$ then $p' \not\!\text{must } a.1 + b.0$, and thus no process p exists that satisfies $r_1 + r_2$; note that the argument above crucially exploits the external non-determinism of $r_1 + r_2$. The client $\mu x.(c.(a.1 + b.x) + c.b.1)$ from Sect. 1 is unusable for similar reasons, the analysis being more involved due to infinite computations.   ∎

We let $(r \text{ after}_{\not\checkmark} s) = \{ r' \mid r \xRightarrow{s}_{\not\checkmark} r' \}$, and call the set $(r \text{ after}_{\not\checkmark} s)$ the *residuals* of r after the *unsuccessful* trace s. We extend the notion of usability and say that r is *usable along* an unsuccessful trace s whenever $r \text{ usbl}_{\not\checkmark} s$, which is the least predicate satisfying the conditions (a) $r \text{ usbl}_{\not\checkmark} \varepsilon$ whenever $r \in \mathcal{U}$, and (b) $r \text{ usbl}_{\not\checkmark} as$ whenever (i) $r \in \mathcal{U}$ and (ii) if $r \xRightarrow{a}_{\not\checkmark}$ then $\bigoplus (r \text{ after}_{\not\checkmark} a) \text{ usbl}_{\not\checkmark} s$. If $r \text{ usbl}_{\not\checkmark} s$, any state reachable from r by performing any unsuccessful subsequence of s is usable [6]. Finally, let $ua_{\mathsf{clt}}(r, s) = \{ a \in \text{Act} \mid r \xRightarrow{sa}_{\not\checkmark} \text{ implies } r \text{ usbl}_{\not\checkmark} sa \}$ denote all the usable actions for a client r after the unsuccessful trace s.

Definition 3 (Semantic client-preorder). *Let* $r_1 \precsim_{\mathsf{clt}} r_2$ *if, for every* $s \in$ Act* *such that* $r_1 \text{ usbl}_{\not\checkmark} s$, *we have (i)* $r_2 \text{ usbl}_{\not\checkmark} s$, *(ii) for every* $B \in \mathsf{Acc}_{\not\checkmark}(r_2, s)$ *there exists a* $A \in \mathsf{Acc}_{\not\checkmark}(r_1, s)$ *such that* $A \cap ua_{\mathsf{clt}}(r_1, s) \subseteq B$, *(iii)* $r_2 \xRightarrow{s}_{\not\checkmark}$ *implies* $r_1 \xRightarrow{s}_{\not\checkmark}$. ∎

Theorem 1. *In any finite branching LTS,* $r_1 \lesssim_{\mathsf{clt}} r_2$ *if and only if* $r_1 \precsim_{\mathsf{clt}} r_2$.

Proof. Follows from [6, Theorem 3.13] and König's Infinity Lemma.

Definition 3 enjoys a few pleasing properties and, through Theorem 1, sheds light on behavioural properties of clients related by $\lesssim_{\mathsf{clt}}$. Concretely, it shares a similar structure to well-studied characterisations of the (standard) must-testing preorder of [12,15], where process convergence is replaced by client usability, and traces and acceptance sets are replaced by their unsuccessful counterparts (modulo usable actions). Unfortunately, Definition 3 has a major drawback: it is parametric wrt. the set of usable clients $\mathcal{U}$ (Definition 2), which relies on an existential quantifications over servers. As a result, the definition is *not* fully-abstract, and this makes it hard to use as proof technique and to ground decision procedures for $\lesssim_{\mathsf{clt}}$ on it.

3   Characterising Usability

We use the behavioural predicates of Sect. 2.1, together with the new predicate in Definition 4, to formulate the characterising properties of the set of usable clients $\mathcal{U}$ (Proposition 1). We use these predicates to construct a set $\mathcal{U}_{\mathsf{bhv}}$ that coincides with $\mathcal{U}$ (Theorem 2); this gives us an inductive proof method for determining usability.

Definition 4. *We write* $r \Downarrow_{\checkmark}$ *whenever for every infinite sequence of internal moves* $r \xrightarrow{\tau} r_1 \xrightarrow{\tau} r_2 \xrightarrow{\tau} \ldots$, *there exists a state* r_i *such that* $r_1 \xrightarrow{\checkmark}$. ∎

Recalling Eq. (3), let $\mathsf{Acc}_{\not\checkmark}(r) = \mathsf{Acc}_{\not\checkmark}(r, \varepsilon)$. Proposition 1 crystallises the characteristic properties of usable clients, providing a blue print for our alternative definition Definition 5. Instead of giving a direct proof of this proposition, we obtain it indirectly as consequence of our other results.

Proposition 1. *For every $r \in$ Proc, $r \in \mathcal{U}$ if and only if*

1. *$r \Downarrow_\checkmark$, and*
2. *if $A \in \mathrm{Acc}_\checkmark(r)$, then there exists $a \in A. \left(r \overset{a}{\Longrightarrow}_\checkmark \; \text{implies} \; \bigoplus(r \; \text{after}_\checkmark a) \in \mathcal{U}\right)$.*

$\square$

The proposition above states that a client r is usable if and only if, for every potentially deadlocked state r' reached via silent moves by r, there exists an action a that leads r' out of the potential deadlock, *i.e.*, into another state r'' where r'' is certainly usable.

Example 3. We use Proposition 1 to discuss the (non) usability of clients from previous example. Recall $r_3 = \tau.(1 + \tau.0)$, $r_3' = r_3 + \tau.0$ and $r_3'' = r_3 + \mu x.x$ from Example 1. Since we have $r_3 \Downarrow_\checkmark$ and $\mathrm{Acc}_\checkmark(r_3) = \emptyset$, r_3 satisfies both condition of Proposition 1, with the second one being trivially true. As a consequence r_3 is usable, and indeed 0 must r_3. On the contrary, we have $\mathrm{Acc}_\checkmark(r_3') = \{\emptyset\}$, thus r_3' violates Proposition 1(2) and thus r_3' is unusable. Client r_3'' is unusable as well, but violates Proposition 1(1) instead. Conversely, client $r_3''' = r_3 + \tau.(1 + \mu x.x)$ satisfies both conditions of Proposition 1, and it is usable. For instance, 0 must r_3'''.

A more involved client is $r_1 + r_2$ from Example 2. There we proved that $r_1 + r_2 \notin \mathcal{U}$, and indeed $r_1 + r_2$ does not satisfy Proposition 1(2). This is true because $\mathrm{Acc}_\checkmark(r_1 + r_2) = \{\{c\}\}$, and $r' \notin \mathcal{U}$, where

$$r' = \bigoplus((r_1 + r_2) \; \text{after}_\checkmark c) = \tau.(a.1 + b.0) + \tau.(a.0 + b.1).$$

In turn, the reason why r' is not usable is that $\mathrm{Acc}_\checkmark(r') = \{\{a, b\}\}$, and Proposition 1(2) requires us to consider every set in $\{\{a, b\}\}$ — we have only $\{a, b\}$ to consider — and show that for some action $a' \in \{a, b\}$, $\bigoplus(r' \; \text{after}_\checkmark a') \in \mathcal{U}$. It turns out that neither action in $\{a, b\}$ satisfies this condition. For instance, in the case of action b, we have $\bigoplus(r' \; \text{after}_\checkmark b) = \tau.1 + \tau.0$ and $\mathrm{Acc}_\checkmark(\tau.1 + \tau.0) = \{\emptyset\}$, so $\bigoplus(r' \; \text{after}_\checkmark b)$ violates Proposition 1(2) and as a result $\bigoplus(r' \; \text{after}_\checkmark b) \notin \mathcal{U}$. The reasoning why action a is *not* a good candidate either is identical. ∎

Definition 5. *Let $\mathcal{F} : \mathcal{P}(\mathrm{Proc}) \longrightarrow \mathcal{P}(\mathrm{Proc})$ be defined by letting $r \in \mathcal{F}(S)$ whenever*

1. *$r \Downarrow_\checkmark$, and*
2. *if $A \in \mathrm{Acc}_\checkmark(r)$, then there exists an $a \in A. \left(r \overset{a}{\Longrightarrow}_\checkmark \; \text{implies} \; \bigoplus(r \; \text{after}_\checkmark a) \in S\right)$.*

We let $\mathcal{U}_{\mathrm{bhv}} = \mu x.\mathcal{F}(x)$, the least fix-point of $\mathcal{F}$. ∎

The function $\mathcal{F}$ is continuous over the CPO $\langle \mathcal{P}(\mathrm{Proc}), \subseteq \rangle$, thus Kleene fixed point theorem [31, Theorem 5.11] ensures that $\mu x.\mathcal{F}(x)$ (the least fix-point of $\mathcal{F}$) exists and is equal to $\bigcup_{n=0}^{\infty} \mathcal{F}^n(\emptyset)$ where $\mathcal{F}^0(S) = S$ and $\mathcal{F}^{n+1}(S) = \mathcal{F}(\mathcal{F}^n(S))$.

The bulk of the soundness result follows as a corollary from the next lemma, which also lays bare the role of non-recursive servers in proving usability of clients.

Lemma 1. *For every* $n \in \mathbb{N}$ *and* $r \in$ Proc, $r \in \mathcal{F}^n(\emptyset)$ *implies that there exists a non-recursive server* p *such that* p must r.   □

An inductive argument is used to prove that $\mathcal{U}_{\mathsf{bhv}}$ is complete wrt. $\mathcal{U}$, where we define the following measure over which to perform induction. We let $MC(r, p)$ denote the set of maximal computations of a composition $r \parallel p$ and, for every computation $c \in MC(r, p)$, we associate the number $\#\mathsf{itr}(c)$ denoting the number of *interactions* that take place between the initial state of c, and the *first* *successful* state of the computation c ($\#\mathsf{itr}(c) = \infty$ whenever c is unsuccessful). Let $\mathsf{itr}(r, p) = \max\{\ \#\mathsf{itr}(c)\ \mid\ c \in MC(r, p)\ \}$. For instance, if $r = \mu x. a. x + b. 1$, we have $\mathsf{itr}(r, \overline{a}.\overline{a}.\overline{b}. 0) = 3$, but $\mathsf{itr}(r, \mu x.\overline{a}.x + \overline{b}. 0) = \infty$.

Lemma 2. *Let* T *be a tree with root* v. *If* T *is finite branching and it has a finite number of nodes, then the number of paths* $v \longrightarrow \ldots$ *is finite.*   □

Lemma 3. *In a finite branching LTS,* p must r *implies the number* $\mathsf{itr}(r, p)$ *is finite.*

Proof. If p must r, every $c \in MC(r, p)$ reaches a successful state after a *finite* number of reductions. Since the number of interactions is not more than the number of reductions:

$$\text{for every } c \in MC(r, p). \ \#\mathsf{itr}(c) \in \mathbb{N} \tag{4}$$

A set of successful computations from $r \parallel p$, e.g., $MC(r, p)$, may also be seen as a *computation tree*, where common prefixes reach the same node in the tree. In general, such a tree may have infinite depth. Consider the computation tree T obtained by *truncating* all the maximal computations of $r \parallel p$ at their *first* successful state, and let $TMC(r, p)$ be the set of all the computations obtained this way. It follows that

$$\{\ \#\mathsf{itr}(c)\ \mid\ c \in MC(r, p)\ \} = \{\ \#\mathsf{itr}(c)\ \mid\ c \in TMC(r, p)\ \} \tag{5}$$

From $\mathsf{itr}(r, p) = \max\{\ \#\mathsf{itr}(c)\ \mid\ c \in MC(r, p)\ \}$, (4) and (5) we know that that $\mathsf{itr}(r, p)$ is finite if the set $\{\ c\ \mid\ c \in TMC(r, p)\ \}$ is finite. This will follow from Lemma 2 if we prove that the tree T has a finite number of nodes. By the contrapositive of König's Lemma [16, 17], since every node in the tree T above is finitely branching, and there are no infinite paths, then T necessarily contains a *finite* number of nodes. By Lemma 2, $\{\ c\ \mid\ c \in TMC(r, p)\ \}$ must also be finite, and hence we can put a (finite) natural number $\mathsf{itr}(r, p) \in \mathbb{N}$ as an upper bound on the number of interactions required to reach success.   □

If the LTS is not *image-finite* then Lemma 3 is false. To see why, consider the infinite branching client r and the server p depicted in Fig. 3. Since r engages in *finite* sequences of a actions which are unbounded in size, and the p offers any number of interactions on action $\overline{a}$, we have that p must r, but the set $MC(r, p)$ contains an infinite amount of computations, and the number $\mathsf{itr}(r, p)$ is not finite. Dually, even if the LTS of a composition $r \parallel p$ is finite branching and finite state,

Fig. 3. Servers and clients to discuss the hypothesis in Lemma 3

it is necessary that p must r for $itr(r, p)$ to be finite. Lemma 3 lets us associate a rank to every usable client r, defined as $rank(r) = \min\{\, itr(r,p) \mid p$ must $r \,\}$. The well-ordering of $\mathbb{N}$ ensures that $rank(r)$ is defined for every usable r. When defined, the rank of a client r gives us information about its usability,[1] where we can stratify $\mathcal{U}$ as follows:

$$\mathcal{U} = \bigcup_{i \in \mathbb{N}} \mathcal{U}^i, \quad \text{where } \mathcal{U}^i = \{\, r \in \mathsf{Proc} \mid rank(r) = i \,\} \tag{6}$$

Lemma 4. *For every $i \in \mathbb{N}$, $r \in \mathcal{U}^i$ implies $r \in \mathcal{F}(\mathcal{F}^j(\emptyset))$ for some $j \leq i$.* □

We are now ready to prove the main result of this section.

Theorem 2 (Full-abstraction usability). *The sets $\mathcal{U}$ and $\mathcal{U}_{\mathsf{bhv}}$ coincide.*

Proof. To show $\mathcal{U} \subseteq \mathcal{U}_{\mathsf{bhv}}$, pick an $r \in \mathcal{U}$. By (6), $r \in \mathcal{U}^i$ for some $i \in \mathbb{N}$, and by Lemma 4 we obtain $r \in \mathcal{F}^j(\emptyset) \subseteq \mathcal{U}_{\mathsf{bhv}}$ for some $j \in \mathbb{N}^+$. To show $\mathcal{U}_{\mathsf{bhv}} \subseteq \mathcal{U}$, pick an $r \in \mathcal{U}_{\mathsf{bhv}}$. Definition 5 ensures that $\mathcal{U}_{\mathsf{bhv}} \subseteq \bigcup_{n=0}^{\infty} \mathcal{F}^n(\emptyset)$, thus $r \in \mathcal{F}^n(\emptyset)$ for some $n \in \mathbb{N}$. Lemma 1 implies that $r \in \mathcal{U}$. The reasoning applies to any $r \in \mathcal{U}_{\mathsf{bhv}}$, thus $\mathcal{U}_{\mathsf{bhv}} \subseteq \mathcal{U}$. □

4 The Client Preorder Revisited

By combining the definition of $\precsim_{\mathsf{clt}}$ with $\mathcal{U}_{\mathsf{bhv}}$ of Definition 5, Theorem 2 yields a fully-abstract characterisation of the client preorder $\precsim_{\mathsf{clt}}$. In general, however, this characterisation still requires us to consider an infinite number of (unsuccessful) traces to establish client inequality. In this section, we put forth a novel coinductive definition for the client preorder and exploit the finite-branching property of the LTS to show that this definition characterises the contextual preorder $\precsim_{\mathsf{clt}}$, Theorem 5. We also argue that this new characterisation is easier to use in practice than Definition 3, a claim that is substantiated by showing how this coinductive preorder can be used to prove the second result in this section, namely that servers offering a *finite* amount of interactions are sufficient and necessary to distinguish clients, Theorem 6. Subsequently, in Theorem 7, we also show that the coinductive preorder is decidable for our client language.

---

[1] Function min is *not* defined for empty sets, thus $rank(r)$ is undefined whenever r is unusable.

Example 4. The use of $\precsim_{\text{clt}}$ is hindered, in practice, by the universal quantification over traces in its definition. Consider, for instance, clients r_4 and r_5,

$$r_4 = a.\,1 + \mu y.(a.r_3'' + b.y + c.\,1) \qquad \text{and} \qquad r_5 = (\mu z.(b.z + c.\,1)) + d.\,1$$

where $r_3'' = (\tau.(1 + \tau.0)) + \mu x.x$ from Example 1. One way to prove $r_4 \lesssim_{\text{clt}} r_5$ amounts in showing that $r_4 \precsim_{\text{clt}} r_5$, even though this task is far from obvious. Concretely, the definition of $\precsim_{\text{clt}}$ requires us to show that for *every* trace $s \in \text{Act}^*$ where $r_4 \; usbl_{\not\checkmark} \; s$ holds, clauses (i), (ii) and (iii) of Definition 3 also hold. In this case, there are an *infinite* number of such unsuccessful traces s to consider and, a priori, there is no clear way how to do this in finite time. Specifically, there are (unsuccessful) traces that r_4 *can* perform while remaining usable at every step, such as $s = b^n$, but also (unsuccessful) traces that r_4 *cannot* perform (which trivially imply $r_4 \; usbl_{\not\checkmark} \; s$ according to the definition in Sect. 2.1), such as $s = d(b^n)$, $s = (db)^n$ or $s = (ac)^n$.

The definition of $r_4 \; usbl_{\not\checkmark} \; s$ does however rule out a number of traces to consider, and Definition 5 helps us with this analysis. For instance, for $s = a$, we have $\neg(r_4 \; usbl_{\not\checkmark} \; a)$ because $\bigoplus(r_4 \; \text{after}_{\not\checkmark} \; a) = (\tau.1 + \tau.r_3'' + \tau.0 + \tau.\mu x.x)$ and, by using similar reasoning to that in Example 3 for r_3'', we know that $\neg((r_4 \; \text{after}_{\not\checkmark} \; a) \Downarrow_{\checkmark})$ which implies $\bigoplus(r_4 \; \text{after}_{\not\checkmark} \; a) \notin \mathcal{U}_{\text{bhv}}$ and, by Theorem 2, we have $\bigoplus(r_4 \; \text{after}_{\not\checkmark} \; a) \notin \mathcal{U}$. □

To overcome the problems outlined in Example 4, we identify three properties of the preorder $\lesssim_{\text{clt}}$, stated in Lemma 5, which partly motivate the conditions defining the transfer function $\mathcal{G}$ in Definition 6. Conditions (ii) and (iii) are explained in greater detail as discussions to points (2) and (3c) of Definition 6 below.

Lemma 5. $r_1 \lesssim_{\text{clt}} r_2$ *implies (i) if* $r_2 \xrightarrow{\tau}_{\not\checkmark} r_2'$ *then* $r_1 \lesssim_{\text{clt}} r_2'$; *(ii) if* $r_2 \xrightarrow{\checkmark}{\not\to}$ *then* $r_1 \xrightarrow{\checkmark}{\not\to}$ *(iii) if* $r_2 \xrightarrow{a}_{\not\checkmark}$ *then* $\left(r_1 \xRightarrow{a}_{\not\checkmark} \text{ and } \bigoplus(r_1 \; \text{after}_{\not\checkmark} \; a) \lesssim_{\text{clt}} \bigoplus(r_2 \; \text{after}_{\not\checkmark} \; a)\right)$. □

Definition 6. *Let* $\mathcal{G} : \mathcal{P}(\text{Proc} \times \text{Proc}) \longrightarrow \mathcal{P}(\text{Proc} \times \text{Proc})$ *be the function such that* $(r_1, r_2) \in \mathcal{G}(R)$ *whenever all the following conditions hold:*

1. *if* $r_2 \xrightarrow{\tau}_{\not\checkmark} r_2'$ *then* $r_1 \; R \; r_2'$
2. *if* $r_2 \xrightarrow{\checkmark}{\not\to}$ *then* $r_1 \xrightarrow{\checkmark}{\not\to}$
3. *if* $r_1 \in \mathcal{U}_{\text{bhv}}$ *then*
   (a) $r_2 \in \mathcal{U}_{\text{bhv}}$
   (b) *if* $B \in \text{Acc}_{\not\checkmark}(r_2)$ *then there exists an* $A \in \text{Acc}_{\not\checkmark}(r_1)$ *such that* $A \cap ua_{\text{bhv}}(r_1) \subseteq B$
   (c) *if* $r_2 \xrightarrow{a}_{\not\checkmark}$ *then* $\left(r_1 \xRightarrow{a}_{\not\checkmark} \text{ and } \bigoplus(r_1 \; \text{after}_{\not\checkmark} \; a) \; R \; \bigoplus(r_2 \; \text{after}_{\not\checkmark} \; a)\right)$

where $ua_{\text{bhv}}(r) = \{ a \mid r \xRightarrow{a}_{\not\checkmark} \text{ implies } \bigoplus(r \; \text{after}_{\not\checkmark} \; a) \in \mathcal{U}_{\text{bhv}} \}$. *Let* $\preccurlyeq_{\text{clt}} = \nu x.\mathcal{G}(x)$ *where* $\nu x.\mathcal{G}(x)$ *denotes the greatest fixpoint of* $\mathcal{G}$. *The function* $\mathcal{G}$ *is monotone over the complete lattice* $\langle \mathcal{P}(\text{Proc} \times \text{Proc}), \subseteq \rangle$ *and thus* $\nu x.\mathcal{G}(x)$ *exists.* □

The definition of $\mathcal{G}$ follows a similar structure to that of the *resp.* definitions that coinductively characterise the must preorder for servers [18, 25]. Definition 6, however, uses predicates for clients, *i.e.*, unsuccessful traces and usability, in place of the predicates for servers, *i.e.*, traces and convergence. Note, in particular, that we use the *fully-abstract* version of usability, $\mathcal{U}_{\text{bhv}}$, from Definition 5 and adapt the definition of usable actions accordingly, $ua_{\text{bhv}}(r)$. Another subtle but crucial difference in Definition 6 is condition (2). The next example elucidates why such a condition is necessary for $\preccurlyeq_{\text{clt}}$ to be sound.

Counterexample 3. *Let $\mathcal{G}_{\text{bad}}$ be defined as $\mathcal{G}$ in Definition 6, but without part (2). In this case, we prove that the pair of clients $(1, \tau. 1)$ is contained in the greatest fixed point of $\mathcal{G}_{\text{bad}}$, and then proceed to show that this pair is not contained in $\sqsubseteq_{\text{clt}}$. Let $R = \{ (1, \tau. 1) \}$. It follows that $R \subseteq \mathcal{G}_{\text{bad}}(R)$ if all the conditions for $\mathcal{G}_{\text{bad}}$ are satisfied: condition (1) in is trivially true, condition (3a) is true because 0 must 1 and 0 must $\tau. 1$, condition (3b) holds trivially because $\text{Acc}_{\not\swarrow}(\tau. 1) = \emptyset$, whereas condition (3c) is satisfied because $\tau. 1$ does not perform any strong actions. It therefore follows that $(1, \tau. 1) \in \mu x.\mathcal{G}_{\text{bad}}(x)$. Contrarily, $1 \not\sqsubseteq_{\text{clt}} \tau. 1$ because the divergent server τ^∞ distinguishes between the two clients: whereas τ^∞ must 1 since the client succeeds immediately, we have τ^∞ m$\not$st $\tau. 1$ because the composition $\tau. 1 \parallel \tau^\infty$ has an infinite unsuccessful computation due to the divergence of τ^∞.* ∎

A more fundamental difference between Definition 6 and the coinductive server preorders in [18, 25] is that, in Definition 6(3c), the relation R has to relate internal sums of derivative clients on *both* sides. Although non-standard, this condition is sufficient to compensate for the lack of compositionality of usable clients (see clients r_1 and r_2 (1) from Sect. 1). Using the standard weaker condition makes the preorder $\preccurlyeq_{\text{clt}}$ unsound wrt. $\sqsubseteq_{\text{clt}}$, as we proceed to show in the next example.

Counterexample 4. *Let $\mathcal{G}_{\text{bad}}$ be defined as $\mathcal{G}$ in Definition 6, but replacing the condition (3c) with the relaxed condition in (3bad) below, which requires each derivative r_2' to be analysed in isolation. We show that the greatest fixpoint of $\mathcal{G}_{\text{bad}}$, $\preccurlyeq_{\text{clt}}^{\text{bad}}$, contains client pairs that are not in $\sqsubseteq_{\text{clt}}$.*

$$\text{if } r_2 \xrightarrow{a}_{\not\swarrow} r_2' \text{ then } \left(r_1 \xLongrightarrow{a}_{\not\swarrow} \text{ and } \bigoplus (r_1 \text{ after}_{\not\swarrow} a) \, R \, r_2' \right) \qquad (3\text{bad})$$

Consider the clients $r_6 = c.r_6'$ and $r_7 = (r_1 + r_2) + \tau. 1$ where

$$r_6' = \tau.r_6^a + \tau.r_6^b \qquad r_6^a = a. 0 + \tau. 1 \qquad r_6^b = b. 0 + \tau. 1$$

and r_1 and r_2 are the clients defined in (1) above. On the one hand, we have that $r_6 \not\sqsubseteq_{\text{clt}} r_7$, because $\overline{c}. 0$ must r_6 whereas $\overline{c}. 0$ m$\not$st r_7. On the other hand, we now show that $r_6 \preccurlyeq_{\text{clt}}^{\text{bad}} r_7$. Focusing on condition Definition 6(3), we start by deducing that $r_6 \in \mathcal{U}_{\text{bhv}}$ (either directly using Definition 5 or indirectly through $\overline{c}. 0$ must r_6, recalling Theorem 2). Now, Definition 6(3a) is true because

0 must r_7, thus r_7 is usable, and thanks to Theorem 2 we have $r_7 \in \mathcal{U}_{bhv}$. Also point (3b) is satisfied, because $\mathsf{Acc}_{\mathscr{N}}(r_7) = \mathsf{Acc}_{\mathscr{N}}(r_6) = \{\{a\}\}$.[2] To prove that the (relaxed) condition (3bad) holds, we have to show that

$$r_6^c \preccurlyeq_{clt}^{bad} a.1 + b.0 \quad and \quad r_6^c \preccurlyeq_{clt}^{bad} a.0 + b.1, \qquad with \ r_6^c = r_6' + \tau.r_6^a + \tau.r_6^b \tag{7}$$

Let $r_7' = a.1 + b.0$. We only show the proof for the inequality $r_6^c \preccurlyeq_{clt}^{bad} r_7'$, since the proof for the other inequality is analogous. We focus again on conditions (3a), (3b), and (3bad). Condition (3a) is true because 0 must r_6^c, and thus $r_6^c \in \mathcal{U} = \mathcal{U}_{bhv}$, and because $r_7' \in \mathcal{U} = \mathcal{U}_{bhv}$ as well (e.g., $\bar{a}.0$ must r_7'). Condition (3b) holds because $\mathsf{Acc}_{\mathscr{N}}(r_7') = \{\{c\}\}$ and $\mathsf{Acc}_{\mathscr{N}}(r_6^c) = \{\{b\}, \{c\}\}$. Finally for (3bad) we only have to check the case for $r_7' \xrightarrow{b}_{\mathscr{N}} 0$, which requires us to show that $\tau.0 \preccurlyeq_{clt}^{bad} 0$; this latter check is routine. As a result, we have $r_6^c \preccurlyeq_{clt}^{bad} r_7'$. Since we can also show that $r_6^c \preccurlyeq_{clt}^{bad} a.0 + b.1$ holds, we obtain (7), and consequently $r_6 \preccurlyeq_{clt}^{bad} r_7$.   ∎

After our digression on Definition 6, we outline why $\preccurlyeq_{clt}$ coincides with $\lesssim_{clt}$. A detailed proof can be found in the full version of this paper [4].

Lemma 6. *Whenever $r_1 \preccurlyeq_{clt} r_2$, for every $s \in \mathsf{Act}^\star$, r_1 usbl$_{\mathscr{N}}$ s implies r_2 usbl$_{\mathscr{N}}$ s and also that for every $B \in \mathsf{Acc}_{\mathscr{N}}(r_2, s)$, there exists an set $A \in \mathsf{Acc}_{\mathscr{N}}(r_1, s)$ such that $A \cap ua_{clt}(r_2, s) \subseteq B$; and that if $r_2 \overset{s}{\Longrightarrow}_{\mathscr{N}}$ then $r_1 \overset{s}{\Longrightarrow}_{\mathscr{N}}$.*   □

Theorem 5. *In any finite branching LTS $r_1 \lesssim_{clt} r_2$ if and only if $r_1 \preccurlyeq_{clt} r_2$.*

Proof. We have to show the set inclusions, $\lesssim_{clt} \subseteq \preccurlyeq_{clt}$ and $\preccurlyeq_{clt} \subseteq \lesssim_{clt}$. Lemma 5 and Theorem 1 imply that $\lesssim_{clt} \subseteq \mathcal{G}(\lesssim_{clt})$, and thus, by the Knaster-Tarski theorem, we obtain the first inclusion. The second set inclusion follows from Theorem 1 and Lemma 6.   □

Example 5. Recall clients $r_4 = a.1 + \mu y.(a.r_3'' + b.y + c.1)$ and $r_5 = (\mu z.(b.z + c.1)) + d.1$ from Example 4, used to argue that the alternative relation $\precsim_{clt}$ is still a burdensome method for reasoning on $\lesssim_{clt}$. By contrast, We now contend that it is simpler to show $r_4 \lesssim_{clt} r_5$ by proving $r_4 \preccurlyeq_{clt} r_5$, thanks to Theorem 5 and the Knaster-Tarski theorem. By Definition 6, it suffices to provide a witness relation R such that $(r_4, r_5) \in R$ and $R \subseteq \mathcal{G}(R)$. Let $R = \{(r_4, r_5), (r_4', r_5')\}$ where $r_3'' = (\tau.(1 + \tau.0)) + \mu x.x$ from Example 1, $r_4' = \mu y.(a.r_3'' + b.y + c.1)$, and $r_5' = \mu z.(b.z + c.1)$. Checking that R satisfies the conditions in Definition 6 is routine work. To prove condition (3b), though, note that $\mathsf{Acc}_{\mathscr{N}}(r_5) = \mathsf{Acc}_{\mathscr{N}}(r_5') = \{\{b, c\}\}$ and that $\mathsf{Acc}_{\mathscr{N}}(r_4) = \{\{a, b, c\}\}$. However $ua_{bhv}(r_4) = \{b, c\}$ and thus the required set inclusion $(\{a, b, c\} \cap \{b, c\}) \subseteq \{b, c\}$ holds.   ∎

The coinductive preorder of $\preccurlyeq_{clt}$ may also be used to prove that two clients are *not* in the contextual preorder $\lesssim_{clt}$: by iteratively following the conditions of Definition 6 one can determine whether a relation including the pair of clients exists.

---

[2] The restriction of the left hand side of the inclusion of Definition 6(3b) by $ua_{bhv}(r_6)$ is superfluous.

This approach is useful when guessing a discriminating server is not straightforward; in failing to define a such relation R one obtains information on how to construct the discriminating server.

Example 6. Recall the clients r_6 and r_7 considered in Counterexample 4. By virtue of the full-abstraction result, we can show directly that $r_6 \not\lesssim_{\text{clt}} r_7$ by following the requirements of Definition 6 and arguing that no relation exists that contains the pair (r_6, r_7) while satisfying the conditions of the coinductive preorder. Without loss of generality, pick a relation R such that $r_6\ R\ r_7$:we have to show that $R \subseteq \mathcal{G}(R)$. Since $r_6 \in \mathcal{U}_{\text{bhv}}$, $r_7 \xrightarrow{c}_{\not\,\,}$ and $r_6 \xRightarrow{c}_{\not\,\,}$, Definition 6(3c) requires that we show that

$$r_6^c\ R\ \tau.r_7' + \tau.r_7'' \text{ where } r_6^c = \bigoplus(r_6\ \text{after}_{\not\,\,} c) \text{ and } (\tau.r_7' + \tau.r_7'') = \bigoplus(r_7\ \text{after}_{\not\,\,} c) \tag{8}$$

and r_6^c, r_7' and r_7'' are the clients defined earlier in Counterexample 4. Since we want to show that $R \not\subseteq \mathcal{G}(R)$, the condition Definition 6(3a) requires that, if $r_6^c \in \mathcal{U}_{\text{bhv}}$, then $(\tau.r_7' + \tau.r_7'') \in \mathcal{U}_{\text{bhv}}$. However, even though $r_6^c \in \mathcal{U}_{\text{bhv}}$, we have $(\tau.r_7' + \tau.r_7'') \notin \mathcal{U}_{\text{bhv}}$, violating Definition 6(3a) and thus showing that no such R satisfying both $(r_6, r_7) \in R$ and $R \subseteq \mathcal{G}(R)$ can exist. We highlight the fact that whereas (7) of Counterexample 4 resulted in $r_6 \precsim_{\text{clt}}^{\text{bad}} r_7$, (8) is instrumental to conclude that $r_6 \not\precsim_{\text{clt}} r_7$. Note also that the path along c leading to a violation of the requirements of Definition 6 is related to the discriminating server $\bar{c}.0$ used in Counterexample 4 to justify $r_6 \not\lesssim_{\text{clt}} r_7$. ∎

5   Expressiveness and Decidability

We show that servers with finite interactions suffice to preserve the discriminating power of the contextual preorder $\lesssim_{\text{clt}}$ in Definition 1, which has ramifications on standard verification techniques for the preorder, such as counter-example generation [11]. We also show that, for finite-state LTSs, the set of usable clients is decidable. Using standard techniques [27] we then argue that, in such cases, there exists a procedure to decide whether two finite-state clients are related by $\lesssim_{\text{clt}}$.

5.1   On the Power of Finite Interactions

We employ the coinductive characterisation of the client preorder, Theorem 5, to prove an important property of the client preorder of Definition 1, namely that servers that only offer a *finite amount of interactions* to clients are necessary and sufficient to distinguish all the clients according to our touchstone preorder $\lesssim_{\text{clt}}$ of Definition 1. Let $\mathsf{CCS}^f ::= 0\ |\ 1\ |\ \alpha.p\ |\ p+q\ |\ \tau^\infty$, and

$$\lesssim_{\text{clt}}^f = \{\,(r_1, r_2)\ |\ \text{for every } p \in \mathsf{CCS}^f.\ p\ \text{must}\ r_1 \text{ implies } p\ \text{must}\ r_2\,\}$$
$$\mathcal{U}^f = \{\,r\ |\ \text{there exists } p \in \mathsf{CCS}^f.\ p\ \text{must}\ r\,\}$$

In what follows, we find it convenient to use the definitions above: CCS^f excludes recursively-defined processes, but explicitly adds the divergent process τ^∞ because of its discriminating powers (see Counterexample 3). Accordingly, $\lesssim^f_{clt}$ and $\mathcal{U}^f$ restrict the *resp.* sets to the syntactic class CCS^f.

Corollary 1. *The sets $\mathcal{U}$ and $\mathcal{U}^f$ coincide.*

Proof. The inclusion $\mathcal{U}^f \subseteq \mathcal{U}$ is immediate. Suppose that $r \in \mathcal{U}$. By Theorem 2 we have $r \in \mathcal{U}_{bhv}$. By Lemma 1, there exists a non-recursive $p \in CCS^f$ such that p must r, thus $r \in \mathcal{U}^f$ follows.   □

Theorem 6. *In any finite-branching LTS $r_1 \lesssim^f_{clt} r_2$ if and only if $r_1 \lesssim_{clt} r_2$.*

Proof. The inclusion $\lesssim_{clt} \subseteq \lesssim^f_{clt}$ follows immediately from the *resp.* definitions. On the other hand, Theorem 5 provides us with a proof technique for showing the inclusion $\lesssim^f_{clt} \subseteq \lesssim_{clt}$: if we show that $\lesssim^f_{clt} \subseteq \mathcal{G}(\lesssim^f_{clt})$ then $\lesssim^f_{clt} \subseteq \prec_{clt} = \lesssim_{clt}$. In view of the Knaster-Tarski theorem it suffices to show that $\lesssim^f_{clt} \subseteq \mathcal{G}(\lesssim^f_{clt})$. In turn, this requires us to prove the three conditions stated in Definition 6. The argument for the first two conditions is virtually the same to that of Lemma 5. Similarly, the arguments for the third condition follow closely those used in Theorem 1 (albeit in a simpler setting of unsuccessful traces of length 1). The only new reasoning required is that servers that exists because of $r_1 \in \mathcal{U}$ also belong to CCS^f, which we know from Corollary 1.   □

An analogous result should also hold for the server-preorder, for the proofs of completeness in [6, Theorem 3.1] rely on clients that can be written in the language CCS^f.

5.2 Deciding the Client Preorder

Figure 4 describes the pseudo-code for the eponymous function isUsable(r, acm), which is meant to determine whether a client r is usable. It adheres closely to the conditions of Definition 5 for $\mathcal{U}_{bhv}$, using acm as an *accumulator* to keep track of all the terms that have already been explored. Thus, if an r is revisited, the algorithm rejects it on the basis that a loop of unsuccessful interactions (leading to an infinite sequence of unsuccessful interactions that makes the client unusable) is detected (lines 2–3). If not, the algorithm checks for the conditions in Definition 5 (lines 4–9). In particular, line 4 checks that infinite sequences of internal moves are always successful (using function convtick defined on lines 11–17) and that partially deadlocked clients reached through a finite number of unsuccessful internal moves, $Acc_{\nsucc}(r) \neq \emptyset$, contain at least one action that unblocks them to some other usable client (lines 7–8). This latter check employs the function existsUnblockAction (defined on lines 19–26) which recursively calls isUsable to determine whether the client reached after an action is indeed usable. isUsable(r, acm) of Fig. 4 relies on the LTS of r being *finite-state* in order to guarantee termination via the state accumulation held in acm. This is indeed the case for our expository language CCS^μ of Fig. 2. Concretely, we define the

```
1   isUsable (r, acm) =
2     if r in acm
3       then false
4       else if convtick (∅, r)
5         then if Acc√(r) == empty
6           then true
7           else BoolSet = map ( existsUnblockAction acm r) Acc√(r)
8                     conjunction BoolSet
9         else false
10    where
11      convtick(acm, r) =
12        if r in acm
13          then false
14          else if r ─√→
15            then true
16            else BoolSet = map (convtick (acm ∪{r})) {r' | r ─τ→ r'}
17                      conjunction BoolSet
18    and
19      existsUnblockAction (acm, r, A) =
20        case A of
21          empty -> false
22          {a} ⊎ A' ->
23            if r ═a═>√
24              then if isUsable (⊕(r after√ a), acm ∪ { r })
25                then true else existsUnblockAction (r, A', acm)
26              else true
```

Fig. 4. An algorithm for deciding inclusion in the set $\mathcal{U}$

set of internal-sums for the derivatives that a client r reaches via all the finite traces $\in \mathsf{Act}^\star$, and show that this set is finite. Let

$$\mathsf{sumsRdx}(r) = \{ \bigoplus (r \; \mathsf{after}_{\!\!\!\!\!/} \; s) \mid \text{ for some } s \in \mathsf{Act}^\star \},$$

Lemma 7. *For every $r \in \mathsf{CCS}^\mu$, the set $\mathsf{sumsRdx}(r)$ is finite.*   □

Proof. Let $\mathit{Reach}_r = \{ r' \mid r \xRightarrow{s} r' \text{ for some } s \in \mathsf{Act}^\star \}$ denote the set of reachable terms from client r, and $\mathit{PwrR}_r = \{ \bigoplus B \mid B \in \mathcal{P}(\mathit{Reach}_r) \}$ denote the elements of the powerset of Reach_r, expressed as internal summations of the elements of $\mathcal{P}(\mathit{Reach}_r)$. By definition, we have that $\mathsf{sumsRdx}(r) \subseteq \mathit{PwrR}_r$. Hence, it suffices to prove that Reach_r is finite to show that PwrR_r is finite, from which the finiteness of $\mathsf{sumsRdx}(r)$ follows. The proof of the finiteness of Reach_r is the same as that of Lemma 4.2.11 of [29] for the language serial-CCS, which is homologous to CCS^μ of Fig. 2 modulo the satisfaction construct 1.   □

Theorem 7. *For every $r \in$ Proc we have that*

(i) $r \in \mathcal{U}$ iff isUsable$(r, \emptyset) =$ true,
(ii) $r \notin \mathcal{U}$ iff isUsable$(r, \emptyset) =$ false.

Proof. For the *only-if* case of clause (i), we use Theorem 2 and show instead that $r \in \mathcal{U}_{\mathsf{bhv}}$ implies isUsable$(r, \emptyset) =$ true; we do so by numerical induction on $n \in \mathbb{N}^+$ where $r \in \mathcal{F}^n(\emptyset)$. For the *if* case, we dually show that isUsable$(r, \emptyset) =$ true implies $r \in \mathcal{U}_{\mathsf{bhv}}$, by numerical induction on the *least* number $n \in \mathbb{N}^+$ of (recursive) calls to isUsable that yield the outcome true. We note that in either direction of clause (i), there is a direct correspondence between the respective inductive indices (*e.g.*, for the base case $n = 1$, $r \in \mathcal{F}^1(\emptyset) = \mathcal{F}(\emptyset)$ implies that $r \Downarrow_{\checkmark}$ and that $\mathsf{Acc}_{\checkmark}(r) = \emptyset$).

For the second clause (ii), the statements $(r \notin \mathcal{U}$ implies isUsable$(r, \emptyset) =$ true$)$ and $($isUsable$(r, \emptyset) =$ false implies $r \notin \mathcal{U})$ contradict the first clause (i) which we just proved. The required result thus holds if we ensure that isUsable$(r, \emptyset)$ is defined for any $r \in$ Proc. This follows from Lemma 7.   □

From Theorems 5, 7 and Lemma 7, we conclude that Definition 6 can be used to decide $\lesssim_{\mathsf{clt}}$ for languages such as CCS^μ of Fig. 2. We can do this by adapting the algorithm of [27, Chapter 21.5], and proving that in our setting [27, Theorems 21.5.9 and 21.5.12] are true. In particular, using the terminology of [27] we have that *reachable*$_{\mathcal{G}}(X)$ is finite, essentially because the *resp.* LTS is finite-state, and thus the decidability of $\preccurlyeq_{\mathsf{clt}}$ follows from Theorem 21.5.12.

6   Conclusion

We present a study that revolves around the notion of usability and preorders for clients (tests). Preorders for clients first appeared for compliance testing [2], and were subsequently investigated in [3,6] for must testing [12] and extended to include peers. The characterisations given in [6] relied fundamentally on the set of usable terms $\mathcal{U}$ which made them not fully-abstract and hard to automate. This provided the main impetus for our study. In general, recursion poses obstacles when characterising usable terms, but the very nature of must testing — which regards infinite unsuccessful computations as catastrophic — let us treat recursive terms in a finite manner (see Definition 5).

We focus on the client preorder, even though [6] presents preorders for both client and peers; note however that [6, Theorem 3.20] and Theorem 2 imply full-abstraction for the peer preorder as well. Our investigations and the *resp.* proofs for Theorem 2, Theorems 5 and 6 are conducted in terms of finitely-branching LTSs, which cover the semantics used by numerous other work describing client and server contracts [6,8,9,18] — we only rely on an internal choice construct to economise on our presentation, but this can be replaced by tweaking the *resp.* definitions so as to work on sets of processes instead. As a consequence, the results obtained should also extend to arbitrary languages enjoying the finite-branching property. Theorem 7 relies on a stronger property, namely that the language is finite-state. In [29], it is shown that this property is also enjoyed by larger CCS fragments, and we therefore expect our results to extend to these fragments as well.

6.1 Related Work

Client usability depends both on language expressiveness and on the notion of testing employed. Our comparison with the related work is organised accordingly.

Session types [14] do not contain unsuccessful termination, 0, restrict internal (*resp.* external) choices to contain only pair-wise distinct outputs (*resp.* inputs) and are, by definition, strongly convergent [25] (*i.e.*, no infinite sequences of τ-transitions). *E.g.*, $\tau.!a.\,1 + \tau.!b.?c.\,1$ corresponds to a session type in our language (modulo syntactic transformations such as those for internal choices), whereas $\tau.!a.\,0 + \tau.!b.?c.\,1$, $\tau.!a.\,1 + \tau.!a.?b.\,1$ and $?a.\,1 + ?a.!b.\,1$ do *not*. Since they are mostly deterministic — only internal choices on outputs are permitted — usability is relatively easy to characterise. In fact [7, Section 5] shows that every session type is usable *wrt.* compliance testing (even in the presence of higher-order communication) whereas, in [26, Theorem 4.3], *non-usable* session types are characterised *wrt.* fair testing. First-order session types are a subset of our language, and hence, Theorem 2 is enough to (positively) characterise usable session types *wrt.* must testing; we leave the axiomatisation of $\mathcal{U}$ in this setting as future work.

Contracts [25] are usually formalised as (mild variants of) our language CCS^μ. In the case of must testing, the authors in [6, Theorem 6.9, Lemma 7.8(2)] characterise *non*-usable clients (and peers) for the sublanguage CCS^f as the terms that can be re-written into 0 via equational reasoning. Full-abstraction for usable clients *wrt.* *compliance* testing has been solved for *strongly convergent terms* in [25, Proposition 4.3] by giving a coinductive characterisation for viable (*i.e.*, usable *wrt.* compliance) contracts. If we restrict our language to strongly convergent terms, that characterisation is neither sound nor complete *wrt.* must testing. It is unsound because clients such as $\mu x.a.x$ are viable but *not* usable. It is incomplete because of clients such as $r = 1 + \tau.\,0$; this client is usable *wrt.* must because, for arbitrary p, any computation of $p \parallel r$ is successful (since we have $r \xrightarrow{\checkmark}$ immediately). On the other hand, r is *not* viable *wrt.* compliance testing of [25] (where every server is strongly convergent), because for any server p we observe the computation starting with the reduction $p \parallel r \xrightarrow{\tau} p \parallel 0$, and once p stabilises to some p', the final state $p' \parallel 0$ contains an unsuccessful client. This argument relies on subtle discrepancies in the definitions of the testing relations: in must testing it suffices for maximal computations to *pass through* a successful state, whereas in compliance testing the *final state* of the computation (if any) is required to be successful. This aspect impinges on the technical development: although our Definition 5(2) resembles [25, Definition 4.2], the two definitions have strikingly different meanings: we are forced to reason *wrt.* *unsuccessful* actions and *unsuccessful* acceptance sets whereas [25, Definition 4.2] is defined in terms of (standard) weak actions and acceptance sets (note that Definition 5(1) holds trivially in the strongly convergent setting of [25]). We note also that our Definition 5 is inductive whereas [25, Definition 4.2] is coinductive. More importantly, our work lays bare the *non-compositionality* of usable terms and how it affects other notions that depend on it, such as Definition 6 (and consequently Theorem 5). We are unaware of any full-abstraction results for contract usability in the case of should-testing [8,24,28].

Future work: In the line of [10], we plan to show a logical characterisation of the client and peer preorder. We also intend to investigate coinductive characterisations for the peer preorder of [6] and subsequently implement decision procedures for the server, client, and peer preorders in CAAL [1]. Usability is not limited to tests. We expect it to extend naturally to runtime monitoring [13], where it can be used as a means of lowering runtime overhead by not instrumenting unusable monitors.

Acknowledgements. This research was supported by the COST Action STSMs IC1201-130216-067787 and IC1201-170214-038253. The first author was supported by the EU FP7 ADVENT project. The second author is partly supported by the RANNIS THEOFOMON project 163406-051. The authors acknowledge the Dagstuhl seminar 17051 and thank L. Aceto, M. Bravetti, A. Gorla, M. Hennessy, C. Spaccasassi and anonymous reviewers for their help and suggestions.

References

1. Andersen, J.R., Andersen, N., Enevoldsen, S., Hansen, M.M., Larsen, K.G., Olesen, S.R., Srba, J., Wortmann, J.K.: CAAL: concurrency workbench, Aalborg edition. In: Leucker, M., Rueda, C., Valencia, F.D. (eds.) ICTAC 2015. LNCS, vol. 9399, pp. 573–582. Springer, Cham (2015). doi:10.1007/978-3-319-25150-9_33
2. Barbanera, F., de'Liguoro, F.: Two notions of sub-behaviour for session-based client/server systems. In: PPDP (2010)
3. Bernardi, G.: Behavioural equivalences for web services. Ph.D. thesis, TCD (2013)
4. Bernardi,G., Francalanza, A.: Full-abstraction for must testing preorders (extended abstract). https://www.irif.fr/gio/papers/BFcoordination2017.pdf
5. Bernardi, G., Hennessy, M.: Modelling session types using contracts. In: SAC (2012)
6. Bernardi, G., Hennessy, M.: Mutually testing processes. LMCS **11**(2), 1–23 (2015)
7. Bernardi, G., Hennessy, M.: Using higher-order contracts to model session types. LMCS **12**(2), 1–43 (2016)
8. Bravetti, M., Zavattaro, G.: A foundational theory of contracts for multi-party service composition. Fundam. Inf. **89**(4), 451–478 (2008)
9. Castagna, G., Gesbert, N., Padovani, L.: A theory of contracts for web services. ACM Trans. Program. Lang. Syst. **31**(5), 1–61 (2009)
10. Cerone, A., Hennessy, M.: Process behaviour: formulae vs. tests. In: EXPRESS (2010)
11. Clarke, E., Veith, H.: Counterexamples revisited: principles, algorithms, applications. In: Dershowitz, N. (ed.) Verification: Theory and Practice. LNCS, vol. 2772, pp. 208–224. Springer, Heidelberg (2003). doi:10.1007/978-3-540-39910-0_9
12. De Nicola, R., Hennessy, M.: Testing equivalences for processes. TCS **34**(1–2), 83–93 (1984)

13. Francalanza, A.: A theory of monitors. In: Jacobs, B., Löding, C. (eds.) FoSSaCS 2016. LNCS, vol. 9634, pp. 145–161. Springer, Heidelberg (2016). doi:10.1007/978-3-662-49630-5_9

14. Gay, S.J., Hole, M.: Subtyping for session types in the pi calculus. Acta Inf. **42**(2–3), 191–225 (2005)

15. Hennessy, M.: Algebraic Theory of Processes. MIT Press, Cambridge (1988)

16. Knuth, D.E.: The Art of Computer Programming, Volume 1 (3rd Ed.): Fundamental Algorithms. Addison Wesley Longman Publishing Co., Inc., Redwood City (1997)

17. König, D.: Über eine schlussweise aus dem endlichen ins unendliche. Acta Litt. ac. sci. Szeged **3**, 121–130 (1927)

18. Laneve, C., Padovani, L.: The Must preorder revisited. In: Caires, L., Vasconcelos, V.T. (eds.) CONCUR 2007. LNCS, vol. 4703, pp. 212–225. Springer, Heidelberg (2007). doi:10.1007/978-3-540-74407-8_15

19. Luo, Q., Hariri, F., Eloussi, L., Marinov, D.: An empirical analysis of flaky tests. In: FSE (2014)

20. Marinescu, P., Hosek, P., Cadar, C.: Covrig: a framework for the analysis of code, test, and coverage evolution in real software. In: ISSTA (2014)

21. Martens, A.: Analyzing web service based business processes. In: Cerioli, M. (ed.) FASE 2005. LNCS, vol. 3442, pp. 19–33. Springer, Heidelberg (2005). doi:10.1007/978-3-540-31984-9_3

22. Memon, A.M., Cohen, M.B.: Automated testing of GUI applications: models, tools, and controlling flakiness. In: ICSE (2013)

23. Milner, R.: Communication and Concurrency. Prentice-Hall, Upper Saddle River (1989)

24. Mooij, A.J., Stahl, C., Voorhoeve, M.: Relating fair testing and accordance for service replaceability. J. Log. Algebr. Program. **79**(3–5), 233–244 (2010)

25. Padovani, L.: Contract-based discovery of web services modulo simple orchestrators. TCS **411**(37), 3328–3347 (2010)

26. Padovani, L.: Fair subtyping for multi-party session types. MSCS **26**(3), 238–302 (2016)

27. Pierce, B.: Types and Programming Languages. MIT Press, Cambridge (2002)

28. Rensink, A., Vogler, W.: Fair testing. Inf. Comput. **205**(2), 125–198 (2007)

29. Spaccasassi, C.: Language support for communicating transactions. Ph.D. thesis, TCD, (2015)

30. Weinberg, D.: Efficient controllability analysis of open nets. In: Bruni, R., Wolf, K. (eds.) WS-FM 2008. LNCS, vol. 5387, pp. 224–239. Springer, Heidelberg (2009). doi:10.1007/978-3-642-01364-5_14

31. Winskel, G.: The Formal Semantics of Programming Languages: An Introduction. MIT Press, Cambridge (1993)

Communication Requirements for Team Automata

Maurice H. ter Beek[1]([✉]), Josep Carmona[2], Rolf Hennicker[3], and Jetty Kleijn[4]

[1] ISTI–CNR, Pisa, Italy
`maurice.terbeek@isti.cnr.it`
[2] Universitat Politècnica de Catalunya, Barcelona, Spain
[3] Ludwig-Maximilians-Universität, Munich, Germany
[4] LIACS, Leiden University, Leiden, The Netherlands

Abstract. Compatibility of components is an important issue in the quest for systems of systems that guarantee successful communications, free from message loss and indefinite waiting for inputs. In this paper, we investigate compatibility in the context of systems consisting of reactive components which may communicate through the synchronised execution of common actions. We model such systems in the team automata framework, which does not impose any a priori restrictions on the synchronisation policy followed to combine the components. We identify a family of representative synchronisation types based on the number of sending and receiving components participating in synchronisations. Then, we provide a generic procedure to derive, for each synchronisation type, requirements for receptiveness and for responsiveness of team automata that prevent that outputs are not accepted and inputs are not provided, respectively. Due to the genericity of our approach w.r.t. synchronisation policies, we can capture compatibility notions for various multi-component system models known from the literature.

1 Introduction

Modern systems are often large-scale concurrent and distributed systems of interconnected, reactive components which collaborate through message exchange. For their correct functioning it is not only important that each component satisfies application-specific properties, but it is also essential that no communication failures, like message loss or indefinite waiting for input, occur during system execution. This requires a deep understanding of the typical communication and interaction policies used in such multi-component systems. To establish that components within a system interact correctly, a concept known as compatibility is useful. In [1], a characterisation was given for compatibility of two components that should engage in a dialogue free from message loss and indefinite waiting. In [2], this binary notion of compatibility was lifted to multi-component systems, in which communication may take place between more than two components at

© IFIP International Federation for Information Processing 2017
Published by Springer International Publishing AG 2017. All Rights Reserved
J.-M. Jacquet and M. Massink (Eds.): COORDINATION 2017, LNCS 10319, pp. 256–277, 2017.
DOI: 10.1007/978-3-319-59746-1_14

the same time (e.g. broadcasting). Compatibility failures detected in a distributed, modular system model may reveal important problems in the design of one or more of its components, to be repaired before implementation. Compatibility checks considering various communication and interaction policies thus significantly aid the development of correct component-based systems.

I/O-transition systems are frequently used as a model for reactive components on which to formally define and analyse compatibility. To express reactivity, I/O-transition systems rely on distinguished output (active), input (passive) and internal (privately active) actions. They come in several flavours, like I/O automata [3,4], team automata [5,6], interface automata [7,8], component-interaction automata [9] or modal I/O automata [10]. Several compatibility notions studied in the literature are influenced by the interface automata approach, which uses synchronous point-to-point communication. Two interface automata are said to be compatible if no illegal state can be reached autonomously in the synchronous product of the two. A state is illegal if "one of the automata may produce an output action that is an input action of the other automaton, but not accepted" [7]. The notion was weakened in [11] by allowing a component to still perform some internal actions before accepting the input. Outputs which are not accepted as input are considered as message loss or as unspecified receptions [12,13]. If any (autonomously chosen) output is accepted, we call this receptiveness [14]. An orthogonal issue concerns the viewpoint of a component waiting to receive an input. It expects an appropriate output to be provided. But in this case the environment can choose which input to serve. Here we refer to this kind of communication requirement (which was already considered as part of a notion of I/O-compatibility in [1]) as responsiveness.

Conditions for receptiveness and responsiveness have been considered in [13] for services and in [2] for team automata. Both approaches support compatibility in multi-component environments for synchronous products, which are known for their appealing compositionality and modularity properties [4,15–18]. A first exploration on how compatibility notions could be generalised to arbitrary synchronisation policies was performed in [14] in the framework of team automata. However, due to the very loose nature of synchronisation policies in team automata, a systematic methodology on how to formalise compatibility conditions in such general settings is still missing. It is the motivation for this work.

The present paper uses as a foundation again the team automata framework, but we additionally define a representative set of communication patterns, called synchronisation types, which help to classify the synchronisation policies that can be realised in team automata. A synchronisation type (snd, rcv) can specify ranges for the number of senders and receivers which can take part in a communication inside the system (possibly based on side conditions). Any synchronisation type uniquely determines a synchronisation policy if the underlying system of components is closed. Otherwise, synchronisation policies with the same type may vary concerning options for interaction with the environment of the system. In any global state of a system $\mathcal{S}$, one of its components or—

more generally—a group of components in S may require certain communications with other components in the system depending on the currently enabled actions. If (common) outputs are enabled in a group of components this leads to requirements for reception. Conversely, enabled inputs lead to requirements for providing appropriate output, i.e. responsiveness requirements. This allows us to define a notion of compatibility for team automata in terms of their compliance with communication requirements. A team automaton is said to be compliant with communication requirements if the desired communications can immediately occur in the team; it is said to be weakly compliant if the communication can eventually occur after some internal actions have been performed.

In this paper, we propose a general procedure to systematically derive receptiveness and responsiveness requirements from any synchronisation type. Then we can check for any team automaton of synchronisation type (snd, rcv) whether it is compliant with the receptiveness and/or responsiveness requirements derived from (snd, rcv). Thus we get a family of compatibility notions indexed by synchronisation types. Our methodology is illustrated with several examples. We show that our notions can be instantiated with well-known compatibility notions from the literature where particular synchronisation types are considered. In particular, our approach can express two different paradigms for compatibility in open systems, often called the optimistic and pessimistic approaches (cf. [19]).

The paper is organised as follows. In Sect. 2, we introduce team automata followed by the notion of synchronisation types in Sect. 3. In Sect. 4, we define communication requirements for receptiveness and responsiveness and the compliance of team automata with such requirements. In Sect. 5, we show how to derive these requirements from synchronisation types, how known compatibility notions from the literature can be captured and how our theory can be applied. We conclude with a summary of our achievements and some pointers to future work in Sect. 6.

2 Component Automata and Team Automata

Component automata and team automata are defined as (reactive) automata without final states which distinguish input, output and internal actions and which can be combined by synchronisations on common actions according to synchronisation policies. First we fix some notation.

Given a finite index set $\mathcal{I} = \{1, \dots, n\}$, we denote the Cartesian product of sets $V_1, \dots, V_n$ as $\prod_{i \in \mathcal{I}} V_i$. If $v = (v_1, \dots, v_n) \in \prod_{i \in \mathcal{I}} V_i$ and $i \in \mathcal{I}$, then the i-th entry of v is obtained by applying the projection function $proj_i : \prod_{i \in \mathcal{I}} V_i \to V_i$ defined by $proj_i(v_1, \dots, v_n) = v_i$.

Definition 1 (Component automaton). *A* component automaton *is a tuple* $\mathcal{A} = (Q, \Sigma, \delta, I)$, *with set* Q *of* states; *set* Σ *of* actions, *such that* $Q \cap \Sigma = \varnothing$, *and* Σ *is the union of three pairwise disjoint sets* Σ_{inp}, Σ_{out} *and* Σ_{int} *of input, output and internal* actions, *respectively;* $\delta \subseteq Q \times \Sigma \times Q$ *is its set of (labelled)* transitions; *and* $\varnothing \neq I \subseteq Q$ *its set of* initial states. □

A (component) automaton (Q, Σ, δ, I) with input, output and internal actions Σ_{inp}, Σ_{out} and Σ_{int}, respectively, may be specified as $(Q, (\Sigma_{inp}, \Sigma_{out}, \Sigma_{int}), \delta, I)$. By Σ_{ext} we denote the set $\Sigma_{inp} \cup \Sigma_{out}$ of external actions. Especially in figures, we may emphasise the role of external actions by appending input actions with ? and output actions with ! For an action $a \in \Sigma$, we define the set of a-*transitions* as $\delta_a = \delta \cap (Q \times \{a\} \times Q)$. We may write $p \xrightarrow{a}_A p'$ instead of $(p, a, p') \in \delta$.

The behaviour of an automaton $\mathcal{A}$ is determined by the execution of actions enabled at its current state. We say that a is *enabled* in $\mathcal{A}$ at state $p \in Q$, denoted by $a \, en_A \, p$, if there exists $p' \in Q$ such that $p \xrightarrow{a}_A p'$. The (finite, sequential) *computations* of $\mathcal{A}$, denoted by $\mathcal{C}(\mathcal{A})$, are those sequences $p_0 a_1 p_1 \cdots p_{k-1} a_k p_k$ such that $k \geq 0$, $p_0 \in I$ and $p_{i-1} \xrightarrow{a_i}_A p_i$ for all $i \in \{1, \ldots, k\}$. For $X \subseteq \Sigma$, we write $p \xrightarrow{X}{}^*_A p'$ if there exists $p_0 \xrightarrow{a_1}_A p_1, \ldots, p_{j-1} \xrightarrow{a_j}_A p_j$ for some $j \geq 0$, with $p_0, \ldots p_j \in Q$, $a_1, \ldots, a_j \in X$, $p = p_0$, and $p' = p_j$. A state $p \in Q$ is *reachable* if $p_0 \xrightarrow{\Sigma}{}^*_A p$ (with $p_0 \in I$) and the set of reachable states of $\mathcal{A}$ is denoted by $\mathcal{R}(\mathcal{A})$.

As usual, we may omit subscripts referring to $\mathcal{A}$ if no confusion can arise.

Team automata consist of component automata that collaborate through synchronised executions of shared actions. When and which actions are executed and by how many components depends on the chosen synchronisation policy.

Let $\mathcal{I} = \{1, \ldots, n\}$ be a finite index set. Let $\mathcal{S} = \{\mathcal{A}_i \mid i \in \mathcal{I}\}$ be a set of component automata defined, for each $i \in \mathcal{I}$, as $\mathcal{A}_i = (Q_i, (\Sigma_{i,inp}, \Sigma_{i,out}, \Sigma_{i,int}), \delta_i, I_i)$ with $\Sigma_i = \Sigma_{i,inp} \cup \Sigma_{i,out} \cup \Sigma_{i,int}$. $\mathcal{S}$ is *composable* if $\Sigma_{i,int} \cap \bigcup_{j=1, j \neq i}^{n} \Sigma_j = \varnothing$ for all $i \in \mathcal{I}$. Thus in a composable system, internal actions are not shared. Note that every subset of a composable set of component automata is again composable.

$\Sigma = \bigcup_{i \in \mathcal{I}} \Sigma_i$ is the set of actions of $\mathcal{S}$, $\Sigma_{int} = \bigcup_{i \in \mathcal{I}} \Sigma_{i,int}$ its set of internal actions and $\Sigma_{ext} = \bigcup_{i \in \mathcal{I}} \Sigma_{i,ext}$ its set of external actions. Moreover, $\Sigma_{com} = \bigcup_{i \in \mathcal{I}} \Sigma_{i,inp} \cap \bigcup_{i \in \mathcal{I}} \Sigma_{i,out}$ is the set of *communicating* actions of $\mathcal{S}$. Hence, an action (of $\mathcal{S}$) is communicating if it occurs in Σ_{ext} both as an input action of one of the automata and as an output action of an automaton.

For an action $a \in \Sigma$, its domain in $\mathcal{S}$, denoted by $dom_a(\mathcal{S})$, consists of the indices of all automata from $\mathcal{S}$ in which it appears as an action. So, $dom_a(\mathcal{S}) = \{i \mid a \in \Sigma_i\}$. Hence in a composable system, the domain of an internal action is always a singleton set. For $a \in \Sigma_{ext}$, we let $dom_{a,inp}(\mathcal{S}) = \{i \mid a \in \Sigma_{i,inp}\}$ be its *input domain* (in $\mathcal{S}$) and $dom_{a,out}(\mathcal{S}) = \{i \mid a \in \Sigma_{i,out}\}$ its *output domain* (in $\mathcal{S}$). Hence an action is a communicating action of $\mathcal{S}$ if both its output and its input domain in $\mathcal{S}$ are not empty.

Finally, we say that $\mathcal{S}$ is *open* if it has external actions that are not communicating (they appear only as an input or only as an output action). If $\mathcal{S}$ is not open, it may be referred to as *closed*; in this case all its external actions are communicating (all have at least one communication partner).

Notation. *For the remainder of this paper, we fix $\mathcal{I}$ and $\mathcal{S}$ as above. Moreover, $\mathcal{S}$ is composable. We refer to $Q = \prod_{i \in \mathcal{I}} Q_i$ as the state space of $\mathcal{S}$ and to Σ, Σ_{int}, Σ_{ext} and Σ_{com} as its set of actions, internal actions, external actions and communicating actions, respectively.*

Definition 2 (System transition). *A tuple* $(q, a, q') \in Q \times \Sigma \times Q$ *is a transition on a (in $\mathcal{S}$) if there exists an $i \in \mathcal{I}$ such that $(\text{proj}_i(q), a, \text{proj}_i(q')) \in \delta_i$, and if for all $i \in \mathcal{I}$, either $(\text{proj}_i(q), a, \text{proj}_i(q')) \in \delta_i$ or $\text{proj}_i(q) = \text{proj}_i(q')$.*

For $a \in \Sigma$, $\Delta_a(\mathcal{S})$ is the set of all transitions on a in $\mathcal{S}$, *while $\Delta(\mathcal{S}) = \bigcup_{a \in \Sigma} \Delta_a(\mathcal{S})$ is the set of all* transitions in $\mathcal{S}$. □

If $(q, a, q') \in \Delta(\mathcal{S})$, then any component $\mathcal{A}_i$ for which $(\text{proj}_i(q), a, \text{proj}_i(q')) \in \delta_i$ is said to be *involved in* (q, a, q'). By definition, in all transitions in $\mathcal{S}$, at least one component is involved through a 'local' transition. Moreover, all transitions in $\Delta_a(\mathcal{S})$ are combinations of existing a-transitions from the component automata in $\mathcal{S}$ and all possible combinations occur in $\Delta_a(\mathcal{S})$. As in earlier papers, we will often refer to the elements of $\Delta_a(\mathcal{S})$ as *synchronisations on a* also when no more than one component is actively involved. In particular, when a is an internal action of a component automaton, then all transitions on a are executed by that component alone. Moreover, for each transition on an external action in one of the automata, $\Delta(\mathcal{S})$ will also contain all synchronisations that involve only that component through that particular local transition. When a synchronisation on an external action a involves both a component in which a is an input action and one in which it is an output action, it is called a *communication*.

All team automata over $\mathcal{S}$ will have Σ as their set of actions, consisting of the external actions Σ_{ext} of the components and the internal actions Σ_{int} comprising all internal actions of the components. In addition, we need to define the sets of *input* and *output* actions. We follow the idea from [6] that components have control over their output actions whereas input actions are passive, i.e. driven by the environment. As a consequence, actions that appear as an output action in one or more of the components are considered to be under the control of the team and hence will be output actions of the team (even if they are input to some other components). Input actions that do not appear as output, are input actions of the team. Formally, $\Sigma_{out} = \bigcup_{i \in \mathcal{I}} \Sigma_{i,out}$ and $\Sigma_{inp} = (\bigcup_{i \in \mathcal{I}} \Sigma_{i,inp}) \setminus \Sigma_{out}$. Furthermore, $Q = \prod_{i \in \mathcal{I}} Q_i$ will be the set of states of every team automaton over $\mathcal{S}$ and $I = \prod_{i \in \mathcal{I}} I_i$ its set of initial states.

Finally, it is the choice of synchronisations, thus the choice of a subset δ of $\Delta(\mathcal{S})$, that defines a specific team automaton. As internal actions are assumed to be under the control of the component automata, all transitions on internal actions will always be included as transitions of any team automaton over $\mathcal{S}$. Subsets δ of $\Delta(\mathcal{S})$, such that $\delta_a = \Delta_a(\mathcal{S})$ for all $a \in \Sigma_{int}$, are referred to as *synchronisation policies* (over $\mathcal{S}$).

Definition 3 (Team automaton). *The* team automaton *over $\mathcal{S}$ with synchronisations δ is the component automaton $\mathcal{T} = (Q, (\Sigma_{inp}, \Sigma_{out}, \Sigma_{int}), \delta, I)$.* □

Each team automaton determines a synchronisation policy over $\mathcal{S}$ and vice versa. Since every team automaton is a component automaton, team automata can be used in hierarchical constructions (systems of systems).

3 Synchronisation Types

We have seen that team automata over a composable system are defined by synchronisation policies. For all states of the system and for each external action enabled at the corresponding local state of at least one of its components, it has to be decided which synchronisations on that action to include as a (team) transition. In practice, this will seldom be decided individually for every candidate synchronisation. The system designer will most likely have a certain synchronisation pattern in mind. In this section, we introduce so-called synchronisation types which allow us to define in a compact way specific synchronisation policies.

Synchronisation types specify lower and upper bounds on the number of components involved in a synchronisation or they indicate that the synchronisation is of an *action-indispensible* or *state-indispensible* type. These notions were originally introduced in [6]. There an action-indispensible synchronisation policy requires for every team transition on a given action the involvement of all components to which that action belongs; a policy is state-indispensible if in every team transition on a given action all components that could be involved (because that action is enabled at the current local state) are involved. Here, we apply this idea to communicating actions and distinguish between their input and output roles. We use *ai* and *si* to indicate the number of input or output components that could maximally be involved in a synchronisation on a communicating action (having that action as input or output, respectively, and for *si* the action is moreover enabled at the current local state).

The next definition introduces synchronisation types as pairs that can be used to specify for a synchronisation on a communicating action, possible numbers of components involved as sending components (for which the action executed is an output action) and as receiving components (for which the action is an input).

Definition 4 (Synchronisation type). *A synchronisation type is a pair* (snd, rcv) *such that for* $x = snd$ *and for* $x = rcv$ *either* x *is an interval* $[k, m]$ *with* $0 \leq k$ *and* $(k \leq m$ *or* $m = *)$ *or* $x \in \{ai, si\}$. *We call* snd *and* rcv *the sending and receiving multiplicity, respectively, of the synchronisation type.* □

Next, we turn to synchronisations. For $(p, a, p') \in \Delta(\mathcal{S})$, the number of automata involved as output or input component in (p, a, p') is denoted as follows:

$$out_a(p, a, p') = \#\{i \in \mathcal{I} \mid (proj_i(p), a, proj_i(p')) \in \delta_i \text{ and } a \in \Sigma_{i,out}\}$$
$$inp_a(p, a, p') = \#\{i \in \mathcal{I} \mid (proj_i(p), a, proj_i(p')) \in \delta_i \text{ and } a \in \Sigma_{i,inp}\}$$

To be able to deal with *si*, we denote the number of automata, for which an output or input action $a \in \Sigma_{com}$ is locally enabled at state $p \in Q$, as follows:

$$out_{si}(p, a) = \#\{i \in \mathcal{I} \mid a \, en_{\mathcal{A}_i} \, proj_i(p) \text{ and } a \in \Sigma_{i,out} \}$$
$$inp_{si}(p, a) = \#\{i \in \mathcal{I} \mid a \, en_{\mathcal{A}_i} \, proj_i(p) \text{ and } a \in \Sigma_{i,inp}\}$$

In what follows, $\ell \in \mathbb{N}$ is said to *satisfy an interval* $[k, m]$ with $0 \leq k \leq m$ whenever $k \leq \ell \leq m$; and ℓ satisfies $[k, *]$ if $k \leq \ell$.

Definition 5 (Typed synchronisation policy). *Let $a \in \Sigma_{com}$, $p \in Q$ and $(p, a, p') \in \Delta(\mathcal{S})$. Then*

$$(p, a, p') \text{ is of type } (snd, rcv) \text{ if } \begin{cases} snd = [o_1, o_2] & and\ out_a(p, a, p') \text{ satisfies } [o_1, o_2] \\ snd = ai & and\ out_a(p, a, p') = \#dom_{a,out}(\mathcal{S}) \\ snd = si & and\ out_a(p, a, p') = out_{si}(p, a) \\ rcv = [i_1, i_2] & and\ inp_a(p, a, p') \text{ satisfies } [i_1, i_2] \\ rcv = ai & and\ inp_a(p, a, p') = \#dom_{a,inp}(\mathcal{S}) \\ rcv = si & and\ inp_a(p, a, p') = inp_{si}(p, a) \end{cases}$$

We say that a synchronisation policy $\delta \subseteq \Delta(\mathcal{S})$ is of type (snd, rcv) if δ contains, for all $a \in \Sigma_{com}$, all transitions on a of type (snd, rcv) and no other transitions on a. A team automaton $\mathcal{T}$ over $\mathcal{S}$ with synchronisation policy δ is of type (snd, rcv) if δ is of type (snd, rcv). □

From Definition 5 it follows that for closed systems where all external actions are communicating, a synchronisation type (snd, rcv) determines a unique synchronisation policy δ and hence a team automaton. Synchronisation types do not apply to non-communicating external actions and so, if the system is open, a synchronisation policy of a certain type may contain any subset of transitions $(p, a, p') \in \Delta(\mathcal{S})$ with actions $a \in \Sigma_{ext} \backslash \Sigma_{com}$. If all of them are selected, then the synchronisation policy is called *maximal*.

Note that a transition in $\mathcal{S}$ may be of several, different types. Furthermore, a team automaton may have a synchronisation policy that includes communications that do not have a common synchronisation type.

Let us now consider some familiar synchronisation types which occur in the literature and in concrete systems.

$([1, 1], [1, 1])$: binary communication, meaning that a communicating action can be executed only as a synchronisation involving exactly one component for which it is an output action and exactly one for which it is an input action.

$([1, 1], [0, 1])$: as directly above, but now over a lossy channel, meaning that a communicating action can be lost (i.e. involving exactly one component for which it is an output action and at most one for which it is an input action).

$([1, 1], [0, *])$: multicast communication, meaning that a communicating action can be executed only as a synchronisation involving exactly one component for which it is an output action and any number of the components in which it is an input action. This is called weak synchronisation in BIP [20].

$([1, 1], si)$: broadcast communication, meaning that whenever a communicating action is executed it occurs exactly once in its output role in that transition with as many as possible (all currently enabled) input components involved.

$([1, 1], ai)$: strong broadcast communication, as directly above, but now with all input components involved. This is called strong synchronisation in BIP.

(ai, ai): transitions on communicating actions are always 'full' synchronisations, meaning that all components that share a communicating action are involved in all transitions on that action. When all external actions are communicating ($\mathcal{S}$ is a closed system), this means that we are dealing with the classical synchronous product of automata (cf., e.g., [2, 14, 21]).

([1, *], [0, *]): transitions on communicating actions always involve at least one
   component where that action is an output action. This is the idea of 'master-
   slave' communication (cf. [6]), according to which a master (output) can
   always be executed and slaves (input) never proceed on their own.
([1, *], [1, *]): as directly above, but now at least one slave has to 'obey' (the
   master). This is called 'strong master-slave' communication (cf. [6]), by which
   a master (output) can always be executed and slaves (input) must be involved.
([0, 1], [0, 1]): not obligatory binary communication (communicating actions may
   also be executed as stand alone) like in CCS [22].   □

These synchronisation types define team automata based on one type of synchronisation only, but for future work combinations could be imagined as well.

Example 1. We consider the system $Sys_1 = \{Runner_1, Runner_2, Controller\}$
depicted in Fig. 1. Here and in all subsequent examples components have exactly
one initial state denoted by 0. All actions apart from the internal actions run_1
and run_2 are communicating. We want to combine these components in a team
in a way that the controller component starts both runner components at the
same time, but each runner can separately signal to the controller when it has
reached the finish line. To this aim, the synchronisation type (ai, ai) with all
transitions on communicating actions being full synchronisations is appropriate.
Thus we obtain the team automaton T_1 of type (ai, ai) over Sys_1. (Since the
system is closed, this team is unique.)   □

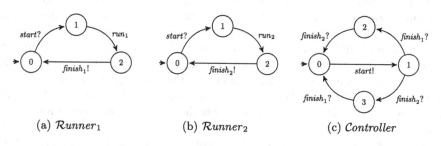

(a) *Runner₁*   (b) *Runner₂*   (c) *Controller*

Fig. 1. Automata *Runner_i*, with $i \in \{1, 2\}$, and *Controller* of Sys_1

Example 2. Now we consider the system $Sys_2 = \{Runner'_1, Runner'_2, Controller'\}$
depicted in Fig. 2. The idea is similar to Example 1. As before, the controller
should start the runners at the same time and each runner should separately send
its finish signal to the controller. The difference with Sys_1 is that both runners use
the same finish signal to communicate with the controller. Therefore we cannot
use the synchronisation type (ai, ai) but choose the type $([1, 1], ai)$ instead. The
sending multiplicity $[1, 1]$ enforces that communication in the system will always
involve exactly one sender, which precludes the two runners sending their finish
signal together. The receiving multiplicity is ai since the two runners must receive

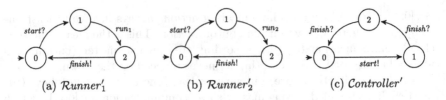

(a) $\mathcal{Runner}'_1$ (b) $\mathcal{Runner}'_2$ (c) $\mathcal{Controller}'$

Fig. 2. Automata $\mathcal{Runner}'_i$, with $i \in \{1,2\}$, and $\mathcal{Controller}'$ of $\mathcal{Sys}_2$

the start signal together. This leads to the team automaton $\mathcal{T}_2$ of type $([1,1], ai)$ over the system $\mathcal{Sys}_2$.   □

4   Communication Requirements

In this paper, we are interested in the communications between components in a team built over the system $\mathcal{S}$. In any state p of $\mathcal{S}$, one of its components or, more generally, a group of components in $\mathcal{S}$ may require certain communications with other components in the system. This is formally expressed by communication requirements. In the following, we represent a group of components in $\mathcal{S}$ by their indices, i.e. by a non-empty subset $\mathcal{J} \subseteq \mathcal{I}$. By abuse of terminology, we will often identify $\mathcal{J}$ with the group of components represented by $\mathcal{J}$.

For a communicating action $a \in \Sigma_{com}$, a group $\mathcal{J} \subseteq \mathrm{dom}_{a,out}(\mathcal{S})$ in the output domain of a may have a communication requirement $(\mathcal{J}, a)$ at some state p, if (output) action a is enabled in the local states $proj_j(p)$ of all components $\mathcal{A}_j$ with $j \in \mathcal{J}$. This requirement expresses that at least one component in the input domain of a should communicate with group $\mathcal{J}$ and receive a in the current state. Thus (synchronised groups of) sending components can have demands w.r.t. the reception of an output action and therefore $(\mathcal{J}, a)$ will be called a *receptiveness requirement*. According to Definitions 7 and 8 below, it will depend on the synchronisation policy of a team whether receptiveness requirements are fulfilled.

Similarly, we consider groups $\mathcal{J} \subseteq \mathrm{dom}_{a,inp}(\mathcal{S})$ in the input domain of a. Then a communication requirement $(\mathcal{J}, a)$ can be given for a state p, if (input) action a is enabled in the local states $proj_j(p)$ of all components $\mathcal{A}_j$ with $j \in \mathcal{J}$. According to this requirement at least one component in the output domain of a should communicate with the group and send a in the current state. Thus (synchronised groups of) receiving components may require output from other components and then $(\mathcal{J}, a)$ will also be called a *responsiveness requirement* (although it is not necessarily a response to a former call). Again it will depend on the synchronisation policy of a team whether responsiveness requirements are satisfied (cf. Definitions 7 and 8).

Communication requirements can be combined by conjunction and disjunction. As we shall see in Sect. 5, the former will be in particular useful for combining receptiveness requirements and the latter for responsiveness requirements.

Definition 6 (Communication requirement)

(i) *A* receptiveness requirement *at* $p \in Q$ *is a pair* $(\mathcal{J}, a)$ *with* $a \in \Sigma_{com}$ *and* $\varnothing \neq \mathcal{J} \subseteq dom_{a,out}(\mathcal{S})$ *such that* $a \, en_{\mathcal{A}_j} \, proj_j(p)$ *for all* $j \in \mathcal{J}$.

(ii) *A* responsiveness requirement *at* $p \in Q$ *is a pair* $(\mathcal{J}, a)$ *with* $a \in \Sigma_{com}$ *and* $\varnothing \neq \mathcal{J} \subseteq dom_{a,inp}(\mathcal{S})$ *such that* $a \, en_{\mathcal{A}_j} \, proj_j(p)$ *for all* $j \in \mathcal{J}$.

(iii) *An* atomic communication requirement *at* $p \in Q$ *is either the trivial requirement* true *or a receptiveness requirement at* p *or a responsiveness requirement at* p.

(iv) *A* communication requirement *at* $p \in Q$ *is either an atomic communication requirement or a conjunction* $\psi_1 \wedge \psi_2$ *or a disjunction* $\psi_1 \vee \psi_2$ *of communication requirements* ψ_1 *and* ψ_2 *at* p. □

When all non-trivial atomic requirements occurring in a communication requirement φ are receptiveness (responsiveness) requirements, we also refer to φ as a receptiveness (responsiveness) requirement, respectively.

Definition 7 (Compliance). *A team automaton* $\mathcal{T}$ *over* $\mathcal{S}$ *with synchronisation policy* δ *is* compliant with *a communication requirement* φ *at* $p \in Q$ *if either* $p \notin \mathcal{R}(\mathcal{T})$ *or* $\varphi = $ true, *or*

(a) $\varphi = (J, a)$ *is a receptiveness requirement at* p *and there exist* $i \in dom_{a,inp}(\mathcal{S})$ *and a transition* $p \xrightarrow{a}_{\mathcal{T}} p'$ *such that* $(proj_k(p), a, proj_k(p')) \in \delta_k$ *for all* $k \in \mathcal{J} \cup \{i\}$;

(b) $\varphi = (J, a)$ *is a responsiveness requirement at* p *and there exist* $i \in dom_{a,out}(\mathcal{S})$ *and a transition* $p \xrightarrow{a}_{\mathcal{T}} p'$ *such that* $(proj_k(p), a, proj_k(p')) \in \delta_k$ *for all* $k \in \mathcal{J} \cup \{i\}$;

(c) $\varphi = \psi_1 \wedge \psi_2$ *and* $\mathcal{T}$ *is compliant with* ψ_1 *at* p *and with* ψ_2 *at* p;

(d) $\varphi = \psi_1 \vee \psi_2$ *and* $\mathcal{T}$ *is compliant with* ψ_1 *at* p *or with* ψ_2 *at* p. □

Note that when $\mathcal{T}$ is compliant with an atomic receptiveness requirement at a state p, then according to (a) above, the output a from the components defined by $\mathcal{J}$ can be received by a component $\mathcal{A}_i$, but this may be realised through a synchronisation at p involving more components from the output and input domains of a. A similar remark holds for compliance with responsiveness requirements.

Communication requirements can be used to express various properties that may emerge during the computations of a team automaton, such as progress properties. As an example, when a team automaton $\mathcal{T}$ is compliant with a nontrivial communication requirement at state p, then *communication progress* is possible at p, i.e. $a \, en_{\mathcal{T}} \, p$ for some $a \in \Sigma_{com}$.

In general, the definition of compliance as we have it now, may be too strong in the sense that it could be natural to allow the team to execute some intermediate, internal ('silent') actions before it would be ready for the required communication. This leads to the notion of *weak compliance* following the ideas of weak compatibility introduced in [11].

Definition 8 (Weak compliance). *A team automaton* $\mathcal{T}$ *over* $\mathcal{S}$ *with synchronisation policy* δ *is* weakly compliant with *a communication requirement* φ *at* $p \in Q$ *if either* $p \notin \mathcal{R}(\mathcal{T})$ *or* $\varphi = $ true, *or*

(a) $\varphi = (J, a)$ is a receptiveness requirement at p and there exist $q \in Q$ with $\mathrm{proj}_j(p) = \mathrm{proj}_j(q)$, for all $j \in J$, and $i \in dom_{a,inp}(S)$ such that $p \xrightarrow{\Sigma_{int}}_T^* q \xrightarrow{a}_T p'$ holds and $(\mathrm{proj}_k(q), a, \mathrm{proj}_k(p')) \in \delta_k$ for all $k \in J \cup \{i\}$;

(b) $\varphi = (J, a)$ is a responsiveness requirement at p and there exist $q \in Q$ with $\mathrm{proj}_j(p) = \mathrm{proj}_j(q)$, for all $j \in J$, and $i \in dom_{a,out}(S)$ such that $p \xrightarrow{\Sigma_{int}}_T^* q \xrightarrow{a}_T p'$ and $(\mathrm{proj}_k(q), a, \mathrm{proj}_k(p')) \in \delta_k$ for all $k \in J \cup \{i\}$;

(c) $\varphi = \psi_1 \wedge \psi_2$ and T is weakly compliant with ψ_1 at p and with ψ_2 at p;

(d) $\varphi = \psi_1 \vee \psi_2$ and T is weakly compliant with ψ_1 at p or with ψ_2 at p.   □

Obviously, compliance implies weak compliance. Observe furthermore that we require that the components defined by J do not change their local state as a result of the execution of the silent actions. This implies that these components do not (have to) execute internal actions to reach the global state where the required communication would be possible. Moreover, the definition given here makes it possible that also components not involved in the eventual communication, take part in the silent computation needed to reach a team state where that communication could take place. This phenomenon is known as 'state-sharing' (cf. [6,23]) and allows components to influence potential synchronisations through their local states without being involved in the actual transition.

Example 3. We consider the team automaton T_1, introduced in Example 1, with synchronisation type (ai, ai). We denote the states of T_1 by triples (q_1, q_2, q_3) where q_1 is a state of *Controller*, q_2 a state of *Runner*$_1$, and q_3 a state of *Runner*$_2$. Examples for receptiveness requirements are:

($\{Controller\}, start$) at $(0, 0, 0)$
($\{Runner_1\}, finish_1$) $\wedge$ ($\{Runner_2\}, finish_2$) at $(1, 2, 2)$

The first one expresses that in the initial state the start signal of the controller should be received (by at least one runner); the second one that in state $(1, 2, 2)$ each runner wants its finish signal to be received (by the controller). Obviously, the team automaton T_1 is compliant with both receptiveness requirements.

Examples for responsiveness requirements are:

($\{Runner_1, Runner_2\}, start$) at $(0, 0, 0)$
($\{Controller\}, finish_1$) $\vee$ ($\{Controller\}, finish_2$) at $(1, 1, 1)$

The first requirement concerns the group consisting of the two runners which together request to be started. The second one expresses that in state $(1, 1, 1)$ the controller expects a finish signal either from *Runner*$_1$ or from *Runner*$_2$. This illustrates the use of disjunctions to reflect external choice of inputs. Note that T_1 is *not* compliant but only *weakly* compliant with this requirement at $(1, 1, 1)$. In this state, neither *finish*$_1$ nor *finish*$_2$ can be sent immediately to the controller, but either one can be sent when the respective component has done its running (an internal action).   □

Theorem 1. *Let T be a team automaton over S and, for each $p \in \mathcal{R}(T)$, let ϕ_p be a non-trivial[1] communication requirement such that T is weakly compliant with each ϕ_p at p. Then at all reachable states of T, at least one action is enabled.[2]*

Proof. For every reachable state p of T there is at least one atomic communication requirement with which T is compliant. Hence, in state p, the requested action a can eventually be executed in the team.   □

5   Deriving Communication Requirements

In the previous section, we have introduced the concepts of communication requirement and compliance of team automata. However, we provided no methodological guidelines outlining when which requirements would be meaningful. Consider, for instance, the team automaton T_2 of Example 2 with synchronisation type $([1,1], ai)$. The global state $(1, 2, 2)$ is a reachable state of T_2 at which for both runner components, the output action *finish* is locally enabled. Hence, $(\{\mathcal{R}unner_1, \mathcal{R}unner_2\}, finish)$ is formally a receptiveness requirement at $(1, 2, 2)$. This requirement does not make much sense, though, because of the sending multiplicity $[1, 1]$ by which always exactly one sender participates in the execution of a communicating action. Therefore, the choice of suitable communication requirements should take the synchronisation type of the team into account.

In this section, we propose a general procedure to derive communication requirements from an arbitrary synchronisation type. The approach was inspired by initial ideas for a generic definition of compatibility of components relative to the adopted synchronisation policy in [14] (where no classification of synchronisation types was considered and no derivation procedure was envisioned). We will do so separately for receptiveness (Sect. 5.1) and responsiveness requirements (Sect. 5.2). Thus, we get for all synchronisation types introduced in Definition 4, a compatibility notion w.r.t. receptiveness (Definition 9) and responsiveness (Definition 10) suitable for all team automata with a synchronisation policy of that type.

5.1   Deriving Receptiveness Requirements

We first formulate receptiveness requirements for each synchronisation type (snd, rcv). We distinguish the following cases.

Case: snd arbitrary, $rcv = [0, i_2]$ or $rcv = si$. In this case, the synchronisation policy allows that sending components progress also when their output will not be received. Thus we have no more than the trivial receptiveness requirement *true* at all states $p \in Q$.

In the following cases, we assume that neither $rcv = [0, i_2]$ nor $rcv = si$ and proceed with a case distinction on snd.

---

[1] i.e. it cannot be logically reduced to *true*.
[2] i.e. $\mathcal{R}(T)$ contains no deadlock states.

Case: $snd = [o_1, o_2]$. In this case, the subsets *relevant* to our considerations are those $\mathcal{J} \subseteq \mathcal{I}$ with $o_1 \le |\mathcal{J}| \le o_2$. Let $p \in Q$ be a global state. For each such $\mathcal{J}$, we consider all communicating (output) actions a which are simultaneously enabled at the current local states $proj_j(p)$ of the components $\mathcal{A}_j$, i.e. a $en_{\mathcal{A}_j}$ $proj_j(p)$ for all $j \in \mathcal{J}$. This leads to the following receptiveness requirement at p:

$$\bigwedge \{(\mathcal{J}, a) \mid \varnothing \ne \mathcal{J} \subseteq \mathcal{I}, \; o_1 \le |\mathcal{J}| \le o_2,$$
$$\text{and, for all } j \in \mathcal{J}, a \in \Sigma_{j,out} \cap \Sigma_{com} \text{ and } a \, en_{\mathcal{A}_j} \, proj_j(p)\}$$

We use conjunction here to reflect that whatever output action will be executed, a corresponding input is required. If the set of all pairs $(\mathcal{J}, a)$ considered above is empty, then there is no proper receptiveness requirement at p other than the trivial requirement *true*.

To conclude, a team automaton $\mathcal{T}$ over $\mathcal{S}$ of type $([o_1, o_2], rcv)$ (such that neither $rcv = [0, i_2]$ nor $rcv = si$) is (weakly) compliant with the receptiveness requirements at p if whenever a group of components wants to perform an output a, then the team can (eventually) carry out a synchronisation such that a is sent by the group and received by some (at least one) other component.

Case: $snd = ai$. In this case, an action a is only executed as an output action if *all* components in its output domain are at a state at which a is enabled. Hence we formulate the following receptiveness requirements for states $p \in Q$:

$$\bigwedge \{(\mathcal{J}, a) \mid \varnothing \ne \mathcal{J} = \mathrm{dom}_{a,out}(\mathcal{S}), \; a \in \Sigma_{com} \text{ and, for all } j \in \mathcal{J}, \; a \, en_{\mathcal{A}_j} \, proj_j(p)\}$$

These receptiveness requirements apply, in particular, to the synchronous product where the synchronisation type is (ai, ai).

Case: $snd = si$. This case is similar to $snd = ai$, but taking into account that now an (output) action can be executed in any synchronisation involving all components where it is locally enabled at p.

$$\bigwedge \{(\mathcal{J}, a) \mid \varnothing \ne \mathcal{J} = \{i \in \mathcal{I} \mid a \, en_{\mathcal{A}_i} \, proj_i(p) \text{ and } a \in \Sigma_{i,out}\}, \; a \in \Sigma_{com}\}$$

Combining the synchronisation types from Definition 4 with the above receptiveness requirements gives rise to the following definition.

Definition 9 (Receptive team automaton). *Let $\mathcal{T}$ be a team automaton of type (snd, rcv) over $\mathcal{S}$. $\mathcal{T}$ is (weakly) receptive if it is (weakly) compliant at all $p \in \mathcal{R}(\mathcal{T})$ with the receptiveness requirements derived above for (snd, rcv).* □

5.2 Deriving Responsiveness Requirements

We now formulate responsiveness requirements for each synchronisation type (snd, rcv). We distinguish the following cases.

Case: $snd = [0, o_2]$ or $snd = si$, rcv arbitrary. In this case, the synchronisation policy allows that receiving components progress also without being triggered by output. Thus we have no more than the trivial responsiveness requirement *true* at all states $p \in Q$.

In the following cases, we assume that neither $snd = [0, o_2]$ nor $snd = si$ and proceed with a case distinction on rcv.

Case: $rcv = [i_1, i_2]$. In this case, the subsets *relevant* to our considerations are those $\mathcal{J} \subseteq \mathcal{I}$ with $i_1 \leq |\mathcal{J}| \leq i_2$. Let $p \in Q$ be a global state. For each such $\mathcal{J}$, we consider all communicating (input) actions a which are simultaneously enabled at the current local states $proj_j(p)$ of the components $\mathcal{A}_j$, i.e. $a \, en_{\mathcal{A}_j} \, proj_j(p)$ for all $j \in \mathcal{J}$. This leads to the following responsiveness requirement at p:

$$\bigvee \{(\mathcal{J}, a) \mid \varnothing \neq \mathcal{J} \subseteq \mathcal{I}, \; o_1 \leq |\mathcal{J}| \leq o_2,$$
$$\text{and, for all } j \in \mathcal{J}, a \in \Sigma_{j,inp} \cap \Sigma_{com} \text{ and } a \, en_{\mathcal{A}_j} \, proj_j(p)\}$$

We use disjunction here to reflect that the choice of a particular input action is made by the environment, but (at least) one of the inputs must be served. If the set of all pairs $(\mathcal{J}, a)$ considered above is empty, then there is no proper responsiveness requirement at p other than the trivial requirement *true*.

To conclude, a team automaton $\mathcal{T}$ over $\mathcal{S}$ of type $(snd, [i_1, i_2])$ (such that neither $snd = [0, o_2]$ nor $snd = si$) is (weakly) compliant with the responsiveness requirements at p if whenever a group of components can perform an input action a, then the team can (eventually) carry out a synchronisation such that a is sent by some (at least one) component of the group.

Case: $rcv = ai$. In this case, an action a is only executed as an input action if *all* components in its input domain are at a state at which a is enabled. Hence we formulate the following responsiveness requirements for states $p \in Q$:

$$\bigvee \{(\mathcal{J}, a) \mid \varnothing \neq \mathcal{J} = \mathrm{dom}_{a,inp}(\mathcal{S}), \; a \in \Sigma_{com} \text{ and, for all } j \in \mathcal{J}, \; a \, en_{\mathcal{A}_j} \, proj_j(p)\}$$

These responsiveness requirements apply, in particular, to the synchronous product where the synchronisation type is (ai, ai).

Case: $rcv = si$. This case is similar to $rcv = ai$, but taking into account that now an (input) action can be executed in any synchronisation involving all components where it is locally enabled at p.

$$\bigwedge \{(\mathcal{J}, a) \mid \varnothing \neq \mathcal{J} = \{i \in \mathcal{I} \mid a \, en_{\mathcal{A}_i} \, proj_i(p) \text{ and } a \in \Sigma_{i,inp}\}, \; a \in \Sigma_{com}\}$$

Combining the synchronisation types from Definition 4 with the above responsiveness requirements gives rise to the following definition.

Definition 10 (Responsive team automaton). *Let $\mathcal{T}$ be a team automaton of type (snd, rcv) over $\mathcal{S}$. $\mathcal{T}$ is (weakly) responsive if it is (weakly) compliant at all $p \in \mathcal{R}(\mathcal{T})$ with the responsiveness requirements derived above for (snd, rcv).* $\square$

5.3 Examples

Example 4. We consider the team automaton T_1 of Example 1 with synchronisation type (ai, ai). It is sufficient to consider communication requirements only for those states which are reachable. First we derive receptiveness requirements according to Sect. 5.1:

$(\{Controller\}, start)$ at $(0, 0, 0)$
true at $(1, 1, 1)$
$(\{Runner_1\}, finish_1)$ at $(1, 2, 1)$
$(\{Runner_2\}, finish_2)$ at $(1, 1, 2)$
$(\{Runner_1\}, finish_1) \wedge (\{Runner_2\}, finish_2)$ at $(1, 2, 2)$
true at $(2, 0, 1)$
$(\{Runner_2\}, finish_2)$ at $(2, 0, 2)$
true at $(3, 1, 0)$
$(\{Runner_1\}, finish_1)$ at $(3, 2, 0)$

All receptiveness requirements are straightforward and express our intuition that if a component can send an action then the other component(s) should be ready to receive it. Obviously, T_1 is compliant with all receptiveness requirements.

Let us now derive responsiveness requirements according to Sect. 5.2. We get:

$(\{Runner_1, Runner_2\}, start)$ at $(0, 0, 0)$
$(\{Controller\}, finish_1) \vee (\{Controller\}, finish_2)$
       at $\{(1, 1, 1), (1, 2, 1), (1, 1, 2), (1, 2, 2)\}$
$(\{Controller\}, finish_2)$ at $\{(2, 0, 1), (2, 0, 2)\}$
$(\{Controller\}, finish_1)$ at $\{(3, 1, 0), (3, 2, 0)\}$

The first requirement at $(0, 0, 0)$ concerns the group of the two runners which both together request to be started. The responsiveness requirements at states $(1, 1, 1)$, $(1, 2, 1)$, $(1, 1, 2)$ and $(1, 2, 2)$ all express that the controller component wants to receive a finish signal either of $Runner_1$ or of $Runner_2$. This illustrates the use of disjunctions to reflect external choice of inputs. The responsiveness requirements at states $(2, 0, 1)$ and $(2, 0, 2)$ express that the controller wants to receive a finish signal from $Runner_2$. The requirements at states $(3, 1, 0)$ and $(3, 2, 0)$ are analogous. As discussed in Example 3, T_1 is *not* compliant with all responsiveness requirements, but it is *weakly* compliant with all of them.   □

Example 5. As an open system, we consider $\hat{Sys}_1$ depicted in Fig. 3. The difference with Sys_1 is that the runner component $\widehat{Runner}_2$ may decide not to wait for the start signal of the controller and start by performing an input action *go*. This is an external action but not a communicating action, which may be called by the system's environment.[3] Thus, in contrast to Sys_1, $\hat{Sys}_1$ has an open input.

We consider again the synchronisation type (ai, ai) but, since the system is open, the synchronisation policy is not uniquely determined by the synchronisation type. Let us first choose the maximal synchronisation policy over (ai, ai). Then the state $(0, 0, 1)$ becomes reachable with the external *go* action. For

---

[3] For instance, a false start signal coming from the outside.

this state, our method derives receptiveness requirement $(\{Controller\}, start)$ at $(0,0,1)$. Clearly, the team is *not* (weakly) compliant with this receptiveness requirement at $(0,0,1)$, since the second runner would also be needed to start. So we must choose a different synchronisation policy. The solution is simple. We just omit the transition with input action go from state $(0,0,0)$ to state $(0,0,1)$. Then $(0,0,1)$ is no longer reachable and the new team is compliant with all receptiveness requirements. Removal of the 'bad' open input transition matches the approach of interface automata in [7], where components are considered to be *compatible* if they can work properly together in a 'helpful' environment.   □

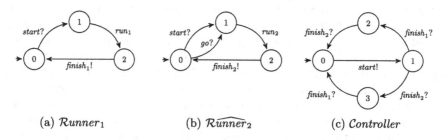

(a) $\mathcal{Runner}_1$ (b) $\widehat{\mathcal{Runner}}_2$ (c) $\mathcal{Controller}$

Fig. 3. Automata $\mathcal{Runner}_1$, $\widehat{\mathcal{Runner}}_2$ and $\mathcal{Controller}$ of $\widehat{\mathcal{Sys}}_1$

Example 6. Consider team automaton $\mathcal{T}_2$, introduced in Example 2, with synchronisation type $([1,1], ai)$. From sending multiplicity $[1,1]$ we derive, for instance, the receptiveness requirement $(\{\mathcal{Runner}_1\}, finish) \wedge (\{\mathcal{Runner}_2\},$ $finish)$ at $(1,2,2)$. It is easy to verify that the team automaton $\mathcal{T}_2$ is compliant with this requirement and with all other derived ones not shown here.

Let us play a bit with this example to see the importance of synchronisation types. Assume we would have chosen the sending multiplicity $[1,2]$ instead. The corresponding synchronisation policy δ' would then allow that the two runners send simultaneously the finish signal to the controller, i.e. we get an additional transition from state $(1,2,2)$ to state $(2,0,0)$ labelled with $finish$. Then we derive responsiveness requirement $(\{\mathcal{Controller}\}, finish) \vee (\{\mathcal{Runner}_1, \mathcal{Runner}_2\}, start)$ at the newly reachable state $(2,0,0)$. Clearly this requirement is not fulfilled by the team with synchronisation policy δ' (and hence it was a good idea to choose the sending multiplicity $[1,1]$ for the system Sys_1).   □

5.4 Related Compatibility Notions

In the literature, compatibility notions are often considered for systems built according to a specific synchronisation type. For instance, interface automata [7] and many others, like [10,19,24,25], consider synchronous compositions of composable I/O-transition systems with (binary) point-to-point communication, i.e. the synchronisation type is $([1,1], [1,1])$. These papers moreover deal with the aspect of receptiveness only. We can say that a team automaton of type $([1, 1], [1, 1])$ over a (closed or open) system of components $\mathcal{A}_1$ and $\mathcal{A}_2$ is receptive in the sense of Definition 9 iff $\mathcal{A}_1$ and $\mathcal{A}_2$ are strongly synchronously compatible in the sense of [25] iff they are receptive in the sense of [1]. Weak receptiveness corresponds to weak synchronous compatibility in [25] and is also captured by unspecified receptions compatibility in [13]. An even more liberal notion of compatibility was used in [24] for assemblies of modal interfaces. It allows that before accepting a message issued by one component the other components can still communicate (cf. Definition 8 and Sect. 5.1 in [24]).

For open systems there are variations of compatibility notions discriminated by so-called "pessimistic" and "optimistic" approaches (cf. [19] for a discussion and formalisation of both of them). The difference is that in the pessimistic approach, followed by [1, 13, 25], *all* states of the synchronous product are considered and responsiveness must be guaranteed for all of them. As we have just seen above, we can express the pessimistic approach. The idea of the optimistic approach, proposed for interface automata in [7], is that responsiveness must only be guaranteed for those states which are *autonomously* reachable when components work together. Then two components forming an open system (with open inputs) are compatible if there exists a 'helpful' environment which avoids to send messages to the system which would lead the system to an illegal state. As we have seen, synchronisation types uniquely define synchronisation policies only for closed systems, while for open systems we can decide to restrict the set of transitions with external, non-communicating actions. Therefore, we can find an appropriate policy to make two components in an open system receptive iff they are compatible in the sense of optimistic compatibility in [7].

We are aware of only a few approaches that consider compatibility w.r.t. responsiveness. In [1], responsiveness is captured by deadlock-freeness and in [13] it is expressed by part of the definition of bidirectional complementarity compatibility which, however, does not support choice of inputs as we do.

5.5   Applications

The contributions of this paper enable to explore component-based modelling and composition according to a wide range of synchronisation policies, not limited to the classical synchronous product, bringing upfront the communication requirements that must be fulfilled to derive a compliant system.

We foresee many application areas where the perspective taken in this paper can play an important role to enhance the interaction and communication policies that are used. In Swarm Intelligence, for instance, agents communicate by means of sensors, actuators and connectors. Such sensors and actuators allow communication through the receiving and sending of signals. This communication often concerns a small selection of agents that changes over time, thus deviating from the synchronous product [26]. Being able to construct swarm networks that fulfil certain compatibility guarantees on alternative communication policies, like the ones considered in this paper, may represent an important step towards their satisfactory application.

Another application area is Software Engineering. In particular, the provision of compatibility theories that go beyond limited formalisms like UML statecharts composed according to the synchronous product, will rise the expressibility level, thus widening the applicability scope to cover much more real-world situations.

Also concurrent asynchronous programming languages can benefit from having a general theory of compatibility such as the one we envision in this paper. Erlang [27] is a prominent example: its asynchronous communication mode allows for a very flexible communication architecture, but if used incorrectly it may lead to invalid/suboptimal system implementations. To the best of our knowledge, current approaches follow a *post-mortem* approach to verify properties like liveness and safety of Erlang programs. Instead, correct-by-construction design might become applicable if the theories described in this paper were used in the specification of Erlang programs.

Finally, the field of Web services may also be a nice application arena for the ideas put forward in this paper. Like in some of the previous examples, we are only aware of notions of compatibility for the composition of Web services defined over the restricted synchronous product [28,29].

We close this section with a more realistic example than the ones of Sect. 5.3, which were intended to illustrate our definitions. Some aspects of this example are covered by our current approach while others cannot as yet be dealt with, but we give a preview of what is needed in the future.

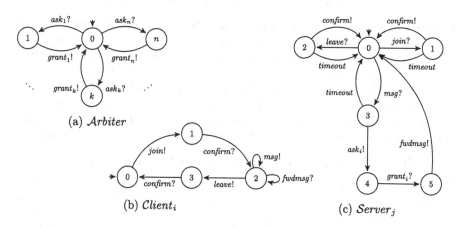

Fig. 4. Automata $\mathcal{Arbiter}$, $\mathcal{Client}_i$ and $\mathcal{Server}_j$, with $1 \leq i \leq m$ and $1 \leq j \leq n$

Example 7. We consider a distributed chat system where buddies can interact once they register into the system. The system is formed by three types of components (cf. Fig. 4): servers, clients and an arbiter. To increase the robustness of the system, not one but several servers are devoted to control both new entries into or exits from the chat, as well as to coordinate the main activity in the chat, viz. forwarding client messages to the chat. Communicating actions are partitioned into chat access actions (*join*, *leave*, *confirm*), chat messaging (*msg*, *fwdmsg*) and arbiter selection of the forwarding server (*ask$_i$*, *grant$_i$*). The overall messaging protocol is that clients communicate messages to the servers (action *msg*) which, upon approval by the Arbiter, broadcast the received messages to the whole set of clients in the chat (through action *fwdmsg*). Note that in some of the states, servers contain an internal action *timeout* to allow a server to return to its initial state whenever it does not participate in the communication.

Consider team automaton $\mathcal{T}_{chat}$ constructed over the aforementioned system with synchronisation type $([1, 1], [1, *])$. We assume the system to contain n servers, m clients and one arbiter. States in this system are expressed as $n + m + 1$ tuples $(q_1, \ldots, q_n, q_{n+1}, \ldots, q_{n+m}, q_{n+m+1})$, i.e. the first n states correspond to server states, the second m states denote client states and the final state corresponds to the arbiter state.

Let us now derive an example of a receptiveness requirement (cf. Sect. 5.1):

$$(\{\mathcal{S}erver_j\}, \ fwdmsg) \ \text{at} \ (q_1, \ldots, q_{j-1}, 5, q_{j+1}, \ldots, q_{n+m+1})$$

The requirement expresses that the message forwarded to the chat by a server will be received by the clients. It is fulfilled by $\mathcal{T}_{chat}$ whenever some client is still in the chat, i.e. $\exists i, n + 1 \leq i \leq n + m : q_i = 2$.

An example of a responsiveness requirement is the following (cf. Sect. 5.2):

$$(\{\mathcal{S}erver_j\}, \ join) \ \vee \ (\{\mathcal{S}erver_j\}, \ leave) \ \vee \ (\{\mathcal{S}erver_j\}, \ msg)$$
$$\text{at} \ (q_1, \ldots, q_{j-1}, 0, q_{j+1}, \ldots, q_n, \ldots, q_{n+m+1})$$

This responsiveness requirement at state 0 of $\mathcal{S}erver_j$ provides a choice concerning the server's functionality: it can either coordinate joining or leaving actions from a client, or messages sent to the chat. The requirement is fulfilled by $\mathcal{T}_{chat}$ whenever there are at least as many clients as servers in the team.

We now continue this example to point out two limitations of our current approach, which can be overcome by two planned generalisations of our notion of compatibility, as mentioned in the previous section and listed as future work in the next section. First, consider the following receptiveness requirement:

$$(\{\mathcal{C}lient_i\}, \ join) \ \text{at} \ (q_1, \ldots, q_n, \ldots, q_{n+i-1}, 0, q_{n+i+1}, \ldots, q_{n+m+1})$$

This requirement expresses that in state 0 of $\mathcal{C}lient_i$, *join* actions should be received by at least one server. This receptiveness obligation is currently not fulfilled by $\mathcal{T}_{chat}$, which can be seen as follows. Assume that we have two clients and one server and note that the server, after communication with one of the clients and the arbiter, is in state 5. If the second client now wants to join the chat, then it expects, according to the $[1, 1]$ output multiplicity of $\mathcal{T}_{chat}$, to find exactly one communication partner, in this case the server, that can receive an input *join*. However, to satisfy the definition of receptiveness in case of weak compliance (cf. Definition 8(b)) the server would be allowed to move to state 0 (where it can indeed receive *join*) only with an internal action and *not* with a communication on *fwdmsg* with the first client (as would be the case for this example). The more liberal notion of compatibility from [24] mentioned in the previous section would allow such a communication before receiving *join*.

Second, a client currently might send a message to two servers, who can then both forward the message (upon approval from the arbiter). This could be avoided by generalising our approach such that synchronisation types are no longer uniform, but can be specified per action, since this would allow us to define the synchronisation type $([1,1],[1,1])$ for action *msg*, thus solving the problem of duplicate message forwarding.   □

6 Conclusions and Future Work

We have investigated compatibility notions concerning receptiveness and responsiveness in the team automata framework. Team automata are characterised by the synchronisation policy they use to coordinate the components of a given system. There is a huge variety of possible synchronisation policies. The synchronisation types as we introduced them here support a systematic approach to the investigation of compatibility notions related to communication. To find appropriate compatibility notions, we first analysed what kind of communication requirements can occur when components are composed. We distinguished receptiveness and responsiveness requirements and we showed how such requirements can be systematically derived depending on a synchronisation type. A team automaton is compliant with a communication requirement if (groups of) components in the team issuing requests for communication can successfully find partners to join. If this is the case for all receptiveness (responsiveness) requirements, then the team automaton is receptive (responsive, respectively). We have also considered weak compliance, where communication requirements need not be fulfilled immediately but only after some internal actions have been executed. We plan to generalise this concept even further by using the more liberal ideas defined for receptiveness in synchronous products in [24] and explained briefly in Sect. 5.4.

Our approach is appropriate for both closed and open systems. A team automaton over an open system is itself a reactive component and thus gives rise to hierarchical composition. One of the next steps in our research will be to study compatibility in the context of hierarchical composition and of synchronisation policies that are not necessarily uniform but combine different synchronisation types. The latter would also concern an investigation of compatibility notions tailored to particular connectors as used, e.g., in BIP and Reo (cf. [30] for a comparison). Also the incorporation of asynchronous communication in synchronisation policies and the study of compatibility notions in this case [25,31,32] is a topic for future research. Then it would be interesting to generalise synchronisation types to the asynchronous context and to consider different types of communication channels. Currently asynchronous compatibility notions are mainly studied for point-to-point communication, like for multiparty session types in [31]. However, when unbounded message queues are used for communication then decidability of compatibility becomes an issue, since it is generally undecidable [12]. Moreover, appropriate notions of equivalences and refinements for team automata and how they behave w.r.t. our receptiveness and responsiveness notions are interesting questions to consider.

Acknowledgments. We thank the reviewers for their comments. J. Carmona is supported by the Spanish Ministry for Economy and Competitiveness (MINECO) and the EU (FEDER funds) under grant COMMAS (TIN2013-46181-C2-1-R).

References

1. Carmona, J., Cortadella, J.: Input/output compatibility of reactive systems. In: Aagaard, M.D., O'Leary, J.W. (eds.) FMCAD 2002. LNCS, vol. 2517, pp. 360–377. Springer, Heidelberg (2002). doi:10.1007/3-540-36126-X_22
2. Carmona, J., Kleijn, J.: Compatibility in a multi-component environment. Theor. Comput. Sci. **484**, 1–15 (2013)
3. Lynch, N.A., Tuttle, M.R.: Hierarchical correctness proofs for distributed algorithms. In: PODC 1987, pp. 137–151. ACM (1987)
4. Lynch, N.A., Tuttle, M.R.: An introduction to input/output automata. CWI Q. **2**(3), 219–246 (1989). https://ir.cwi.nl/pub/18164
5. Ellis, C.A.: Team automata for groupware systems. In: GROUP 1997, pp. 415–424. ACM (1997)
6. ter Beek, M.H., Ellis, C.A., Kleijn, J., Rozenberg, G.: Synchronizations in team automata for groupware systems. Comput. Sup. Coop. Work **12**(1), 21–69 (2003)
7. de Alfaro, L., Henzinger, T.A.: Interface automata. In: ESEC/FSE 2001, pp. 109–120. ACM (2001)
8. de Alfaro, L., Henzinger, T.A.: Interface-based design. In: Broy, M., Grünbauer, J., Harel, D., Hoare, T. (eds.) Engineering Theories of Software Intensive Systems. NATO Science Series (Series II: Mathematics, Physics and Chemistry), vol. 195, pp. 83–104. Springer, Dordrecht (2005)
9. Brim, L., Černá, I., Vareková, P., Zimmerova, B.: Component-interaction automata as a verification-oriented component-based system specification. ACM Softw. Eng. Notes **31**(2), 4 (2006)
10. Larsen, K.G., Nyman, U., Wąsowski, A.: Modal I/O automata for interface and product line theories. In: Nicola, R. (ed.) ESOP 2007. LNCS, vol. 4421, pp. 64–79. Springer, Heidelberg (2007). doi:10.1007/978-3-540-71316-6_6
11. Bauer, S.S., Mayer, P., Schroeder, A., Hennicker, R.: On weak modal compatibility, refinement, and the MIO workbench. In: Esparza, J., Majumdar, R. (eds.) TACAS 2010. LNCS, vol. 6015, pp. 175–189. Springer, Heidelberg (2010). doi:10.1007/978-3-642-12002-2_15
12. Brand, D., Zafiropulo, P.: On communicating finite-state machines. J. ACM **30**(2), 323–342 (1983)
13. Durán, F., Ouederni, M., Salaün, G.: A generic framework for n-protocol compatibility checking. Sci. Comput. Program. **77**(7–8), 870–886 (2012)
14. ter Beek, M.H., Carmona, J., Kleijn, J.: Conditions for compatibility of components. In: Margaria, T., Steffen, B. (eds.) ISoLA 2016. LNCS, vol. 9952, pp. 784–805. Springer, Cham (2016). doi:10.1007/978-3-319-47166-2_55
15. Jonsson, B.: Compositional specification and verification of distributed systems. ACM Trans. Program. Lang. Syst. **16**(2), 259–303 (1994)
16. ter Beek, M.H., Kleijn, J.: Team automata satisfying compositionality. In: Araki, K., Gnesi, S., Mandrioli, D. (eds.) FME 2003. LNCS, vol. 2805, pp. 381–400. Springer, Heidelberg (2003). doi:10.1007/978-3-540-45236-2_22
17. Gössler, G., Sifakis, J.: Composition for component-based modeling. Sci. Comput. Program. **55**, 161–183 (2005)

18. ter Beek, M.H., Kleijn, J.: Modularity for teams of I/O automata. Inf. Process. Lett. **95**(5), 487–495 (2005)
19. Lüttgen, G., Vogler, W., Fendrich, S.: Richer interface automata with optimistic and pessimistic compatibility. Acta Inf. **52**(4–5), 305–336 (2015)
20. Basu, A., Bozga, M., Sifakis, J.: Modeling heterogeneous real-time components in BIP. In: SEFM 2006, pp. 3–12. IEEE (2006)
21. Arnold, A.: Finite Transition Systems: Semantics of Communicating Systems. Prentice Hall, Englewood Cliffs (1994)
22. Milner, R.: Communication and Concurrency. Prentice Hall, Upper Saddle River (1989)
23. Engels, G., Groenewegen, L.: Towards team-automata-driven object-oriented collaborative work. In: Brauer, W., Ehrig, H., Karhumäki, J., Salomaa, A. (eds.) Formal and Natural Computing. LNCS, vol. 2300, pp. 257–276. Springer, Heidelberg (2002). doi:10.1007/3-540-45711-9_15
24. Hennicker, R., Knapp, A.: Moving from interface theories to assembly theories. Acta Inf. **52**(2–3), 235–268 (2015)
25. Hennicker, R., Bidoit, M., Dang, T.-S.: On synchronous and asynchronous compatibility of communicating components. In: Lluch Lafuente, A., Proença, J. (eds.) COORDINATION 2016. LNCS, vol. 9686, pp. 138–156. Springer, Cham (2016). doi:10.1007/978-3-319-39519-7_9
26. Isokawa, T., et al.: Computing by swarm networks. In: Umeo, H., Morishita, S., Nishinari, K., Komatsuzaki, T., Bandini, S. (eds.) ACRI 2008. LNCS, vol. 5191, pp. 50–59. Springer, Heidelberg (2008). doi:10.1007/978-3-540-79992-4_7
27. Armstrong, J.: Erlang. Commun. ACM **53**(9), 68–75 (2010)
28. ter Beek, M.H., Bucchiarone, A., Gnesi, S.: Web service composition approaches: from industrial standards to formal methods. In: ICIW 2007. IEEE (2007)
29. Sheng, Q.Z., Qiao, X., Vasilakos, A.V., Szabo, C., Bourne, S., Xu, X.: Web services composition: a decade's overview. Inf. Sci. **280**, 218–238 (2014)
30. Dokter, K., Jongmans, S.-S., Arbab, F., Bliudze, S.: Combine and conquer: relating BIP and Reo. J. Log. Algebr. Meth. Program. **86**(1), 3–20 (2017)
31. Deniélou, P.-M., Yoshida, N.: Multiparty compatibility in communicating automata: characterisation and synthesis of global session types. In: Fomin, F.V., Freivalds, R., Kwiatkowska, M., Peleg, D. (eds.) ICALP 2013. LNCS, vol. 7966, pp. 174–186. Springer, Heidelberg (2013). doi:10.1007/978-3-642-39212-2_18
32. Fiadeiro, J.L., Lopes, A.: An interface theory for service-oriented design. Theor. Comput. Sci. **503**, 1–30 (2013)

Author Index